THE
Eighties

Also by Dylan Jones

Haircults

Jim Morrison: Dark Star

Ultra Lounge

Sex, Power and Travel

Meaty Beaty Big & Bouncy

iPod Therefore I Am: A Personal Journey Through Music

Mr Jones' Rules for the Modern Man

Cameron on Cameron: Conversations with Dylan Jones

British Heroes in Afghanistan (with David Bailey)

When Ziggy Played Guitar:
David Bowie and Four Minutes That Shook the World

The Biographical Dictionary of Popular Music

From the Ground Up

THE
Eighties
One Day, One Decade

DYLAN JONES

preface

Published by Preface 2013

10 9 8 7 6 5 4 3 2 1

First published in Great Britain in 2013 by Preface Publishing
20 Vauxhall Bridge Road
London, SW1V 2SA

An imprint of The Random House Group Limited

www.randomhouse.co.uk

Addresses for companies within The Random House Group Limited
can be found at www.randomhouse.co.uk

The Random House Group Limited Reg. No. 954009

A CIP catalogue record for this book is available from the British Library

ISBN 978 1 848 09413 0

The Random House Group Limited supports the Forest Stewardship
Council® (FSC®), the leading international forest-certification organisation.
Our books carrying the FSC label are printed on FSC®-certified paper. FSC is
the only forest-certification scheme supported by the leading environmental
organisations, including Greenpeace. Our paper procurement policy can be
found at www.randomhouse.co.uk/environment

Typeset by Carrdesignstudio.com

Printed and bound in Great Britain by Clays Ltd, St Ives PLC

For Terry Jones
One Day, One Decade, One Life
Thank You, Terry

Contents

INTRODUCTION

Not since those star-spangled, guilt-edged nights in 1970–
1971 when Leonard Bernstein threw his Black Panther party
and George Harrison organised the Concert for Bangladesh
have so many of the rich and famous stepped out for the
poor and famished.

OBSERVER

It's twelve noon in London, 7 a.m. in Philadelphia,
and around the world it's time for: Live Aid.

RICHARD SKINNER OPENING THE SHOW.

Today, Saturday 13 July 1985, everyone got up with the same purpose in mind. Everyone got up knowing exactly what they were going to be doing for the rest of the day. For weeks beforehand it was all anyone had been talking about. Some were going to tidy the house before sitting down in front of the television. Some were having friends round, for a barbeque, beer, and lots of wine, on the patio, on the terrace, in the back garden, so they could still hear the TV. Others were going to spend the morning doing chores, visiting the supermarket, picking up the dry-cleaning, and then swinging by the off-licence on the way home.

It didn't matter what you were doing, you knew where you were going to be. Because for weeks, months beforehand, we had talked of little else.

It was going to be a long day.

This was a day when bells should have been pealing out across the Thames, a day with such an air of benevolence you almost expected there to be two rows of stone pineapples greeting you as you skipped up the steps from Wembley Way.

If you were lucky enough to be going, that is.

Some, like me, hadn't even considered the TV. Because we were going. We were actually going to the concert, actually going to Wembley, actually going to sit in the sun for ten hours, listening to the biggest stars in the world sing their hearts out for Africa. We were going to Wembley Stadium to be part of the world's biggest ever charity concert, organised by Bob Geldof, a fading pop star who had been horrified by the famine in Ethiopia, and who was determined to try and do something about it. I was going to have a late breakfast, listen to the radio, throw on some clothes, and flick through the papers before getting on the Jubilee Line, all the way up to Wembley.

I'd woken up that day in my long, narrow, uncarpeted first-floor housing association flat in Brixton – just behind the Ritzy Cinema, overlooking the infamous Coldharbour Lane – made myself and my girlfriend some tea, and spent two hours wandering from room to room in silent anticipation. I was killing time, but enjoying every moment of it.

Before I left the flat, around ten o'clock, I did what I did every day, one of those things I'd inherited from my parents, one of the things which I always did, regardless of where I was living. Which was turn off every electrical appliance in the house. Neither Mum nor Dad would go to bed or leave the house without all of the plugs being pulled from their sockets, just in case some rogue electrical spark had the temerity to attach itself to the nearest piece of man-made fabric and burn the house down. It was a habit I found myself incapable of ignoring, along with going to the window each morning just to check for the weather. Even though you could easily tell from behind the blind what the day had in store for you, I would still make my way to the living-room window and peer through the slats, for my own empirical proof.

Today was going to be hot. Which is just the sort of weather Live Aid deserved.

Because today was going to be a very special day.

I picked up my best friend, and we made our way to Wembley. For us it was relatively simple, as all we had to do was jump on the Victoria Line, change at Green Park and then take the Jubilee Line to Wembley Park. And like 72,000 others, and the millions, the billions, who were going to watch on TV (we had repeatedly been told over the previous few weeks that this was going to be the biggest television audience ever), there was nowhere else I wanted to be that day.

It was going to be a wonderful day.

'Everyone has a common experience of it, everyone remembers where they were, everyone remembers what they felt about it,' said J. K. Rowling. 'It's one of those little pegs that you hang all your other memories on.'

Bob Geldof woke at seven, having gone to bed at two, and with very little sleep in between. His stomach was sore with tension. His penultimate phone call of the night had been with the manager of an American band who said that unless their set was lengthened, they were going to pull out.

'Well, fucking pull out. I'm going to bed,' said Geldof. Minutes earlier he had had a call from U2's office, threatening to pull the band as they hadn't been offered a soundcheck. His response was typical: 'Fuck 'em.'

Geldof quickly dressed himself, throwing on the same clothes he'd worn every day for weeks, a denim shirt and skinny trousers. In a matter of hours he was going to be performing in front of 2 billion people, but dressing up for it didn't somehow seem appropriate. And anyway, he didn't think of it. And probably didn't have any clean clothes anyway.

'I thought about what to wear, but in the end it just seemed preposterous. Seriously, now, what was I dressing up for? A drought? A famine? Television?'

With only four hours to go to the start of the show, Geldof was pacing, listening to the radio, and worrying about all the people he was told were going to be watching today. He could hear television sets tuned in ready for the concert all along his street. According to his team's predictions, at some point during the day, more than 85 per cent of the world's TV sets would be tuned to Live Aid. The sky was blue, the sun was up, and there wasn't a cloud on the horizon.

He climbed into the car outside the house, and stared at the waking world on the other side of the glass. On the drive to Battersea Heliport he could already sense the excitement in the air. He wound down the window and heard televisions blasting out through people's doors, windows, back gardens. 'And now there's just four hours to go,' said the BBC announcer. It was already hot, already barbeque weather, and the denizens of south London were preparing to spend the day outdoors, glued to their TVs.

People waved at him as the limo sped by, wishing him well, excited by the prospect of the day ahead. 'This is it,' thought Geldof. 'Here we go.'

The helicopter flew across London, and as it reached Wembley, Geldof could see people already pouring towards the stadium. He could see it filling up, as people rushed to get the best places. His back hurt, as it had done for ages. Throughout the day he would lie down to relieve the pain, but for now he was content to ignore it.

There was too much to worry about to allow pain to get in the way.

Some artists arrived by car, others by helicopter (Elton John, David Bowie, Spandau Ballet, The Who, George Michael, etc.). These were landing on a nearby cricket field, where in the evening a wedding reception took place; after various complaints from the father of the bride, David Bowie was dispatched to smooth things over, and – obviously – have his picture taken with the bride and groom.

At the time, Gary Farrow was running his own PR company, looking after the likes of Frankie Goes to Hollywood, Paula Yates, Wham! and Heaven 17. A good friend of the Live Aid promoter and organiser Harvey

Goldsmith, Farrow had been called by him to see if he could persuade some of his famous friends to let them use their helicopters for the day, to fly the performers into the stadium from the heliport in Battersea. Due to the number of acts on the bill, and the crowds, there was simply no other way to guarantee them arriving on time. And so Farrow rang the BBC presenter Noel Edmonds, along with some other owners, and they all agreed to supply them. They also arranged for the fuel to be donated, as well as the pilots' time. Because of the number of return flights needed, the operation was quickly labelled the biggest airlift since the Falklands War.

The helicopters were going to land on a makeshift landing strip, complete with windsock and lights, beside the cricket green behind the stadium, where a match was due to be played that day. It was agreed with the teams that the match wouldn't be cancelled, but that they'd simply take the bales away whenever a heli needed to land. This went on all day. One of the security guards told Farrow that not even the Pope had been able to land so close to the stadium. 'That's because he didn't have a laminate,' quipped Farrow.

Harvey Goldsmith left his home in Mill Hill that morning and arrived at the stadium about forty minutes later. His last phone call the previous evening had been to Geldof just after 2 a.m., and he had then had about four or five hours' sleep. 'I looked out the window and thought, "It's going to be a nice day." That's the first thing I thought, "Thank God for that."'

The Live Aid PR Bernard Doherty slept on the paparazzi photographer Alan Davidson's sofa, as he lived in Wembley, just around the corner from the stadium, and Doherty had to be there at 6 a.m. Doherty was working for the PR company Rogers and Cowan, part of a small team that also included Mariella Frostrup, whose day job was working for Bob Geldof's label, Phonogram Records.

Doherty was so disorganised that he had to arrange for a suit to be couriered up from his home in Greenwich, as he knew he had to be in the receiving line for Charles and Diana, introducing the prince and the princess to the artists. Having realised that he didn't have any cufflinks for his shirt, he used paperclips instead.

'It was the first time we had done something on this scale, and actually it was the first time anyone involved had done anything on this scale, which made Live Aid even scarier than we had thought it might be,' said Doherty. 'I was a roadie, production manager, everything. It was chaotic, but there was ordered confusion. In fact it had a very British feel, with everyone mucking in. You felt that everyone was involved because they had been affected by the cause, not just because they'd been corralled into doing it.'

Mark Ellen was one of the BBC presenters at Wembley, and at one point early in the afternoon he had to get to Regent Street, where they were broadcasting the American leg from. He had been at the stadium since nine that morning, and hadn't been out since then. What he found was shocking.

'I just couldn't believe how quiet everything was,' he said. 'It was as though they'd dropped the bomb. It was such a hot day and London was deserted. It was *so* eerie. I dashed into a taxi to take me to the West End and just as I was about to ask the driver to turn his radio on, I realised that he already had it on, that every car had it on, as well as every taxi, every van, everybody. When I told him what I'd been doing he couldn't believe it. "You've just come out of it?! It's amazing!" He was so excited. I sat there and talked to him about it for half an hour and he was very impressed. Every house you passed, every open window, everyone was tuned to the BBC, everyone was watching it. It was so, so odd. I got him to drop me at a pub near Broadcasting House as I wanted a drink and something to eat. There was no one in the bar, as everybody was at home watching on TV. There was just me and the barman, and the telly. It was so intense. People could not bear to miss one single second of this thing.'

Then Ellen heard a car screech to a halt outside the pub and saw a chap jump out and run towards the entrance. He didn't park properly, didn't wind the windows up, he may not even have shut the door. He just dashed in and ordered a drink and looked up around the bar. 'You could feel this palpable relief pass over him as he realised that there was a TV and they had it on and he wouldn't be missing anything . . .

'London was alive. Everybody was glued to this thing. That's all they could talk about. It was absolutely beautiful. It was really unexpected.'

All over London there was an awesome silence.

Everyone knew that Live Aid was a proper event. A big one. One that everyone in the country knew about, had an opinion about. It wasn't necessarily something you had to be at – how could everyone squeeze into Wembley? – but there was no way you could not watch it on TV. This was appointment television. Why on earth would you be anywhere else? Honestly, this was the event to end all events. And it was happening here, in London, smack bang in the middle of the Eighties. This wasn't a Sixties 'happening', or a hip Seventies gig taking place upstairs in a west London pub, this was an all-inclusive event to which everyone was invited. Want to be involved? Then just get involved! All you needed to do was turn up in your living room, pour yourself a cup of tea or pop open a beer, sit down in front of the TV, and you were there.

Across town, my friend Richard was about to spend the whole day in bed with his girlfriend, completely intoxicated by the thought of watching television for sixteen hours. Twenty-three, and single, Campbell principally wanted his girlfriend to stay in bed all weekend, and Live Aid was the perfect opportunity. He watched the show in his flat in Beaufort Street in Chelsea, on a new set bought specifically for his bedroom that weekend. 'Usually there wasn't an excuse to stay in bed all day,' said Richard, 'but Live Aid was a great excuse to stay in bed and, frankly, have sex. It was this constant roller coaster of performers – it was properly amazing. We watched the whole Wembley show and then the US show and by the time I got to work on Monday I felt like I had jet lag.' He remembers getting out of bed only to open bottles of wine, prepare food or open the window, but other than that it was Live Aid all the way. From soup to nuts, via two or three bottles of Le Piat d'Or.

Richard wasn't unconcerned or dismissive about the cause; he loved the whole idea. He understood that this was the first time aid had been marketed in such a way, he understood that this was the first time pop had been used to fund-raise on such a scale, and he liked most people on the bill (although like everyone I knew he wasn't that enthralled by Nik Kershaw, Paul Young or Howard Jones, who were makeweights before they were pop stars, and destined to revert to type). Like all of us he understood that this was a colossal event, and not something to be treated lightly. And it needed to be celebrated, like a moon landing, or a Wimbledon final. Or a Wimbledon final on the moon.

For my parents it was equally exciting, as it was a legitimate excuse to sit and watch telly all day, plugging themselves into the zeitgeist while not needing to know anything about it. This was a big charity thing, and it would last until it reached the end of the road. Everything in their house was eaten on trays that day, from tea in the morning right through to Horlicks at night.

Another friend of mine had just moved into a flat in Blackheath, in south London, with his new wife, and he spent the whole day sanding their floor. Together they watched the whole thing, turning off the sander when a band they liked came on the TV, and turning it on again when Phil Collins or Dire Straits came on. They drank beer, and made ratatouille with baked potatoes. They had no furniture to speak of, so watching Live Aid felt quite glamorous, as the TV pumped out all this music to a large empty room, as though it were an auditorium. The newlyweds were going to do nothing all day but sand their floor and watch television, and they actually couldn't think of anything else they'd prefer to be doing, nowhere else they'd prefer to be.

Another friend, Kathy, who had just had a baby, had to use four VHS tapes in order to record it all. Jane, a St Martin's girl, watched it at her father's house in Windsor, recording it on a format that was soon to die an ignominious death, Betamax. She was paying close attention as a friend of hers, Chester Kamen, was playing at Wembley with Bryan Ferry that day. The brother of Eighties models Nick and Barry Kamen, Chester was a successful session guitarist, and also played on Ferry's *Boys And Girls* album.

Live Aid was organised in just nineteen weeks, from scratch, immediately after the end of a Boomtown Rats tour on 3 March. Not only did Bob Geldof want to put on a stadium show that would be televised worldwide, he wanted there to be two venues for the show, one in London and the other somewhere on the East Coast of the US (it had to be on the East Coast because of the time difference). The idea was to create a bill featuring the biggest contemporary acts in the world, mixed in with some heritage acts, and then use the concert as a massive fund-raiser for the victims of the Ethiopian drought. It was only an eight-hour flight from London to Ethiopia, yet it may as well have been a different planet.

Live Aid was preceded by the Band Aid charity single 'Do They Know It's Christmas?' nine months earlier, a record that changed the nation's psyche in the space of only a few days.

It all began for Geldof late on 24 October 1984, as he sat in his Chelsea home watching the BBC *Six O'Clock News* with his girlfriend Paula Yates. This was in the days when the *Six O'Clock News* had an audience of around 10 million, or roughly a sixth of the population. They were watching BBC reporter Michael Buerk's second film on the Ethiopian famine, and it was harrowing. In particular, it was the sight of a young English Red Cross worker that really shocked Geldof, as she had to decide which of the starving children she could try and help with her limited supplies.

Michael Buerk's second BBC report on the Ethiopian famine, first broadcast on 24 October 1984, was the catalyst for Live Aid. In many respects it's possible to say that the Eighties finally began that day.

A long-term drought and secessionist wars in the Eritrea and Tigre regions had caused the failure of most food crops in Ethiopia and Sudan, and so a terrible famine struck the area. As the summer of 1984 dragged on and on, the fields withered and died, and the human tragedy grew worse. Western Aid was organised immediately, but it was far too little to have any real impact. Geldof recalled the dignity of those condemned to death, hiding, almost cowering behind a low-lying wall.

'I remember them staring over it,' he told the *Radio Times*. 'There was no rancour in their faces at all. That, more than anything, shocked me profoundly.'

Buerk's seven-minute report started with these two emotive sentences: 'Dawn, and as the sun breaks through the piercing chill of night on the plains outside Korem, it lights up a biblical famine, now, in the twentieth century. This place, say workers here, is the closest thing to hell on earth.'

'I was based in Johannesburg at the time and was the BBC's correspondent in Africa,' said Buerk. 'The rains that should have come in around August to Ethiopia had failed again for the sixth season running and it tipped over from being a crisis to a catastrophe. People suddenly realised they were going to die and this huge mass migration started. It tipped very quickly.

'We flew and then drove up there and the roads were just littered with dying people. It was extraordinary, it was just on such a huge scale. At Korem there were 40,000–45,000 people, and in Makele there were another 80,000–90,000. They tended to congregate along the spinal road that led north from Addis, where they thought relief would get to them.

'It's difficult to express the inadequacy I felt. You take refuge in the technicalities of filming, finding sequences, working out the logistics and so on. There were two films, two pieces that finally aired. I knew they wanted about three minutes, but I cut eight and thought, fuck 'em. In those days as a foreign correspondent, communications being what they were, I tended to work on the basis that they got what they were given. I knew it was a very powerful film.'

I remember the BBC broadcast well – so many people you know had seen it, although not everyone had been horrified by what they saw – and bizarrely heard Geldof discussing it a few days later. The infamous Eighties chronicler Peter York was launching his *Style Wars* sequel, *Modern Times*, at Heinemann's then rather swanky offices in Grosvenor Street, and a bunch of us were going. I was the editor of *i-D* at the time, and went along with various editors from *The Face*, the *Evening Standard* and the *Sunday Times*. At the event, Geldof told me, and indeed anyone who would listen, about the terrible images he had seen. The BBC's *Arena* arts programme was filming at the launch, as a segment of a modern-day *Pygmalion* they were producing, called *Ligmalion*, about making your way in the Swinging London of the Eighties. Geldof was caught on camera describing the awful scenes he had seen on TV, and that night – inspired by the party guests' apathy as much as anything else – he decided to make a record to raise funds for those affected by the famine.

Geldof said: 'To die of want in a world of surplus is not only intellectually absurd, it is morally repulsive.'

'It did not look like television,' said Geldof. 'Vast . . . grey . . . these grey wraiths moving about this moonscape . . .'

The next day Yates left a message for him on their kitchen noticeboard, encouraging them both to try and raise some money from their friends; but then Geldof decided that a better way to raise money would be to make a charity record. So he called Ultravox's Midge Ure, Sting and Duran Duran's Simon Le Bon, and proceeded to plan the Band Aid record. Geldof called every pop star he knew (and many he didn't) and persuaded them to record the single under the title 'Band Aid', for free.

A day later, Geldof called a friend and explained his idea for Band Aid. 'Fucking good craic, eh, Mike?' he said. The friend explained: 'He wasn't thinking in terms of salvaging his rock career. By "craic", he meant pulling a stroke on the world.'

On Saturday 24 November 1984, a star-studded group of musicians convened in a London studio to produce Geldof's folly: Duran Duran, Spandau Ballet, Wham!, Paul Weller, Phil Collins, Culture Club, the Police, Bananarama, Bono, and many others.

'Band Aid was actually incredibly competitive,' said Spandau Ballet's Gary Kemp. 'Even people who came from the same club as us, like Boy

George, Wham!, Duran, whoever it was. We hardly ever saw each other, but now we were all going to be in the same place at the same time.

'A few days after the Michael Buerk programme I was in an antiques shop on the King's Road and I was in the window pointing at something I wanted to see and Geldof pressed his face up against the window and he said did I see Michael's programme, and I hadn't. And he said, "Look it was so moving and I feel that we could all do something about this." We all liked Geldof, as he was quite cool about hanging with the newer generation of kids. He and Paula came to some of those clubs [Blitz, Le Beat Route, Club For Heroes, etc.] and I think he was one of the few from that era who got what we were doing and wanted to kind of be part of it. And I always loved Paula. Even though he wasn't having hit records at that point, he was still a cool guy. When you're in a room with Bob – I mean he's incredibly powerful. It's difficult to ignore him, you wanna be in his trench.

'He said, "Do you fancy doing a single, making some music?" I thought, "Dunno, it's a good idea," but totally cynically thinking, "Who the fuck's going to want to sing on that?"'

Spandau were off to Japan that day, and Kemp asked Geldof to call if any more came of the idea, thinking that absolutely nothing would. But he got the call the very next day, and was coerced into joining Geldof in his mission to get every major British pop star to sing on his charity record. The band had to travel to Germany to do a TV show before coming back to Britain to sing on the record, by which time Geldof had managed to co-opt most of the top thirty. While Spandau were in Germany they bumped into Duran Duran for the first time since they had come to see Spandau play at the botanical gardens in Birmingham, when Spandau had just signed to Chrysalis Records. They decamped to the studio bar and proceeded to drink themselves into a stupor. 'It was a big drinking match,' said Kemp, 'and they were completely wrecked. I remember talking to Nick Rhodes who said, "Oh yeah, we've got a make-up artist meeting us at Heathrow so we can look half decent when we get out the other side." I thought, "Fuck me, we're going to be in trouble now."'

'So the actual day of recording became a very competitive day. We both got our private planes back, literally trying to beat each other to Heathrow. We were told that there were security guards waiting to meet us at Heathrow, but when we got there the place was empty, because all the press were down at Sarm Studios waiting for everybody to arrive to record Band Aid.'

Spandau got their arrival at Sarm spectacularly wrong. They allowed cars to be organised for them, and when Martin Kemp got out of his limo in front of the studio, he actually said, 'We're back,' showing a complete lack of empathy and tact.

'Everyone knows how to be humble now, but not then,' said Gary Kemp. 'Sting got it perfectly right. He walked up the road with a copy of the *Guardian* under his arm. He probably got his driver to drop him off round the corner, but it looked as though he was completely on-message. He knew what to do immediately. Bollocks, he fucked us. But I'll never forget the day, because that was the best day, to have all those musicians in that studio, all trying to make it work and all getting on. U2 were there and we were all thinking, "Why the fuck are U2 here? They're nobody, they're punk wannabes." And their bass player Adam said to Steve, our manager, "Can I talk to you? What do you do about screaming girls because we're starting to get them?" And Steve said, "We love them."'

'Do They Know It's Christmas?' was released two days later, immediately going to number one and becoming the fastest-selling single ever in Britain. The single raised £8 million worldwide (rather than the £50,000 or so that Geldof had originally envisaged), money that was used to buy and transport food, including 150 tons of high-energy biscuits, 1,335 tons of milk powder, 560 tons of cooking oil, 470 tons of sugar and 1,000 tons of grain.

The single was not only a huge hit, it seemed to tap into a new zeitgeist, one that initially appeared to be counter-intuitive compared to everything else that was happening in Eighties Britain. In 1984 we were living in a world rapidly becoming obsessed by status, obsessed by the trappings of the designer lifestyle, full of newly empowered yuppies wrapping themselves in the spoils of style culture. In 1984, our new Swinging London had monetised itself, and bought into (literally) a world of Italian espresso machines, lifestyle magazines, designer fashion, matt-black hardware, silver sports cars and lobotomised pop music. 1984 meant style over content, a Paul Smith suit, a Sade record (soon to be on CD!), and a fancy European holiday.

Immediately the Band Aid record became part and parcel of the festive period, and that Christmas, and for most Christmases until the end of the decade, primary schools would sing the song as the finale of their carol service or nativity plays. Suddenly everyone was channelling Sting, George Michael or Tony Hadley. Until Elton John's re-recording of 'Candle In The Wind', written for Princess Diana's funeral in 1997 (with all the proceeds going to another charitable venture, the Diana, Princess of Wales, Memorial Fund), it was the best-selling British single of them all.

'When Midge and I did "Do They Know It's Christmas?", I'd thought, 72,000 sales, give the money to Oxfam and Save the Children and get the fuck out,' said Geldof, as the decade ended. 'It was just a personal gesture, the only thing I could do at the time. I didn't have any money, we weren't successful, so I couldn't do the song myself, it would have been disastrous. The Rats wouldn't have sold anything.

'The song became, completely unwittingly, the focus for what must have been lurking about out there, a sense of impotence and compassion, a rejection of selfish values. I can't explain the song any other way. Musically it wasn't the greatest thing ever written, forget it. 3 million sales in Britain alone cannot be explained except as a social phenomenon. People must have tapped into this thing. What they'd seen on TV had appalled them, and they'd found no instrument to articulate that sentiment, and suddenly this silly piece of plastic came along, a fairly duff song, and that was it.'

A few months later, emboldened by the record's extraordinary success, and frustrated by the way in which the aid agencies were distributing the money, Geldof decided that there should be a concert, too. He felt there was much more to do, and – Geldof being Geldof – he felt that he was the person to do it.

'Bob then said we needed to break this trucking cartel in Ethiopia and buy a fleet of trucks and spares to deliver the aid,' said Midge Ure, who had co-written and produced the Band Aid single. 'We didn't have the money so Bob came in with this little drawing of the world with a knife and fork and the idea to do a concert. This mad, mad idea just grew.

'I didn't really get a chance to say no. Bob arrived in my office and basically said, "We're doing this." It started from there.'

As many have said, death confers dignity on the famous only for a short time. Within a year or so their reputations begin to dip, often staying that way for decades. Then, as the wheel turns, so time reconfers dignity and importance, and the dead are rediscovered and reappraised, their legacies balanced out.

It's often the same with decades. 'The recent past always seems tawdry and passé in comparison to the more distant past, and this applies to the people who were celebrities in it,' wrote A. C. Grayling. 'Look at images of the people and fashions in the Eighties, and compare them to images from the Fifties; the latter seem far more interesting because they're more remote and magical. The Eighties just seem old hat. While the past moves through old hat to its magical stage, the personalities in it have to suffer the same fate.'

The Eighties have changed, though, and the farther away they become, the more interesting they appear. In Britain the decade has been demonised, held collectively responsible for the divisive economic and social policies of Margaret Thatcher – with her ocean blue suit and predatory smile – while at the same time celebrating the trivial, the shallow and the expensively produced. But the farther away we get from it, the more the decade is reassessed, its legacies re-evaluated and re-graded.

One of the events of the Eighties that never needed re-evaluating was the mother of all benefit gigs, Bob Geldof's Live Aid, a touchstone of the decade, a pinch point, an event that was deemed to have enormous relevance and a lasting legacy weeks, months, before it actually happened. Live Aid was a global village Woodstock with a mission. One of the reasons it caused such a stir was because of the environment in which it blossomed. On paper, a global charity concert featuring the likes of Bob Dylan, Elton John, the Rolling Stones and a Beatle should have happened in the Seventies, not the selfish, grasping Eighties, surely. In the Sixties or Seventies, the benevolent gesture politics of the Sixties were still being taken seriously, the shockwaves still reverberating around the music industry. But by the midway point of the Eighties we appeared to be far more interested in Boy George's make-up, the drum machines on the new Phil Collins record and the four-wheel drive option of the new Golf GTI.

1985 wasn't meant to be the year that Britain remembered to celebrate the Sixties. It wasn't meant to be the year of benevolence, charity or global empathy. We were living in the Reagan/Thatcher era, when political intransigence was king, and market forces determined everything. In this environment, Live Aid seemed positively contrary.

Which is possibly why it struck such a chord.

There was a direct through-line from Live Aid back to the Sixties, the decade that witnessed the birth of the mass media through Telstar, the first television satellite (as well as the title of an international hit for the Tornadoes, produced by the maverick record man Joe Meek), and ushering in the age of emancipated pop and the counter-cultural call for love and peace. Like the Sixties, Live Aid started in London and then spread around the world.

Live Aid was positively bipartisan, as it celebrated both the new guard and the old. It celebrated the 'new pop' groups, the loose amalgam of New Romantic bands who had grown up out of punk, and who had all recently taken America by storm: Duran Duran, Spandau Ballet, Culture Club, Wham!, the Thompson Twins, etc.; while it also celebrated the likes of Status Quo, Elton John and Paul McCartney, acts who were making records back when God was a boy. You could look at the Live Aid bill and think that punk had never happened, as though the social insurrection and class warfare of 1976 had been just a fantasy dreamed up by a couple of bored music journalists who had got sick of listening to their Iggy Pop and Lou Reed records.

In a way, pop had never been bigger. Record sales had certainly never been bigger, while the music business was now a fully-fledged part of the entertainment industry. It was certainly no longer a novelty when *Arena*,

Omnibus or *The South Bank Show* produced a programme about a pop star. Live Aid gave birth to a new form of pop that didn't rely on anything but its ability to connect with a large audience. By the time of Live Aid, pop was exactly thirty years old, and in a way the event was pop's apotheosis. After this, everything would eventually start to fragment, as the power shifted from rock to dance, from white to black, from the cult of celebrity to the cult of the dance floor.

Live Aid caused a quantum shift in the entertainment industry. The stadium became the de facto benchmark of success (if you couldn't fill a stadium three nights running then you weren't properly successful); while the underground did what it always does in situations like this, it burrowed even deeper. From 1985 onwards, Britain's alternative culture would revolve around dance music, a groundswell of activity that involved nightclub culture, DJ culture, dance music, and the re-emergence of black music as a form of insurrection. This wasn't just about rap and hip-hop, this was about rap and hip-hop becoming the dominant force in pop (the Beastie Boys would hit in 1986); this wasn't just about the 12" remix, this was about dance music becoming the lingua franca of underground cool.

This was the point where pop diverged again, where mainstream rock acts went in one direction, and underground dance music created an alternative culture that would soon rival rock in its omnipotence. In the thirty years after Live Aid, dance music would become the dominant force in pop – so much so that if a Live Aid anniversary concert were organised today, one might imagine that most of the acts would be what we used to call dance acts.

Billed as the 'global jukebox', that day there were also concerts in Philadelphia, Sydney, Cologne, Holland and Moscow, but it is the concert at Wembley Stadium which immediately became representative of a new kind of global celebrity culture, a concert which rubber-stamped the decade like no other before or after it, an event that would soon come to define the Eighties. Not only that, it was the largest-scale satellite link-up and television broadcast of all time: an estimated global audience of 1.9 billion, across 150 nations, watched it live.

Everyone was involved in Live Aid – everyone that is except Bruce Springsteen, who apparently wanted some time at home with his new wife. Paul McCartney was there, along with U2, Bob Dylan, Queen, Sting, Elvis Costello, Hall and Oates, Billy Joel, Elton John, Madonna, Phil Collins, The Who, George Michael, Dire Straits, Bryan Adams, Mick Jagger and David Bowie and dozens more.

Apart from Queen – who on 13 July would redefine what it meant to be a rock band – the other highlight of the day was the performance by U2. During 'Bad', Bono pulled a girl up from the audience and started to dance with her, something he would do again in other shows, but in the context of Live Aid, which was all about reaching out, touching, connecting, it was a magical moment. (The girl he danced with claimed in 2005 that he actually saved her life. She was being crushed by the throngs of people pushing forwards; Bono saw this, and gestured frantically at the ushers to help her. They didn't understand what he was saying, so he jumped down to help her himself.)

Phil Collins famously performed at both Wembley and JFK Stadiums, using Concorde to get him from London to Philadelphia. Noel Edmonds piloted the helicopter that took Collins to Heathrow Airport to catch his flight. Apart from his own performance at both venues, he also provided drums for Eric Clapton and Led Zeppelin at JFK.

The whole point of Live Aid was to raise money for Ethiopia, to extend the charitable efforts of Band Aid. Nearly seven hours into the Wembley concert, Bob Geldof enquired how much money had been raised. When he was told that so far they'd managed to raise £1.2 million, he marched to the BBC commentary box, and gave the infamous interview in which he used the word 'fuck'. The BBC presenter David Hepworth, conducting the interview, had attempted to provide a list of addresses to which potential donations should be sent; Geldof interrupted him in mid-flow and shouted: 'Fuck the address, let's get the numbers!' After his outburst, giving increased to £300 per second.

There were some extraordinary moments at Live Aid, although there were some travesties, too. When Bob Dylan broke one of his strings on stage in Philadelphia, Ronnie Wood took off his own guitar and gave it to him, meaning Wood was left standing on stage guitarless. After shrugging to the audience, he started playing air guitar, even mimicking The Who's Pete Townshend by swinging his arm in enormous circles, until a stagehand brought him a replacement.

After Live Aid the music industry was never really the same again. From here on in, success was quantifiable in such obvious ways; pop suddenly had the ability to reach the four corners of the earth. To achieve anything less was a disappointment, a failure. For many who performed that day, their appearance was a blink, a blemish, a fleeting dream, something that they're still not sure really happened to them. So many people who performed at Wembley, and indeed in Philadelphia, did so in some sort of a daze – blinded by the crowd, cowed by the occasion, or simply overcome by nerves. Consequently many of them have extremely particular memories of the show, memories that have a huge bearing on what happened to them afterwards. Some only remember what they were feeling by watching themselves on tape.

As I went home that night, having spent all day in the Wembley sun, huddled on the Tube, along with thousands of others who had sung along to the finale of 'Do They Know It's Christmas?' in the hot summer air, I felt as though pop had somehow entered another dimension, pushed itself through a vortex.

Live Aid was the greatest stadium concert of all time, possibly the most important rock spectacle of them all, with as much cultural resonance as Woodstock or Altamont, and one shared by billions of people as opposed to tens of thousands. It was a spectacle in so many different ways, and in a way the day unfolded like a thriller, from the hours before the performance to the finale in Philadelphia and into the small hours after.

For ten hours on Saturday 13 July 1985, exactly halfway through the decade, Wembley Stadium became one vast, electronic begging bowl, a massive exercise in choreographed compassion. But while Geldof was expert at milking human kindness more efficiently than it had ever been milked before, Live Aid stood for something else: in some respects it was the pinnacle of post-war pop culture, its defining moment, the realisation of Canadian academic Marshall McLuhan's 'global village' party. At the start of the Sixties McLuhan wrote: 'Postliterate man's electronic media contract the world to a village or tribe where everything happens to everyone at the same time: everyone knows about, and therefore participates in, everything that is happening the minute it happens.' Electronic media was to become the Esperanto of its day, while Live Aid would be the event that finally saw humankind move – albeit temporarily – from a state of individualism and fragmentation to something resembling a collective identity. A 'tribal base'.

Tom Wolfe may have identified the Seventies as the Me Decade, but the idea really came to fruition in the Eighties. The extraordinary transformation of lifestyles occasioned by the Sixties confronted a generation with decisions they had never been asked to make before – decisions of taste. In the Eighties, those decisions became even more fundamental as society became more market-driven, and choice became a lifestyle decision in itself. Even when it came to charity.

1985 had already been a something of a tumultuous year, albeit one intertwined with trivia. On 1 January the first British mobile phone call was made (it was a stunt: the comedian Ernie Wise calling Vodafone), prompting British Telecom to announce it was going to phase out its famous red telephone boxes. On 20 January, US president Ronald Reagan was sworn in for a second term in office, while barely two months later, Mikhail Gorbachev became the General Secretary of the Soviet Communist Party and therefore de facto leader of the Soviet Union. At fifty-four he was the youngest member of the Politburo, and not only looked more youthful than any previous Soviet leader, but came armed with new ideas to boot. He eagerly wanted a dialogue with the West, and would seek internal reforms completely alien to previous regimes. He was driven by change, and by ambition: this was a man who had graduated from driving a harvester to a law degree from Moscow University.

The US was still recovering from the international horror at the gas leak from an American facility in the Indian city of Bhopal at the very end of

1984, where several thousand people died in the worst industrial accident in history. Nearly forty tons of a highly toxic mix of methyl isocyanate, cyanide and phosgene was accidentally released into the atmosphere, causing not only the initial deaths, but also excessive rates of cancer, breathing disorders and birth defects. Nearly 500,000 suffered from some form of poisoning, while over 150,000 people were disabled because of it. This was seen as yet another example of imperialistic American negligence. (In 1992, the Bhopal Court of Justice would issue an arrest warrant for the company's CEO, although the Indian authorities failed to have him extradited.)

In some respects the world was a simpler place in 1985, with broadly defined ideas of good and evil. The Cold War was still raging, and a poll conducted in Britain in 1980 found that 40 per cent of adults were convinced that nuclear warfare was likely in the next ten years. The threat was referenced everywhere in pop culture, from Frankie Goes to Hollywood's 'Two Tribes' to Hollywood's own *War Games* via Martin Amis's *Einstein's Monsters*. For many, the only sure-fire weapon against communism was Rocky Balboa, who managed to bring about world peace in *Rocky IV* by beating Russian boxing machine Ivan Drago. On 12 June 1982, over one million people demonstrated in New York City's Central Park against nuclear weapons and for an end to the cold war arms race. It was not only the largest anti-nuclear protest ever, it was also the largest political demonstration in American history. As Freddie Mercury would sing on the Wembley stage on 13 July, 'For we who grew up tall and proud/ In the shadow of the mushroom cloud/Convinced our voices can't be heard/We just wanna scream it louder and louder and louder.' Economic instability in the Soviet Union and the country's inability to match Ronald Reagan's arms spending would eventually lead to a massive reduction in nuclear stockpiles, but by then there was another threat to world peace on the horizon. Towards the end of the decade we were offered a glimpse of how other ideologies would change the religious and political nature of the country, with the furore that greeted the publication of Salman Rushdie's *The Satanic Verses* in 1989. Thereafter, religious militancy would take on a whole new meaning.

Elsewhere, on 16 February 1985 Israel started withdrawing its troops from Lebanon, while twelve days later the IRA carried out a mortar attack on the Royal Ulster Constabulary police station in Newry, killing nine officers; it was the highest loss of life for the RUC on a single day.

3 March saw the end of the year-long miners' strike, one of the most fractious periods of the Thatcher government's second term, although its place on the evening news was soon taken by the newly ascended football yoberati. English football hooliganism was fast becoming one of the country's worst exports. On 13 March rioting broke out at the FA Cup quarter-final between Luton Town and Millwall at Kenilworth Road, Luton; hundreds of hooligans tore seats from the stands and threw them on to the pitch before a proper pitch invasion took place, resulting in eighty-one people injured (thirty-one of them members of the police force). Two months later a fire engulfed a wooden stand at the Valley Parade stadium in Bradford, killing fifty-six people and injuring more than 250 others. On 29 May, at the European Cup Final between Juventus and Liverpool at the Heysel Stadium in Brussels, thirty-nine spectators were killed in rioting on the terraces, casting an even larger shadow over the state of English football. On 2 June UEFA banned all English clubs from European competitions indefinitely, suggesting that Liverpool serve an extra three years of exclusion.

Just three days before Live Aid, at the behest of President Mitterrand, French DGSE agents sank the Greenpeace vessel *Rainbow Warrior* in Auckland harbour. Humbled by the outcry that followed, the French government decided to abandon nuclear testing for ten years.

In April, worried about the continuing onslaught of Pepsi – who appeared to have decided that the Eighties were going to be their decade – Coca-Cola had done the unthinkable and announced a new formula, New Coke ('The best just got better'). It had already been such a disaster that three days before Live Aid they had been forced to reintroduce 'Classic Coke'. Pepsi couldn't believe this gift of such a self-inflicted PR disaster by their fiercest rival. Coincidentally, on 13 July their logo was flying above the Wembley stage.

Just a few days before Live Aid, the seventeen-year-old German Boris Becker had become the youngest ever male Grand Slam singles champion and the youngest ever men's singles winner at the Wimbledon Championships, beating the South African Kevin Curren. His athleticism, power and drive (as well as his soon-to-be-famous 'boom boom' serve) signalled the dawn of a new era in tennis, as the hegemony of Jimmy Connors, John McEnroe and Bjorn Borg gave way to a faster, harder, less flamboyant type of player.

This was also the year the BBC launched its own soap opera – jumping ahead of the curve for once by using the increasingly popular conceit of abutting two words and inserting a medial capital letter, thus: *EastEnders*. This was also called CamelCase, or bicapitalisation – compounds in which words are joined without spaces: CinemaScope, FedEx, InterLink, PlayStation, HarperCollins, WordPad, SureStart, etc. This was what Tom Wolfe called the new lean, mean fashion of jamming names together 'as if that way you were creating some hyperhard alloy for the twenty-first century'. In the case of *EastEnders* it was curiously unnecessary, but it had the effect of making the BBC seem a little less stuffy than the competition. Not that the BBC would need worry about being stuffy, as with Live Aid they were about to be the feeder broadcaster for the largest television event in history.

Terry Waite, the Archbishop of Canterbury's special envoy, negotiated the release of four British hostages from Beirut, while the civil war continued. The Shias took over the city and the Lebanese Cabinet fell. The conflict then spread to a wider stage as the Israelis bombed PLO offices in Tunis. In June, a TWA jet was hijacked and diverted to Beirut and its thirty-nine American passengers held hostage by Shia terrorists for sixteen days until 700 Lebanese Shia prisoners were released from Israel. Slightly less successful was the hijacking later in the year of the Italian cruise ship *Achille Lauro* by a group of Palestinian pirates.

Violence was also escalating in South Africa, with a broad pattern of racial strife spreading through the townships. While the ban on mixed marriages had ended, there was escalating pressure for international sanctions to be imposed. A state of emergency was declared, and press restrictions imposed.

1985 was an eventful year for the music industry. In both the UK and the US, record and cassette sales were up 14 per cent from the previous year, with cassettes outselling vinyl albums in Britain for the first time. The number of albums certified platinum in the US increased by 46 per cent over 1984, while compact discs accounted for 21 million of the 643 million total units sold, an astonishing increase of 250 per cent. In some respects 1985 was the year of Madonna, who in twelve short months had become the most famous sex symbol since Marilyn Monroe. In Britain alone, she had seven zeitgeist-defining top-five hits: 'Material Girl', 'Crazy For You', 'Into The Groove', 'Holiday', 'Angel', 'Gambler' and 'Dress You Up'. However, it was the year that the second British invasion reached its zenith, with the likes of Duran Duran, Culture Club, Tears For Fears and Wham! crowding the US charts. It would soon begin a precipitous decline, as the sparkling video revolution would help spur a backlash. Perhaps sensing a zeitgeist shift, Wham! became the first Western pop group to perform in the People's Republic of China and to release records there. Ironically this was also the year in which heavy metal and hard rock started their renaissance: Kiss came back with a silver-tongued vengeance, WASP reared their ugly codpiece, and Ratt's *Out Of The Cellar* and Motley Crue's *Shout At The Devil* both went double platinum. Whitney Houston also had a good year, as her eponymous debut became the best-selling debut album by a female act. Michael Jackson paid $40 million for the rights to the ATC Music catalogue, which included over 5,000 songs, including many written by Lennon and McCartney. A group of influential if overly earnest Washington housewives, including Tipper Gore, formed the Parents' Music Resource Center, which pressured the music industry to establish a rating system that would warn potential record buyers of sexually explicit and violent lyrics. They may as well have carried stickers emblazoned with 'THIS RECORD CONTAINS SEX AND DRUGS AND ROCK 'N' ROLL!'

On the legal front, blues performer Willie Dixon filed a complaint alleging that Led Zeppelin's 'Whole Lotta Love' was plagiarised from his song 'You Need Love', recorded in 1962 by Muddy Waters. Dead icons proved more than enduring: the US Postal Service issued an Elvis Presley stamp commemorating what would have been his fiftieth birthday; a record-breaking 500 million Elvis stamps would eventually be sold. Not only that, but John Lennon's psychedelic Rolls-Royce went for over $2 million at a New York auction. The co-founder of the Rolling Stones also died this year, although unlike his partners, he was never an icon: pianist Ian Stewart died of a heart attack at the age of forty-seven.

Elsewhere, it was more than fitting that British *Elle* launched in 1985 as this was the year that British fashion truly went global, with Vivienne Westwood, Bodymap, Scott Crolla, Rachel Auburn, John Galliano and a whole host of other younger designers at the forefront of a movement which looked as if it were about to take over the world. Perhaps the most successful designer of the year was Katharine Hamnett, who briefly swapped places with Christo as her shirts seemed to cover the planet like huge silk shrouds. She had become a household name the year before when she had worn one of her protest T-shirts – '58% Don't Want Pershing', a reference to a poll showing public opposition to the basing of Pershing missiles in the UK – to Downing Street to meet Mrs Thatcher.

The Eighties were the decade of power dressing, concocted by the likes of Gianna Versace and Karl Lagerfeld, while the maxim of the moment was 'If you've got it, flaunt it.' Hermes even produced a leather harness for carrying your bottle of Evian. The decade started with businessmen being knighted for go-getting, and then jailed when it was discovered how; began with keeping your valuables in a vault, and ended by pretending you used unleaded petrol.

It was more than appropriate that Live Aid was the event of the decade, because if the Seventies had been the Me Decade, then if anything the Eighties were the Media Decade, ten years in which cable TV took over the world, and where satellites gave us deep dish. VCRs (and for a while, Betamax) meant that we could now record everything, while CDs meant that the past was brought right up to date, remixed, burnished, and with a shiny, metallic modern sheen (which a lot of people hated). Twenty-four-hour news meant that the world continued to shrink, and as the proliferation of newspapers and magazines continued in a seemingly exponential gear, so lifestyles became content. It would be hyperbolic to say that hype replaced art, but it appeared to replace just about everything else.

Those in the know were reading Oliver Sacks's *The Man Who Mistook His Wife for a Hat* and anything by Tama Janowitz, the literary Cyndi Lauper, while the London glitterati were listening to Phyllis Nelson, Grace Jones, Cameo and an awful lot of Blue Note. They quaffed champagne, watched *Prizzi's Honor* and dashed off to Barcelona to escape *EastEnders*. The cool magazine face of the year was Mickey Rourke.

Stephen Sondheim and Studs Terkel both won Pulitzer Prizes, while the Oscar winners included F. Murray Abraham (*Amadeus*), Sally Field (*Places in the Heart*), Haing S. Ngor (*The Killing Fields*), Peggy Ashcroft (*A Passage to India*), Milos Forman (*Amadeus*), Robert Benton (*Places in the Heart*), Chris Menges (*The Killing Fields*) and – rather ridiculously – Stevie Wonder, for the use of 'I Just Called to Say I Love You' in *The Woman in Red*. The top five grossing movies were *Back to the Future*, *Rambo: First Blood, Part II*, *Rocky IV*, *The Color Purple* and *Out of Africa*. 1985 was also the year when we saw the last of Orson Welles, Yul Brynner, Rock Hudson, Simone Signoret, Margaret Hamilton, Ricky Nelson, Michael Redgrave, Louise Brooks, Phil Silvers and Wilfred Brambell. Hudson's death was especially notable as he was the first high-profile star to die from AIDS.

It was also the year in which Steve Jobs gave the following quote to *Playboy*: 'A computer is the most incredible tool we've ever seen. It can be a writing tool, a communications center, a supercalculator, a planner, a filer and an artistic instrument all in one, just by being given new instructions, or software, to work from. There are no other tools that have the power and versatility of a computer. We have no idea how far it's going to go. Right now, computers make our lives easier. They do work for us in fractions of a second that would take us hours. They increase the quality of life, some of that by simply automating drudgery and some of that by broadening our possibilities. As things progress, they'll be doing more and more for us.'

Not that many people believed him.

London was changing beyond recognition, as new money swept into the city, and we all tried to embrace the trappings of the upwardly mobile. We started defining ourselves in different ways, too. At the start of the Eighties, there were hardly any good restaurants in London, yet as the decade wore on, they appeared to arrive every hour, on the hour. Lindsey Bareham was then a food writer for the London listings magazine *Time Out*: 'Suddenly we knew the names of top chefs in the same way that we knew the names of the Beatles: the Roux brothers, Anton Mosimann, Nico Ladenis and Raymond Blanc. Rose Gray and Ruth Rogers tentatively launched the River Café as a works canteen for Richard Rogers' architectural practice next door; Alastair Little, Marco Pierre White and Simon Hopkinson, and the late Rowley Leigh at Kensington Place, all opened trend-setting restaurants within months of each other.'

As Bareham and every other traditional recipe writer soon discovered, while these new chefs' coffee-table books inspired a generation of newly confident home cooks, the meals they were making required unusual, esoteric ingredients, prompting the likes of Marks & Spencer to broaden its range of upmarket ready meals, bringing flat-leaf parsley, banoffee pie, rocket and plum tomatoes to the masses.

And we hoovered it up, thinking ourselves on the cusp of some great new foodie dawn. Not all of it was as advertised, though. I remember once taking a colleague to Marco Pierre White's restaurant Harvey's in south London, to thank them for a project they'd been researching for me. The waitress was *extremely* French, almost comically French, acting a little bit as though she were in a prime-time sitcom, making sure she accompanied every laying of a fork and every rustle of a napkin with something suitably *exclamatif*.

The food was predictably, reassuringly extraordinary, and we both felt that the journey south had been worthwhile. However, the evening's coda was completely unexpected, although rather telling. As our oh-so-French waitress approached our table with the bill, she knocked a fork on to the floor, and as she did so, it wasn't a knee-jerk 'Merde' that slipped from her lips, but rather a fully loaded 'Shit' in broadest cockney.

This just showed how important appearances were becoming, in the restaurant business as well as everywhere else. Those in the metropolitan West were worrying about the provenance of their loose-leaf lettuce, while all over north-east Africa, people were literally starving.

The day of Live Aid, the biggest pop concert the capital had ever seen, the British charts were as confusingly anodyne as ever, with Sister Sledge's 'Frankie' at number one, followed by Harold Faltermeyer's 'Axel F', Madonna's 'Crazy For You' and Kool & the Gang's 'Cherish'. Bruce Springsteen, Fine Young Cannibals, Scritti Politti and the Eurythmics hovered about below, but the top thirty wasn't exactly a testament to great pop. But then Live Aid itself wasn't, merely being a barometer of popularity. And the world's biggest charity event, lest we forget. The 164-page perfect-bound Live Aid programme cost £5, with a Peter Blake illustration and the words 'THIS PROGRAMME SAVES LIVES' on the cover. Geldof's introduction was impassioned, to say the least:

I must try and show you this.

There is a child, I think maybe it's four months old. The doctor says, 'No, it's two years old.' It squats on baked mud, a tattered dusty piece of cotton hangs from one shoulder on to its distended stomach. Its face is huge. A two-year-old face on a four-month body.

The eyes are moons of dust and flies caked by tears so big they don't dry until they reach the navel.

Its mother is squatting also, behind her and slightly to the left. She is faint. She falls over a lot. I notice hundreds falling over.

The child stares. Between its legs flows a constant stream of diarrhoea. The immediate earth around its legs is damp with it.

I am watching a child die. In total silence and surrounded by its family it eventually begins to shit out its own stomach.

I am tired with grief and despair and a consuming rage for humanity.

He dies soon. He just dies. Big deal. A jumble of bones and dry skin, wet eyes, flies and shit. His mother hasn't noticed. She is too weak. Eventually they will come and tie his hands and legs in the approved manner, wrap his weightless body in anything and he will be buried hurriedly in a fruitless attempt to lessen the disease that flies ceaselessly through the scorching air.

At 2 a.m. it is freezing. At 2.30 the noise begins. Bodies too small and skinny to produce heat, too impoverished to have clothing, too weak to be able to digest, too thirsty to do anything but croak, too cold to do anything but die, too full of despair and hopelessness to live.

At 10 a.m. it is a cauldron. There is no noise except shuffle of feet moving forward in the endless procession of the intensive feeding lines, the soft keening of the bereaved, the moaning of the dying and the endless drone of the carrion flies.

It is a discreet, soft background sound, like afternoon tea in the Bath Tea Rooms I think. The almost soothing sound of famine. Inside the corrugated iron huts, it is beyond Dante's Inferno. At night freezing, by day an oven.

The living lie beside the dead on the earth or concrete platforms. Expediency rules. Famine is not polite. There is no beauty but in the faces, there is no dignity but in the eyes, no nobility but in the bearing, no privacy but of the mind.

The open letter went on and on, by turns shocking and heartbreaking. He ended by saying that eight weeks previously, the EEC spent £265 million destroying 2 million tons of vegetable and fruit . . . 'The shame, the shame, the shame.'

ONE

12:02

Status Quo: 'Rockin' All Over The World', 'Caroline', 'Don't Waste My Time'

The day before the concert I went out and bought 20 or 30 very large clocks and just stuck them everywhere. I sent notes round to every single act saying, I don't care what time you go on . . . I only care what time you come off'

HARVEY GOLDSMITH

The day was going to be as glorious as England's 1966 World Cup win. At least that was the feeling out front, as 72,000 people quickly assembled in front of the stage. A Goodyear airship floated benignly above them, and all was right with the world; well, all was right with this little patch of north London, anyway. Anticipation was so high there were queues outside the stadium as early as six in the morning. The doors opened at 10 a.m., two hours before the start of the show, and everyone wanted in. Some people had seats in the stands, others had pitch tickets, and all of us had smiles. Some of us brought jackets, others blankets.

Although by 1985 Wembley Stadium was already world famous, it wasn't used as a music venue until 1972, when it hosted the London Rock 'n' Roll Show, featuring Jerry Lee Lewis, Little Richard, Screaming Lord Sutch, the MC5 and Bill Haley and his Comets as well as Chuck Berry, who at the

Throughout the day, TV viewers were urged to donate money to the Live Aid cause. 300 phone lines were manned by the BBC, so that the public could make donations using their credit cards.

time was enjoying a massive chart success with his awful novelty single, 'My Ding-A-Ling'. By the time of Live Aid, the stadium was thought of as the best, and certainly the biggest, music venue in the country.

But it had never seen anything like this.

This was the sixteen-hour Leviathan: the tickets had cost £25, which was not an inconsiderable amount in 1985, not when Jobcentres were advertising employment opportunities at £1 to £1.25 per hour. Even though the event was officially sold out, there were still turnstiles letting people in for cash. This was truly going to be a day of numbers. Along with the 72,000 people in Wembley, there were another 90,000 in Philadelphia, with 2 billion watching worldwide on 500 million TV sets, via fourteen satellites. £11 million was raised in the UK that day, with another £36 million raised in the States. There were £50 million pledges. 50,000 £5 programmes and 10,000 £2.50 posters had already sold out before Status Quo had even reached the stage. The T-shirts were being sold for £8, although they ran out almost immediately.

Ninety-six countries broadcast at least a portion of the event; the Philippines broadcast four hours, while Luxembourg showed the full sixteen. The Soviet Union decided to record the shows, and then edit them and show them later. A group of about 800 VIPs were invited to the Gosteleradio Concert Hall, at the time the USSR's main television centre, to watch the Soviet band Autograph play their set and to view some of the Live Aid broadcast. Another sixty-five countries – those that couldn't receive the Live Aid satellite feed, or who couldn't afford the £20,000 to show it – were given a four-hour taped version.

13 July had not been an especially auspicious date in the annals of rock 'n' roll. Jim McGuinn was born on this day in 1942, the man who would change his name to Roger as part of his Subud religion, having already formed one of the most influential rock bands of all time, the Byrds. It was the day in 1881 that Pat Garrett shot Billy the Kid, and which was famously memorialised by Bob Dylan. And it was the day that Queen released their first album, simply titled *Queen*, in 1973.

There were other historical echoes: 13 July 1960 was the day the US Democratic party nominated John F. Kennedy as its presidential candidate, and the date seven years later of the infamous Newark race riots, in which twenty-seven people died. It was also the date, in 1939, when Frank Sinatra had made his recording debut, and the date, in 1923, when the Hollywood sign ('Hollywoodland') was officially dedicated in the hills above Los Angeles (it would lose its last four letters in 1949). Strangely, Ronald Reagan was not president on the day of Live Aid, Vice President George Bush having become acting president for the day as Reagan underwent surgery to remove polyps from his colon. Perhaps more pertinently it was the day, in 1935, when Emperor Haile Selassi rejected Italian suggestions that Abyssinia fall under the Italian sphere of influence. On 13 July 1955, Ruth Ellis became the last woman in England to be executed, at Holloway Prison in north London, with thousands of people outside protesting against the death penalty. Twenty-one years later on the same day, the first issue of the punk fanzine *Sniffin' Glue* appeared, including articles on the Ramones, the Flamin' Groovies, the Stranglers, Blue Oyster Cult, the Runaways, Television, Eddie & the Hot Rods and the 101'ers. Exactly a year later the Sex Pistols were in full flight, kicking off a proposed two-week

Scandinavian tour with the first night at Daddy's Dance Hall in Copenhagen.

13 July was, on average, the hottest day of the year in England, although in 1985, the omens for respecting this figure were slim, as the weeks leading up to Live Aid were full of grey gloom. But today the sun shone, emerging with gusto, as though nothing was going to stand in its way. No clouds. No obstructions. 'In this most dismal of English summers the sky was, for once, blue, and there was not a cloud in sight,' said Bob Geldof.

In 1973, *Elvis: Aloha From Hawaii* had been simultaneously broadcast to over a billion people worldwide, but this event was different, as this event was all about altruism. The thing was, would it work?

Some had been camping outside the gates of Wembley Stadium all night in order to get a good spot when the doors opened the following morning. One such person was seventeen-year-old Sharon Craig from Worcestershire, who remembered the night as 'one long party, with people singing and getting excited. We knew something great was going to happen.' There were even a few people who, being unable to get tickets for the Philadelphia show, had flown to England and bought tickets for Wembley, and so luckily for them saw Queen instead of Kenny Loggins.

Out front, there was a feeling of calm expectation, a sense that today was going to be a great day, regardless of how much anyone willed it to happen. There was a sense of inevitability about it, a sense that this wasn't going to be a day of anticlimaxes. Backstage, there was rather less optimism, as the stage crew were still tinkering with the revolving stage. Over the previous few weeks a circular, three-section stage had been developed, in which one band would be getting ready to perform while another played, and the third were dismantling their equipment. It was an inspired idea, yet no one was quite sure if it was going to work or not, especially considering the time constraints. Each artist was supposed to have exactly eighteen minutes on stage. There was a traffic-light system at the side of the stage, and when the amber light went on it meant they had one minute left. 'You won't see it turn red because that is when the power goes,' said the stage manager. Harvey Goldsmith said he didn't care what time bands went on stage, as all he cared about was what time they went off.

'The night before the biggest problem we had was the bloody turntable stage didn't work,' said Goldsmith, 'and that was a real issue. There was quite low morale with all of the crew, and I had to go and pep them up. Then I got a phone call about midnight from Tommy Mottola, from Sony. He said that if we didn't make sure Hall & Oates were on the ABC two-hour special, as well as the MTV broadcast of the whole show, then he was pulling Mick Jagger. And I told him, it is what it is. It's too late now and if you want to pull Mick Jagger then pull him, but I don't actually think you're going to succeed on that one. And then Bill Graham, who was organising the JFK show, phoned me up and said, "I'm making this plea, if you want me to really get my head around this you've got to put Black Sabbath on because I've got a merchandising deal with them." Love it! The crew had been working for thirty-six hours, so with all this going down it was quite demoralising for all of us.'

Geldof had spent much of the night on the phone, calling Postmaster Generals all over the world, trying to make sure that people's payments wouldn't be held up by unnecessary bureaucracy.

'I was calling Norway and all these places in the South Pacific checking what I remember as locked-box systems. I've no idea what that was, I've no idea what it is now. But I was told to call all the Postmaster Generals and find out had they put in place their locked box. That's what it was like for me. Boring shite. Were the satellites in place? I remember calling up to say are all the satellites now booked? Have we got total blanket coverage? I went to sleep just hoping people would turn up to play, as there were no fucking contracts.'

Goldsmith was obsessive about the timings, as he only needed one act to go over their limit and the whole schedule would fall to pieces. So he sent out for about thirty big Smiths clocks and put them everywhere backstage. 'Also, I can't work in clutter, so I cleared the stage for every performance. If you look at the stages in Wembley and Philadelphia you'll see the difference, as the US stage was littered with people. You couldn't work out who was playing and who wasn't. I can't work that way, and knowing that we had such a limited time to change over, I told everybody not to hang on the side of the stage.'

So it was, and so it began.

'It's twelve noon in London, 7 a.m. in Philadelphia, and around the world it's time for Live Aid,' said the DJ Richard Skinner over the Wembley PA system, his emphasis on the word 'Aid', as the term had yet to properly enter the vernacular. 'Wembley welcomes their Royal Highnesses the Prince and Princess of Wales.' At eleven o'clock, Charles and Diana had arrived to receive the stars, going backstage half an hour later. Everybody showed – Bowie, Elton, the lot – Diana even adjusted Bowie's tie, as it was a little crooked. They lined up around the edge of the banqueting room with its shiny floor and stood looking at one another, a little embarrassed, but also rather intrigued to meet the princess. Adam Ant thought she looked slender-faced, skinny and 'dinky', while she told him she was worried that he'd melt in his leather trousers.

Diana's PR people were as revolutionary in their own way as she was, as they said the TV crews should come as close as they wanted to. They were determined to make sure the photographers got pictures of them having a good time.

'I remember Charles and Diana were the guests of honour and there were strange things happening throughout the day,' said U2 manager Paul McGuinness, 'like Steve Wozniak from Apple asking to meet them. For some reason he was attached to the group of people that I helicoptered in with earlier in the day to suss things out, and I remember – hilariously – he was extremely keen to meet Charles and Diana, and whoever it was who was in charge – probably Geldof or Harvey Goldsmith – negotiated this. They said, "Well, if you write a very big cheque to Live Aid, we'll make sure you meet the royal couple." And I think he did. Backstage was great fun, because it was like the United Nations of the rock world.'

'Diana and Charles were hugely symbolic of the age, and it was a very big symbol that they came,' said Geldof. 'It was a huge endorsement. And getting them to come was a major fucking thing because I'm not sure Charles really wanted to be there. Diana certainly liked pop stars, and she was always flirting with them. Charles was saying, "I don't really want to commit to something that isn't the Prince's Trust," but I'd say, "hold on, Harvey Goldsmith organised the Prince's Trust. To all the rock guys, this is payback time." I was so glad when they came. There were all these moments that came together on the day. You had this amazing galaxy of rock stars, and yet Diana was the most famous woman on the planet. Get her, and you've tuned in a whole section of American society. As soon as I knew she was going to come, I knew that the Americans would tune in. I could hear them, "Everyone look at this." That's literally what was in my fucking head. I really pushed this home in the States, as I knew it was the biggest button to push.'

Live Aid PR Bernard Doherty was actually underneath the Royal Box as Quo hit the stage, and as they lurched into 'Rockin' All Over The World', three Special Branch officers pinned him against the wall, unsure as to his security status, worried he might be a royal stalker. 'They said, "We don't care how many passes you've got, just stand right there and don't move,"' said Doherty. He was so overwhelmed that he actually burst into tears; he wasn't scared by the police, but relieved that the event that he had spent so long helping to organise was actually happening. Eight weeks after being hired, Geldof's mad vision was actually happening!

Doherty had tried to arrange as many face-to-face interviews with Geldof as possible that day, and had positioned various groups of journalists around the backstage area, so that he could suddenly deliver Geldof and get maximum exposure. 'I quickly realised that walking around with Bob was like being with the prime minister or the president of the United States,' said Doherty. 'His back was killing him, and he had to keep lying down all the time, but he kept going, giving sound bite after sound bite after sound bite.

'I had a notebook full of all these lists, and every time I did something I crossed it off. NBC. ABC. *NME*. *Melody Maker*, etc. Everyone had to be fed, everyone had to be given something exclusive, even if it wasn't exclusive.'

'I don't remember sitting down all day,' said the legendary music industry PR Alan Edwards, who was representing various record companies and artists at Live Aid, including David Bowie, through his Modern Publicity company. 'I'd arrived that morning way before the bands started, maybe half-ten, eleven, as it was important to get the lay of the land. Everyone was there. The head of every record company, every PR, every music journalist; well, the ones who had been sanctioned or had bought tickets. There was a festival atmosphere at Wembley, although it already felt more important than that. Even before Status Quo went up on stage you could tell that this wasn't going to be just another industry get-together. The place just fizzed with excitement, it was electric. Ironically, it was quite luxurious backstage, with good food, plenty of drinks, and a bizarre, heightened atmosphere. No one's feet touched the ground that day.'

Geldof had arrived at Wembley with Paula Yates and their small daughter, Fifi Trixibelle. He appeared to be so haggard that someone said he looked as though he was wearing Fatigue by Max Factor. According to Jill Sinclair, a producer of the Live Aid DVD, they had to stop at a petrol station on the way to Wembley because Yates remembered she hadn't got any flowers for Princess Diana. 'Just as her daughter Fifi was about to hand over the flowers during the royal line-up, she realised that the price was still on these cheap garage-bought flowers. Fifi hadn't wanted to present the flowers, so Paula had bribed her with the promise of some more smoked salmon. When Fifi handed over the flowers she said to the princess, "More fish, please."'

Wembley erupted as Charles and Diana eventually shuffled into the Royal Box, accompanied by Geldof in his denim shirt. Appropriately, they sat right in front of Queen.

In the same way that you don't bring a flute to a gunfight, so you shouldn't really bring timpani to a rock concert. Consequently, as soon as the band of the Coldstream Guards had finished their performance of 'Royal Salute', so Status Quo were ushered on to the Wembley stage to officially begin Live Aid.

'Hello, are you all right?' asked the band's Francis Rossi, and 72,000 people said that yes, they were very much all right, thank you very much.

Suffused with a sense of purpose, the band tore into 'Rockin' All Over The World', and Live Aid was off.

The choice of Quo to open the show was perfect in its imperfection, and the quintessentially reductive nature of their look, their sound and their legacy was more than apt for an event that was all about scale. And as for the opening song, it had already become something of an unofficial anthem for the event as the BBC had repeatedly used it to advertise their TV coverage. There had been some discussion about whether the song should open or close the show, but in reality there was no way that the band were going to be in a fit condition to play it at 10 p.m., and anyway there was a certain logic to opening the show with it.

Status Quo hadn't ever been hip, not ever, and the group themselves would have conceded that creatively their glory years were behind them, trapped in the early Seventies, over a decade earlier, when they lit up the British singles charts with heads-down-we'll-see-you-at-the-end barnstormers such as 'Roll Over Lay Down', 'Caroline' and 'Rain'. There was much to enjoy but little to admire in their twelve-bar boogie, and they appealed to the crowd gathered at Wembley in the same way the Queen Mother would have, or Cliff Richard. They were blue-denim rock royalty.

If you were to have chosen artists who best personified 1985, who best summed up the state of pop at the halfway point of the Eighties, you wouldn't have chosen Status Quo. The Smiths, yes, or Prince, the Jesus and Mary Chain, Prefab Sprout, Cameo, Trouble Funk or Bruce Springsteen. But not a bunch of long-haired denim-clad rockers whose musical offerings appeared to impress in ever-decreasing circles. It was often joked that Status Quo were perfectly named as everything they did sounded the same; but rather than continually sounding the same, everything they released was at least 20 per cent worse than whatever had preceded it.

For Live Aid, though, they were perfect. Everyone knew who Status Quo were, even those who despised them. And while they were unlikely to espouse the charitable aspects of the show with the same conviction as Bob Geldof, the same could be said for so many others on the bill that day. Although they were children of the Sixties, having had a massive psychedelic hit in 1967 with 'Pictures Of Matchstick Men', it was the early Seventies when Quo managed to grab our attention. With anglicised twelve-bar blues-rock, denim waistcoats, air guitar and a cheery, if beery disposition, Quo were the band for the grown-up Slade fans, a knockabout party group. In the space of three or four years, and with singles like 'Break The Rules', 'Down Down' and 'Mystery Song', they became a national institution, as British as HP Sauce, an errant royal or a disco headbutt. But having achieved somewhat extraordinary success throughout the Seventies, they became lazy, druggy (Francis Rossi once pushed a cotton bud through his ravaged nose on a chat show on Sky TV to demonstrate the effect of his relentless cocaine abuse), and shamelessly repetitious. Yet the hits kept on coming, proving that the Quo Army (a veritable denim battalion of banner-waving, head-shaking pubgoers) were more interested in the idea of Status Quo than the actuality. In the mid-Seventies the *NME* posed a question: 'The worst band in the world, or the true progenitors of working class punk heavy metal?'

Who knew?

The press were equally scathing about them as punk became the new orthodoxy. In a review by the *NME*'s star critic Paul Morley in 1978, he asked some further questions: 'What is beyond Status Quo, I often wonder? What is beyond tracks with titles such as "I'm Givin' Up Worryin", "Gonna Teach You To Love Me", "Long Legged Linda" and "Like A Good Girl"? What is beyond the boogie, the grimace, the superstition, the stagnation, and the gaps between their legs? What is beyond the mere myth . . . ?'

I remember walking out into the stadium as they were halfway through their first song, and although I hadn't bought a Quo record since their *Piledriver* album in 1972 (which included their classic single 'Paper Plane', about which John Peel said, 'Now this, boys and girls, is a real gem. If it's not a number one single then you all deserve to be horsewhipped'), the whole spectacle seemed to make sense. It was simple and it was effective, and their noise positively *filled* the stadium. As 'Rockin' All Over The World' (a song written and recorded by John Fogerty back in 1975) rang around Wembley, you could immediately sense a feeling of goodwill, one that you could also feel escaping the stadium, like gas, a sense that today was going to do some good, and that in doing some good we were all going to have a good time, a thoroughly good time. Walking into the stadium you immediately imagined that the whole world could hear what was going on inside, and that people all the way from Stockholm to Adelaide, and from Nairobi to Buenos Aires could hear the D, G and A chords pumping through the crowd. What Status Quo served up was never going to be the truth raw, it was going to be cooked, overcooked, which for the assembled multitude made the whole idea of Live Aid far more palatable. And what they did sounded great: no one today was going home with their timbers unshivered.

The band wore what they always wore, Rossi in jeans, white shirt and waistcoat, and Parfitt in jeans, bright billowing shirt (today it was pink) and wristband. The rest of the band wore denim, and everyone wore plimsoles. As ever they looked just like their roadies, as though they could move from the public bar to the saloon bar with ease.

Everyone backstage appeared to be nervous, apart from Status Quo, that is. Everyone said it. The Quo just weren't nervous. They weren't fussed. For them it was going to be fun. Only a gig. Just another day at the fair.

'Status Quo were the only people who weren't nervous,' said Harvey Goldsmith. 'Everyone was hanging around backstage, most of them in the Hard Rock Café at the back. Everyone was very aware of adhering to the schedule, of playing ball, so everyone was being mindful of the timings. And most people, believe it or not, were actually very nervous. David Bowie was nervous, Elton was nervous, Freddie Mercury was pacing around. The only people who weren't were Quo.

'As soon as we knew Charles and Diana were coming, we knew we had to alter the show, as we needed a big beginning, a grand opening. We knew the royals wouldn't stay all day, so we had to open big. That's when we decided that Status Quo were the right people to open the show. I had always assumed that Bob would open the show, but after a while it made sense for Quo to do it, with "Rockin' All Over The World". They did it as a bit of a favour, believe it or not, but we kind of thought they would fit in somewhere in the show, an iconic British group. And it worked perfectly. Everybody remembers "Rockin' All Over The World", *everybody*. It was like a stroke of genius. The atmosphere in the audience was fantastic, and it set the day up perfectly. At the end of the day everyone kind of left it to me to sort out the running order, and I sort of did it using common sense, but primarily because of changeover times. So everybody accepted that because there was a logic to it.'

Status Quo were also an important choice, because they were completely apolitical, and while many might have assumed they were closer to the left than the right, they didn't appear to be that bothered by either. At the time, if you said you were apolitical, or admitted that you were ambivalent about Thatcher – which a lot of people were – you were assumed to be right wing, as anyone who didn't profess to support the left was deemed, by the music press at least, to be politically suspect. The groundswell of independent media that swirled up around punk quite soon became ideological, as it was thought that politics and culture should walk hand in hand, and that anything not of the mainstream, anything counter-cultural, had to be driven by a socialist agenda. To admit anything else made you a pariah, and slightly worrisome, as though you might have nationalistic tendencies.

So in this respect, the blue-denim neutrality of Status Quo was crucial.

Most of the acts were watching in the Royal Box, keen to get a sense of where the day was headed. There had been no rehearsals, and no one really knew what the day would bring. 'We weren't on until later, but we went down for the opening and sat in the Royal Box with Princess Diana and Prince Charles,' said Queen's Brian May. 'Then Status Quo came on and started. I thought they rose to the occasion *magnificently*.'

Like many other acts on the bill, Status Quo had come to the party falteringly. The band had actually broken up, and had no intention of performing again, so Geldof's request put them in an odd position. They told him they were not really together as a band any more, but Geldof wouldn't take no for an answer. 'I spoke to Bob Geldof two to three months ago in our record company and he was very depressed,' said Francis Rossi on the day of the concert. 'He couldn't get Wembley or the police to do it for free. Then it all snowballed and we said, "Let's go for it." We had some hesitation at first about playing live again after we said we'd given up forever, but it's only two or three numbers. I said to Bob, "I don't know about this," but he said, "It doesn't *matter* how good or bad you are."'

'It went by in such a flash,' said Rossi. 'I remember I got my face burnt because the sun was hitting the stage. It was a scorching day, a perfect day, one of those days that nobody who was there will ever forget, perhaps the greatest rock festival of all. Yet I'm amazed Rick [Parfitt] and I have any shared memories of Live Aid at all, we were so out of it for the whole thing. I do remember the trumpeters and trombonists from the Guards regiment that played a few bars of "God Save The Queen" just before we went on, then Radio 1 DJ Tommy Vance booming over the PA: "And now, to start the sixteen hours of Live Aid, would you welcome Status Quo!"'

Rossi says that Live Aid was the most significant gig they ever played, but 'that said, in other respects Live Aid was no different to me from any other day back then. I had already done a gram of coke and half a bottle of tequila before we went on stage. I think we did exactly one rehearsal beforehand. The feeling was, we're only doing ten minutes, we can knock that off. Quo didn't really exist any more, so who cared anyway?'

The band had met that morning at a pub in Battersea, near to the riverside flat where Parfitt lived. This is where Rossi had his first quadruple vodka of the day. They were then helicoptered into Wembley.

'There were a lot of egos there that day, but everyone knuckled down and got into the spirit of things,' said Parfitt, who had once said that his industry was full of insecure little show-offs, including himself. 'There was no complaining about the flowers in the dressing room, it was just go on, do your gig, then get off again.'

'Freddie from Queen came over and gave me a big hug,' said Rossi 'picking me up and swinging me round. He was so strong. With the exception of Elvis Costello, who it appears thought so highly of himself he refused to even speak to me when I tried to say hello, all the artists were friendly backstage. Nearly all of them were wasted, too. By the end of the day there were some real casualties walking around, not least yours truly. David Bowie astounded everyone by doing the opposite and looking better and better as the day wore on.'

Neither Rossi nor Parfitt remember being on stage for the finale, although both of them were there. They were not the only ones who overindulged, as so many people backstage had little sinners' grins that day, from the booze and the coke that appeared to be readily on tap; the indulgences weren't as excessive as they had been during the recording of the Band Aid single, but they were significant. As soon as the band came offstage they started drinking even more heavily, content to let the rest of the day go by in a blur. They had been given some new mobile phones, huge great things that you had to run off a battery, but nobody ended up using them as they couldn't get any reception in the stadium.

'It was 1985 for chrissakes, it was a sea of cocaine backstage,' said Bernard Doherty. 'It wasn't a horrible atmosphere though, it just happened to be the drug of choice at the time, and so everyone was on it. It was carnage. Cocaine was everywhere, you couldn't move for the stuff.'

'There was a lot of gear backstage,' said Gary Farrow. 'If there had been a Lance Armstrong-style blood test, there wouldn't have been many people who would have passed.'

Live Aid had the green room of all green rooms, with everyone milling about, wanting to mix, connect, chat, and – some – perk themselves up a little. The Hard Rock Café had built a tented replica of its London restaurant, giving burgers away for free, but supplying dozens of huge buckets for donations. Consequently everyone spent a great deal more. Backstage enmity was largely absent, with even Paul Weller and George Michael being cordial to each other; Michael says that during the recording of the Band Aid record, Weller berated him in front of the rest of the stars assembled that day. 'I said, "Don't be a wanker all your life. Have a day off."'

'Backstage in the Green Room we were all thrown in together,' said Midge Ure, who was performing with Ultravox that day. 'Ultravox and the Rats, the Style Council, Nik Kershaw, Adam Ant, Spandau, Sting, Sade and Phil Collins, an ill-matched, mixed-up collection of pop and rock stars. But once Status Quo kicked off the show with "Rockin' All Over The World", irrespective of what genre of music you were tied in with, it was fabulous.

'Everyone had stupid grins on their faces. Even Paul Weller. Live Aid was real, tangible; it was happening. We all knew that we were part of history in the making. It didn't matter how long our careers had been, how many hits we had had before or might have in the future, none of us had ever done anything like this.'

'The atmosphere backstage was unbelievable,' said Gary Farrow. 'You didn't really know what was going to happen next, and that was part of the excitement. Everybody got on, everyone watched each other on stage on the screens backstage, there was a real sense of community.'

In the months following Band Aid, Geldof had attended a meeting of the Band Aid trustees every Thursday, and went into the Band Aid offices every two or three days. In the run-up to Live Aid he was spending an average of fourteen hours a day in meetings, and then another four or five on the phone to America. In 1985 people were still communicating by telex. There were no mobile phones and no computers, making Live Aid even more of a logistical miracle. Back then, faxes were almost futuristic. Miles Kington in the *Independent* described the 'mini-symphonic sounds' created by the machine as it prepared to receive a message, 'like a robot orchestra tuning up for a conductor'.

'Live Aid from start to finish was an enigma,' said Harvey Goldsmith. 'When Bob asked me to get involved I wasn't available as I was involved in taking Wham! to China as well as looking after Roger Waters, who was launching his solo career in North America. I couldn't get my head around Bob banging on the door. I just didn't have the time to devote myself to it fully. As much as he was getting frustrated even I know there's a limit to how much I could do. However, in hindsight the short time we had to do it in meant that it had to work. I've always been a believer in this – if it's meant to be, it will happen.'

The truth is that Live Aid became a global event because of the BBC. Geldof had originally done a deal with Channel 4, 'but the BBC got involved because Channel 4 fucked it up,' said Harvey Goldsmith. 'They didn't really understand what they were doing to some extent. I told him they weren't the right people to do it, but Bob went to see them anyway. They were going to do a two-hour show, which wasn't the point at all. So the BBC got involved.

'Luck and timing are absolutely major in anything of this nature. Bob was obsessed with having one show on each side of the Atlantic, and having the whole thing televised on both continents. It was unheard of then, as no network had ever done such a thing. To have sixteen, seventeen hours of non-stop TV for an event, it was unheard of. You couldn't sell the concept then, and you certainly couldn't now. Plus, we needed American TV, we needed a US network to make it work. But we somehow managed to do it. We went down the route we knew, which was approaching Mike Appleton at *The Old Grey Whistle Test*, who in turn put us on to Roger Laughton, the head of daytime programming. It transpired that Roger was a huge advocate for change and for understanding that there were problems in the world, like Africa, that needed solving. It was his personal belief. He was privately supporting a lot of activities that were going on with famine. So when we pitched it to him, he was hugely in favour of it. He went to Michael Grade and the rest is history.

'People forget, but we were in the middle of a Test match, and their problem was scheduling the show in spite of it. Because you can't interrupt a Test match. It was a big deal. And so we were moved from BBC2 to BBC1. I think Michael Grade realised it was groundbreaking. When the BBC agreed to broadcast it, this opened up negotiations all over the world, as we could use them as leverage. And that was really important. Otherwise it would have been a local event with an anomaly of having something going on in America.

'In the end we were on the phone calling around all these different countries to make sure they had the signal and that it was working ok.

'I think we only got £200,000 out of the BBC.'

One man who didn't have a good Live Aid was 'Whispering' Bob Harris, the laid-back radio DJ and former presenter of *The Old Grey Whistle Test*, back in its Seventies heyday. As Geldof and Goldsmith had contacted Mike Appleton and the *Whistle Test* production team, this relatively marginal late-night music show ended up producing the biggest television event of all time. And 'Whispering' Bob, the man who had made *Whistle Test* famous, the man who had helped give 'alternative' rock a profile at the Beeb, was nowhere to be seen, working for local radio and still licking his wounds after being consigned to the broadcasting bin of history.

'My career reached its lowest point on the day Live Aid was broadcast in 1985,' he wrote, in sub-Alan Partridge-style in his lamentable autobiography. 'I was on air at Radio Broadland, doing my *Bob Harris Music Show*, watching the concert on the monitor in the studio. Mike Appleton collaborated with Bob Geldof to co-ordinate worldwide television coverage of the event and it was very much a *Whistle Test* day, using all the programme's facilities and expertise. I desperately wished Mike had asked me to be involved. I felt sad and unwanted, like I was a million miles removed from it all. I knew nobody had tuned into my show. I actually asked for people to phone in, just to reassure me someone was listening. I got one call.'

2 billion people in over fifty countries would see today's show at Wembley, while the watching millions would donate a total of £150 million to aid the starving people of Africa. More people would see Bob Geldof swearing on television than saw Neil Armstrong walk on the moon.

Suddenly this wasn't a concert, wasn't two concerts, this was now all about television.

'This was going to be a TV show,' said Geldof, who had suddenly changed his tune. 'It wasn't a concert. Never to me. It was a TV show, and the TV show was to get at one end. *Money.* It was all a pragmatic exercise.'

The novelist and journalist Pete Hamill said it best: the Live Aid concerts were welding together popular art and human politics, using the power, energy and invention of rock 'n' roll to accomplish something of practical social value. 'For that single day, a group of the richest, most spoiled and safest human beings on the planet assembled in concert to try and feed another group of human beings, a group that has been ravaged, humiliated and imperilled. This is no small thing.'

The performances weren't taking priority, the fund-raising was. Throughout the day, viewers were urged to donate money to the Live Aid cause. 300 phone lines were manned by the BBC, so that the public could make donations using their credit cards. The phone number and an address where viewers could send cheques were repeated every twenty minutes. In between the acts at Wembley, and then at the JFK Stadium, various other acts were beamed into Wembley from some of the other participating countries. There was Autograf from Moscow, Loudness from Japan, B. B. King from Holland, Yu Rock Mission from Yugoslavia and many more, although it's assumed that donations were scant during these performances.

David Bailey had been asked to photograph everyone backstage, and so had constructed a makeshift studio, catching them as they came offstage (much to the annoyance of Brian Aris, who had been told that he was the only photographer backstage). The acts would pour through their set of unalloyed classics, wait for the stage light to turn from green to orange (one minute left), and then dart off and nip to the Hard Rock Café backstage, to be entertained by Elton John or Freddie Mercury, both of whom were treating the day with the irreverence that only comes from the properly famous. 'That was a crazy experience, as it was so unreal,' says Bailey. 'Everyone was famous, and it was like being at some sort of party that never ended. It was hectic. Things always are at charity dos. Everyone was great – Elton, Bowie, Paul McCartney, U2, everybody. Freddie Mercury was funny because he French-kissed me quite aggressively – he grabbed me, swung me round and said "I have to kiss you!" – and the only people who were a bit off were George Michael and Sade, who didn't want her picture taken. We auctioned off all the pictures afterwards. I was meant to fly across the Atlantic with Phil Collins, but I didn't go as I knew I had enough [material].

'I loved it because I was one of only four people who had the magic pass, the pass where you could go everywhere. Bob Geldof had one, Midge Ure had one, Harvey Goldsmith had one, and I had the other. It was like Willy Wonka's Golden Ticket. I could even have gone on stage if I'd wanted to. It was funny. Diana was there, although I didn't see her that day. Diana was a nice, upper-class Sloaney girl, but she was no great beauty. They used to call Prince Charles handsome and dashing, too, which really is a stretch. Diana was all right, but she insisted on having that terrible hairdo, the one that looked like a wig. She had terrible posture.

'Live Aid was an incredible event, and I'm glad I was there, but I wasn't moved by the day. Photography protects you in a way, and helps keep you removed from reality. Don McCullin once told me that he'd been taking these pictures in the Congo for the *Sunday Times Magazine*, and he'd seen some pretty horrific stuff, but it was only when he developed the pictures when he got home that he was shaken by them. That's what got him. He said he had to leave the darkroom and rush to the toilet and throw up because it was only when he looked at his pictures that he understood the true horror of it all. At the time he was too busy trying to get the pictures.'

A similar thing happened to Bailey when he had gone to the Sudan at the end of 1984. He'd gone at Geldof's behest, to take photographs for a Band Aid book project that was to be called *Imagine*. He spent a week touring the refugee camps and feeding centres along the Ethiopian/Sudanese border and in the Red Sea Province of Sudan.

'That was a tough shoot as we didn't take any sleeping bags and had to sleep under the trucks,' said Bailey. 'It was only eight days, but it was enough. They even thought I was a spy at customs, simply because I didn't have an entry stamp. I tried to convince them that if I was a spy I might have bothered to actually get a stamp, but that logic didn't work on them. It was quite scary because I was locked up in this little room and I didn't know what was going to happen. So I had to get round it by putting $100 in my passport and the passport of my assistant. That seemed to work as suddenly we weren't spies any more and we had entry stamps. In the end we missed the return flight so I had to buy more tickets. But it was an extraordinary shoot, and I'm really proud of the book.'

Imagine was one of those books that really was all done for charity. No one took a fee, not even Thames & Hudson, the publishers, and Bailey paid most of the costs himself. 'Some of the images were heartbreaking, and it was awful to see all these poor, diseased people who were literally dying all over the place,' said Bailey. 'I was quite surprised by the reactions of some of the doctors, as they were quite rude to me, and accused me of being sensationalist, which was the last thing I was trying to be. I was shocked. The heat. The flies. The lack of food. You'd go back to look for a child you'd photographed a few hours previously and he'd be dead. Some of the men's hands were no bigger than a child's. It broke your heart.'

Bailey's pictures would turn out to be the Nag Hammadi of Live Aid, and while he ignored the human carnival outside in the stadium, his pictures of all the acts who performed that day form one of the most important galleries of the decade. If *Goodbye Baby and Amen*, his ode to Swinging London, was a testament to the Sixties, then these photographs turned out to do the same for the Eighties. It was a narrower band of talent for sure – this was just the pop aristocracy, rather than the politicians, scene-shifters, journalists and business-tyros who normally might have been included – but it was laden with meaning. The pictures remain as powerful as they were the day they were taken, beautifully carved portraits of moments that were only meant to be fleeting. They sit today, these hundreds of pictures, in large A2 boxes in chests in Bailey's ramshackle Bloomsbury studio – negatives, contact sheets and prints, all labelled, numbered and expertly categorised by his small team of long-suffering assistants. Bailey will grudgingly pull them out for you if you ask, grasping your arm as he talks you through them, telling you that they were merely snapshots, and that all he had to do was shoot what was there in front of him. And yet they have a power and a majesty that jumps out at you.

'He was a funny cunt, Geldof,' said Bailey. 'The whole day was mad, and it was sort of organised chaos backstage, but you could tell that Geldof knew where everything was, and where everyone was meant to be. I'm sure most of the day was accidental, but you felt that Geldof somehow made it all happen, even if he always looked like he didn't know what the fuck he was doing.'

Back on the Wembley stage, Status Quo were coming to the end of their set, having put a smile on the faces of 72,000 people. So successful was their performance that it encouraged the band to question their decision to retire. It also helped focus the minds of everyone else who was going to perform that day. The bar had been set, and the bar was high.

'With a large audience like that you do usually get a good vibe, but there was something totally unique and I'm not sure I've ever felt it since,' said Rossi. 'They weren't just people paying to see a show, they were part of it. There was such a euphoric feeling in that arena.'

When Geldof came up to Rossi and told him that 2 billion people had just seen his performance, he said, 'I'm glad you didn't tell me that before.'

TWO

12:19

The Style Council: 'You're The Best Thing', 'Big Boss Groove', 'Internationalists', 'Walls Come Tumbling Down'

'The Face reflects the aspirations of a generation who no longer see a chic lifestyle as the sole birthright of the idle rich.'
SUNDAY EXPRESS

Punk's greatest moments are replayed incessantly. Some of us were there, and some of us weren't, but even those of us who were didn't see it all, and so we replay those classic moments in our minds and on our music boxes and computers as though they were part of the Zapruder film of the Kennedy assassination, trying to assign more and more meaning to them, watching or imagining them again for clues as to the true meaning of punk. Was it the time the Sex Pistols played the Screen on the Green, the night the Damned played the Roxy for the first time, the Clash CND gig in Victoria Park, Public Image attempting to play on the roof of Beaufort Market in the Kings Road, the night Sid Vicious attacked the *New Musical Express*'s Nick Kent, that extraordinary night at Aylesbury Friars when Talking Heads and the Ramones occupied the same stage, seemingly beamed down from two completely different planets?

There was a night at the 100 Club when the Jam played there that will always stick in my mind. I was standing right in front of the stage, right in front of Paul Weller, as one of the speaker stacks began to teeter. As the bass reverberated through the wooden stage, the speaker swung forwards, swung back, swinging away as though it were being pushed back and forth by a wind. I caught the eye of a roadie, who, like me, expected the speaker to topple at any minute. He couldn't do anything about it as it was too high, and in the end it just kept swinging back and forth, and even seemed to speed up the longer the gig went on.

This motion seemed to mirror the jutting chins on stage, as all three members of the band kept pushing their chins forward like chickens, metronomically keeping up with 'All Around The World', 'This Is The Modern World', 'Away From The Numbers' and all the others, little horizontal pogos that were copied by all of us in the crowd. The Jam were hugely influenced by Dr Feelgood, and the way they stuck their necks out was copied exactly from Feelgood's guitarist Wilko Johnson. I remember seeing them upstairs at the Nag's Head in High Wycombe in 1975, and marvelling at Wilko's ability to duck-walk around the stage, like Chuck Berry on speed, seemingly oblivious to the band, the crowd, or indeed the sweating walls around him.

Punk was jittery. The atmosphere at punk gigs was so heightened, so aggressive, that it made you jittery. Everything about it was jittery. The way we sipped our drinks, the way we pulled at our cigarettes, the way we hunched our shoulders or pulled up the collars on our (plastic) leather jackets. Any second someone could throw a punch, or a glass, and then we'd have to duck, or dart sideways. I remember another night at the 100 Club, when Jordan was still singing with Adam and the Ants, and as she walked through the crowd to the stage, an empty pint jug flew by my ear, landing God knows where. And so you were always on your guard. Everything about punk was short. The songs. The hair. The conversations (terse). The looks you gave skinheads as you passed them on the stairs of the Roxy or the Hope and Anchor, before quickly scurrying in the opposite direction.

And Paul Weller looked like the tersest man you'd ever have the misfortune to meet. John Lydon looked as though he'd shout at you, Sid Vicious looked as though he'd hit you, and Joe Strummer looked as though he'd give you a lecture. Weller, meanwhile, just looked as though he'd tell you to fuck off and be done with it. He seemed deliberately, almost confrontationally inarticulate, as though having a good vocabulary might somehow be a betrayal of his class. Yet even at that young age, when he was as callow as he was ever going to be, he could write on occasion with the subtlety of Van Morrison or the ferocity of Pete Townshend.

While he was the son of a taxi driver and a cleaner, and had a thoroughly working-class Secondary Modern education, nevertheless Weller was embarrassed about being from Surrey. Weller came from the London overspill, the no-man's-land of belonging, neither one thing nor another. One of the most evocative songs from the Jam's first album, *In The City*, was 'Sounds From The Street', which contains one of Weller's latent insecurities writ large: 'I know I come from Woking and you'll say I'm a fraud/But my heart is in the city where it belongs.' Part of the Greater London Urban Area and the London commuter belt, Woking was fundamentally parochial; visitors were once greeted with a billboard that proclaimed 'All-Weather Shopping And Sparkling Entertainment', a promise too dull even to contemplate.

'When I was a kid I remember asking my dad how long a mile was,' said Weller. 'He took me out into our street, Stanley Road, and pointed down to the far end, towards the heat haze in the distance. To me there was a magical kingdom through that shimmering haze, the rest of the world, all life's possibilities. I always return to where I came from, to get a sense of my journey and where I'm heading next.' As a boy he would accompany his father to Heathrow to watch the planes, and when he hit his teens would travel up to London by train, and record the traffic noises, which he would play back in his bedroom in Woking (Weller was from a generation who were already feeling excluded from inner-city cool). He appropriated urbanity by developing an interest in clothes, an adolescent obsession that has never left him. Modernism enveloped him, to the extent that he wouldn't talk to other children unless they were wearing the right clothes (to this day he still, rather childishly, distrusts those he thinks are poorly dressed).

Having formed the Jam when he was in his early teens, his influences were the Beatles, then Dr Feelgood, and then anything with a pulse emanating from London. Unlike punks (dirty, subversive), the band wore bank-clerk suits, the bassist Bruce Foxton even sporting one of those 'Dmitri'-style haircuts you used to see advertised in barbers' windows. Weller hated being labelled a throwback, though, and once wore a placard around his neck on stage that asked, 'How can I be a revivalist when I'm only fucking eighteen?'

He was obsessive about guarding against hypocrisy, to the point of pomposity. He also had an incredibly old-fashioned and traditionally working-class attitude towards masculinity. When he recorded his first real ballad, 'English Rose', released on the Jam album *All Mod Cons* in 1978, he cleared the studio while he recorded the vocals, and refused to let the lyrics be printed on the sleeve along with those of the other songs on the album.

Weller wrote proper songs, too; fuelled by bolshieness, power chords and shouting, for sure, but there were real tunes there, so many that he never worried about moving on and leaving punk behind.

The Jam were the ultimate Secondary Modern pop group, a suburban expression of teenage urban angst, folded into the punk mix before it exploded, nationwide and then globally. 1977 was made for them, or rather they were made for 1977.

I lost count of the number of times I saw the Jam. The 100 Club, the Marquee, the Nag's Head, the Red Cow. I probably saw them – and their more than occasional support band, the decidedly mediocre New Hearts – a dozen times, sweating through their suits, jutting their chins and pumping out the likes of 'In The City', 'All Around The World' and 'The Modern World' with the sort of sincerity that these days just looks forced and nostalgic. Then they ditched punk, became the most popular band in Britain, and bowed out in a blaze of retroactive glory.

One of the salient reasons he disbanded the Jam in 1982 was because of their success, and the fact that the crowds at the band's concerts often turned ugly, and started to resemble those at football matches. The cultural aggression felt at early punk concerts had swiftly morphed into a gang mentality that made the crowd at a Jam gig not that much different from the crowd at one by Sham 69. The political sentiments broadcast from the stage may have been poles apart, but the crowds were nearly as unruly. So, sensing a change in the zeitgeist, and enjoying the sort of cross-fertilisation between New Romantic pop and jazz-funk he heard on records such as Spandau Ballet's 'Chant No. 1', he decided to ditch the Jam, buy a pair of white socks and reinvent himself as a sort of tongue-in-cheek New Wave soul boy. His next vehicle, the Style Council – a great band with a terrible name – were often mannered and gauche, yet they sounded like the Eighties, all spic and span and shiny. Keen exponents of faux jazz (they were the Nescafé Society), they enjoyed getting up the noses of those fans and critics who would have preferred him to keep on making Jam records in perpetuity.

When Weller finished off the Jam, he was looking forward, not only to a fresh start with new musicians (a new career in a new town), but also to a period of relative normality, for a superstar at least, when the paparazzi wouldn't be parked outside his Solid Bond studios, when he wouldn't be accosted in Oxford Street by hordes of Norwegian parka-clad Jam fans. In 1983 Weller was looking forward to being an un-pop star. Much like Paul McCartney when the Beatles split (and he would always hate the comparison), Weller surrounded himself with a few select musicians and started getting on with his life, making records every now and then, not really caring if his old fans warmed to his new direction. He almost took a perverse delight in denying his past, refusing to play any of the vast number of excellent Jam songs, or even talk about them. This was what modernists did, moved forward. And Weller couldn't resist telling you what a modernist he was. In the Jam Weller was as synonymous with his two-tone shoes as Humphrey Bogart was with his Chesterfields, and he wasn't going to wear them any more.

Unlike many of his generation, who hadn't got a clue how to further their careers after punk began to wane, Weller had talent, tenacity and a thirst for change. And the Style Council turned out to be one of the best things he ever did, actually better than the Jam (that's right, better than one of the best epoch-making singles bands of all time), and certainly as good as the Steve Winwood-driven solo career he would pursue in his thirties, forties and fifties.

Not that he was happy with his lot, oh no. Along with his partner in crime, Mick Talbot (ugly mug, played keyboards), Weller went out of his way to distance himself from the game of self-promotion. One way in which the Style Council combated their image as a 'quirky Eengleesh pop band' – which is what they almost immediately became in the eyes of the music press – was to send the whole thing up. Irony was always big in their world, and what was often seen as gross pretentiousness was actually a giant wind-up. It was in this way that Weller defused a lot of the contradictions thrown up by him being on one hand a recognisable icon in *Smash Hits*, and an opinionated political animal on the other. For the maudlin pied piper, donning a silly hat let him off the hook, but for many of their fans the irony was lost. They just liked their records.

Ironically, as he became more obviously fashionable, his lyrics got angrier. Weller's agit-prop lyrics were everywhere, not least on his 1985 album, *Our Favourite Shop*: 'Come take a walk among these hills/And see how monetarism kills/Whole communities, even families.' He was as distrustful of Labour MPs as he was of their Tory opposites: 'He always did say to me, "You know they're just using us,"' said Billy Bragg. 'And I would say, "Yeah, but we're using them too, Paul."'

Many people were surprised to see the Style Council on the bill. Weller had looked extremely uneasy on the video accompanying 'Do They Know It's Christmas?', as though by singing alongside the likes of Duran Duran, Wham! and Culture Club he was somehow endorsing what they did. The Style Council followed Status Quo at Live Aid, and the contrast could not have been greater.

The Style Council came bounding on to the Wembley stage as though they were on a children's television programme, all dressed in tennis whites, blazers and primary colours, looking like extras in an early Cliff Richard film. When they launched into 'You're The Best Thing' nothing could have been breezier on this hot, sunny afternoon. This was a moment that deserved ice-cream, jelly, and lashings of ginger beer. But the song lasted a little longer than it needed to, with an endlessly repeated riff, and so they lost those parts of the crowd who were basically just at Wembley for a singalong. They followed this with 'Big Boss Groove', and lost even more of the audience, who weren't necessarily Style Council fans, and had come for the hits and little else. For a while the band looked as though they were on stage at the Newport Jazz Festival. This would no doubt have pleased them enormously, although they didn't exactly set the Live Aid crowd alight. They were energetic enough, but they didn't really click. Mistake number three was choosing to play 'Internationalists' as their next song; the sentiment may have been right – Weller introduced the song thus: 'This shows what can happen when people get together, and this song is dedicated to that spirit' – yet it was another random tune unknown to the bulk of the crowd (including me, who actually quite liked the Style Council). They finished on a high with 'Walls Come Tumbling Down' but by then the audience was already looking forward to whoever was coming next.

Weller was expected to make some sort of political statement as he introduced the band, but this didn't materialise – largely because Weller himself was so nervous. Even though he had been in one of the most successful British groups of the last ten years, he found the scale of the event completely intimidating. For Weller, all of the attention was drenching, a great noise, overpowering.

However, Weller seized the initiative a few months after Live Aid by helping, along with Labour leader Neil Kinnock, Billy Bragg and the Communards, to create Red Wedge, a pressure group that sought to engage young people with left-wing issues, and with the Labour Party in particular. The collective took its name from a 1919 poster by Russian constructivist artist El Lissitzky, *Beat the Whites with the Red Wedge*. Despite echoes of the Russian Civil War, Red Wedge was not a communist organisation, although it was flagrantly socialist. With a logo designed by Neville Brody, the whizz-kid designer behind the look of *The Face*, *City Limits* and soon *Arena*, Red Wedge was launched at a reception at the House of Commons on 21 November 1985 hosted by the Labour MP Robin Cook, with Weller, Bragg, Strawberry Switchblade and Kirsty MacColl. For a while it became the cause *du jour*, and its first tour, in the early few months of 1986, featured appearances by Elvis Costello, Madness, Heaven 17, Spandau Ballet's Gary Kemp, Junior Giscombe, Jerry Dammers, Bananarama, Prefab Sprout, Sade, Tom Robinson, the Beat, Lloyd Cole, the Redskins (a hard-line Trotskyite trio from Yorkshire led by public-school revolutionary Chris Dean, the scourge of the bourgeoisie, who called Band Aid 'Egos for Ethiopia. Bob Geldof is the third-division international statesman of pop with the political perception of a dead slug') and the Smiths. There was even a Red Wedge magazine, *Well Red*, and a Red Wedge comedy special, starring Ben Elton ('Up the workers!'), Robbie Coltrane and Harry Enfield, who all appeared under the banner 'Move On Up and Vote For Labour'. The Blow Monkeys financed their own Red Wedge leaflet featuring a cartoon of their singer Dr Robert, and asked, 'How can you complain about the state of the nation; your vote to cast is your only salvation.' It rhymed. Because the proposition was so potentially drab, levity was the order of the day. When announcing his involvement, Kinnock tried a joke about how Red Wedge wasn't a reference to his haircut. He paused for the big laugh, but none came. On the campaign trail in Llandrindod Wells, a small spa town in Brecon, a Tannoy system outside the Labour Party HQ blared out the following message: 'The Labour Party is the fun party, the good-time party. Come and enjoy yourselves.' Later that day, at a free concert organised by

Billy Bragg, autograph hunters approached the singer. 'And will you sign this one for Marie?' asked one woman. 'She couldn't come because her mum votes Conservative.'

'I suppose the Wedge came about because we all kept meeting at benefit gigs for Nicaragua or whatever,' said Bragg, whose whole career appeared to be devoted to modern interpretations of the protest song. 'The same faces kept showing up, like Jimmy Somerville, Weller, Tom Robinson – and we all shared similar ideals. Those were the darkest days of the Thatcherite Eighties, as well. There was a feeling that something had to be done.' Bragg had previously played benefit shows for striking miners, miners' wives support groups, CND, Amnesty International, the GLC, Greenham Common Women, anti-apartheid, and rate-capping schemes in Liverpool and Sheffield.

What had to be done was an earnest jolly, a sort of dour *Magical Mystery Tour*, basically a loose collective going on tour like no bands had done since the Sex Pistols/Clash Anarchy coach tour of 1976. The venture owed something to the Anti-Nazi League as well as to Rock Against Racism, the alliance between the Socialist Workers Party and various rock and reggae musicians, which used local concerts and open-air festivals (the most famous of which was held in Victoria Park in Hackney in the summer of 1978, headlined by the Clash), to promote the fact that racism was unfashionable.

The Red Wedge bands would roll into town, hook up with local community leaders, union leaders and Labour MPs, and attend rallies, shows and press conferences. Events were organised in key marginal seats across the country, hoping to mobilise the normally apathetic youth vote. Pop stars signed autographs while politicians kissed babies. It was as much of an eye-opener for the politicians as it was for the artists themselves, because while the bands were shocked by the way in which the politicians expected so much stage time, they in turn were rather shocked by the attitude of the youngsters turning up for the events – most of whom weren't that interested in traditional Labour Party policies, but instead wanted to discuss gay rights, the environment, the marginalisation of minorities, etc. On a flying visit to Finchley, Billy Bragg offered to play a free victory show at a local school if Mrs Thatcher lost her seat. At one debate in south-east London with the Communards and a hopeful local Labour candidate, a trainee teacher asked about education policies, an art student asked about cuts, and a Labour supporter made a short speech about cuts. Minutes after the Red Wedge crew moved on, the college administrators had put their Tory election posters back in the windows.

'The atmosphere on the bus was electric,' said Neil Spencer, the former *NME* editor who was handling press relations for the organisation. 'There had been nothing like this since the package tours of the Sixties. Musicians in the Eighties tended to live very segregated lives, but when they had a chance like this to collaborate they really loved it. Everybody left their ego at the door and mucked in.'

Which obviously wasn't true of the politicians or the union leaders, who loved the attention, and the fact that the music press was now following them all around.

'The artists got along very well, but these politicians would turn up and want to go on stage,' said Tom Robinson, whose breakthrough hit had been 'Glad To Be Gay' back in 1977. 'The last thing we wanted was hard-line party blokes going out there and lecturing the crowd on the evils of capitalism. That's not how you change the minds of rock fans. We had to keep finding ways of keeping them off.'

The aspirations were to keep creating some kind of common ground between the fans and Labour, and to seed people into local parties. But it was an uneasy mix, and although Red Wedge would continue for a year or so, there is little evidence that it made any difference. Youth support for Labour in the 1987 election (which the Conservatives won, their third eletion win in a row) was marginally higher than it was in 1983, although it would be difficult to attribute this to Red Wedge, as by then support for Margaret Thatcher was starting to slowly decline anyway. Red Wedge was a turn-off because not only was the proposition dull, but the politicians involved came across as self-serving and crass. While the Conservatives knew nothing about pop culture (the best they could get in terms of generating support in the entertainment industry was Gary Numan, the borderline racist comedian Jim Davidson and the Hot Chocolate singer Errol Brown), at least they didn't try to co-opt it.

'The Style Council obviously topped the bill at all the Red Wedge gigs,' said Gary Kemp, who thought Weller tried to take too much ownership of the organisation. 'One night when I was playing I remember being in the dressing room with Billy Bragg and Johnny Marr, and one of Paul's roadies came in just before we were all going on to play and he said: "When you go on stage, don't play too loudly because Style Council fans don't like guitars."

'And we're thinking: "Hang on a minute, this isn't a Style Council gig, they're all here to see everybody, it's a Red Wedge gig." And in any case, what a prick. When we went on stage – it was a bit like showing a red rag to a bull – I think Johnny and I played [Curtis Mayfield's] "Move On Up". Now, I'm never going to play it like it's heavy metal. I'm playing funk guitar. At one point, Weller came to the back and said, "Turn that fucking thing down." Later on that evening we're sitting in a bar and he said, "Gary why do you not write any songs about the miners?" Honestly!'

When *Melody Maker* held a debate featuring some of the Red Wedgers, there were howls of protest from the paper's readers: 'Billy Bragg and Paul Weller are the most boring individuals in the whole music business,' said one reader. Another wrote, 'We all know what the Tory government is doing to us, especially if you're on £28 a week. Raising money for people who need it is one thing, but what we don't need is a bunch of pop stars with big egos telling us to vote Labour.'

Red Wedge gave politicians a liking for this new kind of limelight. Politicians increasingly turn to pop culture to try and make themselves appear more relevant and credible, but obviously run the risk of making themselves look opportunist, irrelevant and behind the curve. At the time the Tories were incapable of harnessing any serious cultural support, and so it left all channels open for the Labour Party to exploit (although Liberal leader David Steel did make an excruciating rap record – 'I Feel Liberal, Alright'). Why else would Neil Kinnock, the leader of Her Majesty's Loyal Opposition, turn up on *Saturday Swap Shop* in early 1987, sharing airtime with the lead singer of Dr and the Medics? He had already appeared in a cameo role in a Tracey Ullman video and been a guest presenter at the BPI Awards. Compared to Kinnock, Tony Blair would turn out to be a wallflower.

From a critic's point of view, while a worthy enough enterprise, in terms of content Red Wedge was actually a completely enervating experience. 'The problem is the fundamental modesty of the aspiration,' wrote Simon Reynolds in *Melody Maker*. 'Because [while] there's a potential for romance in streetfighting and revolution . . . how *can* you make the Labour Party seem exciting? That's the flaw in Red Wedge – their chiding logic of pragmatism is in fundamental antagonism to pop's intolerant utopianism.'

Weller himself was soon off. 'We felt [the Labour Party] were totally out of touch,' he said. 'We wanted to find a way of closing the gap between youth and the party, but there were so many factions within the Wedge, and so much red tape to go through within the party – it took ages to change anything.'

'Red Wedge was a joke,' said Bob Geldof. 'It was so old hat they may as well have been in the Twenties with no concept of what modern politics was about. The only one I've got a lot of respect for in this area is Billy Bragg, who has an idea of politics that he's utterly true to and maintains it with great integrity and makes fantastic music. He sees himself clearly in the Woody Guthrie vein, but for me it's very old hat. It's like a Depression-era romanticism with no basis in reality . . .

'Forget protesting. Forget marching around Trafalgar Square singing, "We Shall Overcome". It fucking gets you nowhere! So get real. You want to stop something then put your guitar down and engage. Otherwise fuck off and make a hit record. You either stop and engage utterly or don't do it at all because we can all write a nice little song like "Give Peace A Chance" because music does not change things.'

As much as anything, the organisation was trying to quickly move pop from a world of image, escapism and conspicuous consumption into one of more overt political commitment. But this wasn't going to happen. Not with Red Wedge, anyway. Taking Live Aid as something of a template may have seemed like a good idea on paper (at least in terms of propaganda), but the failure of Red Wedge only highlighted the fact that activism can't be genuinely manufactured to any lasting effect.

During the Eighties, much like the Seventies, you weren't allowed to be on the other side of the political divide. Being the most divisive prime minister in living memory made Margaret Thatcher the most visible manifestation of right-wing authority the so-called counter-culture had ever had, at least in Britain. To the British she was that generation's Nixon, a wall on which to project all of society's evils.

The country was becoming a very different place under her leadership, and the way she rapidly took ownership of Britain's psyche was more than remarkable. And even by 1985 the country had changed dramatically since her arrival in Downing Street. However, as Alwyn W. Turner points out in *Rejoice! Rejoice! Britain in the Eighties*, it would be a mistake to conflate these two things, 'for it was by no means certain that the changes that Britain went through were in the direction she wished. Rather it was as though she had unlocked a Pandora's box and released forces into a society over which she had little or no control. She called for a return to thrift and good housekeeping, and presided over a massive increase in credit card and mortgage indebtedness; she sought to encourage the entrepreneurial spirit, and saw the City of London overrun by what detractors viewed as a generation of spivs and speculators; she wished to reverse the effects of Sixties permissiveness and found herself in a country . . . where home video recorders and satellite television made pornography ever more available.'

In 1937, when George Orwell wrote that 'all of us owe the comparative decency of our lives to the poor drudges underground, blackened to the eyes', virtually all the energy consumed in Britain was produced by miners. By the early Eighties this was no longer the case – in its last full year of operation, British Coal made a loss of over £400 million, a figure that excluded the subsidy from the electric companies – which is why the government saw fit to try and dismantle the industry. As a coal strike in 1974 had brought down Ted Heath's government, this could have been a risky strategy, yet Thatcher knew she was made of stronger stuff than Heath. One of her economic policies was the privatisation of industries she didn't think should have been nationalised in the first place, not when they required such massive subsidies.

The first pit closure to be announced was Cortonwood near Barnsley in Yorkshire, which was enough of a spark to ignite the wrath of the Marxist leader of the National Union of Mineworkers, Arthur Scargill, who used the 1981 NUM ballot (which legislated that strike action was permissible if any pit was threatened with closure 'unless on grounds of exhaustion') as a call to arms.

And what a call it was. In Britain, the miners' strike turned out to be the most bitter, fiercely fought industrial battle of the decade. This wasn't just eradication, this was ideological warfare. As Godfrey Hodgson wrote in the *Independent*, 'As we went into the Eighties, the miner with his ravaged lungs and aching muscles was still as potent a symbol of division in British society as he had been for a hundred years, a black legend of pride and militancy for the working class and of middle-class guilt and fear.'

Arthur Scargill used the miners' strike as a way to claim the soapbox as often as possible, but made a strategic error in not devising a plan based on trying to win public support rather than just using industrial muscle.

It didn't matter how often the government emphasised that inefficiency was the only reason that pits were being closed, didn't matter how many times it repeated its mantra of what it considered to be more than generous severance terms – no compulsory redundancies, early retirement on better terms than any other nationalised industry, and larger redundancy payments to younger miners – Scargill was going to call a strike. And once it began, on 6 March 1984, parts of Britain became as dangerous and as confrontational as pockets of the Middle East. Scargill used the strike as a way to claim the soapbox as often as possible, but made a strategic error in not devising a plan based on trying to win public support rather than just using industrial muscle. Consequently most of the country, and most of the press, turned against him. He may have been able to use television to exaggerate his personality, but it wasn't a personality it was easy to warm to. He was tireless, however. As Patrick Wintour said in the *Guardian* the following year, 'his resilience and ingenuity in keeping the momentum of the strike going through twelve months were remarkable'.

In July, having largely kept some judicious public distance from the National Coal Board's attempts to control the strike, Thatcher compounded what the left saw as her party's audacity to try and neuter one of the country's most inviolate national industries by making a speech so incendiary that it galvanised those who had previously just been shouting from the sidelines. Like, for instance, many of the participants in and organisers of Red Wedge. That month she told the 1922 Committee of Conservative MPs that the striking miners and their violence were 'a scar across the face of the country . . . We had to fight an enemy without in the Falklands. We always have to be aware of the *enemy within*, which is more difficult to fight and more dangerous to liberty.' She continued: 'There is no week, no day, nor hour when tyranny may not enter upon this country, if the people lose their supreme confidence in themselves, and lose their roughness and spirit of defence. Tyranny may always enter – there is no charm or bar against it.'

While this added fuel to the miners' fire, and gave them even more of a reason to keep on fighting, it also added an ideological top note to the government's rhetoric, which many on the left took to be a declaration of class warfare. This more than anything made Thatcher the bogeywoman – more than her hard-line economic policies, more than her intransigent response to the riots, or the way in which she had dealt with the Falklands; in a few short sentences she created a cultural divide as well as a political one, as she had now kick-started a generational antipathy that would inform all the entertainment worlds. She had been railed against ever since she got into power, but these few words somehow sealed her legacy.

Not that it stopped her. Thatcher's myopic nature was not just one born of arrogance, however. Not only did she have little interest in what people said about her, most of the time she didn't actually *know* what people said about her, which probably came as a surprise to many of those journalists, leader writers and newspaper editors who perhaps thought that she hung on every trenchant word. She certainly had no interest in pop culture, and was rather proud that she knew nothing about it. As Andy McSmith pointed out in *No Such Thing As Society*, his history of Britain in the Eighties, in her memoirs, she had nothing to say on Africa, Third World aid, Live Aid or Bob Geldof, subjects she just had no interest in.

I had lunch with Thatcher's former chief press secretary, Sir Bernard Ingham in July 2009, exactly twenty-five years after Thatcher's speech, and he confirmed that his former boss had little interest in the white noise of Fleet Street tittle-tattle. He turned out to be no great fan of the dark arts of spin, especially as practised by the likes of Alastair Campbell or Peter Mandelson. Over haddock and chips, Mrs Thatcher's former gatekeeper spent two hours bemoaning the way in which party attack dogs had been trained to feast on Fleet Street political editors. In his own day, Ingham would occasionally brief against the government's own ministers – he once described the Leader of the House of Commons, John Biffen, as a 'semi-detached' member of Government – but he said he regrets this.

In his book *Kill the Messenger*, Ingham writes that Thatcher almost never read newspapers, and would rely on him to cut out and photocopy the things she needed to see. He reiterated the point over lunch, stressing that she never read leader columns, and would only do so if Ingham shoved one under her nose. 'She didn't see the point,' he told me, as he nibbled on his fish. 'To her it was a waste of time. Didn't watch much television either, maybe just the headlines on the radio.'*

The IRA attempt on her life in Brighton that October, at the Tory Party Conference, only strengthened Thatcher's resolve. Her battle with Scargill now took on a personal dimension (although she had always regarded him as a Marxist revolutionary rather than a normal trade union official), and as one minister said at the time, 'Our leader will not be satisfied until Scargill is seen trotting round Finchley tethered to the back of the prime minister's Jaguar.'

In turn, Thatcher's intolerance served as an accelerant for Scargill's activities. Given their backgrounds it was almost as if both of them had been preparing for the final battle all their lives.

In the end there was no quarter given, although the government's tactics had to be altered, especially where it counted, outside the pits, in front of the television cameras. If it hadn't been for the 1981 riots, in particular those in Toxteth, it's unlikely that the government would have been so confident of defeating the miners. They knew that industrial action would inevitably lead to violence, and it was their steep learning curve in terms of crowd control that summer that had forced the police to seriously improve everything from weaponry to strategy, from body armour to on-the-ground communication.

Christmas 1984 was tough for families who hadn't seen any income for nine months, and men began heading back to the pits. On 3 March, at a

---

* Ingham was amused when I told him that the only photograph in Andy Coulson's office when he worked for David Cameron was a framed print of Margaret Thatcher sitting on a park bench reading the *News of the World* (the paper Coulson used to edit before going to work for Cameron). Ingham thought that both Cameron and William Hague had grown in stature, and believed both to be capable of being great statesmen. 'I just wish I knew what Cameron stood for,' he said. Finally we discussed the possibility of Mandelson getting rid of Gordon Brown – who was still PM – if the Irish ratified the Lisbon Treaty referendum in October (if Ireland backed the treaty, it would only remain for it to be signed by the presidents of Germany, Poland and the Czech Republic to come into law), suggesting that Mandy could use a bus. Which, of course, allowed Sir Bernard to recall the famous Lord Carrington story: when Thatcher's first Foreign Secretary was asked what would happen if she was run over by a bus, he replied, 'The bus wouldn't dare.'

specially convened conference, NUM delegates voted by ninety-eight to ninety-one to call off the strike and go back to work. And so began the beginning of the end of the mining industry, as the pit-closure programme accelerated. Some saw this as collective punishment, but in reality it was simply part of the Conservatives' obsession with the privatisation of the energy sector.

It was a victory, but not much of one. As Hugo Young wrote in his remarkably deadpan biography of Mrs Thatcher, *One of Us*, 'Scargill's own imperishable extremism successfully placed him in the folk-memory alongside the Argentinian leader General Galtieri as an important accessory to the Tories' continuing political domination.'

There were other legacies resulting from this victory. By 1991, trade union membership would be down by 4 million, or over 30 per cent. In 1979, for every 1,000 people in work, 1,274 workings days were lost through strikes. By the end of the decade the figure was down to 108 days. Thatcher would take this victory with her everywhere she went, and it gave her the confidence to do so much over the next five years. What she didn't do, however, was seriously look at the consequences of her actions, and while she had successfully started to dismantle the coal-mining industry, she had paid little mind to the havoc that this would wreak, turning entire communities into ghettos, diminishing fathers in the eyes of their sons, and helping build an underclass that hadn't been seen on this scale since the nineteenth century.

Which was certainly enough to rebel against if you were that way inclined, although there were predictable contradictions. One of the greatest songs of the period was Elvis Costello's 'Shipbuilding' – which he wrote with the producer Clive Langer for Robert Wyatt – a blistering condemnation of the Falklands conflict and a brutal – if elegantly composed – sideswipe at government policy ('Diving for dear life . . . When we could be diving for pearls'). Yet the label it was released on, Rough Trade, was an independent, arguably a model of Thatcherite entrepreneurial flair; these inconsistencies were obviously not acknowledged by anyone involved.

While it was her dedication to the free market and to monetarism (protecting the economy) that had already polarised the media, it had been

DIGGING DEEP

WE told you we'd be there and by Arthur, we were, cutting a rug at The Miners' Benefit down at the Wag Club a mere Tuesday ago. And what a night, brothers and sisters, *what* a night. While Ol' Toothless Dammers span the discs, hordes of punters got into their groove and a splendid £1,200 was taken to help pay off those desperate miners' bills. Above, in all their bevvied up finery, are a typical clutch of those who should be congratulated — left to right: HARRY ENFIELD ("Spitting Image" — he does Prince Philip's voice), BARRY and GRAHAM (Durham miners), DYLAN JONES (deejay), BEDDERS (a bassist), VAUGHAN TOULOUSE (an ex-pop star) and DAMMERS (a hero). Good on 'em all.

say this

While few had much sympathy for Arthur Scargill, public sentiment for the miners was heartfelt, as it was obvious that the death of the coal industry was about to have a ruinous effect on communities all over the country.

Thatcher's stand against Argentina over the Falkland Islands in 1982 that really proved to be divisive in the entertainment industry (not that many members of Red Wedge would have considered themselves to be part of it at all). It was impossible to be ambivalent about the way she went to war with the Argentinians, and so one was forced to come down on one side or the other. And in the British entertainment industry you couldn't find many who would admit that they felt rather gung-ho about the whole thing. It was the British victory in the Falklands, plus her own in the 1983 election, which gave Thatcher the confidence to be even more radical with her policies, particularly where the miners were concerned and with scant regard for the communities she was shattering in the process. It was this draconian interference in particular that the politically activated on the left of the industry so objected to.

Having fleetingly expressed some admiration for the Conservatives when the Jam first started attracting attention in 1977, in a volte-face Weller quickly embraced the Labour Party, almost to the point of obsession, turning himself into a class warrior in the process. The rise of Thatcher only exacerbated this. His lyrics would often sound idealistic and naïve, although this was forgivable considering how sweet his melodies were. A self-proclaimed 'moody bastard' (whenever I hear the Style Council song 'My Ever Changing Moods' I think, ah yes, all the way from taciturn to grumpy), Weller was the champion of everyone he knew with a 'bingo accent'; he was eighteen in 1976, and was almost fully formed when he became famous. There were three principal figureheads of punk: John Lydon, an unreconstructed sociopath; Joe Strummer, a slumming busker; and Weller, who managed to articulate the desperate aspirations of the suburbanite while cataloguing the striplit nature of late Seventies Britain.

So it was odd to see him all spangly and tanned on the Live Aid stage. For all the emotion they displayed the band may as well have been appearing on a German TV show. Weller looked out of sorts. The Style Council certainly looked committed – maybe more committed than some of the others appearing that day – yet they didn't seem remotely grand enough. Weller, who was usually so cool, was feeling a riot of emotion, namely fear. His blood pressure had stabilised at about the level of a gecko's, and his eyes were pinned. This was the big time. This was not the kind of gig where the audience hung on every flicker of an eyelid, this was the quintessential stadium gig, the arena for the grand gesture, and Weller was worried that they weren't up to it.

However far he thought he'd come from the punk ethic, and from the punk noise, Weller was still a surly punk at heart. Throughout the Eighties he had a true punk sensibility; no, he didn't get a Mohican like Joe Strummer, during the Clash's death throes, and no he didn't drink and swear a lot like John Lydon; but he remained true to his intransigent nature.

Weller adored Pete Townshend, yet The Who's guitarist always tried to keep him at arm's length. 'One of the most difficult people for me to cope with was Weller,' he said, 'because he was a huge fan of mine, but he would sit in a club with me and say, "Don't look back." And I would think, actually your whole mod thing is about looking back.'

I interviewed Weller and his Style Council cohort Mick Talbot for *The Face* exactly three years after Live Aid, when the Eighties looked as though they were going to limp to a close, and they were as mordant as ever, especially Weller. I met them in the Solid Bond studios (which Weller then owned) near Marble Arch, right at the north-east corner of Hyde Park. As I sat down opposite them in a small boardroom in the basement, and tried to make small talk, Talbot turned and stared across at his partner and said, 'This could come out sounding as if we're very dour.' To which Weller replied, typically, 'I don't give a shit how it comes out.'

I said at the time that it was unlikely that either Weller or Talbot would ever read my article. Both had spent the previous five years in the company of merciless, retarded, fawning, cut-throat, unprepared, badly briefed journalists. The Style Council had been championed and then slagged off by every other music critic in the world (or so they thought), and Weller and Talbot had had enough; they no longer read what was written about them. They still cared, but were loath to admit it to anyone within typing distance.

Nevertheless they agreed to a few interviews in support of their latest Polydor LP *Confessions Of A Pop Group*, and *The Face* had priority. As expected, they asked for the cover, and were politely turned down. This was just as well, because there seemed to be some kind of problem over the photo session. They wouldn't do one. 'I'd already done two for the record company and didn't want to do any more,' said Weller, not unreasonably. Then there was a problem with the two existing sessions. We weren't allowed to see them. After a seemingly endless bout of phone calls the Style Council conceded, and some pictures were prised out of them. They weren't suitable, so back we went . . .

This game of PR ping-pong went on until we finally got our pictures and our interview, though neither Weller nor Talbot seemed overexcited by the prospect of spending two hours with some complete stranger and then having their private indiscretions itemised inaccurately in a magazine which Weller had once referred to as being full of people wearing lampshades instead of trousers.

Initially courteous and amenable, seemingly resigned to the PR rigmarole, Talbot and Weller offered tea and sympathy in equal measure. Both were immaculately dressed, something you tended to take for granted after seeing them in numerous photo sessions styled to the nth degree. But when we met there were no stylists, just the Style Council living up to their name – very spartan, very clean, very modernist. Paul Weller was still a remarkably attractive man; tall, tanned, slim, with a bright complexion and recently lightened thatch. The man looked like a pop star. I made the mistake of mentioning this, and the atmosphere immediately turned sour.

'We aren't pop stars,' said Weller, 'that's the kiss of death. The music isn't the trap, that's the way forward. The traps you find yourself in are because of all the other stuff that goes with it. Having to argue with the record company, having to talk to journalists. By and large, doing press is a massive drag. Take *Top of the Pops*. You either do it and it puts your record up ten places, or you don't and it slips. We've often talked about knocking it on the head, but then we come up with something really strong, like the material on the new LP, and we think, fuck it, of course we'll carry on. It's worthwhile us continuing if only to show people that there are other sides to pop music. We're still firmly in the middle ground between the two polarised areas of pop, the teenyboppers on one side and the serious artists and all that crap on the other. We're not either, never have been. We're the inbetweenies.'

For Weller, press was an imposition, poor love, but why object to doing it?

'It's about making records. The rest is all crap. I spend my life trying to make records, trying to better myself and the band through the songs I write and the records I make.'

'The reason most people do press,' said Talbot rather obviously, 'is so that people buy their record. Pop stars are now just young economists.'

'After a while I wonder what I've got left to say to people,' Weller continued. 'It's hard to judge. When I read the articles afterwards I think, why did I bother doing that? Being a celebrity has got nothing to do with music, it's utter bullshit. Celebrities are one thing, and musicians, artists and writers are another. I don't think there's anything wrong with trying to elevate what you do to a higher level.'

'That kind of mentality is not expected to exist within pop music,' said Talbot. 'Without being po-faced about it, we regard ourselves as musicians. You're allowed to be dignified and well known if you're in jazz, or in any other field of music, but not pop. If Paul were a novelist, a different kind of attitude would attach itself to him.'

Well, Weller wasn't a novelist and at the time it would have been difficult finding a more po-faced pop star. Even though the oxygen of publicity surrounding punk had been the fuel that eventually allowed him to escape it, Weller was still complaining about one of the core components and one of the key relationships of the pop world. In this he would forever be naïve, refusing – like Van Morrison, the man he would unwittingly use as a role model, not least in his relationship with the press – to understand that one of journalism's salient tenets is finding out what people don't want you to know. During the Eighties Weller continued to develop his hatred of critics, those conduits employed to tell the consumer whether or not they should keep their money in their pockets or not.

Weller was the result of a groundswell of entrepreneurialism, a DIY ethos that, in the space of about eighteen months, produced an entire generation of musicians. There was also an ancillary army of journalists, film-makers, fashion designers, illustrators, publishers, promoters. This entrepreneurial spirit was one that continued as the Seventies turned into the Eighties, and as times became tougher, so we had to be swifter on our feet. As society's safety net was swiftly reeled in and folded up, the pioneering spirit became the order of the day, and whether we went to work in advertising agencies or in nightclubs, going to work was what we tried to do. Punk had also encouraged many of us to take more care with how we dressed, beginning to understand that the way you looked determined not just how you were perceived, but also how you might be employed. On face value, you could safely say that the Eighties were the decade of dressing up and looking busy.

All over the country the post-punk generation were dressing up to get ahead. Britain's obsession with youth culture seemed to intensify during the last few months of the Seventies, and it was only natural that it would soon start to be reflected in the media.

In 1985 the ad campaign for the Style Council's current album saw Mick and Paul atop surfboards, while the photo session accompanying the piece in *The Face* included them sporting false moustaches and spoofing English stereotypes. It was in this way that Weller defused a lot of the contradictions thrown up by him being on one hand a recognisable icon in *Smash Hits*, and an opinionated political animal on the other, although for many the irony remained lost. Well, according to Mick Talbot it was.

'We have a problem with our sense of humour, definitely,' he told me. 'Sometimes when we're trying to be pretentious, just on a humorous level, it's totally missed, and other times, when you're deadly serious, people just think, what a prat.

'In the end you think, why bother? When we were listening back to some of the semi-classical things on the first side of *Confessions Of A Pop Group*, my mind was cast back to when we played this secret gig at the Shaw Theatre. I was playing a little classical thing just before we went into a tune, and there were all these people down the front going "Whooargghh! Mickey! Essex! Essex!!" What's all that about? Sometimes you wonder what you're up against.'

1987 turned out to be not such a good year for the Style Council. In February they released a pedestrian LP called *The Cost Of Loving*, a soporific affair that sounded like a collection of Kashif outtakes from 1980. Then they offered up an expensive home movie, *Jerusalem*, the Style Council's very own *Magical Mystery Tour*, and what a lot of nonsense it was. Both products were critically maimed, and though Weller admitted that *The Cost Of Loving* was not their best work ('it's sometimes difficult to know when you're putting out rubbish'), he thought that *Jerusalem* would one day be seen as a classic of its kind. 'In ten years' time some anthropologist will find it and start showing it at all the fringe cinemas, believe me.' Unsurprisingly, this never happened.

For Weller, 1988 looked more promising, not only because the Style Council produced what was probably their most engaging LP to date, brimming with haunting ballads and political sideswipes, but at the time of the interview, Style Council member Dee C. Lee was about to give birth to Weller's first child. For Weller, popular miserablist and miserable populist, *Confessions Of A Pop Group* was the pinnacle of the Style Council's brief but prodigious career. The only problem he saw was convincing other people that this was the case.

In September 1966 the Modern Jazz Quartet had spent a week in Paris recording with the Swingle Singers. The resulting LP, *Place Vendôme,* was an unqualified success, a unique mixture of abstract jazz devices and elegant vocal harmonies, Ward Swingle's singers interpreting original songs by the MJQ's leader John Lewis (the song 'Vendôme' written in 1952 being one of the songs which brought the MJQ worldwide acclaim) as well as classical tunes such as Bach's 'Air On A G String' and Purcell's 'When I Am Laid To Earth'. For quite some time a favourite of Paul Weller's, the album inspired him to ask Ward Swingle and his latest amalgam of vocalists to contribute to 'The Story Of Someone's Shoe', one of the songs on the first side of *Confessions*, with an emotionally explicit lyric unnervingly at odds with the lush arrangement, much in the vein of Elvis Costello. Again, the collaboration worked (somewhat facetiously Weller always said the Style Council were meant to be a cross between the Small Faces and the MJQ), this time emphasising Weller's immersion in quasi-classical music.

The stinging love songs and soapbox rhetoric were still there, though on half the album at least the Style Council had gone pastoral. It was a long way from 'In The City', and Weller appeared to have grown out of suburbia and moved to the country.

In the years since Weller had formed the band, there had been a revolution in black music, what with the global appreciation of soul, pop appropriation of dance music techniques by everyone from Bruce Springsteen to boy band Bros, the emergence of hip-hop, rap, scratching, electro, Go-Go, house, acid house, sampling, the unearthing of rare groove, etc. Although the Style Council occasionally made the odd concession, up until this point they had mined an almost traditional vein, sometimes even accused of being reactionary, soul fundamentalists.

Much of the new stuff left him cold, he admitted. 'You can call us reactionary, but that's only because we can't understand how to use the fucking machines! We have to hire people to turn them on! No, I think the sampling thing is OK, but some are just lousy records, really boring. As for house music, most of it sounds like "Stars On 45" to me, this incessant disco beat. I don't know much about it but I think it sounds like boring Seventies disco music. If we made a house record we could call it a Council House . . . that would be nice.' Ironically, a year later the band would record their own lousy, boring house record, *Modernism: A New Decade*, which their record label Polydor quite sensibly rejected.

In 1988, after five years of hit-and-miss records, five years with an uneasy and uncertain public profile, five years of countless refusals to play the publicity game, Weller had come to an impasse, or so he thought. He didn't crave the fame that had all but killed off Boy George (when you consider just how big Culture Club were in 1983 it almost makes it inconceivable that they weren't involved in Live Aid), but he did want acceptance by his peers as a major songwriter, something he felt he still didn't command. For a man who had written some of the finest songs of the previous decade, he felt he had been slighted by the critics, his public and his peers. Although one of Weller's defining characteristics was having a chip on his shoulder the size of a baked potato.

I asked Weller if it wouldn't be better if he put a stop to the Style Council, stopped being marketed as a pop group. After all, what was an old punk doing in the Eighties anyway? He said it wasn't that easy. As I left Solid Bond studios that day a saccharine but enduring refrain from the early Seventies came wafting across from the in-house stereo: 'Band on the run, band on the run . . .'

On 13 July, Paul Weller was something of an anomaly, a man involved yet a man apart. He said many things about Live Aid, before, during and after, but unfortunately – for him – the most memorable is this: 'There's no one backstage I particularly want to meet. I can't talk to those people.'

THREE

12:44

Boomtown Rats: 'I Don't Like Mondays', 'Drag Me Down', 'Rat Trap'

I was anchoring that part of the broadcast, up in the boiling hot Perspex box in the roof of Wembley, and, following one of Geldof's finger-pointing rants, went to the appeals procedure. 'Here's the address,' I said. 'Fuck the address,' he said. I've never looked at a tape of that incident since the day, but I was amazed to watch the 'give us your fucking money' myth blossom. People who had watched it told me with great certainty what had happened, as did people who hadn't

DAVID HEPWORTH

Nearly twenty years before Live Aid, the England football squad had prepared for their own momentous day at Wembley Stadium in a typically prosaic way. The night before England's glorious 4–2 victory over West Germany on 30 July 1966, Bobby Moore, Bobby Charlton, Geoff Hurst and the rest of manager Alf Ramsey's squad were all staying at the ivy-clad Hendon Hall Hotel in a discreet corner of north London, not too far from Wembley, but just far enough from the distractions of the West End. So instead of rum and Cokes and dancing girls in Soho, the team was treated to the delights of *Those Magnificent Men in Their Flying Machines* at the local fleapit. There was no police escort, no press officers, no minders, and no cameras. In fact almost nobody noticed them. This small group of men who would soon become the most famous team in the country – in the world, for a while – had no need for anyone other than themselves.

The players who would score the winning goals the next day – Martin Peters and Geoff Hurst – were sharing a room together at Hendon Hall, and as they turned in for the night, having made themselves a pot of tea and called their wives, they both let each other know that they'd been picked for the final. Each player had been told by Alf Ramsey privately that night, but then asked to keep it a secret. Hurst and Peters sat opposite each other on their beds and just smiled.

The next day, as the team loitered in the Wembley tunnel, gently kicking the air in front of them,* waiting for the Germans to emerge from their dressing room, each of them was gripped with nerves. They'd waited for what seemed like several minutes when suddenly they could hear them coming, 'their boots resounding on the concrete surface of the tunnel,' said Martin Peters. 'It was a chilling moment as the Germans filed up to the mouth of the tunnel. I glanced across – Seeler, Weber, Beckenbauer, Haller, Schnellinger, Overath. Yes, they had some great players.

'Before that thought had time to take root, we were ushered forward. Both teams walked together into the sunshine to be greeted by a wall of noise. My life was about to change.'

Nineteen years later, as Bob Geldof walked on to the Wembley stage, about to participate properly in the biggest shared experience in human history, he felt a similar surge of emotion. His life would never be the same again.

By rights the Boomtown Rats didn't deserve to be on the bill, but it was Geldof's band and Harvey Goldsmith basically told him he ought to do it. Had to do it. Having organised the event, and having rarely been

---

* A couple of days before the final, most of the players had agreed to wear a pair of Adidas boots during the match, for the princely sum of £300 each. As many of them didn't want to wear new boots for the game, they simply painted three white Adidas stripes down the side of their old boots.

Bob Geldof wrote 'I Don't Like Mondays' as a knee-jerk response to the 1979 shooting spree of the sixteen-year-old Brenda Ann Spencer, who had fired at children in a schoolyard in San Diego, killing two adults and injuring eight children and one police officer.

off the television for the last six months, Goldsmith thought it would have been perverse for Geldof to ignore the fact that he was the lead singer in a still-almost-relevant pop group.

So Geldof grabbed the opportunity. Sod the consequences, he thought, this is my day as much as anyone else's. Wasn't it just. The band had already played their biggest hit, 'I Don't Like Mondays', before Geldof announced to the crowd, 'I've just realised today is the best day of my life.'

Geldof remembers people in the crowd swaying like corn in the wind, but mostly he remembers being scared. By the time he was on stage he knew that the day was going to work in at least one way; there were bands backstage, the television coverage was working, and Status Quo had turned a benign crowd into a benevolent one. For months, weeks, days, and even hours beforehand, though, he had had this overwhelming sense of fear, of dread, a terror of failure. 'Let's imagine the simple failure of no one turning up. Fifteen hours of the Boomtown Rats would have been a little hard to take. I had no contracts with any of these people. And what if there wasn't any money. I'd look completely stupid.'

But so far it was going all right. So far he had seen little of the show, as he was doing what he would be doing all day, namely running around between the TV trucks, the stage, the appeals office, the studio and the Royal Box, checking on Charles and Diana (she was obviously enjoying herself but Geldof wasn't so sure about her husband, who although he was smiling was also looking a little nervous), making sure everyone was where they ought to have been, and generally being busy. At some point he ate a BLT sandwich, not that he can remember exactly when. He remembers lying down at the back of the stage because of the tremendous pain in his back, and he remembers shouting at a few members of the road crew who he thought weren't working fast enough. But by the time the Boomtown Rats went on stage most of it was already a blur.

All over the world, money was pouring in. Old ladies in Ireland were pawning their wedding rings, while one couple sold their first home and gave Band Aid the proceeds. But it wasn't coming in as quickly as Geldof wanted it to.

At one point he was sitting in the presenter's box, surrounded by Billy Connolly, Pamela Stephenson, the Cult's Ian Astbury and co-presenter David Hepworth. At this point Hepworth announced that there had been a significant donation, and then Geldof read out the details, of the £1 million pledge from Sheik Mani Al-Makhtoum and the Dubai government. He then went on to implore people not to go to the pub tonight, and to phone in donations instead. 'Please, stay in, and give us the money. There are people dying now' – slaps leg – 'so give me the money. And here's the number . . .' And then, as Hepworth tried to read out the address, Geldof said, 'Fuck the address, let's get the numbers, because that's how we're going to get it.'

Geldof would repeatedly say how shocked he was when he eventually walked on to the Wembley stage with the Rats. He drank it all in, like he never had before, and would rarely do again. The quotes would be a variation of the following: 'It was only when I walked on stage with the band that the romance of it and the hugeness of it got to me. There was the dawning realisation at that point of exactly what it was, as opposed to what it was organisationally. It was a very tangible, emotional feeling that overwhelmed me, the enormity of it – not just the size of the crowd but to be aware that there was someone in China or somewhere watching that specific moment. A million different things hit me at once and scared me, an amazing overwhelming sense, almost physical in its power.'

Geldof's big moment was halfway through the first song, 'I Don't Like Mondays', the song he had written as a knee-jerk response to the 1979 shooting spree of the sixteen-year-old Brenda Ann Spencer, who had fired at children in a school playground in San Diego, killing two adults and injuring eight children and one police officer. Spencer had showed no remorse, casually saying that 'I don't like Mondays. This livens up the day.' When Geldof got to the line, 'And the lesson today is how to die' the song was brought to a halt by the massive roar of the Wembley crowd. 'I let them shout and then lifted my hand aloft with my fist clenched, and the audience fell into a massive breathing quietness. That moment when I pull up sharp on "Mondays" – time became elastic, like I stood there for hours and my hand just stayed in mid-air. My dad was there – not a great time with him, but he was there – and every person I had ever met in my life in the world was probably watching.'

This moment lent a poignancy to the day that had so far been absent. The air was punched a lot after that, real 'fight the power punches', acknowledging the symbolism and shooting the sky for Bob.

Spandau Ballet's Gary Kemp, who was watching from the wings (they would be on in an hour's time, and were already dressed in their duster coats), said that the moment Geldof stopped the song and raised his fist in the air was evangelical. Kemp says Geldof was statesmanlike, and had so much charisma he'd make a frightening politician. '[He was] a link between punk and the New Romantics and the Eighties.'

After Status Quo's hoary old canter through 'Rockin' All Over The World', this was Live Aid's second iconic moment. There would be a few more, but this was one we were all definitely going to remember.

'When I stopped dead in the middle of "I Don't Like Mondays", my brain was working ahead of me. Before I got to sing it, I thought: I'm going to sing that line out loud. I'd done stadiums before, but this was different, and I had the feeling that everyone I'd ever met in my life would be watching it. So I thought to myself, I'm going to stop and take that in. It was a unique moment and one that I knew would never come again. Everything just pulled me up sharp. You can see me going from right to left, taking it in around the stadium. This is what I was in the middle of and suddenly I understood another meaning to "the lesson today is how to die", and I wanted that to impact anyway. Of course it was one of the moments when the fucking floodgate just opened and cash poured in because suddenly it hit home. I looked at the guys in the band who were a bit freaked out that I stopped, as I'd never done that, and they all just looked at me and carried on.

'That was a big moment for me, the big romance of it. The emotion really grew after that. You could see the figures scale up, as people got more involved and started competing with how much they could pledge. Then when I was being interviewed by David Hepworth – who had started acting in this Smashey & Nicey way, even though he isn't like that – the money really started pouring in. I just couldn't be bothered with the formality of it all. You had Billy Connolly crying his eyes out, and all this BBC formality about the address. Fuck writing in. What the fuck are you talking about? Just give us the fucking money, OK? People aren't going to lick stamps and send it in – do it now, over the phone. And don't go to the pub. So they didn't go to the pubs. That was it.'

Geldof knew that the only way he could rationalise his band's appearance was by playing the hits. He put one recent single, 'Drag Me Down', in between the hits, although people forgot about this faux pas almost immediately. He finished the Rats' Live Aid set with 'Rat Trap', which was the first 'New Wave' song to make number one in the UK, seven years previously, in November 1978. At the time it had replaced 'Summer Nights', the massive hit single by John Travolta and Olivia Newton-John, from the *Grease* soundtrack. This had just spent two months at the top of the UK charts, and when the Rats performed the song on *Top of the Pops*, various band members tore up photographs of Travolta and Newton-John (with Geldof miming the saxophone part on a candelabra like a demented student).

Originally called the Nightlife Thugs, the band changed their name to the slightly less preposterous Boomtown Rats after a gang Geldof had read about in Woody Guthrie's autobiography *Bound for Glory*. Even though they were releasing records in 1977, the Rats were very much a second-generation punk band, more New Wave than anything else.

This was the start of an era in which other music genres were fused with the presentational sheen and urgency of punk, moving towards what would soon become known as skinny tie pop. Many of these bands were hopelessly late to the party, and so all they could offer was style. At least the Rats had an Irish gobshite Mick Jagger lookalike who apparently didn't care what he said to the press. 'Somebody once asked me what I thought of Thatcher,' said Geldof, not long before Live Aid. 'And I said that because she has the bottle, the courage of her convictions, I admire her. So they put in the paper that Geldof admires Thatcher and they printed a picture of me kissing her. In fact, what I said was no matter how asinine, how pigheaded her policies are, she's still a person with convictions, who believes in what she's saying. This was before things got so incredibly bad that she knew she was wrong. Tony Benn himself later said he agreed with her politics of conviction, but disagreed with her. Yet it's me who is vilified! It's me who's fucked in the face!'

The Rats were exuberant and aggressive, even if their inauthenticity made them a laughing stock among the first generation of punk bands. So much of punk was based on the standard obnoxiousness of adolescence, dressed up with postmodern manifestos by sharp-eyed managers, but by the time they were being photographed for music magazines and appearing on television, the Rats just looked like overgrown schoolboys using punk as a way to get themselves noticed.

Geldof admitted that he was once jealous of those members of his peer group who had the credibility he lacked, especially the Clash's Joe Strummer. 'Yes, I did envy the credibility, but it wasn't that I wanted people to say: "Hey this guy's so deep, look at what he's saying!" It wasn't that at all, but there's a fairly highly developed sense of irony in the songs and that irony stems from taking what I do too seriously, and then laughing at myself for taking *anything* I do too seriously. I don't take myself too seriously, but the things I do, I do the best I can. And the things I have written, believe me, are sincere. You can argue the toss, but I think some of the things I've done are still valid.

'I'm glad we contributed to the '76 thing simply because retrospectively it was so exciting and so important. But at the time there was a cultural

Taliban, and the Rats were not deemed to be cool. The only people who liked us were the Yanks, bands like the Ramones. I got on with Johnny Rotten as he was Irish, but no one else was friendly. There was intense rivalry, dissing each other's records – we sold out faster than you, our tickets were more expensive . . .'

He has never understood why critics thought he was cynical, either. 'Why was it we who were calculating? We'd literally stumble from one situation to the next. I think we were clever, sure, but never calculating. We were desperate and hungry, and so were our record company and I think they're the prerequisites of being in a successful rock 'n' roll band.'

'Rat Trap' is an odd record, as the lyrical content had almost no relationship to the music, and while the record sounds quite exhilarating, the words express frustration at being confined in a dead-end town. It sounds like knock-off Springsteen, almost as if Bruce had written a tune for a Broadway show, yet it has a certain effervescence, and when Geldof's working-class hero says he's 'Gonna get out of school/Work in some factory,' he sounds as though he's actually looking forward to it. Geldof claimed not to have heard of Springsteen at this point in his career, which, while unlikely, could explain why 'Rat Trap' isn't imbued with any sense of cool. '"Rat Trap" was meant to be a take on Van Morrison, or maybe even a Phil Lynott take on Van Morrison,' said Geldof, 'creating something slightly mythical out of the people and the suburbs where I'd grown up.'

The song is actually based on Geldof's time working in an abattoir. He recalled to *Mojo* in February 2011: 'I wrote "Rat Trap" in the abattoir in 1973, two years before the Rats were around. But I wasn't particularly writing songs. I was just writing loads of words.'

Mojo asked Geldof how much of his songwriting with the Boomtown Rats was journalistic and how much was what he felt, like a psychic download. He replied: 'The very first interview I did with the *NME*, with Angie Errigo, I said I wanted to be famous, because I wanted to use fame to talk about things that bothered me. And I have. But with "Rat Trap", there was just as much, as you say, psychic download going on. That really was me working in the abattoir.'

Who knew? Clocking in at five minutes, and with no discernible chorus, the song wasn't an obvious hit, yet it was picked up by the DJ and TV presenter Kenny Everett, who had also championed 'Bohemian Rhapsody' three years earlier, and with some success. What 'Rat Trap' had was a catchy saxophone riff, and it was this that resonated with Everett, who asked the band to appear on his TV show.

'We were on the road, and our manager says, "You're not going to believe this, but we've got 360,000 pre-orders of a track that isn't even going to be a single,"' said Geldof. 'This was at the absolute apex of *Grease*-mania, so getting to number one meant that you had to sell 450,000. Well, that was a good enough reason to release it. If we could knock John Travolta off the top of the charts, let's go!'

'Rat Trap' was a far more important record that many of us thought at the time, including Geldof himself, if he's honest. It's one of those records that can still easily slip into Radio 2-style drive-time programming, segued between Gerry Rafferty's 'Baker Street' (yet more soaring saxophones!) and the Motors' 'Airport' as a perfectly adequate example of mainstream late-Seventies pop, yet it can also be included on punk compilations, squeezed between 'Hong Kong Garden' by Siouxsie and the Banshees, say, and 'Complete Control' by the Clash without any sharp intake of breath or Hanna–Barbera eye-popping. Like many of his contemporaries, Geldof used punk as a way to get on in the business and not because of any particular ideological bent, making the occasional great pop record in the process. Of course 'Rat Trap' was terribly affected, but then wasn't all great pop affected in some way? Why on earth wouldn't it be? Why so little in common?

In essence, Geldof was the great pragmatist. 'It boiled down to the fact that I did not believe that *Top of the Pops* was the main problem with the world and they [the London punks, including the Clash] did. Of course, they'd all say they didn't want to be on *Top of the Pops* when I knew for a fact they were all trying desperately to get on and as soon as the Pistols got a chance to be on, they were on. Then everybody turned around and said it was a great victory.'

Geldof worked wonders with the song at Live Aid, the largest group of people who had ever heard it played. Those watching on TV got a very distorted view of the relative popularity of people lower down the bill, as you saw these acts playing in front of 72,000 people and you assumed they were bigger than they actually were. So viewers of Live Aid, all 2 billion of them, saw that rock music was alive and kicking, thriving, flourishing. I don't think anyone thought the Boomtown Rats were thriving, not that it mattered though. Geldof could have gone on stage and solemnly recited a nursery rhyme and the audience would have loved it, and loved him for it. Even if they had stopped buying his records.

'Our records were still good but the audience had long moved on and dismissed us,' said Geldof. 'And I say that without bitterness, as that's what happens. I was a pop journalist for long enough to encourage that.'

On this sunny afternoon the song felt full of exuberance, as though it were a generic summer anthem, as though the Rats were a traditional good-time festival band, knocking out the hits for giddy students, weekending thirtysomethings and seriously overhung bikers. It was surprising how many people in the crowd knew the words, as everyone appeared to be singing along. Everyone! Not only that, but almost as many of them were impersonating the sax breaks too, swinging their arms up in the air to replicate playing the instrument, but looking instead like baby elephants pouring water over their backs. This was a moment we could all enjoy should we want to. After all, the Rats were a fairly inclusive band. Also, there were a lot of teenagers in the audience, at least there were around us, and so many of them probably first heard 'Rat Trap' when they were seven, eight, nine or ten, and you could tell that it evoked some giddy collective childhood memories out there on the field. The Rats had been perfect primary-school fodder, and Geldof still looked like an overgrown kid, a dishevelled overgrown kid at that, as did the rest of the band, in their funny hats and pyjamas. If it all went wrong (which it looked as though it already had, to be honest), the band looked as though they'd make a fair fist of being children's television presenters. In fact the idea of Geldof as a sweary *Blue Peter* presenter was actually quite funny. Just imagine it: 'Give us yer foocking sticky-back plastic!'

'Ambition is a variable,' said Geldof. 'You have an idea, your ambition is to achieve it, and that's what I realised a long time ago. I'll do stuff for no money whatsoever, just simply because I think I want to get that idea done, and there's an intense satisfaction in achieving that. A lot of businesses I start, I take no money whatsoever, nothing, for years, just to see it work. That's never varied. You start a band, you really want it to work and you're just laser-focused on this happening. It's not just timing, talent and looks, it's really working it, being really focused on where you want to go and where you want to be and gathering the people around you who can enable that.

'The Boomtown Rats was like that. We were completely focused, as that was the only way I knew it would work.

'A band is a classic, if you want to put it into contemporary economics: people with an entrepreneurial idea who put around themselves a skills base that they don't have for themselves. I can't play guitar very well, so I get a really good guitar player. I can't play piano, so I get a really good piano player. A piano player can't sing, so he gets a really good singer. That's how it works, and then you try and form a coherent identity and a plan that will drive it forward.

'That's what we did with the Rats. At a certain point you've got to have the modesty to stand aside and let an enabler take over and serve the managing role; someone who can enable the central ideas and enthusiasm. What I'm good at is finding people who are better than me at any particular skill around me, articulating the idea, formulating the way forward with that idea and asking them to help me enable it, so that's it. Live Aid would be seen as a classic example of that; as would the Boomtown Rats, as would the Commission for Africa with Blair.

'I can't see the point in doing something if it's not going to work. Being personally successful is a different thing. I want the idea to succeed. What happens to me, my satisfaction comes from the idea of succeeding, it's not me being a success. I'm not driven by that, only by the fact that whatever idea I have, I noodle it around in my head, and I want it to work.'

The odds determined that Live Aid would have been someone's first concert – it just had to have been – and what a way to start! I'm fairly sure my first gig was watching some completely unprepossessing band upstairs at the Nag's Head in High Wycombe, but imagine if your first gig was Live Aid. How could you come back from that? It would be like kicking it all off at Woodstock, or the 100 Club. Imagine if your first gig was not only the defining concert of the year, but the most important concert of the decade, and what would almost immediately become one of the most discussed gigs of all time. It had already been determined that you were doomed to live your concert-going life in reverse, because – seriously – what gig was ever going to top this? Imagine that your rock 'n' roll baptism had been Live Aid, and then your next gig was a local band in a dodgy pub, or Love and Money at the Town and Country Club. Imagine going to the Street Sounds all-dayer at Wembley Arena in 1986 and wondering why there was no love in the room, why there wasn't any sense of euphoria.

We certainly felt that this was the first gig for some of the people around us, as these kids, who couldn't have been more than fifteen or sixteen, were bouncing up and down and pogoing around as though they had just discovered a pantechnicon of amyl nitrate capsules in the Wembley centre circle. They looked as though they would bounce up and down to anything, although the pumped-up pop of the Rats seemed like the perfect sort of thing to work off all that energy. Their songs were energetic, they were vaguely angry (well, angry enough for your average bouncy teenager), and they had the kind of melodies that kept you interested up to and beyond the middle eight. I seem to remember that a lot of the more energetic Rats enthusiasts were wearing scarves, which made me think of the boys down the Marlow rugby club during their Bay City Rollers phase ten years earlier (boys obviously didn't like the Rollers, but they liked the girls who liked them, so what was the harm in investing in a cheap tartan scarf and singing along to 'Bye Bye Baby' after the DJ had finished playing 'Hi Ho Silver Lining'?).

Musically, 'Rat Trap' was not exactly influential, yet its lyrical themes would be picked up by the Specials three years later in a far more demonstrative fashion, when they released 'Ghost Town', not only one of the most important records of the early Eighties, but still one of the most evocative. While punk was largely a cultural insurrection, repeatedly using thematic working-class imagery – the 'brutalist' modern tower block being the most obvious manifestation of this, a symbol of post-war progress that very quickly became a totem of social deprivation – 'Ghost Town' was a direct response to the deprivation that the Specials' leader Jerry Dammers saw around him. The band had already had huge success as the standar-bearers of the 2 Tone organisation, and had had hits with 'Gangsters', 'A Message To You Rudy' and 'Rat Race', amongst others. Even though the Rats were supposedly a punk band, by the time of the Specials, most of their contemporaries had had their edges sanded away; and the Specials were edgier still. Inspired by punk, they had their own grudges to articulate, and they were doing it through the medium of ska. The Rats had experimented with ska with their 1980 hit 'Banana Republic', though it was hardly their proudest moment.

'Britain was falling apart,' said Dammers. 'The car industry was closing down in Coventry. We were touring, so we saw a lot of it. Liverpool and

Jerry Dammers' Specials were the quintessential post-punk band: mixing the best of the past with a post-modernist nod to the future, weaving in a little socio-economic insurrection along the way. They made great singles, too.

Glasgow were particularly bad. The overall sense I wanted to convey was impending doom. There were weird, diminished chords: certain members of the band resented the song and wanted the simple chords they were used to playing on the first album. It's hard to explain how powerful it sounded. We had almost been written off and then "Ghost Town" came out of the blue.'

The Specials were advocates of late-Seventies postmodern ska, the inventors of 2 Tone, and quite simply one of the coolest, most important British bands of all time. In the space of just two years, from 1979 to 1981, the original Specials managed to embody the new decade's violent energies, morals and conflicts – though always with an ironic and often sardonic detachment that kept the band cool as the Eighties grew increasingly hot. Their records defined a generation who weren't sure they wanted to be defined in the first place. Sure, the band were earnest, but they were studiedly sarcastic, too, which endeared them to everyone at the time who mattered. Not only that, but they came from Coventry, Britain's very own answer to Detroit, the epitome of the post-war urban wasteland, the quintessential concrete jungle, and felt they had a right to bleat about anything they wanted to, especially the onslaught of Thatcherism.

They weren't the Boomtown Rats, but then by 1981 not even the Boomtown Rats wanted to be the Boomtown Rats. Their last three singles had been failures, even in Ireland.

1981 was a desperate year in the UK, and not just for the Rats. Youth unemployment was rife as the country felt the bite of Thatcher's cuts, and riots were erupting all over the country, riots that appeared, with eerie synchronicity, at the same time as 'Ghost Town'. Dammers' record was an apocalyptic portrait of inner-city oppression set to a loping beat offset by an unsettling and vaguely Middle Eastern motif: 'Government leaving the youth on the shelf . . . No job to be found in this country . . .' The single sounded like the fairground ride from hell, complete with strident brass, madhouse wailing, and dub-style breaks. The video was just as bleak, featuring a road trip through some of the least salubrious streets of central London.

The week after the song was released, there were riots and civil disobedience all over the country.

'It wasn't a surprise when it went to number one – most things 2 Tone became hits,' said Pauline Black, the lead singer of fellow 2 Tone band, the Selector. '"Ghost Town" epitomised the 2 Tone idea that black and white can operate in the same unit and speak to the youth. And its sense of melancholy spoke clearly: there was the "sus" laws [the informal term for the "stop and search" law that enabled the police to stop, search and potentially arrest suspects], inner cities not functioning, racism dividing the working class. There was fighting at our gigs; there were lots of National Front people around. There was frustration about 2 Tone falling apart. We were Seventies bands in a time of two-man synth bands. The record companies were happy to leave 2 Tone's problems behind.'

'Seventeen months separate the Specials' two number one singles, and a million musical miles,' said Simon Price of the *Independent on Sunday*. 'Their first, a live recording of "Too Much Too Young", was essentially the Sex Pistols' "Bodies" gone ska, but the intervening year saw the Specials ditch that punky-reggae template. Jerry Dammers experimented with lounge-noir on their second album, causing intra-band friction. "Ghost Town" initiated a strand of spooked British pop that has lived on in Tricky and Portishead's trip-hop and the dubstep of Burial and James Blake.'

Realism? This was urban decay writ large, accompanied by a kick drum and a muted horn.

Geldof loved the Specials, as he had always had a penchant for the sharper end of reggae, and had even shoehorned it into the Rats' sound. Both 'I Don't Like Mondays' and 'Like Clockwork' were originally written as reggae records, while their 1980 hit 'Banana Republic' – a scathing knee-jerk description of Ireland, written in response to the band being temporarily banned from performing there – was itself a portmanteau mixture of reggae and ska. Geldof had already made his 'denunciation of nationalism, medieval-minded clerics and corrupt politicians' on *The Late Late Show* in 1977, and this simply added insult to injury.

In some respects 1981 was defined by the riots as much as by the music they inspired. Yes, there was a royal wedding, in sharp juxtaposition to inner-city decay, a wedding that would produce a genuine royal superstar, yet the riots – the worst for a century – would resonate throughout the country for years. Motivated by racial tension, a perception of inner-city deprivation, and heat, the defining factor was the ongoing war of attrition between the black community and the police. The four main riots occurred in Brixton in London, Handsworth in Birmingham, Chapeltown in Leeds and Toxteth in Liverpool, although there were disturbances in at least twenty other towns and cities, including Derby, Bristol and, almost unbelievably, High Wycombe.

The worst were in Brixton, on 10–12 April. Dubbed 'Bloody Saturday' by *Time* magazine, the main riot took place on the 11th, and resulted in a mass confrontation between the mob and the Metropolitan Police. There were forty-five injuries to members of the public, and nearly 300 to the police; over 5,000 rioters were involved, many of who had simply come out to fight as they had nothing better to do, and nowhere better to do it.

The riots were more than a collection of urban disturbances, they were a media flashpoint that drew international attention to the huge rift in ideologies between the left and the right in the country, as well as the gap between perception and reality in terms of how the government were coping with the economy. There was also a growing sense that the Tories had no understanding of, and no pastoral interest in, the have-nots under their care, those who hadn't benefited from financial deregulation, privatisation or Thatcher's changes to the welfare state. While she would always say that she was empowering those who had previously been beholden to the state, Thatcher was criticised most often for having no idea what to do with communities when the safety net had been withdrawn.

The forgotten riot is the one in Brixton riot that started on 28 September 1985. It was sparked by the shooting of Dorothy 'Cherry' Groce by the police, while they were looking for her son Michael Groce in relation to a suspected firearms offence. They thought Groce was hiding in his mother's home, raided it, and shot Mrs Groce, paralysing her from the waist down. As news of the attack spread, so hostilities began, and the police lost control of the area for two days, during which time dozens of fires were started and shops looted. Photojournalist David Hodge

The forgotten riot was the Brixton riot of 1985, sparked by the shooting of Dorothy 'Cherry' Groce by the police, while they were looking for her son Michael in relation to a suspected firearms offence.

died a few days later, after a gang of looters he was trying to photograph attacked and beat him.

The Broadwater Farm riot in Tottenham, in north London, a week later, was dominated by two deaths. During a police search of her home on 5 October, an Afro-Caribbean woman called Cynthia Jarrett died of heart failure, triggering a sequence of events which resulted in a full-scale riot on the Broadwater Farm council estate, involving youths throwing bricks, stones and Molotov cocktails, as well as using firearms. At 9.30 p.m. Police Constable Keith Blakelock was trapped by a gang of local balaclava-clad boys, blowing whistles and ringing bells, who tried to decapitate him using knives and machetes. He was butchered to death. According to a man watching from his second-floor flat, the mob was relentless, like 'vultures tearing at his body'. When he was examined later Blakelock had forty-two different wounds. Winston Silcott, Engin Raghip and Mark Braithwaite were convicted of murder and sentenced to life imprisonment, although all three were cleared by the Court of Appeal in 1991 after it emerged evidence had been tampered with (Silcott remained in prison for the separate murder of another man, Tony Smith, finally being released in 2003).

I spent the years between 1981 and 1987 knocking about in south London, living in various housing association flats in Brixton, Peckham, Herne Hill and the Oval. The 1981 riots happened just a quarter of a mile from where I lived in the Oval, while the 1985 riot happened right outside my front door. 28 September was a Saturday, and having just come back from a trip I had spent the whole day indoors, writing, listening to music, and cleaning the flat, not bothering to go outside for a paper, or turn on the radio or TV. The flat was right behind the Ritzy cinema, just off Coldharbour Lane, a first floor, two-bedroomed housing association flat that backed on to a small courtyard, and faced Brixton's Front Line. The first I knew that something was up was around five o'clock in the afternoon, when I started to hear screaming, windows being smashed, and the sound of running past the window. I looked through the vast, seven-foot-wide venetian blind that faced the street and I saw dozens of local residents – almost exclusively young black men – running by my window carrying stolen record players, televisions, CD players, radios, amplifiers, microwaves, small fridges, speaker systems, anything they could carry. They'd been looting in and around the shops in Brixton market, and in a second I realised I was in the middle of a full-scale riot.

Now I was attuned to everything, including the sound of looters breaking in through the front door of our building. They steamed into the four ground-floor flats, and took anything they wanted that they could carry (again, audio equipment, vinyl, TVs). I had already barricaded our own front door with various pieces of random furniture, although this was largely to try and appease my girlfriend, as I knew that any concerted push from the other side would have caused them to come tumbling down the corridor as the door flew open. The looters (even though they were ostensibly rioting all they were really doing was stealing) did actually run up to the first floor, although they immediately headed back down again as the sound of sirens approached. Police ran into our building but by then most of the looters had run in the direction of Railton Road, and safe havens.

These were small gangs, little groups of boys who had grown up together, becoming disenfranchised together.

When I rang my friend Robin, who had gone with me to Live Aid, and who lived up the road on Brixton Hill, and told him about the dozens and dozens of people still running by my window with enough stereo equipment to start their own branch of Currys, he laughed and rather unhelpfully suggested that I nip out and find something for myself. We had both lived in Brixton for some time, and had become almost immune to the attritional nature of the place. It was our version of gallows humour, as we were no longer surprised by break-ins, muggings or harassment from the locals.

The next morning Brixton looked as though it had been turned inside out, as everything that was usually inside someone's house appeared to be outside, all the household detritus that looks so pathetic and parochial when removed from its natural habitat. The area soon went back to normal, although the fact that there were even more boarded-up windows in the market and along the high street just made you think that whatever forms of gentrification were taking place, Brixton was never going to get any better, as every time it did, there would always be those who would find a way to destroy it (most of whom lived there).

As we eventually moved out – to Shepherd's Bush, in west London – so others took our place, and a gentrification of sorts did occur, the kind that increasingly appealed to those who couldn't afford to get onto the housing ladder anywhere else. By the end of the decade, those pockets of gentrification that had started to pop up around central London would become so oversubscribed that those on the bottom rungs were pushed further and further out, so those previously out-of-bound areas east of Battersea and south of the Thames started to be marketed as close-to-the-city villages that promised the sort of luxurious loft-living the young bankers in Docklands had been promised a decade before. Some thought this was progress, although what was rarely advertised in the *Sunday Times'* Home section was the fact that most of these new developments were nothing less than gated communities. They didn't need to say anything, as it was implicit. The gentrification of London was continuing at an unusually fast pace, one that reflected the new money swirling around and rushing into the city, and the way in which it was being used as an architectural hothouse; but what was rarely discussed was the divisive way in which we were all now being forced to live, the rich rubbing up against the poor, and neither of them appreciating it very much.

London wouldn't experience riots again for another twenty-six years, when the looters couldn't even be bothered to swathe their frustration with their own plight with anything tangible; the looting in 2011 was simply an excuse to steal some new trainers. The gangs were bigger, more organised, more resigned to living outside of society; no explanations or excuses were needed or offered. Compared to the two-speed society of the Tweenies (as economists are still trying to describe the second decade of the twenty-first century), 1985 seemed almost quaint.

Bob Geldof didn't think so, though. Speaking ahead of a show at Islington Assembly Hall in May 2012, the sixty-year-old said he did not believe the previous summer's disorder, which saw pockets of looting and arson even in Islington, was 'emblematic of a wider malaise'. He explained: 'I didn't feel it was that significant to be honest with you. I say that with all respect to the people that suffered with it. I thought it didn't have the weight of the Notting Hill riots or the Poll Tax riots which seemed very specific, one was about racism and lack of opportunity and the other about economic constraints.'

He also criticised modern music for a 'lack of relevance', preferring the musical insurrection of the past. 'In the Seventies the music sounded like how it felt to live around then – that frustration and demand for change. In places like Tottenham today, it's not great out there, it's pretty grim. I am desperate for the new sound – it needs to be of its time and it needs to articulate the now.' Later he would say, 'Rock 'n' roll needs to be against something. It can't just be. Of course there are great songs. There will always be great songs that don't suggest anything other than being a great song. But where are our Ramones or our [Sex] Pistols today?'

Geldof was always fairly political in what he wrote, even if the music was often quite sanitised. His lyrics to their 1980 song 'Elephant's Graveyard', about the race riots in Overtown and Liberty City in Miami that year (when five white police officers were acquitted of charges relating to the murder of an African American called Arthur McDuffie after a high-speed car chase), were as strident as anything written three years earlier during the height of punk, supposedly the ultimate working-class cultural revolution.

A week before Live Aid, the *Observer* profiled Geldof exhaustively, calling him 'a showman of intense energy and organising ability, deeply flawed by a wild, destructive urge.' They called him a mass of contradictions: 'A man without a drop of conventional show-business sentimentality in his veins, an apparently well-adjusted loner in a noisily gregarious trade, an entrancingly literate conversationalist whose altruism is impossible to reconcile with his coarse cynicism, a disciplined professional whose ungovernable egotism has torpedoed his own career.' Maybe, maybe not, but it was this mass of contradictions that made him such a powerful songwriter in the first place.

The paper was referring to a story concerning a radio programmers' national convention in San Diego in 1979, shortly after the release of 'Rat Trap'. The Rats were topping the bill, as they were in the States to plug their album, *A Tonic For The Troops*. It was a huge opportunity for them to break into the US market, although as soon as Geldof hit the stage that night he launched into an attack of the radio stations, causing all the VIP programmers to walk out, vowing to bury the Rats' album and ban it from all their stations. Consequently the band never made it in the States.

Geldof had once said that most people get into the music industry for three reasons: to get laid, to get famous and to get rich. This marked him down for retribution, as he went on to claim that many rock stars went out of their way to lie about the poverty of their background. 'Rat Trap' was deliberately written in the third person for this very reason: Geldof didn't want to try and exploit or exaggerate his own past. He fully understood righteous anger, and wanted to express it in his own way (he once described the Rats as anti-establishment and anti the anti-establishment).

The Eighties riots were devoured so much by the international media that the burning oil drum became as much a part of modern British iconography as the white suits in the 1981 television adaptation of Evelyn Waugh's *Brideshead Revisited* – and for a while seemed to appear in any film about the British underclass, surrounded by a gang of RADA-trained professional cockneys and a smattering of generic gangsters and drug dealers. To the outside world it looked as though rioting was what any youth cult worth their salt did when they'd grown tired of posing for style magazines or making bad pop records.

Living in London you certainly got the feeling that you were somehow living under siege. In south London, conflict gave an edge to every transaction in a corner shop, every late-night walk home from the Underground. Walk into a Brixton pub and you felt eyes upon you. Television coverage of the riots painted them clearly as battles between residents and the police force, although what they really did was create even more racial tension between blacks and whites on the street, between neighbours of different ethnic backgrounds, between people who knew each other and those who didn't. I had a friend who was chased down Gresham Road near Brixton Police Station by some of his black neighbours just because he happened to be white at the wrong time of day. He sought refuge in a (black) neighbour's house, who promptly called out to the gang chasing him, who ran in and kicked the living daylights out of him. Police aggression made everyone paranoid, and made people who had previously lived quite happily side by side turn against each other because it seemed like the safest thing to do.

The morning after the first 1981 riot was almost as bad as the riot itself, as the mess and the devastation made you feel as though you were living in a place that was never going to improve, that was only ever going to get worse. And so you started treating the place with the same disdain; what was the point of throwing an empty cigarette packet in a bin if the bin was going to be thrown through the off-licence window later in the day? Back in 1981, walking around Electric Avenue and Atlantic Road after the first night's disturbance was nothing if not surreal. You couldn't quite believe that things would ever return to normal, what with the broken glass, the boarded-up windows, the dozens of overturned cars, the smoke billowing from the shops in the market. The carpet shop always seemed to suffer, not that any of the stock was ever taken. What had the rioters got against carpet shops? The looters concentrated on the electrical shops, on the ghetto blasters, television sets and radios. Coldharbour Lane always looked like a fairly unforgiving place at the best of times, but for weeks after the riots it felt as though it had been transported directly from some post-apocalyptic wasteland, a tunnel of terror. Walking down the Lane at night you felt a little like Orpheus walking out of the underworld, too anxious to turn around and see what might be behind you. Everywhere there was tension. One afternoon that autumn, a few months after the 1981 riots, I had walked from a squat in Peckham up to the Oval, and was just about to enter the Underground when I was approached by a gang of about a dozen skinheads. They were all over the place at the time, although they tended to leave Brixton and its immediate environs alone, so whenever you saw them in the area you suspected there might be trouble. I assumed that my dyed hair, red bandana and Chinese slippers had probably caused my shorn-haired friends to think I was a lily-livered liberal with a penchant for Afro-Caribbean culture, so as soon as I saw one of them reach into his pocket for his knife I turned on my heels and ran. All the way to Brixton. And, unlike Orpheus, without looking back – I had recently been stabbed by a gang of casuals as I left the Hemingford Arms in Islington, and didn't fancy repeating the experience.

When Mrs Thatcher first arrived in Downing Street in 1979 there were many who thought she would become as much a prisoner of the Whitehall machine as her predecessor, Edward Heath, yet she quickly used her abrasiveness to slap down the mandarins. 'She gives the civil servants hell,' said one observer soon after she became prime minister. 'She writes these brusque, caustic notes accusing them of woolly thinking, and they are absolutely terrified of her.' The Cabinet were terrified too, as her treatment of her colleagues was appalling. There would be no woolly thinking in Mrs Thatcher's government. Elected against a background of rotting refuse and unburied bodies following the Winter of Discontent, she took her mandate for governing as a mandate for change.

No woolly thinking.

Thatcher dismissed the idea that racism, heavy-handed police tactics and unemployment were behind the Brixton disturbances – even though police brutality and continual harassment of young black men had been one of the prime motivators behind the riots – saying 'Nothing, but nothing, justifies what happened . . . What aggravated the riots into a virtual saturnalia was the impression gained by the rioters that they could enjoy a fiesta of crime, looting and rioting in the guise of social protest. They felt they had been absolved in advance.' She was criticised for this outburst, but she wasn't entirely wrong. She was, though, when she claimed that money couldn't buy either trust or racial harmony. What many forget about the peace process in Northern Ireland was that it was as much to do with prosperity as political and sectarian will. Of course large-scale investment would have helped Brixton, although the more disquiet there was, the more unlikely any investment seemed. However, it was to come sooner than anyone thought, as Tesco bought a site on Acre Lane the day after the 1985 riots. Gentrification eventually came to Brixton, inadvertently moving it upmarket; not by much, but by enough. Pride followed prosperity, and in the summer of 2011, when opportunistic revellers attending a street party used the excuse of the riot in Tottenham a few days earlier to loot and burn a string of shops in Brixton, local residents were incensed, calling the thugs 'pathetic . . . It's just an excuse for the young ones to come and rob shops. We are going to get people blaming the economy and what happened last week but that's not the real reason this happened. This is costly for our community reputation.' It would have been difficult to imagine the residents displaying the same sentiments in 1981 or indeed in 1985.

Brixton would change over the next thirty years, especially after the Millennium. From 2001 to 2012, the Afro-Caribbean population of Lambeth, the borough that houses Brixton, fell by 8 per cent, even though the borough's overall population rose by 9 per cent. As *The Economist* pointed out at the time, this was largely due to black flight. To escape crime, and to buy bigger houses and to get their children into better schools, they fled to suburbia, specifically to the areas on the outskirts of south-east London.

Gentrification continues apace, as Lambeth Council has spruced up the area, preventing the conversion of houses into flats to attract middle-class house buyers, and transforming the old covered market into a shopping mall with upmarket cafés and restaurants. A year after Brixton Village opened in 2011, just as the Noughties ended, house prices had risen by as much as 20 per cent, in a market where residential property was largely flat.

Around the same time, if you happened to be reading the classified ads in the arts pages of your favourite national newspaper, you would have seen that revival tours were all the rage. ABC, the Human League, The Who, Lloyd Cole, Ultravox, Deep Purple, the Eagles, Golden Earring and Simply Red were all treading the boards again, seemingly regardless of how these opportunistic outings would ultimately affect their legacies. And who could blame them? People at the time would pay good money to see bands they enjoyed in their youth, sometimes regardless of how many original members they contained. That weird little band from 1983 whose only hit you devoured as though it were the essence of life itself? Yup, well they were probably back too, playing the Shepherd's Bush Empire the night after Joe Jackson, and probably supporting Orchestral Manoeuvres in the Dark, or the Happy Mondays. With all the original members, too, strangely – apart from the drummer, who had no doubt died in a bizarre gardening accident in what the rest of the band at the time thought was a misguided, if not completely unfunny, homage to Spinal Tap.

At the time, as far as music was concerned, there was nothing quite so *au courant* as nostalgia.

And, if you looked carefully, you would have seen that the Specials were back too, churning out the old hits as though they were a human jukebox. They were greeted with open arms by the critics and public alike, only they weren't really the Specials at all, because the most important member, Jerry Dammers, the man who invented them, who gave the band their political edge, who wrote most of their songs, and who was responsible for making them truly memorable, was not encouraged to participate in the reunion ('I founded the Specials, and now they've excluded me,' said Dammers when the band first reunited, in 2008). There had always been friction between

Dammers and the group's singer – Terry Hall, one of the most miserable men in pop – and that friction continued; obviously to the extent that they found it difficult to work together.

Dammers was the creative genius behind the Specials, the man who gave them their idiosyncratic musical tropes, and who set them apart from the likes of the Selector, the Beat, or Bad Manners. The Specials without Dammers were like the Doors without Jim Morrison, Queen without Freddie Mercury, Wham! without George Michael, or Morecambe and Wise without Morecambe or, er, Wise. I saw the re-formed Specials support Blur at their last gig in Hyde Park in 2012, and the band looked like a bunch of fiftysomething cab drivers and sounded like the musical equivalent of a Sunday morning football match. They didn't play 'Ghost Town', but then how could they? The man who wrote it wasn't there.

I knew Jerry extremely well for about five years in the Eighties. I would regularly hitch up to Coventry to sit in sullen working men's clubs with him and his extraordinary circle of friends and acquaintances, discussing socialism (we differed), the provenance of Prince Buster and the validity of Heaven 17. We went clubbing together, spent a few memorable New Year's Eves in Bristol (where Jerry's parents were from), spent birthdays together, and once DJ'd together at a miners' benefit at London's Wag Club in 1983 (he played politically correct funk while I played right-of-centre disco). I even sat through some of the tortuous recording of the 1985 album *In The Studio* by the Special AKA (as the Specials morphed into), containing Jerry's defining moment, the monumentally influential 'Free Nelson Mandela'. Inspired by Live Aid, this ultimately led to the Mandela Seventieth Birthday Tribute concert at Wembley Stadium in 1988, and helped add to the groundswell of support that led to Mandela's release from prison in February 1990.

Dammers was always a genuine bohemian, and it's no surprise to me the way his career panned out (DJing, production, forming various esoteric dance orchestras). However, I also thought he might turn out to be our generation's John Barry, scoring important movies with solemn yet iconic orchestral themes, balancing Jacques Derrida with Francis Lai, Scott Walker with Dr John. To me, Dammers was the Lennon and McCartney of ska, one of the most important voices of the post-punk generation, a man who always appeared to be carrying his generation's hopes and dreams on his shoulders, as well as his own. That he didn't turn into John Barry was a disappointment to me, but probably not to him.

Yes, he should have been at Live Aid, and having the Specials play would have given the event an added perspective, an extra resonance, especially if they had played 'Ghost Town'. Hearing 'Can't go on no more . . . The people getting angry' played by probably the most important multiracial band in the country wafting through the stadium would have had as much of an impact as the 'Drive' video that would be broadcast a few hours later at the end of David Bowie's set.

In the end, we had 'Rat Trap' instead, possibly a more inferior song, but given the man who wrote the song and who sang it so plaintively under the Wembley sun, perhaps a more appropriate one.

In the same way that tragedy plus time equals satire, so coincidence goes a long way in creating drama. During the Brixton riot of 1985, the only real respite in our flat was the kitchen, which faced a tall, narrow courtyard; so narrow that the windows of the other kitchens facing it were only a few feet away. We would often sit there during the summer, as it was cool and quiet, the sun never daring to show its face. There was plenty of room as well, as ironically, for such a small flat, the kitchen was enormous, the largest room of all. We'd sit in here, our feet naked on the lino, and listen to the radio, pretending that the concrete prairie of Brixton was miles away.

That autumn, the radio was full of Live Aid acts, and while it was customary to play only chart songs, both the BBC and commercial radio stations went out of their way to swamp the airwaves with the greatest hits of those who were deemed to have made a success of Live Aid. A list that obviously included the Boomtown Rats. Many of the songs that had been performed at Live Aid were now shrouded in context, so whenever Radio 1 played 'Drive' by the Cars, for instance, all anyone could think about was the mashed-up video of starving Ethiopian children. Similarly, whenever you heard 'Rockin' All Over The World', 'Let It Be' or 'Radio Ga Ga', there was only one image that came to mind, that of a sun-drenched Wembley Stadium full of sunburnt smiling bodies, their ribcages vibrating beneath a pale blue dome of sky.

And while 'I Don't Like Mondays' generally took on the most shadow-filled poignancy, a defining song for the ages, 'Rat Trap' became our own unofficial anthem. The day that marauding looters broke into our building, Geldof's Springsteen homage was the song playing on the radio in the kitchen, sandwiched between the weather and a Billy Idol song. For one fleeting moment, Bob Geldof's paean to urban paranoia had become as loaded with meaning as Jerry Dammers' 'Ghost Town' had four years previously. It didn't sound as ominous or as threatening, yet it somehow captured the mood in a general journalistic sense, if not an expressive one. As it echoed around the courtyard, the day suddenly took on a surreal hue, one which actually made the whole experience somewhat less fraught. Of course, as soon as the lubricious strains of 'White Wedding' started bouncing around the yard, the mood was shattered, and all we could hear was the sound of windows being smashed and front doors being kicked in downstairs.

'The memory of Live Aid was far more important than the actuality of it,' said Geldof. 'For once in pop music the emotion transcended what was happening and you walked away with that as your memory more than any individual performance.

'I was on stage, and the emotive quality of the day, which I hadn't predicted at all nor planned for, struck me. It was an electrifying moment, to be aware that there was someone in Shanghai or Tierra del Fuego or wherever watching that specific moment, and it was strangely calming. I felt very centred. And maybe the first time that I was aware of feeling that sense of being and place, of being right, was at that moment.'

'Bob was God and it was his day,' said the PR Alan Edwards, who was also backstage. 'Just a year ago he was the leader of this no-hope band, a band nobody wanted anything to do with, and suddenly he's the most important person in the music industry. He was messianic after a while, and when he walked into a room it was like Elvis had just turned up. You couldn't ignore him. He'd always had character, always been larger than life, but Live Aid, Band Aid, they gave him power, they gave him the edge. Whether by luck or design, Geldof showed that you could so something on this scale and get noticed.'

'You needed an extraordinary character to make all of the elements work, and it wouldn't have happened without Bob,' said Gary Farrow. 'Every problem that cropped up, he'd say, "Get them on the phone. Let me talk to them." He was proper. In the run-up to Live Aid he was continually being told he couldn't do something, or the Civil Aviation Authority wouldn't allow it, or whatever, and he'd always get on the phone. He would literally not take no for an answer. He just got numbers and called people up.'

'Backstage there was a great deal of love and support for Bob, and if it wasn't for him, I don't think anyone would have come together in the way they did,' said Gary Kemp. 'He had the determination to make it work; determination and incredible perseverance. But also, we all knew what it felt like to record that single. That was really the most extraordinary moment. If the single hadn't been the way it was, and felt the way it did in studio, then I think we would have been much more cynical about it, because usually everyone's hustling in the backstage areas, their management are looking for better facilities for their artist or a slightly larger Winnebago – usually everyone wants an extra velvet rope.

'I remember seeing Geldof punching the air at the moment when he took his applause. I thought that was great theatre. Bob always understands the dynamic of theatre and he delivered it that day. It was wonderful.'

Trevor Dann, of BBC2's *Whistle Test*, said, 'In my view, this has polished Bob off as a rock star. He can't be a symbol of youthful alienation – James Dean and Mick Jagger promising a riot on stage – *and* be sending food to Africa. From now on, he's the guy who organised Live Aid.'

On Terry Wogan's early-evening television programme the night before Live Aid, Wogan had asked Geldof if he was going to go back to the Rats after Live Aid was all over, to which he responded, 'That's what I like doing, what I get satisfaction from, and that's what I hope to do. This is just an aberration in my life. I'll go back and do what I think I'm better at. And I'll have some fun then. I'm motivated by boredom, and as soon as I get bored I go off and do something else. It's all under way now, and all these people have suddenly come out of the woodwork and they're doing their job and you sit back and watch them and enjoy their professionalism; and you, a rank amateur, sit there and smile and say, it worked.' He finished by saying that when Live Aid was all over he could go back to being a complete pain in the neck.

Of course, before Live Aid, Geldof had been something of a busted flush. 'I was a fading pop singer, certainly no longer relevant,' said Geldof. Things had got so bad that behind his back, he was often called Mr Paula Yates.

'He was dying on his feet,' said Tony Powell, who was the marketing director of Geldof's label, Phonogram. 'We'd got to a stage where we were thinking, well, we'll let him make one more record. And we'll see how this goes.'

After Band Aid, there was a brief uplift in attendance at Rats gigs. 'I was a Boomtown Rats fan, and I really liked them,' said J. K. Rowling. 'I saw them at university, and was annoyed at how many thousands of people wanted to get in to see them, because I was a fan. But people were there to worship at the shrine of St Bob, and rightly so. He'd done such an incredible thing. But I was annoyed because I'd been there at the beginning.'

However, as soon as Live Aid was over, Geldof (the 'big-headed twat', according to David Bowie) knew his band were over.

A week after the concert, the Boomtown Rats' record company contract lapsed, and wasn't renewed. Consequently the band broke up.

FOUR

13:00

Adam Ant: 'Vive Le Rock'

Ultravox: 'Reap The Wild Wind', 'Dancing With Tears In My Eyes', 'One Small Day', 'Vienna'

Spandau Ballet: 'Only When You Leave', 'True', 'Virgin'

I flew in with the rest of the band and Kenney Jones, the drummer with The Who. It hit us then, flying over the stadium and seeing the thousands of people coming into the stadium. There was this sense of a grand event going on that could equal England winning the World Cup in 1966 or the Coronation of 1953. This was something that would be stamped on everybody. It was a day when, no matter how young you were, you remembered where you were.

GARY KEMP

One of the commonest complaints about London in the Seventies was that there was nowhere to go. Towards the end of the decade, when the streets were piled with rubbish due to the dustmen's strike, and when the city was grey both literally and metaphorically, there was nowhere to go but home. There were only pubs, pricey West End nightclubs and gig venues, places like the Marquee, the 100 Club and the Nashville, dingy little dives with sticky floors and low ceilings. Towards the end of the decade, there had started to be cocktail bars, where you could go if you were in the dressing-up business, and you wanted your alcoholic beverage to flatter your new threads.

And if you were a New Romantic in a frilly shirt, this is where you would have gravitated to, somewhere with some pink strip lighting, a lot of chrome and drinks that came with little paper parasols. In the mid-Seventies the Covent Garden vegetable market had moved to Vauxhall, over the river in South London, leaving the old site ripe for redevelopment. As the leases were cheap, designers such as Paul Smith moved in, along with trendy little bars and restaurants, Peppermint Park, Café Pacifico and Zanzibar included. The Zanzibar was a members' club unlike any other, and catered mainly for the advertising community.

At the time the only members' clubs were the gentlemen's clubs in and around Pall Mall, which catered specifically for politicians, the legal fraternity, landed gentry or the theatrical community, and many of which had had to resort to trading on past glories by selling memberships to businessmen in the provinces. So at the time the Zanzibar was unique, although in 1985 it suddenly had a rival in the Groucho Club, in Dean Street, a club which would inspire an entire generation of similar places in the city.

The Groucho was conjured up by a group of fifteen writers, publishers and agents who were tired of having nowhere to meet in London, and who wanted somewhere that reflected the changing social attitudes of the city. It was famously named after a Groucho Marx quote: 'Please accept my resignation. I don't want to belong to any club that will accept people like me as a member.'

'I was one of the original members,' said the PR guru Lynne Franks, who was very big in the Eighties. 'London was buzzing in a way that it has hardly done since. You would go there and see your friends and there would always be some amusing tale. I keep seeing Julie Burchill sitting in that corner with her little voice and those red lips. To me, that completely represents

The Groucho Club became 'London Legendary' almost as soon as it opened, bang in the middle of a decade that made a point of celebrating nightclubs, hotels and private members' clubs.

that time. You would sit down in the club, two or three of you, and then someone else would come along, and someone else, and you would end up with as many people as you could fit around a table, having an awful lot of fun and gossiping. There was a huge change going on in the UK at the time, and the Groucho Club was at the heart of that. Whatever was going on in politics, in the media, in fashion, you got to hear about it there.'

I was in the Zanzibar when I first heard about the Groucho. It was late 1984 and I was having a drink with Peter York, discussing the pros and cons of this and that, and the ups and downs of the current ins and outs. As we were leaving we stopped at the table of some high-flying advertising bods, who started discussing this brand new media watering hole that was opening up in Soho in a few months' time, by the very same people who had started Zanzibar. What did we think? Who was going to join? Who would they let in? Who was already barred? Would it work? How long would it take for investors to get their money back? And, more importantly, for the high-flying advertising bods at least, would the Groucho Club (as this new designer den of iniquity was going to be called) kill off the Zanzibar?

Well did it? You bet. Stone dead. The Groucho became legendary almost as soon as it opened its doors, which, in a decade that made a point of celebrating nightclubs, hotels and private members' clubs as though they were churches or palaces, maybe wasn't so surprising. A lavish watering hole catering for every Tom, Dick and Tarquin, a mediacentric wet bar for every publishing wannabe, every aspiring film director, every copywriter and hack, the Groucho immediately became the centrepiece of trendy media London.

Which meant from the off it was loathed as much as it was loved. And boy did some people hate it (and that included many of the original members).

The first time I went there was a hot Friday evening in the summer of 1985, to meet pop archaeologist Jon Savage. We were ostensibly there to discuss work – I wanted Savage to leave *The Face* and join *i-D* – but Jon spent the entire evening slagging off everyone in the bar. 'Hate him.' 'Hate her.' 'Talentless.' 'Fool!' 'What on earth is *he* doing here?' Etc.

Wow, I thought to myself, as my head spun round like a Hanna–Barbera cartoon, this is definitely the place for me.

A short while later I joined, although it only took me a few visits to realise that the place was just as debauched as the nightclubs I was in the process of disembarking from. I remember being shocked the first time I saw a celebrity emerge from the downstairs Gents with small rocks of cocaine falling out of his nostrils, but I soon got used to it. In fact, during a short period in the Eighties, if you paid a visit to the loos and weren't confronted by the sight of an internationally famous television comedian rushing into a cubicle with a rolled-up £10 note in his hand, you felt short-changed (I know I did). Towards the end of the decade I found a credit card belonging to someone who had appeared on *Have I Got News for You*, on the top of the cistern in one of the cubicles. Nothing shocking about that you might think, other than the fact it was liberally coated with what looked like Colombia's finest (either that, or baby laxative). The club was meant to be patronised by those in the advertising and media worlds, although the worst repeat offenders, those regulars who appeared to take pride in their bad behaviour, were artists. Will anyone who was in the club that night forget the Class A Brit Artist crawling along the floor in the downstairs bar begging for sex at the top of his voice?

There was a lot of sex at the Groucho. There was the night a travel PR serviced an entire table of newspaper executives (under the table, one at a time); the night a Hollywood superstar fucked a restaurateur in one of the upstairs hotel rooms; the night a supermodel lasciviously tore the clothes off a Fleet Street legend in the downstairs bar. Because the Groucho had a licence till one, people would forever be falling into the club after eleven, looking for 'entertainment', whatever form that might take. Drink. Drugs. Sex. And if they were lucky, sometimes all three.

This was the place the old world met the new, where deviants and innocents shared the same barstool, where columnists such as Jeffrey Bernard could be seen cavorting with comedians like Keith Allen, where ex-members of the Clash sank tequila with the likes of John Mortimer and Howard Jacobson. 'Damien Hirst pissed in a sink in an ice tray once and forgot about it,' said Allen. 'So people's vodka and tonics must have tasted somewhat different the next day.'

You'd see Stephen Fry hobnobbing with Uma Thurman, Zoë Heller having dinner with Toby Young, or Gary Oldman arguing the toss with Alex James.

'My football team QPR and Fulham announced a possible merger between the clubs, so I and my mate Spike, who supports Fulham, went to the Groucho at about 11 a.m., just as the bar opened, and began plotting ways to block the merger,' said the broadcaster Robert Elms. 'By 3 a.m., we were still there. Our bar bill totalled up to seventy-eight bottles of Becks, one bottle of champagne and a sandwich. It was the biggest bill for two people on a single binge-drinking session that they had ever had at the Groucho, and they had it framed up on the wall for ages. But something we thought of during the session must have worked, because the merger didn't happen.'

At one point during the early Nineties the club had such a reputation for bad behaviour that management made concerted efforts to clean up the place, coming down hard on members who broke the rules. The club's PR wasn't helped by the rumour that one member (allegedly a chef) was selling stories of celebrity indiscretions to the tabloids. Many people made the Groucho their second home, and in the case of some people I think it was their only home. Julie Burchill and her lapdog husband Cosmo Landesman regularly held Friday night soirées, accompanied by journalists like Sean Langan, Sean Macaulay and Tom Shone.

I once saw the editor of a monthly glossy who was so drunk that when his companion nipped off to the lavatory, he keeled over and actually headbutted his dessert. He stayed in this position until said companion came back and woke him up.

An old cartoon shows a receptionist directing a Groucho guest to the restaurant via the bar. 'Turn right at the drunken actors, straight past the failed novelists, left at the film-makers with pretensions but no ideas, right at the hacks with plenty of ideas but no one to commission them.'

Like the famous bar in *Cheers*, the Groucho became the place where everyone knew your name. This, obviously, presented you with a fundamental problem, and you could guarantee that if you had spent all day avoiding someone's phone call, as soon as you walked into the club, their clammy hand would fall heavily on your shoulder. My policy tended to be simple: capitulate, commission the piece and then deny all knowledge of it the next day.

The late writer and broadcaster John Diamond used to say that the clientele of the Groucho was divided into two groups: 'One group uses the club and is fairly laid-back about it. The other group uses it and can't believe their luck that they've actually got in.'

The Groucho quite quickly became the haunt of not just the new pop fraternity – Duran Duran, Ultravox, Spandau Ballet, etc. – but also an oasis for rock royalty. Pete Townshend would no longer have to carouse the night away at Club For Heroes or the Wag Club; in the Groucho he could do everything behind closed doors, beyond the prying eyes of the public. The Groucho would become a home from home for most of the Live Aid acts, and it would not be unusual to pop in there on a Thursday night and find Mick Jagger, Freddie Mercury or Eric Clapton standing at the bar; they may only have been sipping sparkling water, but at least they were away from the throng. Instead of propping up the bar at Dingwalls or the Marquee, Sting, Bono or David Bowie could curl up in one of the sofas and pore over the papers. Launch parties were held here, as were press conferences, private views and book signings. It became a popular place to conduct interviews, as no one would dream of disturbing you by walking up and asking for an autograph. Membership was cheaper than a hotel suite, and you didn't have to suffer the paparazzi stalking you in the lobby or the public spaces.

I remember having drinks there one night with Bob Geldof and the music journalist Adrian Deevoy, discussing the pros and cons of Jim Morrison, as it had just been announced that Oliver Stone was going to direct a movie about him. 'He is exactly the sort of pop star who should have played at Live Aid,' Geldof said. 'What's not to love? The leather trousers, the Oedipal complex, the booze. I reckon I would have got on with him extremely well. He was such a great performer, and he certainly would have been much better than the Hooters.'

It became an institution almost immediately, and continued to be a celebrity haunt throughout the Nineties and Noughties. 'Once I managed to orchestrate it so that Moby played the piano and Mick Jones sang a Clash song, while Coldplay and New Order did the backing vocals,' said Keith Allen. 'Damon Hill was sat there watching, allegedly, and Wayne Sleep was there, and I got him up and he danced.'

'At Christmas a few years ago, Bill Clinton walked in with his minders,' said the PR James Herring. 'He'd only been out of office a few weeks. The jaws of the normally hard-to-impress Groucho clientele were on the floor. About five minutes later, Bono and the Edge from U2 walked in. Soon, Bono was playing the piano and singing "Happy Birthday, Mr President", serenading Clinton.'

There would be many other members' clubs that would come in the wake of the Groucho, but few of them would feel so lavishly louche. Once, when there was a power cut in Dean Street, those inside numbered Jools Holland, who had just arrived with Tom Jones, and Paul McGuinness, who was hosting a dinner in a private room. 'Tea lights were lit and suddenly there was Jools on the piano, Tom Jones singing "Sex Bomb" and Bono duetting with Tom,' said one onlooker.

For the rest of the Eighties the Groucho was like the green room at Live Aid, and it was not unusual to walk in to find one, two, sometimes three people who had been on the Wembley stage on 13 July sipping a Budvar. You'd see Midge Ure, Gary Kemp, Simon Le Bon, Nick Rhodes, Bryan Ferry, Daryl Hall, Bryan Adams, Sting, Ronnie Wood, David Gilmour, Madonna and sometimes, when the stars were aligned, Bob Geldof himself.

You'd often see Adam Ant in the Groucho, dressed up to the nines, usually in leather trousers. He was an exotic creature, a lynchpin of the early punk days, a teen idol, and – after Live Aid – a bit of a casualty.

At Wembley, Ant went on stage after Geldof, and so it was perhaps unreasonable to expect him to make any sort of mark. Honestly, were we going to remember this? He hadn't had a hit since 'Apollo 9' the year before, and was deemed to be on the slide. He was managed by Miles Copeland, who also looked after Sting, and there was a suggestion that Copeland had had a quiet word with Geldof – a kind of 'No Ant, no Sting' thing – a plausible enough explanation when you consider that he was only allowed one song. Rather stupidly, Ant decided to use the opportunity to plug his new single, a fairly terrible glam-rock song called 'Vive Le Rock'. When he was asked if he was scared about appearing in front of such a large crowd, he rather sweetly said that being in the stadium when it was empty was bad enough. He should have maybe worried a bit more, because not only did many people not recognise him when he came on stage, but the song he performed actually went down the charts the following week. Adam Ant split that day, his body going in one direction, his career in another.

As his band got ready backstage, Ant had said to them, 'The world is watching, let's feed it.' Watching the acts that followed him, he realised that he had a long way to go in the industry. 'As I watched Sting, Bowie and Queen play their numbers it all clicked. I've only just begun . . . There's no point moaning, just get on with it, I told myself. Write great songs. As Bowie played "TVC 15", "Rebel Rebel", "Modern Love" and "Heroes", I gaped in awe. Here was a lesson in how to be a star. How far I had yet to go.'

'Adam Ant didn't work, didn't work at all,' said Harvey Goldsmith. 'The audience hated it. I think there were a couple more in the middle of the day that probably didn't work as well as they might, but overall everybody went that extra mile and rose to the occasion. Except Adam Ant. He looked out of sorts with the time, and didn't fit in. He just wasn't "Live Aid" enough, I suppose.'

The closest relationship he had with anyone else performing at the event was a tangential one at best. In the mid-Sixties, his mother used to clean Paul McCartney's St John's Wood home, and the young Ant (born Stuart Goddard) would wangle his way in as often as possible and take McCartney's dog Martha for walks. However, he only actually saw the Beatle once: 'I saw him through a crack in the door, going up the stairs chatting with my mum,' he said. 'It was quite a precious moment.'

Far more precious than his moment at Live Aid, one that would be remembered as an epic failure. He was due to perform 'Stand And Deliver' and 'Goody Two Shoes' as well, although his set kept being cut back. Ant thought 'Vive Le Rock' was the most appropriate for the day, coupled with the fact that his band didn't know his old songs as well as the ones they'd just recorded.

'God bless Adam,' said Gary Kemp. 'His career may have been faltering at the time, but he opened the door for so many people. What he was doing visually eased the way for acts like ourselves in a way.'

Unfortunately for Adam Ant, his role at Live Aid was to be the mote in the eye.

Midge Ure was another shadowy character, both in and out of the Groucho, a man who was more than willing to let Bob Geldof take the lion's share of the acclaim for both Band Aid and Live Aid. Although he was instrumental in the creation of the record and the concert, he was content to let Geldof immerse himself in the organisation of Live Aid. Here was the man responsible for 'Do They Know It's Christmas?' and yet he really only had a walk-on role in Live Aid. His band were obviously granted a spot, and not a bad one at that, slipping between the awful Adam Ant (how could Ultravox not compare favourably?) and their *Top of the Pops* oppos, Spandau Ballet. They had originally been promised a better slot, but as Midge wasn't a big complainer, they had gradually been bumped down the bill (they were originally going to appear where Queen were).

Ure had already been pushed somewhat into the background, something that was made apparent to the waiting world when Geldof arranged the Live Aid press conference six weeks before the show, without involving him. Ure had been told it was happening, and had been summarily invited along, but was given no official duties, and when Geldof finally started reading out the list of bands who had agreed to play, Ure was in an anteroom, waiting to be called . . . or so he thought. 'The conference kicked off without me,' said Ure, obviously distressed. 'I was a bit miffed, a bit left out. I was standing next door talking to Gary Kemp and Adam Ant and I heard the conference start. All the Band Aid trustees were sitting down in front of the stage, apart from me.'

'Well, he had nothing to do with Live Aid,' said Geldof, indignantly. 'That's it, that's the reality of it. And I would have said, if he wants to do something he can, but it was never suggested to me, and I would have thought it redundant really.'

Ultravox were another band who were disregarded by the music press, not least because of their fondness for eyeliner, duster coats and wantonly enigmatic pop videos. The band had passed through a Bowie 'beam' (in the words of the *NME*'s Paul Morley), but then every band at the time had done exactly the same thing. They came along at a point when meaning was everything in pop, and only to *pretend* to have meaning, or to disregard meaning completely, was deemed unacceptable. It didn't help that a lot of the records were also rather mediocre.

'Ultravox always attempted to blend their influences into something as provocative as early Roxy, as challenging as early Floyd,' said Morley. 'They never had the art or the heart and, despite themselves, never looked the part. They tried to be so much more than just a pop group. Ure had disciplined their pretensions into something more realistic. Ure was never quite there, Ultravox was never quite there, together they make inessential but stylish synergic pop.

'*Vienna* is their fourth album but it has the feel of a first, and for Ultravox an unusual consistency. It is the most listenable record either Ure or Ultravox have made, something sweet to play after you've sweated through Cabaret

Voltaire and want to flick through some magazines. For everyone else, the thing is not to take them seriously, and then for the first time you might see a point in Ultravox's existence. This is pop, with style, within reason, without too much pretention.'

At Live Aid they equipped themselves well, playing with passion and gusto, careering through 'Dancing With Tears In My Eyes' as though it were a genuine stadium anthem. At this moment in their career they sounded like a fairly orthodox rock band with a drum machine, which in a way was perfect for the times. They were the poor man's Simple Minds, only with slightly better tunes. At Wembley they also played 'Vienna', one of the better turns, but also one of the most portentous records ever to have appeared on *Top of the Pops*. There was no reason why Ultravox should have been any good in a stadium – as Midge Ure once said, 'We made music that fitted into clubs like the Blitz – nothing more' – yet the Wembley crowd didn't mind them at all. Not one bit.

Ure obviously thought the reception was good enough, as, having released a solo album, he quit the band shortly after Live Aid, convinced he had another life ahead of him. 'With hindsight, which as everyone says is a wonderful thing, the biggest mistake I made was walking away from Ultravox in 1985,' he said. 'The band was still riding high and probably had a lot more to give. But by then, possibly, delusions of grandeur had kicked in for me. The chance to go off and do stuff without having to work within the realms of a band was very appealing. Success brings many things, one of which is an ego. You believe you're utterly invincible; you have a sniff of success on your own and think you don't need to take anyone else's ideas or feelings into consideration. I'm sure we all go through that sometimes.

'But of course when you leave a successful situation like that, you have to start all over again. It's like snakes and ladders – all of a sudden you're at the bottom again. I just felt that maybe Ultravox had had its day and it was time to move on. But the reality is, when you make an album that's not all that great, that doesn't sell that well, it's nobody's fault but yours. Sometimes it's easier to throw the toys out of the pram and walk away rather than be big and say, "This is my mistake, but there's better stuff to come." Looking back, I never realised that the most interesting thing I was doing at that time was actually with Ultravox. But sometimes it's not until you revisit things that you can see them clearly.'

Ultravox were followed by Spandau Ballet, another group fronted by a singer with a penchant for imperious wailing. Today Tony Hadley was also sporting a ridiculous duster coat, looking like he'd just been for a little light lunch and a shopping spree down South Molton Street. Spandau were another band the critics didn't have much time for. They were hated by the left, especially when they found out that Tony Hadley voted Tory. 'But the link between Spandau Ballet and Thatcherism is about more than the personal politics of Tony Hadley,' said the *Guardian*, pompously. 'It's about the emptiness of Spandau, the aspiration to do nothing more than look good in a nightclub, the happy embrace of style over substance. Billy Bragg has even attributed his decision to become a performer to them: "One day [I] saw Spandau Ballet on *Top of the Pops* wearing kilts and singing 'Chant No. 1' and something in me snapped. I was waiting for a band to come along to play the kind of music I wanted to hear, and none was forthcoming, so it was that moment I finally realised it was gonna have to be me."'

Like Duran Duran (or Diana Diana, as Paul Morley liked to call them), Spandau Ballet tended to espouse success, wallowing in extravagant and escapist pop promos, and behaving like minor members of the Royal Family. The hard-core New Romantics were definitely all about the clothes, cosmetics, travel and showing off; as a response to grievous, turbulent times, Steve Strange, Spandau Ballet, Wham! and Duran Duran preferred the dolled-up posing in pampered cliques inside VIP sections of exclusive nightclubs. But then why wouldn't they?

The music press didn't just dislike them because of their music, but they also hated the way in which Gary Kemp would continually point out the inconsistencies of many rock stars' backstories, especially those of white, middle-class heroes such as Bob Dylan and Bruce Springsteen. Spandau were the sort of working class the largely white middle-class music journalist couldn't cope with.

'The collected rabble-rousers, cynics and savage wits at the *NME* lost little time in deflating any ego I might have been nurturing since getting in front of the cameras,' said Danny Baker, himself an *NME* hack. 'They found particular joy in my apparent endorsement of Spandau Ballet – a group who, though generally unknown, were already veterans of the review-room toasting fork. When I presented a similar show about some other newcomers called Iron Maiden they all but debagged me and made me walk up Carnaby Street wearing a bell and a placard around my neck.'

To Live Aid PR Bernard Doherty, the boys were heroes. 'Spandau were my go-to guys when I needed someone to do a press conference, an interview or give a quote,' he said. 'They were stand-up guys, and so enthusiastic about the project. They were great and never said no to anything. Any time I wanted them, they were there, smiling, always ready with a quote, whether it was the *Radio Times* or *Melody Maker*.'

Spandau were one of the few bands who did a soundcheck the day before, as they had flown in from Ireland (where they were recording) early to do a press conference at the stadium with Elton John. Kemp then spent the night at his house in Highbury (he lived next door to Sade), before being driven down to Battersea to catch a helicopter into Wembley with the rest of the band. Even though Spandau had soundchecked, one of the most remarkable things about Live Aid was the quality of everyone's live sound. Most festivals at the time suffered from inadequate sound, and it was unlikely that every band would sound as good as they could have done. But as everyone at Live Aid was using the same PA, this wasn't going to happen.

'We ended up in Noel Edmonds' helicopter, flying with Kenney Jones from The Who,' said Gary Kemp. 'To fly over the top of the Twin Towers, it was my brother's dream. He [Martin] was signed to Arsenal briefly, as a youngster, and it meant the world to him. To see the people all pouring in on this beautiful sunny day to Live Aid and then to land and go backstage where everybody he'd ever known in the music business was milling around.'

Kemp actually has little memory of the band's performance during their twenty minutes, as all he was doing at the time was worrying. Like everyone on stage that day he was performing in front of millions of people and was thinking about them rather than the gig. 'Any fuck-up and then it's there forever and ever. If you weren't thinking about your performance you were thinking about your position and your hierarchy. You know, "Am I worthy and why are they on after us?" It was all of that. There was a natural fan response as well; part of the reason why we allowed certain artists to rush before us in that finale was because we were fans. I do remember wishing we had had a later slot, but all the later slots were for the bigger bands, the Seventies acts.

'It's a bit like being an athlete: when you go on and you know it's that important and you only have twenty minutes to get it right, I find it very hard to concentrate.

'The difference between people's perception of Live Aid and what it was actually like being there is the same as their impression of celebrity in general. They think it's a rather glamorous world of very confident people clinking glasses and hugging each other, when the truth is everyone is terrified and intimidated and wondering about their own self-worth and where they sit in the hierarchy of the room. I think there was a lot of fear backstage. People were on a level playing field performing with virtually every major artist in the world and someone was going to fall. It was the greatest hundred-metre line-up you'd ever seen and I think people don't fully appreciate that. And of course it was mainly alpha males don't forget, as there were very few women performing.

'Performance-wise, we made a faux pas. Our manager Steve Dagger holds his hand up and blames himself for this. We decided to do a new song. We did "True" and "Only When You Leave", and they went down really well. We then did this song called "Virgin" which was from the new album. I think we thought it was a good piece of exposure, some variety, but it was just the same as George Michael doing "White Light" at the end of the Olympics. It was that kind of a faux pas. Not that anyone was upset by it, but it wasted our moment because we only had twenty minutes. Apart from that I thought we played really well.

'Tony [Hadley] was probably overdressed for the weather as he was wearing a long leather coat, so the image wasn't perfect. But I think we played really well. We already understood how to play a big audience. But what we didn't really get was that we should have been doing our greatest hits and that's why Queen was so successful that day.

'We went on in the afternoon, not a great time to go on, but we took what we got. And it got the blessing of Paul McCartney. I'm a big Who fan, and talking to Pete before they went on – they hadn't played together for years – Pete said, "When I go on just walk with me, and come and stand right by the side of the stage." It was a childhood fantasy. So I'm standing at the side of the stage watching John Entwistle's bass amp, or whatever it was, go wrong and I got a tap on the shoulder and it was McCartney and Linda, and he went, "You were great this afternoon." He gave me one of those Scouse thumbs up.

'People say there were a lot drugs around but I don't remember any. There might have been dope, but I wasn't into dope so I don't remember. We certainly didn't do any drugs. I think probably the older school may have indulged, like Status Quo. Certainly at Band Aid, those two boys were feeding it. We played hard but would always work first; while there was a job to be done I think we always stayed clean.'

Both Spandau and Ultravox made music that is still synonymous with the times, yet if you had to choose a record from the period that somehow represented Britain, I doubt it would be one of theirs. Whenever you see a television documentary about any aspect of the Eighties what you'll tend to hear is 'Relax' or 'Two Tribes' by Frankie Goes to Hollywood (a band who, ironically, had nothing to do with Live Aid), perhaps juxtaposed with the unnaturally deep voice of Margaret Thatcher coining one of her famous phrases, such as 'There is no such thing as society.' The effect is usually quite powerful, as it's hard to know which is more intimidating.

While Spandau may have thought they were the new bastions of the underground, they quite quickly became tied up with the whole New Romantic idea of imperialism, escapism and dressing up. The television adaptation of *Brideshead Revisited* was screened in 1981, and while it was obviously a ruthless examination of aristocratic values, on a surface level it was also an endorsement of a fantasy, one that plugged right into the wedding that summer of Charles and Diana; fiddling while Brixton and Bristol burned.

'Spandau Ballet's records are an important part of the evolution of British pop music,' said the band's leader and songwriter Gary Kemp, perhaps unsurprisingly. 'And I'm enormously proud of them. We were part of the golden age of pop. We were a gang who made records.

'It was madly competitive as we were all tribal. Duran Duran wanted to be more successful than us, we wanted to be more successful than ABC, or Culture Club, or Duran themselves. We spurred each other on.

'We went from playing electronica, then funk and then blue-eyed soul, and after that, like a lot of bands who suddenly find themselves selling out Wembley Arena for six nights in a row, music that sounds good in very large sheds. It was a fairly vertical take-off and one we thought we might never come down from.'

The first time that anyone outside London clubland knew about Spandau Ballet was in May 1980 when they appeared on a little-known TV arts programme called *Twentieth Century Box*. An annoyingly trendy magazine show, it nevertheless had its finger on the pulse (or at least its researchers did). The show that week was solely concerned with a new youth cult, the Blitz Kids – a weird nightclub collective comprised of soul boys (and girls), art students with aerodynamic haircuts, trainee hairdressers and the sort of TV researchers who worked for annoying TV arts shows. They were obsessed with Bowie, imported funk and Kraftwerk, obsessed about the way they looked, and were intent on making London nightlife a pool where only the very coolest could swim. And they succeeded. If they were the In Crowd, then the In Crowd's band were Spandau Ballet, whether anyone liked it or not.

'We had no interest in the rest of the music scene, as we grew out of club culture,' said Kemp. 'We started at [the club] Billy's, then the Blitz, and all these places where you didn't rub up against the rock world. We were particular in those days. It was a gang mentality, and one that kept us very close.'

Ushering in a new era of visually dominated pop, their dissatisfaction with their musical peers manifested itself in a mechanical, stylised sound that was born and bred on the dance floors of the West End – white soul boys who had rejected funk and rock while embracing electronica and frilly shirts. The Blitz Kids believed in fashion as though it were a religion. Wear the wrong shoes and no one would talk to you. Wear them twice and no one would ever talk to you again.

Spandau Ballet's biggest hits are part of the pop radio continuum. You can't escape them; turn on Melody or Smooth, or walk into any hotel bar from Baku to Las Vegas and you'll hear the strains of 'Gold', 'I'll Fly For You', 'True' and all the rest. The group's songs – well, actually Gary Kemp's songs – have been heard in *Spin City*, *The Wedding Singer*, *Ugly Betty*, *The Simpsons* and frequently turn up in TV ads.

The band was born in north London in 1979. That winter would determine which bands were going to escape the dark, dank Seventies intact. Fashion was paramount in their appeal, but so was their music: so much so that the bidding war to sign them was fevered. They eventually signed to Chrysalis, releasing their first single, 'To Cut A Long Story Short', in 1980.

'We didn't talk to the music press, as we had no interest in trying to persuade them that what we were doing was good,' said Kemp. 'They didn't believe we were working class and wanted to paint us as middle-class Tories. The music papers at the time were full of middle-class white boys who didn't like the fact that we were from council estates. They wanted to believe something else. They wanted to believe that we were right wing when we were anything but.

'We all came from the Essex Road in Islington and we had no sympathies with anything remotely Thatcherite. We were also commercial – that in those days was a political act in itself. We just wanted to get on and improve our lot. We wanted to be successful, we wanted to be famous, and we didn't see why we should be embarrassed about it.'

Kemp's band was more than just timely – the music they made was genuinely groundbreaking, whether you liked it or not. No, the critics were not kind, painting them as dim, inner-city mannequins, yet their songs resonated with a generation of young men and women who were determined to explore social mobility in much the same way that their parents had in the Sixties. Their most important record from this early period was 'Chant No. 1 (I Don't Need This Pressure On)', a song that had something in common with 'Ghost Town' by the Specials.

'"Chant No. 1" was all about urban paranoia,' said Kemp. 'I wanted to make a Soho film-noir song, something that was evocative of an urban experience. Dark shadows, dark corners. A fear of living on the edge in an urban environment as a young man. The early Eighties were rough for most people, and we wanted to reflect that in the song. It's a very dark track and one that mirrored the economic plight of the time.'

The promotional video for the song was filmed at Le Beat Route, a long, narrow basement club in Soho that was frequented by the Blitz Kids – which was what the New Romantics were called before the media got hold of them. I was there the night the video was filmed, a night when the Blitz crowd came out in force – many of whom would go on to form bands of their own: Wham!, Sade, Swing Out Sister, Visage, Culture Club, Haysi Fantayzee, Dead or Alive . . . George Michael even composed a song about the place, 'Club Tropicana'.

Spandau took success to new heights. They spearheaded the second British invasion of the US charts, becoming more famous in the US than they'd been in Britain or Europe.

'We were an underground band for eighteen months, but then we were on *Top of the Pops* six times, and it's very difficult to be alternative when you're on TV all the time. So "True" was a conscious effort to write some blue-eyed soul that would get us into the charts. I stopped worrying about the rhythm or the sound of the synthesiser and started worrying about the melodies.

'We were becoming bigger and bigger, and when you start to play bigger halls you need different types of material, which is why we changed our sound so much.'

In a way the facts say it all: twenty-three hit singles and worldwide album sales of 25 million, topped off by their performance at Wembley Stadium on 13 July.

At the end of the decade, the band split up. 'It didn't feel like a gang any more – we had drifted apart and it just wasn't fun. Plus the second Summer of Love had arrived in the shape of acid house. And that wasn't really us.' It wasn't really anyone at Live Aid.

Kemp and his brother Martin went back to their acting roots, securing the lead roles in *The Krays*, while Gary went on to star in the Kevin Costner blockbuster *The Bodyguard*, and Martin became a household name by taking a part in the BBC's *EastEnders*. Gary stayed in LA for three years, but his marriage to the actress Sadie Frost began to disintegrate, and, not wanting to bring up his children in Hollywood, he came home.

'Look, it was tough,' said Kemp. 'My marriage was crumbling and Sadie had had enough of LA. She wanted to come home and so it made sense for me to come too. There were films to be made and films I ended up making in Europe, but it just felt right to come home. I missed England, missed London and wanted to see what it would feel like to come back. So we did.'

And he walked straight into a court case. Various band members had decided Kemp ought to have shared the spoils more, and so they ended up before a judge.

'The case was all about the publishing, which it always is, and there was an assumption I was going to share what I'd written, which I wasn't. And so we went to court. None of us lied – we just have our own versions of a truth. The judge had to choose, and he did. But even though I did OK, no one came out of that case smelling of roses and that includes me. It had besmirched a great history, a great legacy, and had cost everybody a huge amount of money and stress. And yet it brought us back together. Suddenly we were the old gang again. Ironic, really.

'The whole thing was very theatrical – almost like an old Spandau Ballet show. Tony and I eventually settled our differences in a pub in Highgate. And we've had a great relationship ever since.'

As for Live Aid, it was sobering to say the least.

'It made all of us feel a little different about our success, I think. These were shallow times, whether we liked it or not, and Live Aid was a bit of a reality check. In fact it was a huge one. Usually when we came off stage, there were people waiting with towels, drinks, all sorts of things,' said Kemp. 'Here, I fell over, and no one gave a toss.'

FIVE

Elvis Costello: 'All You Need Is Love'

Nik Kershaw: 'Wide Boy', 'Don Quixote', 'The Riddle', 'Wouldn't It Be Good'

> Some people seemed a bit reluctant at first. The argument which swayed them was when I said, 'I actually couldn't care less myself if you get up and play – the only point is that if you do, people who like you will contribute thousands of pounds.' That seemed to be the argument that persuaded them.
>
> BOB GELDOF

L ive Aid was the world's biggest variety show. There was such a weird mix of acts on the bill it was almost like a circus. The whole idea had been to create a bill full of the most popular acts in the world; they didn't necessarily have to be that good, they just had to be popular. Geldof constructed his bill pell-mell, and his rationale was simple: the more popular an act was, the more people would be inclined to buy tickets for the gigs, the more people would be inclined to watch television and pledge money.

At first it had been impossible to get anyone to commit. After all, at the time Bob Geldof was a washed-up ex-punk who'd put together a one-off charity single, something that, while laudable, was considered by many in the industry to be little but a gimmick. Having had so few genuine commitments, when he announced the concerts at the first Live Aid press conference, he had to fudge a few names. 'When I announced it, one of the acts who was dithering, as ever, was Bryan Ferry. So I just said, " . . . and Bryan Ferry,"' said Geldof. 'And he rang to say, "I didn't say 'Yeah.'" I said, "Well, say 'No', then. You're the one who can announce it though."'

'People now say, how could an artist refuse to be on a show like that?' said Live Aid production manager Andy Zweck. 'But my memory prior to the event was how Bob and Harvey Goldsmith struggled to get the artists and struggled to get the show in America. Bob had to play some tricks to get artists involved. He had to call Elton and say Queen are in and Bowie's in, and of course they weren't. Then he'd call Bowie and say Elton and Queen are in. It was a game of bluff.'

This was less a case of the world saying no until Geldof forced it to say yes, as Geldof refusing to take no for an answer. 'If he doesn't get you with the poetry, the spittle won't be far behind,' said Bono.

Geldof's assistant Marsha Hunt would call people up and say, 'It's going to be sometime in July, not sure where it's going to be, don't know if it's going to be on the telly, oh and by the way you can probably only play for about twenty minutes, you won't get a contract, and you have to pay for it all yourselves.' She was told to fuck off more than a few times.

By the time the bulk of the roster was announced, Geldof started to be criticised because there weren't many black acts on the bill, and was accused of treating the event in a traditionally colonial fashion, and yet many black acts simply weren't interested in appearing.

'We were criticised endlessly for not having enough black acts on the bill, but nobody wanted to do it,' said Harvey Goldsmith. 'We couldn't find any acts that were either available or that wanted to do it. Honestly, we tried every major black act both here in the UK and in the US and none of them were interested. It was embarrassing. Some even wanted money. Stevie Wonder eventually agreed to appear, but then he phoned me up and said, "I am not going to be the token black on the show." The only one who actually ended up doing anything was Lionel Richie because his manager really got what we were doing and he ended up doing "We Are The World" with Michael Jackson. The others no, they were just not interested. We just kept saying, without being rude, you're always harping on that you don't get recognition within the industry and so on but then you're not getting involved.

'We just went through the cards, and we tried everyone. It's always hard to get acts to commit to do things like this, because they've got to give up their time, services, whatever. You're juggling balls and then hoping that the balls don't drop. But it was extremely disappointing.'

When Geldof had been to Ethiopia in January he had been travelling with Jesse Jackson's wife, and a representative of Africare, a black American aid agency. He told Geldof that he had found it difficult getting black entertainers and sportsmen to do anything for them as they had 'little or no social responsibility'. Geldof was not only finding a similar response, he was also being attacked for not having approached any reggae acts. 'If Bob Marley were alive, I'd be on my knees begging him to play,' said Geldof at the time. 'But no one's heard of Aswad outside the universities. Put them on telly and people will switch it off . . . If I have a choice between Steel Pulse or Wham! on this show, I'll take Wham!'

And he did.

'My main problem at the time was with the American acts,' he said. 'Michael Jackson just didn't seem to want to do it. I rang Quincy Jones to talk to him. I rang his manager, Frank DiLeo, I rang Walter Yetnikoff, the chairman of Columbia records to talk to him. I was having real problems with all the American black acts.'

This was ironic as 'We Are The World', the US answer to Band Aid, had been prompted by Harry Belafonte's dismay at seeing 'a bunch of white English kids doing what black Americans ought to have been doing'.

'As the show grew, Bob Geldof had a certain number of acts which had committed to him,' said the US promoter Bill Graham. 'He had no black acts. It was obvious to me right away. Certain major black acts were not available. People could say, "They *should* be available for their brothers and sisters in Ethiopia." That was not for me to say. What I could say was that I contacted every single major black artist. I won't name them . . . But they *all* turned down Live Aid. I also turn things down. That doesn't mean they didn't care. But all the major black artists? *All* the biggest ones? You name them. They *all* turned Live Aid down.'

Diana Ross was making a record in LA, Lionel Richie was doing the same, and Prince had 'retired'. Prince apparently supplied a black-and-white film instead, of him saying 'Feed the world' while lying naked on his bed. It was politely turned down. He also sent a pre-taped video of an acoustic version of his song '4 The Tears In Your Eyes', which was played during the concert. He was there in spirit, however, as he helped Madonna with the choreography for her performance. She spent a few days with him in Minneapolis before the show, as he took her through her dance moves.*

The writer Pete Hamill thought that in terms of black music, or at least its roots – tangentially at least – that Live Aid was really just a way of saying thanks. 'For rock 'n' roll came from the blues, and the blues were made by the American children of Africans who had been ripped from their homes and taken across oceans and sold to other human beings. From that crime against Africa came the greatest music of the twentieth century: the blues, jazz and rock 'n' roll.

'That music has since reached every corner of the earth, so it was only fitting that this event was broadcast to [so many] countries in the global village.'

There were many other acts who said no to Geldof, or who avoided getting involved. The Eurythmics' Dave Stewart turned it down – '[He] just didn't want to know,' said Midge Ure. 'I wonder if he regrets that now' – as did Liza Minnelli, Yoko Ono and Cyndi Lauper. Billy Joel, Waylon Jennings and Kris Kristofferson were all included in early promotional material for the Philadelphia concert, but none of them made the show itself. Huey Lewis & the News and Paul Simon both accepted requests to play but later

---

* When Prince had failed to appear on 'We Are The World' the industry was all of a sudden alive with stories about the singer's petulance. Garry Trudeau even lampooned Prince for this in his *Doonesbury* cartoon strip, depicting Prince asking Quincy Jones to remove all of Michael Jackson's lines before he would consider contributing to the record.

issued press statements stating they had chosen not to appear because of disagreements with the promoter of the Philadelphia concert, Bill Graham.

Rod Stewart wasn't touring and couldn't get a band together in time, while Talking Heads didn't appear as David Byrne was too busy finishing his film *True Stories*. Various heavy metal-bands were asked, too: AC/DC were invited to play but declined. The re-formed Deep Purple were also due to appear from Switzerland via satellite before changing their mind, and Def Leppard were originally going to perform, but due to drummer Rick Allen's car accident bowed out.

Culture Club should have been there, but singer Boy George was having serious drug problems at the time. 'I found it difficult to speak the truth because it was such a worthy cause,' said George. 'I didn't want to appear, even though I'd made half-hearted promises to Bob Geldof and excuses to the band. It was a mixture of fear and loathing. I didn't think we could cut it in front of 2 billion people, and disliked the rock pomposity of it all. Culture Club flew back to London on the day of Live Aid. I watched the concert round at [a friend's] flat in Chiswick. Madonna's howling confirmed all my fears. Except for Bowie and Queen I found it boring and self-congratulatory. All my friends went on at me for not being there. Jon, Roy and Mikey [the rest of the band] were bitter. I'd ruined their chance of a part of history.'

Apparently Frank Zappa was asked, but refused because he thought the money raised by Live Aid did not address the core problems facing the developing world. He was also determined to shock, later questioning the legitimacy of the event by saying, 'I think Live Aid was the biggest cocaine money-laundering scheme of all time.'

Geldof would sit in the Band Aid office in the West End, and spend hours on the phone, building the gigs like he was building a house. Commitments were made by some early on: John Weller promised that his son Paul would be there, Miles Copeland delivered Sting, and Phil Collins had said he was in. But there were some people he just couldn't get.

Tears For Fears, for instance, who at that point were one of the biggest bands in the world.

'[We] had been touring for a year, really hard work,' said the band's Curt Smith. 'We had five days off and planned a holiday in Hawaii. Then Bob Geldof announced that we were playing Live Aid. He never asked us. Geldof thought he was so powerful that if he announced it, we'd have to say yes, or we'd look like bad people. I was pissed off. Whether we played or not wasn't going to make a difference to the amount of money raised. So we went on holiday, because that was the only break we had.'

Big Country, Fish and the Moody Blues were too late, as was Cat Stevens, who was prepared to come out of retirement to play, and who actually turned up on the day at Wembley with his guitar, having written a song especially. As he hadn't told anyone he was interested in appearing, he wasn't allowed on stage.

Geldof had a couple of bum steers, too, as apparently Bill Wyman told him not to approach the Stones, 'Cos Keith doesn't give a fuck.'

The Smiths hadn't been invited to perform, principally because they weren't yet big enough to be asked, although Morrissey's condemnation of the Band Aid single might not have helped: 'One can have great concern for the people of Ethiopia, but it's another thing to inflict daily torture on the people of England. It was an awful record considering the mass of talent involved.'

Geldof's biggest disappointment was Bruce Springsteen, who he had circled for months. Springsteen declined to play Live Aid, something which he now regrets, saying that he 'simply did not realise how big the whole thing was going to be'.

However, at the time the answer was a big fat no. Harvey Goldsmith says it was never going to happen.

'It wasn't a disappointment to me because it was a reality. I was working with Springsteen, and I knew exactly what was going on. I knew he had to go back to America because his daughter just started horse riding, was in a competition and because he travelled so much he insisted on going back to see her compete. Bruce told me this at the beginning and I told Bob that and he just wouldn't have it. Bob kept saying, "He has to come back." He couldn't stay that week and that was the end of it. Then Bob moved the dates.'

The concert was originally scheduled for 6 July, but in order to try and accommodate Springsteen, Geldof moved the date to the 13th.

'He moved the date because he thought Springsteen would do it, and still he wouldn't,' said Goldsmith. 'I kept telling Bob he wasn't going to do it, but he wouldn't listen. He just wasn't going to do it. Springsteen has never done any of those events; the only thing he ever did was the Amnesty shows. I think Bruce Springsteen only wants to do shows he can control. No one is going to tell him what he should and shouldn't do and that's the end of it. He's never done any of these since. In that respect Bruce Springsteen is the only person ever to get one over on Bob Geldof. Springsteen left his stage behind at Wembley so we could use it, which was kind of him, but he was never going to perform on it.'

As late as 6 p.m. on the day of the concert in Philadelphia, the MTV presenters were still discussing whether or not Bruce was going to show up, based on the fact that 'he'd just flown into Philly', 'Bill Graham was using one of his lighting rigs' and his drummer Max Weinberg was actually in the stadium.

However, my wife has a vivid memory of seeing Springsteen open the American part of the show, playing 'Born In The USA' and, remarkably, 'Philadelphia', a song that wasn't recorded until seven or eight years later. She also remembers seeing Annie Lennox ('Doing one of her slow songs, you know the ones'), and – of course – Elton John leaving Wembley by helicopter in order to take Concorde to New York. She also thought Bananarama were rubbish, which must have been news to Bananarama, who weren't even on the bill. I had a small-scale argument in the car back from Wales one Sunday afternoon when I asked her what she remembered of Live Aid, and then suggested that she may have been having more of a good time at her friend's party in St John's Wood that day than she thought she was.

'Are you sure Bruce Springsteen didn't play at Live Aid?' was her final salvo. 'I thought he was rather good. We watched him on the TV at the end of someone's garden. If he didn't then he really should have. It would have been great.'

Even better if Springsteen had duetted with Annie Lennox.

The rumours beforehand were rife: the Beatles were going to re-form with Julian Lennon on guitar, Sting was going to parachute into Wembley Stadium, Michael Jackson was going to ride on to the stage in Philadelphia on his llama, while the computer-generated TV presenter Max Headroom was going to MC the whole event. *Smash Hits* came up with others: Bono was planning to perform a twenty-seven-minute a cappella version of Deep Purple's 'Smoke On The Water', Duran Duran's Andy Taylor and Frankie Goes to Hollywood's Nasher were going to organise a backstage beer-drinking contest, and the reason that Madonna was prevaricating over performing was because she was actually scheduled to marry Prince that day, in St Charles' Church, Cincinatti. My favourite piece of spurious gossip was the one concerning Gary Kemp, who had been going through a rigorous keep-fit campaign in preparation for the big day. Why? Because he had challenged Bruce Springsteen's guitarist Nils Lofgren to a backflip competition, while playing the guitar refrain from their hit 'True'. Mini trampolines were being supplied free by Adidas.

Oh, how we all lapped this stuff up.

Extraordinarily, the Beatles rumour was true, and there was actually a meeting between Paul McCartney, George Harrison and Ringo Starr where they discussed re-forming with Julian Lennon playing piano. However, as soon as the story leaked – and it leaked instantly – they shut the whole thing down.

It was bizarre that Frankie Goes to Hollywood weren't on the bill, as for the previous year they had been the biggest, most notorious band in Britain. 'We were invited and I wanted to do it but all the other members of the group and so-called manager didn't want to do it,' claimed singer Holly Johnson. 'This was the biggest management mistake of Frankie's career.'

Apparently Frankie refused to play on the grounds they were suspicious of the motives of some of the performers. 'Whatever their fucking motives, who cares?' said Geldof. 'What difference does it make to Frankie Goes to Hollywood if other people's motives are dubious? That's not a reason. They should have said, "Our reasons aren't, we wanna be there." So they're worried about the moral rectitude of some of the people involved? I find that a little funny coming from the Frankie camp.'

While Geldof was getting support from all corners, and would eventually end up with the bill of all bills, he couldn't persuade either Ronald Reagan or Margaret Thatcher to record a video message to intersperse in between the broadcasts. In 1985 events like these were unknown quantities, and as Live Aid was considered by many to be a political rally, was deliberately ignored by those who potentially had too much to lose from being involved. It's impossible to imagine the respective leaders of those countries not lobbying to get involved in a similar event today; it would be too good a photo opportunity to turn down. But neither Reagan nor Thatcher were interested.

Many acts fought for time slots. Some wanted to be early, some late, most wanted the maximum TV exposure both in the UK and the States, and others just wanted to make sure they didn't follow Queen. No one apart from Geldof and Goldsmith actually knew exactly who was performing, and while performers had a rough idea, they wanted to try and protect themselves as much as possible.

Elvis Costello was one act who didn't fight for a particular slot, and so understanding was he that he didn't flounce when his set kept being cut. (Elvis was originally meant to play three songs, and when his manager was told that the set had been cut to two, and then to one, he said that if they were going to cut any more numbers then Elvis wouldn't play at all.) On a show of this size, things were always going to have to give, and Costello gave in more ways than one.

On the day he decided not to play one of his own songs, but a song that meant so much more. He had only been on stage for a few moments before he asked the crowd to 'help [him] sing this old northern English folk song'. As he started singing, you could see he had the words written on his hand, probably meaning that this was a spontaneous gesture, rather than something preconceived. Making it all the more special. The song was 'All You Need Is Love' by the Beatles, and the crowd loved it. Few had seen him performing in such a benign way, and he looked almost lovable.

'All You Need Is Love' was the first Beatles song to be played at Live Aid.

Costello had not only chosen a song that best epitomised the day's message, but also one that was built for purpose. 'All You Need Is Love' was written by John Lennon especially for a 125-minute BBC1 programme called *Our World*, the world's first televised satellite link-up, connecting thirty-one TV networks in as many countries worldwide, on 25 June 1967 (and on which the Beatles would appear – Lennon on speed, McCartney smoking a joint – surrounded by garlanded hangers-on, singing the song as though it were a nursery rhyme). The show was designed to allow each country a small segment in which to show off its cultural highlights (bringing 'man face to face with mankind' was the rather pompous sell, 'in places as far apart as Canberra and Cape Kennedy, Moscow [not true, as it happened] and Montreal, Samarkand and Soderfors, Takamatsu and Tunis'), and was there any cultural highlight with more traction than the UK's biggest cultural export? The Beatles had been told that the whole world would see them recording a new song, and while the reality of that was obviously never going to work (how strange that people still thought the band went in and knocked out a song every couple of hours), they found the idea suitably intriguing to write some material for it. 'The general idea was that the television viewers would actually see the Beatles at work recording their new single – although, modern recording being what it is, we obviously couldn't do that for real,' said the band's producer George Martin, diplomatically.

The BBC had asked if the song could be as simplistic as possible, as it was obviously going to be devoured by hundreds of millions of people, and they wanted the message to be simple, clear, and completely understandable. Which is why the lyrics are so uncharacteristically straightforward (for Lennon, anyway, who at this stage was used to writing down any stream-of-consciousness ramblings that might occur to him to be worthy of posterity). The song's message encapsulated the optimistic if simplistic mood of the Summer of Love, although it was slapdash in its construction as well as its production ('All you need is love?' said Keith Richards. 'Try livin' off it.'). An inelegant song at the best of times, the engineers at Olympic Studios, where the backing track was prepared for the television broadcast, were astounded by the cursory way the mix was done. By rights they shouldn't have had a backing track anyway, as the BBC had made it a condition that everything on the show needed to be live, but as George Martin was worried about the inability of his charges to perform in public with any semblance of professionalism, he made it a precondition that the backing track was used. The track took five days, and fifty-eight takes to record, and included a thirteen-piece orchestra playing snatches of one of Bach's Brandenburg Concertos, 'Greensleeves' and 'In The Mood' over the musical funhouse of the fade, as well as 'La Marseillaise' being stuck on to the front of the song. In an inspired act of self-parody, as the song drifts away, Lennon started singing 'She loves you, yeah, yeah, yeah . . .'"

Lennon may have thought himself a sloganeering revolutionary artist, although perhaps the real revolutionary was standing in a CBC TV studio in Toronto, dressed in a sombre suit and tie, making his own pronouncements about the contracting world as part of the country's own contribution to the show: Marshall McLuhan, the man who had coined the term 'global village', and the prophet of the electronic age. Saliently, he suggested on

Our World was the world's first televised satellite link-up, connecting thirty-one TV networks in as many countries worldwide, on 25 June 1967, and bringing together Canberra, Cape Kennedy, Montreal, Samarkand and Takamatsu.

the show that one of the fastest manifestations of electronic media was the eradication of the generation gap, where children grow up more quickly than they ever have before, and where parents have to acclimatise to the ever-changing world of the teenager.' A state that was exemplified by the global Live Aid audience.

The show had actually begun with the Vienna Boys Choir singing its theme song in twenty-two different languages, before moving to Canada, and then on to Glassboro in New Jersey, where the American and Soviet leaders were meeting, before going to Melbourne, Tokyo and beyond. McLuhan called the show 'a humming, buzzing confusion'. He went on: 'Everyone will look at this programme as something they have already seen before, with just a little addition of this or that, because that is the inevitable way in which we look at everything. A huge mosaic has been created, which is in effect a kind of X-ray of world cultures. Not a storyline, not a perspective, not a point of view, but a kind of mosaic . . . in which everybody can participate. This show today will have some unexpected repercussions – people will be drawn into it as participants, whereas they're merely viewing themselves as spectators at the moment.'

At this stage in their short career, the Beatles thought they were pretty much beyond reproach, and as Ian MacDonald said in *Revolution in the Head*, 'Creativity was merely the childlike play of the imagination,' and therefore had to be taken seriously. Weren't we all artists? The Beatles certainly thought they were. So convinced were they at the time of their divinely dispensed gifts, throughout the recording of the song George Harrison insisted on playing a violin, an instrument he had never previously shown any aptitude for.

'We were big enough to command an audience of that size, and it was for love,' said Ringo Starr. 'It was for love and bloody peace. It was a fabulous time. I even get excited now when I realise that's what it was for: peace and love, people putting flowers in guns.'

The Beatles began recording the backing track just a few weeks after the release of *Sgt Pepper*, and they were brimming with confidence, energy and songs. Why would they worry about a potential television audience of

400 million? (The potential audience was initially thought to be closer to 500 million, until the Soviet Union and East Germany pulled out.) They had originally considered two new McCartney songs, 'Hello Goodbye' and 'Your Mother Should Know', but had quickly decided on Lennon's new suggestion (even though George Harrison had criticised it during Lennon's first demo performance: 'Well, it's certainly repetitive,' he had said to McCartney: the song would later inspire him to write 'It's All Too Much').

'"All You Need Is Love" was John's song,' said Paul McCartney. 'I threw in a few ideas, as did the other members of the group, but it was largely ad-libs like singing "She Loves You" or "Greensleeves" or silly things at the end and we made those up on the spot. The chorus, "All you need is love", is simple, but the verse is quite complex; in fact I never really understood it, the message is rather complex. It was a good song that we had handy that had an anthemic chorus.' On the show that chorus contained contributions from Mick Jagger, Keith Richards, Eric Clapton, Marianne Faithfull, Graham Nash, Keith Moon, Jane Asher, Mike McCartney, Patti Harrison, the Small Faces (all wearing clothes from Granny Takes a Trip), three representatives from the Fool (which made hippy clothes and accessories that would shortly be sold through the Apple boutique), Walker Brother Gary Leeds and the Beatles biographer, Hunter Davies (most of whom had been found and co-opted at various West End nightclubs – the Scotch of St James, the Bag O' Nails and the Speakeasy – the night before. Keith Moon, having been warned that the show was live and would probably be seen by over 400 million people, decided to carry on partying, and turned up for the recording not having gone to bed). Large placards with the message 'ALL YOU NEED IS LOVE' in a variety of different languages were paraded in front of the cameras.

Ian MacDonald was not a fan of the finished recording. 'During the materialistic Eighties, this song's title was the butt of cynics, there being, obviously, any number of additional things needed to sustain life on earth,' he wrote, his tongue only partially in his cheek. 'It should, perhaps, be pointed out that this record was not conceived as a blueprint for a successful career. "All you need is love" is a transcendental statement, as true on its level as the principle of investment on the level of the stock exchange. In the idealistic perspective of 1967 – the polar opposite of 1987 – its title makes perfect sense.'

Its sentiment, too, which is why Costello chose to play it, tempered by the distance and cynicism of two decades. 'When Elvis Costello revived the song for his Live Aid appearance,' said the Beatles biographer Tim Riley, 'his vitriolic snarl implied how far there still was to go rather than how far we'd come.' Also, by deciding not to play one of his own compositions, he rather snootily remained aloof from the whole enterprise. After all, Live Aid was 'a noble enough cause,' said Costello, 'but it was such an incredible shame that so little good music came out of such a gigantic event'.*

Still, at the time the song's message resonated with so many. Discussing 'All You Need Is Love', the Scottish psychiatric guru R. D. Laing said, 'The times fitted [the Beatles] like a glove. Everyone was getting the feel of the world as a global village – as us, as one species. The whole human race was becoming unified under the shadow of death. We knew we were one, because we could now commit suicide together. For some years, we had been able to kill ourselves by poison and plagues, and now we had nuclear devices. Short of complete suicide, we could and did inflict terrible havoc on ourselves. And it seemed it could break out anywhere. We were unified, but terrified of being unified. We feared ourselves maybe no more than before, but in a new way . . . One of the most heartening things about the Beatles was that they gave expression to a shared sense of celebration around the world, a sense of the same sensibility.'

'It was seen by an estimated 400 million people,' said George Martin. 'Not quite the 1.9 billion who watched Live Aid, but pretty awesome for its day.'

---

* John Lennon and Paul McCartney had met almost exactly twenty-eight years previously, on 6 July 1957, at a Saturday evening fête in St Peter's Church, Woolton, in Liverpool, where the sixteen-year-old Lennon's skiffle group, the Quarry Men, were performing. 'All You Need Is Love' was released almost exactly ten years later, on 7 July 1967. Nine days later there would be a 'Legalise Pot' rally in Hyde Park, followed a week later by a massive 'Love-In' in Los Angeles. At the end of the month, homosexuality would finally be legalised in the UK, while Mick Jagger would win the appeal against the jail sentence relating to his drug conviction.

Costello didn't look as though he was especially enjoying the Wembley experience, however. He was used to playing big crowds, yet recently had tried to distance himself from the pop arena. He was sporting a beard, one that he would intermittently grow throughout this period of his career, in an attempt to throw off the shackles of stardom that had successfully snared him for the last three years of the Seventies (when he had been perfectly happy to embrace the trappings of the music industry, cleverly exploiting it through his ad campaigns with Stiff and Radar, his record labels at that point).

By 1985 he had already started to step back a little from the pop merry-go-round, so in a way it was odd to see him on the Wembley stage. He was hardly having a creative impasse, however, and the following year would release what many would consider to be his best ever record, *Blood And Chocolate*, an album of searing guitar pop that was as innately savage as anything he had recorded ten years previously, during his first flush of fame. 'All You Need Is Love' was completely out of character, though, which made the performance rather odd. He had always been so associated with his own anger — he could channel bile better than almost anyone — and it was strange to see him so eloquently interpreting this classic hymn to altruism. Perhaps a more overtly political statement — 'Shipbuilding', say — would have made more of an impression, although this was hardly a reason to criticise him. It would be easy to say that Costello was another performer whose success during the punk years was making it difficult for him to adjust to the demands of the Eighties, yet he had actually already established himself as a singer/songwriter with such conviction — as well as success — that he was already considered to be a member of the establishment. This was a remarkable achievement in itself, considering a decade earlier he had been lampooned for daring to co-opt the Christian name of the King.

Costello's moment at Live Aid could — should — have been one of the defining moments of the day. Here was one of the industry's greatest talents, a man who had been thrown up by punk, and who had very quickly become one of the music business's greatest assets, appreciated throughout the world for being one of the foremost songwriters of his day, deciding to forgo the opportunity to play one of his own songs on the biggest stage in rock 'n' roll's short, thirty-year history, only to decide instead to play a song that really meant something, a song from the past, a classic, that would – could! – resonate around the world.

Yet for some reason it didn't really work. Perhaps he was on too early, perhaps it was the odd way he looked – not iconic enough, frankly – perhaps because the crowd were still in party mode and not quite ready for any kind of reflective 'moment', perhaps his voice wasn't necessarily suited to the song, or his arrangement of it, perhaps his performance was slightly off kilter. Maybe it was because the guitar sound was too thin (perhaps he should have been backed by John Oates's old guitar partner, Wild Willy Barrett). Perhaps the song really did need an enormous, shambolic mess steering it home, maybe it did need a full orchestra and a chorus full of angels. After a while it turned into a fireside sing-song, yet in a way it seemed so terribly old-fashioned, even though it should have had the opposite effect (prescience). There is nothing quantifiably wrong about the performance, apart from the fact that it doesn't work. No mind, as a gesture it was magnanimous in the extreme, and Costello deserved more plaudits because of it.

Elvis's performance was important less for its quality than its content: Elvis Costello, that bastion of post-punk vitriol, who came along in 1976, the punk Year Zero, whose stage demeanour was almost as intimidating as Joe Strummer's or Jimmy Pursey from Sham 69, and whose lack of tolerance was almost legendary . . . here he was performing a sappy Beatles song at an industry love-in along with the likes of Status Quo and Spandau Ballet, and basking in the acclaim.

In essence, 'All You Need Is Love' had reach, which was what Geldof had wanted all along. Reach. Scale. Songs which everyone could sing along to.

'With the Band Aid record, I wanted to make something that could be sung all around the world, like "All You Need Is Love". It didn't have to be any good, just popular. Given where we [the Rats] were at in our career, there was no guarantee that the tune would be a hit, and I needed the guarantee that there would be a pragmatic focus coming in. So you get the guys who you've met over ten years in pop who are making the running now, gather them together and get them to make it, because they're the ones on televisions all over the world.

'I was always trying to create a political lobby for change, which is what a lot of people still don't get. That's where I was at; they confuse it with the cultural event it was, which it became. That wasn't my intention. My intention was to create a political lobby and the financial outpouring of that would be the cash. That was it, very simply. It was the same with Live Aid. You had the biggest bands playing their hits. The end. There was nothing to do with personal taste. If it was up to my personal taste, we'd have had John Lee Hooker, Van Morrison and the Rats. Seventeen hours of the Boomtown Rats would be perhaps a little too much, even for me. That was it. The logic for the political lobby was simple. So how do we alter the politics? You create a vast political lobby, you harness it and you drive it forward. It took twenty years but we got there. That was it, and that's what it was for me.'

Live Aid was a different kind of Year Zero, a different kind of level playing field. Here there were denim-clad boogie boys, dodgy New Romantics, old-school pop entertainers, ersatz soul stars, rock royalty, *Top of the Pops* stalwarts . . . and Nik Kershaw. There was no Prince, no Bruce Springsteen and no Michael Jackson. But here was Nik Kershaw instead.

In all the interviews Geldof gave after the event, you could tell that he was a little embarrassed about some of those on the bill. After all, he was born in 1951, and his heart lay in the Sixties, in the original rebel music made by Bob Dylan, the Stones and The Who. Like many musicians his age, punk was a convenience more than anything, a chance to shoehorn whatever it was they were doing into a convenient and expedient form of expression. Joe Strummer wasn't a punk, nor were the Stranglers, the Vibrators or Elvis Costello; but if wearing bondage pants and sneering got them on the cover of *Sounds*, then punks were what they were going to be. A quick look at Geldof's *Desert Island Discs* from 1992 shows where his affections lay, and they lay in the past: Bob Dylan's 'My Back Pages', the Beatles' 'In My Life' (the Lennon song), Loudon Wainwright III's 'Central Square Song', Howlin' Wolf's 'Smokestack Lightnin'', Bob Marley's 'Them

Belly Full (But We Hungry)', etc. The most incendiary record was 'Lust For Life' by Iggy Pop, one of those records that had galvanised if not an entire generation, at least those parts of it who were listening. Geldof's rebellious nature was what fuelled him throughout his time with the Rats, even if this didn't always show itself in their music. He certainly knew the right touchstones (after all, he was a music critic for a while).*

At twenty-two minutes past two, Kershaw followed Costello on to the stage, for one of the least prepossessing performances of the day. He had actually been the very first person Geldof had asked to perform at the concert, as he had shared the idea for Live Aid with Kershaw when they'd bumped into each other at Heathrow. But he was never going to violate his amateur standing. He may have attempted passion and depth in his songs, but his sedulousness was agony to watch. Nik Kershaw was far too tentative to be a proper pop star.

Live Aid was nicknamed the 'global jukebox' for a reason: it was a concert full of hits, whether old or new, which was why Kershaw was on the bill. This was a popularity contest, and as long as you were popular, you were in. Bob Geldof wasn't stupid. Kershaw had been riding high for the previous eighteen months, and in 1984 had been in the charts for fifty weeks of the year, something of an achievement in itself. He looked rather old to be a teen idol (he was twenty-seven at Live Aid), yet that was exactly what he was.

His USP was his colour-by-numbers boy-next-door appeal, as he was probably the least idiosyncratic pop star of the whole decade. If Throbbing Gristle or the Bad Seeds were at one end of the pop continuum, then Kershaw was at the opposite end, sitting cross-legged in a slightly bemused

---

* Geldof had been typically acerbic on *Desert Island Discs*. The presenter at the time was Sue Lawley, who at one point scolded her castaway: 'Let's get down to your eight desert island discs, which despite months of warning, you still only decided on in the past few days. Is this because it's such a weighty decision, or is it sheer laziness?' Geldof's reply was equally curt: 'It's not sheer laziness. It's because right at the moment I'm up to my neck with a million things, and it's the little minutiae of life that really bore me. I dismiss them until the last moment because they're not important. And though I know that this is a venerable British institution it is, after all, another radio show.'

fashion in his white picket-fence playpen surrounded by cheap fluffy toys and plastic guitars in primary colours.

He was about as anodyne a pop star as it was possible to be. To his credit, he never pretended otherwise, and a quick trawl of his website (yes, he still tours and makes records) shows how much store he sets by his normalcy: 'It was at Northgate [Grammar School] that he met Russell Chesterman. He had a Gibson 335 (copy) and wasn't afraid to use it. Sunday afternoons would never be the same again, throwing shapes to Black Sabbath and Deep Purple whilst Russell's mum made light refreshments. It was here that Kershaw was first introduced to the shady underworld of lime cordial and fish paste sandwiches.'

He hailed from Ipswich, which is not the sort of place you should be caught living in if you're one day going to be a member of any group aspiring to be Primal Scream or the Velvet Underground. But as he apparently only ever wanted to be Nik Kershaw, then coming from Ipswich wasn't as bad as it could have been. A few years later, when Steve Coogan launched Alan Partridge, East Anglia was chosen as his place of birth, as there was no county more comic, more prosaic, or more naff. Hailing from Norwich, Ipswich, or anywhere in Norfolk or Suffolk was somehow at odds with any notion of cool. Especially if your provenance was unwittingly exposed while you were sitting on a breakfast television sofa.

'He left school in 1975 in order to concentrate on his music career. To this end, he secured a job in Ipswich Unemployment Benefit Office. By day he was mild-mannered clerical officer Nik Kershaw [crazy name, crazy guy!], by night he wore loon pants and tie dyed batwing shirts.'

He did the group thing, then the solo thing, got a manager, a deal, released a few singles and for two or three years was ridiculously famous. He was the kind of chap you'd always see on early-evening television, gurning, and playing his rather nasal hits – 'I Won't Let The Sun Go Down On Me', 'Wouldn't It Be Good', 'The Riddle', 'Human Racing', 'Wide Boy' and 'Don Quixote', none of which were ever going to be classics, but which would occasionally be adapted by Radio 1 DJs, who inserted their own names into the choruses. I couldn't stand his records, although they were ridiculously catchy, and often found myself singing along to them on the radio, always against my better judgement. Still, there was no need for Kershaw to be more interesting or more talented than he was, which was just as well, as he wasn't.

Would it have helped if he had been called Mingus? Probably. But his records wouldn't have been any better.

I remember looking at the Live Aid bill when it was announced and deciding which sections could be skipped, in case anyone wanted to go to the bar, or the loo, or go for a wander. Both Kershaw and Howard Jones's sets were on this list, and in fact I have no recollection of seeing them on the day, so I'd either successfully managed to find something better to do – searching the many pockets in my MA-1 flying jacket for loose change, perhaps – or I've simply blocked them from my memory. I suppose if Live Aid had been attempted four or five years earlier, then Gary Numan might have filled this slot, but then imagine how people would have sniggered if Numan had performed at the 13 July concert.

According to Geldof's rationale for inclusion, if Live Aid had been organised a few years later no doubt the bill would have been full of Rick Astley, Kylie Minogue and all the other singers who fronted Stock Aitken Waterman records. Instead we had Nik Kershaw, a publicist's dream, and someone who couldn't really believe he was appearing at Wembley. 'The music business is too often associated by its critics with things trivial, negative and destructive, so I feel pleased to be able to play even a small part in an event which proves otherwise,' he said afterwards. He even found time to mention his family. 'I didn't enjoy it really. It was a bit fraught – a lot more so than supporting Elton John last year,' he told *Smash Hits* when he came offstage. 'Is there anyone I'd like to meet backstage? Yeah, Sheri, my wife . . .'

SIX

14:55

Sade: 'Why Can't We Live Together', 'Your Love Is King', 'Is It A Crime'

This British future style is a dandy one – it's software rather than hardware. What they're setting up is the cellar club of the future rather than the next shuttle station. They're working on the great look, rather than the five-year plan.

PETER YORK

If, in the Nineties, the prefix of choice was 'luxury' – luxury clothes, luxury hotels, luxury bath soap, luxury breakfast cereal, etc. – then it shouldn't have come as much of a surprise that it was swiftly followed in the Noughties by 'bespoke', a word used by the marketing departments of luxury-goods houses to flatter those customers of theirs who had become rather alarmed at just how many people could now afford 'luxury'.

They banged on about 'bespoke' as though it were some new form of Viagra, a consumer principle with the capacity to empower anyone who came into contact with it. King Midas was born again and he had a flagship store on Bond Street, with a little room on the first floor where you could get your suit altered (here, why don't you have a new silk mauve lining!) or some initials put on your handbag.

Designers and marketers began obsessing about provenance and heritage and legitimacy and history, as though true luxury was something defined only by a calendar. In the Nineties and early Noughties we were subjected to a multitude of alternative ways to describe this so-called affluent lifestyle: 'old luxury', 'true luxury', 'real luxury', 'contemporary luxury', and my favourite, 'super luxury'. We were spared 'super duper luxury', but for the life of me I don't really know why.

It was the same with cars, and it was no longer enough for them to be luxurious, as they had to be 'high-end luxury' or 'ultra-luxury'. It was no longer a consumer jungle out there, it was a zoo, one with so many alternative choices. It was the same with the hospitality industry: why stay in a simple five-star hotel when you could be ensconced in a mega-suite in a 'five-star deluxe', a 'six-star' or, in the case of Dubai's already iconic Burj Al Arab, 'seven-star'? Why indeed.

Status frenzy caused some of those lunatics whose consumer habits once helped prop up the luxury industry to travel far and wide in search of their next hit. It could have been an Alpine spa, could have been a sabbatical in Patagonia – accompanied only by your Brazilian girlfriend, a pair of neoprene-lined Hunter's wellingtons and half a dozen fully charged credit cards. There were even those whose obsession with luxury caused them to seek out ever more exotic fabrics, the sort of oddballs who described their predilections with the sort of arcane language once used by Damon Runyon and S. J. Perelman. You know the kind of thing: 'His waistcoat felt as though it had been fashioned from the nether regions of several rather fastidious otters.' Or, a real one this, and the most precise outfit I recall Perelman ever describing: 'A shower-of-hail suit, lilac gloves, a split-sennit boater, and a light whangee cane.'

Back in the Eighties, things were slightly more prosaic, as the prefix of choice back then was simply 'designer'. This was everyone's favourite retail tag, used in conjunction with everything from cars, double-breasted suits and supermodels to personal organisers, kitchen fittings and vegetables, and was one we were all encouraged to embrace with gusto. 'Designer' was originally used adjectivally to describe the notionally elitist Gloria

Vanderbilt designer jeans produced by Murjani in the Seventies. It is often said that the company had actually wanted Jackie Onassis to lend the brand her name (and thus enormous added value), but when it could not get the former first lady, it called in the New York socialite. These garments were advertised on the sides of buses with the slogan 'The end justifies the jeans', alongside photos of a line-up of Vanderbilt-clad (signed) bottoms.

The idea caught on, though, and soon the word 'designer' was being stuck in front of everything, even pop groups.

Which is how Sade became the first designer pop group, a band who dared to whisper about the good life, the thread of the exotic. In various obvious ways Sade were the quintessential Eighties act, adored and vilified in equal measure because of it.

At the time, the very idea of Sade was anathema to the music press in the UK, principally because she was so different to pretty much everything that had gone before.

'The whole thing is extraordinarily composed, very *civilised*,' wrote a *Melody Maker* journalist just a year before Live Aid. 'Which makes her arrival as a bona fide pop star even more incongruous. Is this music for young marrieds? Songs for the Habitat generation? A voice for the discerning adult?

'Fact of the matter is there are no easy categorisations for Sade. One of the reasons she's so fascinating is that she conforms to *nothing*. She straddles all manner of age, creed and market, confounding the rules of the business at every turn, but doing it with such style and charm that after a while you just don't care any more. A woman for all seasons and the first lady of '84.'

The way she looked was discussed almost as much as her music; in fact for many journalists this was her biggest problem – her beauty, and the way in which she dressed. 'In England, 'twas ever thus,' wrote Charles Shaar Murray in *Rolling Stone* just six weeks before Live Aid, in an attempt to explain her to a potential American audience. 'Before the hit records, before the acclaim, before even the voice . . . there comes The Look. And what a look Sade has: the high forehead; the svelte shape; the luminous, almost oriental eyes, the generous, sensual mouth. Without pastel cosmetics or a hedge-clipper haircut, Sade has a look that's both distinctive and unconventionally alluring.'

The thing about Sade was the fact that she, and her band, was obsessed with *less* as opposed to *more*, a distaste for wildness and flash that was reflected in Sade's public persona. 'It's now so acceptable to be wacky and have hair that goes in 101 directions and has several colours, and trendy, wacky clothes have become so acceptable that they're . . . conventional,' she said at the time. 'From being at art college, I've always hated people that have the gall to think they're being incredibly different when they're doing something in a very acceptable way, something safe that they've seen someone else doing. I don't look particularly wacky. I don't like looking outrageous. I don't want to look like everybody else.'

As the Eighties blossomed, so did design as a cultural force. Designers assumed godlike status, as young urban professionals surrounded themselves with the trappings of the upwardly mobile: the Tizio lamp, the Breuer chair, the Dualit toaster, the Alessi kettle, the Tag-Heuer watch, the Golf GTI convertible . . . and of course the Paul Smith Prince of Wales check suit. Smith sold suits to managing directors, but also to art directors and plumbers, and became famous for clothes which screamed when you wanted them to, not when you least expected it. We were told that everyone could have a designer lifestyle if they were so inclined. Money wasn't mentioned, but then how on earth could it be? That was the illusion: money was no object.

This was the decade when air conditioning was a luxury good, when chilled air became a rarefied perk. All of a sudden we were surrounded by things previously denied us. Bottled water, imported cheeses, 12″ remixes, designer clothes in all their finery. We could get money from a hole in the wall, and magazines were beginning to write about people in the lifestyle industry as though they were heroes – club runners, photographers, restaurant managers, the designers of board games – as though they were all choosing careers in the same way that they might choose lifestyle cultures; if they were given the opportunity, that is. The Pet Shop Boys sang 'I've got the brains, you've got the looks, let's make lots of money,' and they were only half joking. This was rare in itself, as jokes were thin on the ground in the Eighties, as irony had to elevate itself in order to be taken seriously.

The Eighties were reduced to one word: cool. Everything was cool, or not. There was a complete anorexia of language. And Sade was accused of being complicit in this time and time again.

'I do care about clothes and glamour, but not because I'm a singer,' she said, in her defence. 'When you have a photograph taken of you it's a permanent thing so you make an effort. If someone comes up to you at a party with a camera you don't then start scratching your ear unless it's for a joke. If I have a picture taken of me for the cover of a magazine I don't want to look gruesome 'cause I have to look at it. The same way I don't want to look gruesome walking about the streets. I pay attention to detail 'cause it's a frozen image that reports you. I have to project myself. But I only do that because that's the way I want to be.

'I didn't want to be signed up because I was glamorous, because I might make glamorous records.'

If the Seventies in Britain had suggested that the country was a shrinking state on the verge of collapse, in the Eighties all anyone could talk about was growth. The nationalised industries may have been taking a pounding, unemployment may have been rising as quickly as the shiny new buildings in Canary Wharf, and the poorer pockets of the country may have been starting to become disenfranchised as the disparity between rich and poor began to escalate; yet everywhere you looked things were getting bigger, grander, more expensive. As Alwyn W. Turner said in *Rejoice! Rejoice! Britains in the Eighties*: 'Models mutated into supermodels, supermarkets into superstores, cinemas into multiplexes. Building societies became banks and humble record shops developed delusions of grandeur, turning themselves into megastores. High streets were eclipsed by out-of-town shopping centres, and the number of television channels, newspapers and magazines simply grew and grew. If something wasn't already big, then advertising – one of the great growth industries of the time – could make it seem so, or else the overblown price tag would suffice, as with the rise of nouvelle cuisine or the trend away from drinking in pubs towards bottled beers in bars.'

You only had to look at the 1982 advertising campaign for Stella Artois to understand how the Eighties were starting to define themselves. The 'Reassuringly Expensive' slogan was created by Frank Lowe, formerly of Collett Dickinson Pearce, who had worked on the Stella brand in the Seventies, and who took the account with him when he left to form his own agency in 1981. Within a year he had turned a considerable negative (the beer's high alcohol content made it more expensive due to greater duty) into a positive, convincing the consumer that because it was more expensive than its competitive set, it was better. This rationale would start to be applied to everything, from clothes and cars to apartments and holidays, from food and drink (the more expensive the cocktail, the more we wanted it) to art and design. Taste was suddenly an intangible it was acceptable to buy; so what if you didn't know anything about white leather Italian furniture or Scandinavian kitchens, you could simply buy the most expensive and be done with it.

Taste as a commodity became big business in the Eighties, as it became a growth industry in the media. Magazines, newspapers and lifestyle television programmes were aimed not just at teenagers hungry for culture but avaricious adults who had enough money to buy into the good life. If, in the Sixties, taste was something discovered by the few, in the Seventies it became something owned by the few; in the Eighties taste started to become something that not only did most people want, but something a considerably larger number of people could afford.

At least this was what we were told.

The illusion of affluence played such an enormous part in the designer-lifestyle boom of the early to mid-Eighties, creating a divisive culture in which the yuppie dream was allowed to thrive as though it were a religion. If you were on the right side of the fence then the party went on all night.

Perhaps predictably, 'designer' became a pejorative almost as quickly as it became a prefix, while the consumers of anything 'designer' were brutally lampooned. This was death by acronym. Peter York's *Style Wars* ushered in the Eighties (it was published in 1980, and was as prescient as the first number one of the decade being 'Brass In Pocket' by the Pretenders), and it brought with it a series of acronyms used and abused by every aspiring style guru as pigeonholing went global. And inside the glassy whirlpool – surrounded by guppies (gay urban professionals), dinkies (double income no kids), dockneys (docklands London yuppie), poupies (Porsche-owning urban professionals) and buppies (black urban professionals) – was the first urban tribe, the yuppies; young urban professionals.

The yuppies' hobby was money, their aim self-fulfilment, and they surrounded themselves with the accoutrements and occupational hazards of the newly empowered: the waterfront conversion, the better-buffed personal trainer, the foreign domestic help and the Golf GTI convertible with the personalised number plate. If you didn't have a Barcelona chair, a Richard Sapper anglepoise or a Braun shaver, then there was really no point in turning up at the office. And like *The Face* said, all was black, matt black, in the matt black dream home: this was the matt black dream conversion, with a black hi-fi on a black shelf, and black clothes in the black wardrobe. Having parked your black BMW in the underground car park, you settled down on a black sofa (pre-1987, bought from Habitat; post-1987, bought from the Conran Shop), your sublime good taste confirmed, and then read with horror the red bank statement.

Of course, as you settled into your evening, perhaps reclining in a tubular steel and leather Breuer chair, you would be listening to a Sade CD. As a metaphor for the Eighties, the CD is as good as any other. Like Madonna, the black Gucci loafer, MTV, privatisation, shoulder pads or Terry Farrell's truly dreadful postmodern architecture (such as the MI6 headquarters in Vauxhall, for instance), the CD was the defining symbol of the age, an age when presentation wasn't just paramount, it was pretty much everything. The compact disc compartmentalised its content; cleaned it up, washed behind its ears, and then dressed it up for the market; it digitally improved it, shrunk it and then enshrined it in a transparent pocket-sized jewel case. Albums were messy things, and didn't fit in with the ideas the decade had about itself. Albums were OK if you went back to a flat filled with grey metal office shelving units, all the better for showing off your adolescent good taste. But having good taste in music didn't matter as much in the

The Band Aid single became the default Christmas present of 1984,
a record that broke records and saved lives. With an original cover by Peter Blake

The BBC Arena programme *Ligmalion* (an Eighties update
of *Pygmalion*) includes Bob Geldof's first reaction to the
Michael Buerk film of the Ethiopian famine

Saturday July 13th, 1985 was the day of days, the pinch-point
of the decade, the day the Eighties came alive. There will never
be another day like it

In November 1983 *Rolling Stone* announced the third British invasion, as
Culture Club, Duran Duran and Spandau Ballet put their tanks on the White House Lawn.
Courtesy of *Rolling Stone*

By rights, Bob Geldof should have been washed-up by 1984, as his band the Boomtown Rats were somewhat on the slide. Yet Band Aid and Live Aid caused a generous revaluation of their career

New York was the quintessential city of the decade, a big town of big money, big nightclubs and the biggest book of the Eighties, Tom Wolfe's *The Bonfire Of The Vanities*. Yet New York mayor Ed Koch couldn't get Live Aid

Queen's performance at Live Aid
was not just the highlight of the day,
it was also one of the greatest stadium
performances of all time, perhaps
the greatest. Freddie Mercury
was simply mesmerizing

David Bowie and Mick Jagger
had originally planned
to perform a duet separated
by an ocean with one of
them performing in London,
and the other in Philadelphia.
In the end they recorded a
camp knockabout version of
'Dancing In The Street'

Sade and *The Face*, two icons of the Eighties. Sade's music was perfect for the designer decade, as they took elements from the past, fused with elements of the present, creating a modern symbiotic sound that had sheen and distance

Eighties as it had in the Seventies; taste had changed, anyway, drifting off to the borders and corners, diversifying in extraordinary ways. But even music that determinedly originated in the dark on the edges of society, or was designed to appeal to those for whom music had become too commercial, too blemish-free, even this was codified, commodified. The CD made a commodity out of everything.

Yes, the CD occasionally had a rather large and unnecessary photograph of Mick Hucknall, Phil Collins or Wet Wet Wet on it, but let's face it, no decade's ever perfect. Its size was in one sense contradictory, as it was largely impossible to amplify or appreciate the CD covers themselves. When U2 released *The Joshua Tree* in 1987 – the revenge of the gatefold sleeve – the CD version looked almost apologetic. No, CDs weren't visual (surprising, for a decade obsessed with looks), they were artefacts, popular for the way they felt, and the way they made you feel, rather than for their innate attractiveness. And while they were a commodity, they soon became rather disposable. When CDs first arrived, they cost a fortune, as the record companies liked to say that they needed to be expensive to pay back all the research and development costs (they even offered their artists smaller royalty rates for the same reason, and many of them believed it); but, late at night, having come in from a tapas bar or a trendy new wine bar, aspiring yuppies would use their CDs as coasters, on which to put their new designer glasses, bought from a shop that desperately wanted to be Heal's.

Like the designer decade it would soon become synonymous with, the CD was an emblem of burnished success – a smarter, more upmarket version of everything that had gone before it. The CD was a designer accessory like no other, and heralded an era when music became a supermarket product. Almost overnight, as design started to infect every area of our lives, from clothes and interiors to cars and household accessories, so music became a lifestyle accessory, a muted background fizz to be played at designer dinner parties in designer lofts in designer postcodes. 'CD music' became pejorative, as did the likes of Sade, Anita Baker and Luther Vandross. Critics – the sweaty guys at the back with the bad teeth, the bad shoes and more opinions than they would ever have money – said that this was just music with the edges rubbed off, with the soul extracted. 'Sade?' they said, almost as one. 'Those guys are so boring their dreams have muzak. And barely audible muzak, at that.' But then the arbiters of taste who were indulging themselves in their new-found designer trinkets didn't hear the barrage of envy around them, probably because they were too busy listening to Sade. And, aspirational in essence, if you didn't have the wherewithal to surround yourself with the occupational hazards of yuppiedom, then a few CDs left casually on the sub-Matthew Hilton coffee table would suffice.

What the cloth-eared, dog-eared critics didn't understand was that the Eighties generation wanted designer dreams just as much as their predecessors did – and what the market wants, the market tends to get. Or at least it did in the Eighties. Which is probably why Sade became one of the biggest bands of the decade, 'designer' or not.

People weren't kind about them in the early days, but then most of the criticism came from those critics – yes, them again – who were championing the likes of the Birthday Party, The The and German avante-garde nonsense like Einstürzende Neubauten. Elsewhere the band – and Sade was always a band, never just a gorgeous Nigerian-born singer called Helen Folasade Adu – were welcomed with open arms, cutting through class, culture, age, race and sex, while their first album, *Diamond Life* ('Smooth Operator', 'Your Love Is King', 'Hang On To Your Love', 'Why Can't We Live Together', etc.) sold 6 million copies in the UK, and in the region of 17 million in the US. Which, as Robert De Niro says at the end of *Midnight Run* (a film released in 1988, and one of the first to use the icon of Seventies cinema as a mainstream knockabout action entertainer; De Niro wanted to stretch himself, and plumped for comedy, even pursuing – unsuccessfully – the lead role in Penny Marshall's *Big*, the role that eventually went to Tom Hanks), is a very respectable neighbourhood. One of the reasons they were so successful was because they slotted nicely into 'Quiet Storm' programming, the sexy, late-night radio format featuring soulful slow jams, smooth R&B and misty-eyed soul, pioneered in the mid-Seventies by DJ Melvin Lindsey at WHUR-FM in Washington DC.

The brilliant thing about the band was their almost total ambivalence towards success, and no sooner had they conquered the world, than they would run back home again (to London, Cheltenham, New York or the Caribbean), only to emerge, sleepy-eyed, three or four years later when it was time for another record. Their initial appeal was that they didn't appear to have any 'issues'; they were modern, they made contemporary-sounding soul music, yet they weren't in any way angry, thus appealing to the widest demographic. Previously, their kind of music might have been developed to aid revolution, whereas it was actually enjoyed as a lifestyle soundtrack.

But at least Sade had their own sound, their own sonic world. Much of the commercial music produced in the Eighties was swathed in artificiality, manifested by the Fairlight synthesiser, the Australian-manufactured machine used by the likes of Thomas Dolby, Peter Gabriel, Alan Parsons, Herbie Hancock and *Miami Vice* composer Jan Hammer. If you wanted to sound futuristic, modern, then the Fairlight was your studio toy of choice. In the Eighties, every established pop star from Bob Dylan to the Rolling Stones began using drum machines, in the hope of being embraced by the new MTV generation, and grasping another lifeline. If you wandered through a Virgin Megastore in the Eighties, you'd hear the time-capsule *clank* of over produced synthesised drums. Boing!

For a while, it felt as though music on CD all sounded like CD music, every track coated in thin synthesised swirls, every hook punctuated by piping sampled horns (trumpets delivered at the punch of a button rather than because of a serious intake of breath), and every crescendo building on banks and banks of overlaid keyboards, as though the dynamics of Led Zeppelin or Derek and the Dominoes (say) could be replicated mathematically. And then there were the drums, the dreaded computerised drums, the great slabs of digitised cardboard. Music on CD sounded cleaner, leaner, less down and dirty. Initially it suited soul, heavily organised rock and gentle singer-songwriter stuff, but wasn't so good at replicating the noise and squabble of punk or the energy and naïvety of rockabilly or early rock 'n' roll.

To their credit, Sade didn't go down this route, and while their music couldn't have been made during any other decade, it actually sounds rather old-fashioned.

There are so many records that defined the era, although not many of them stand up now (does anyone listen to Tracy Chapman any more? What about Erasure? Foreigner?). It was the decade when David Bowie (trying, for the first time since the Sixties, to make music he thought people wanted) made his worst records; when the Stones (trying to please themselves) made their very worst records – on 1986's *Dirty Work*, Mick Jagger didn't even play guitar; when Terence Trent D'Arby's debut LP (*Introducing The Hardline According To . . .*) spent eight weeks at number one, and the follow-up (*Neither Fish Nor Flesh*) died something of a spectacular designer death.

Prince's 1987 opus *Sign Of The Times* was probably the best album of the Eighties (the Clash's much-lauded *London Calling* was actually released in 1979, even though its slightly later American release caused *Rolling Stone* to call it the best album of the Eighties), a sexy smorgasbord of a record, the buffet at the porno party of your dreams. It was all there: love, sex, religion, drugs, politics (sexual and otherwise), and a real home-made sense of fun. It was a record that couldn't have been made in any other decade, layered as it was with drum machines, samples, and the kind of studio wizardry that just wasn't possible in the Seventies. (It's the record that studio maverick Todd Rundgren would have made if he'd perhaps been born ten years later and actually knew how to dance.) And while *Sign Of The Times* had the trademark studio sheen of any record made in the Eighties, compositionally it was about as eclectic as it's possible to be and still retain a substantial fan base. Not only that, but Prince largely did everything himself: he wrote the songs, played most of the instruments, recorded and produced it and delivered the final product to the record company (rumour has it, in a purple Mustang), who then simply distributed and marketed it.

Prince was a maverick, someone for whom social interaction was a distraction, not a welcome respite. He operated in a vacuum, whereas every new pop star in London appeared to know each other. The early Eighties were the years when you'd bump into George Michael in the Wag Club dancing to one of his own records, or stand behind David Bowie in the queue for the Gents at the Mud Club, or see one of Spandau Ballet chatting up Bananarama.

There was one particular party, bizarrely enough in Harrods in 1985, just a few weeks before Live Aid, when Harrods decided it wanted a bit of designer *jus* itself, where a group of luminaries included former Labour leader Neil Kinnock – slumming it for a bit of tabloid and style magazine exposure – Simon Le Bon, PR guru Lynne Franks, Boy George, fashion designers Jean Paul Gaultier and Katharine Hamnett, the American artist Julian Schnabel and one of London's most notorious transsexual prostitutes. Oh lordy, it was as if social boundaries had yet to be invented, as though social mobility was the birthright of anyone in a loud jacket with shoulder pads and a pair of bulbous patent leather shoes. London was like the Sixties only with its own new prefix.

Pop stars were everywhere, propping up the bars and piling into toilet cubicles. Walk into Club for Heroes, Heaven or the Wag Club and you'd see someone from Spandau Ballet or Duran Duran, Madonna, Shane McGowan, Depeche Mode, August Darnell from Kid Creole & The Coconuts, the Pet Shop Boys, Boy George, Spear of Destiny's Kirk Brandon, Pete Townshend, George Michael and Andrew Ridgeley. (You went to Rio, Monte Carlo, New York, LA, Tokyo and Toronto, and they were all there too, propping up the bar and nodding as you walked in as though they were still drinking cocktails in Soho. Twenty years later and the pop stars *du jour* would be doing the same at film festivals, but in the Eighties it was almost exclusively nightclubs.)

During the Eighties the media went fashion crazy as London became a crucible of self-expression. Club culture had produced a generation of show-offs, and they were as desperate to be photographed as the papers were desperate to feature them. Everyone wanted to buy into the dream, even pop stars. Club culture was trendy, and there was no better photo opportunity than the bar at the right nightclub. In 1986 I wrote a long and rather inflammatory piece in *i-D* about a silly Italian youth cult called the

Paninari. In a style that now seems excited (actually to be fair it's a lot worse than that), I catalogued the Paninari obsession with casual sportswear, their predilection for riding little red motorbikes through the streets of Milan and hanging out in sandwich bars (hence the name: a *panino* is a bread roll) and of course their reactionary prepubescent machismo. Acting on disinformation, I also wrote that the Pet Shop Boys – who were apparently big fans of Paninari fashion – had even recorded their own paean to the cult, called, simply enough, 'Paninaro'. When the song appeared a few months later I thought nothing of it. Until about three years later, that is, when I read an interview with the Pet Shop Boys in *Rolling Stone*. They had read my piece: 'We read that we'd recorded this song,' said Pet Shop Boy Chris Lowe (the laconic one). 'Of course we hadn't but we thought it was such a good idea that we soon did.'

Style culture actually became the binding agent of all that was supposed to be cool. Catwalk models were no longer simply clothes horses, they were rechristened supermodels. Fashion designers were no longer just considered gay iconoclasts or hatchet-faced prima donnas. They became solid-gold celebrities to be fawned over and profiled. Designers who had previously been demonised for their outrageous abuse of models and staff were now being sanitised for everyday consumption. Pop stars were no longer considered to be council-house Neanderthals, they were suddenly elevated to front-page sex symbols, whose every word was copied down, amplified and endlessly repeated in the gossip columns of the national press. It was a sartorial melting pot, a visual mélange of crushed-velvet miniskirts, high heels and lipstick. And that was just the men. It was almost as if there was a blueprint for the celebrity interface with the fashion industry, one that determined that the best place to be at any given time was either propping up the bar in the Wag Club, or grinning your rictus grin at a shop opening.

Before the Eighties, our reading matter in this area was principally American, and our perceived sense of style came from magazines such as *Interview*, *New York* or the now defunct *Punk*. We might have taken a lead from something in the *New Musical Express* (then selling in excess of 250,000 copies each week), or maybe *Tatler* or *Vogue*, but there was no magazine for the generation of young people who had been inspired by punk. Sure, there was a fanzine industry, a thriving independent sector that was responsible for some of the most important music journalism of its time; but there was nothing that had a wider brief.

Until 1980 that is, when in the space of three months, three magazines would launch that would help define the decade. Nick Logan, Terry Jones and, to a certain extent, Carey Labovitch started a small publishing revolution by launching, respectively, *The Face*, *i-D* and *Blitz*. Logan, former editor of the phenomenally successful *NME* and creator of *Smash Hits*, and Jones, a former art director of British *Vogue*, both independently realised that style culture, or what was then simply known as 'street style', was being ignored by much of the mainstream press. Labovitch, an Oxford graduate, was thinking the same thing, and although *Blitz* was never held

i-D was the first magazine to reflect the new generation of consumers, many of them male. Along with *The Face*, it gave voice to a generation who had grown up by dressing up, spreading out from the hub of the third wave of Swinging London.

in the same regard as *i-D* or *The Face*, it was fundamental in exploring the surface matter of the new decade. These magazines were launched not only to catalogue this new explosion of style, but also to cater for it. *i-D*, *Blitz* and *The Face*, which were aimed at both men and women, reflected not only our increasing appetite for street style and fashion, but also for ancillary subjects such as movies, music, television, art and zeitgeisty things in general – everything that was deemed to have some sort of influence on the emerging culture. They soon became style bibles, cutting-edge manuals of all that was deemed to be cool. Fashion, nightclubs, art, pop – if it clicked, it went in.

1980 was Year Zero in terms of independent British magazine publishing, in much the same way that 1976 was Year Zero in the music industry, the date when lifestyle suddenly became an end in itself rather than a by-product of success, when teenagers became more concerned with fashion than music, and when magazine publishing houses started to realise that men and women might be able to buy the same magazines. During the Nineties, style magazines would become commonplace, fascinating little parish tip sheets called things like *Touch*, *Citizen K*, *Big*, *Scene* and *Dazed & Confused* (which was often called *The Face* of the Nineties). Not a week went by without some wide-eyed, new-moneyed fool throwing his cash at some plastic-laminated homage to the increasingly nebulous worlds of fashion, beauty, music, nightlife, politics and celebrity trivia.

Yet the style decade had an unlikely birth, one that actually happened back in the Seventies. While the success and influence of *i-D*, *The Face* and *Blitz* were so huge and so far-reaching – it would not be unfair to say that Jones and Logan changed the face of magazine publishing – there was actually a time before Year Zero, a period in the late Seventies that produced some of the most inventive magazines ever launched in Britain. Today they are long gone, available only in libraries, vintage-magazine shops and those dark corners of the Internet where few dare to venture, gone to the great reading room in the sky. They are the style magazines that time forgot.

And what wonderful things they were: *New Style*, David Bailey's and David Litchfield's *Ritz*, the slightly more cerebral and arty *ZG*, the ridiculously large (four foot by three) *Midnight*, and *Viz*, not the scatological comic, but a London-based monthly that featured what all these magazines featured: art (usually home-grown stuff by Allen Jones, Duggie Fields, Peter Blake), fashion (Antony Price, Claude Montana and a newcomer called Jean Paul Gaultier), furniture (Memphis, Tommy Roberts), sub-erotic photography, nightclub vox pops, arch celebrity profiles, restaurant reviews, gossip (back when gossip was a novelty, not a publishing genre), lots of articles about the *Rocky Horror Show*, and dozens and dozens of ads for long-forgotten King's Road boutiques. In these post-punk gazettes the motif was always leopard skin, the cultural touchstone Biba (which had closed down a few years before, in 1975), the club always the Embassy, the Bond Street haunt that was Mayfair's answer to Studio 54. In broad brushstrokes, these magazines were a cross between *Tatler* and the *New Musical Express*, a mixture of uptown and downtown, of street life and park life, of toffs and commoners colliding in a giddy world of fashion, music, cocktails and lifestyle, before lifestyle became what we know it as today.

One of the most impressive titles was *Boulevard*, a monthly large-format London-based style magazine that was launched at the end of 1978 by someone called Baron S. Bentinck. Containing the usual *Ritz/Viz/New Style* mix, *Boulevard* also had about it a certain hi-lo punk pizzazz, a certain sense of what was right for the times, a certain energy that was missing from the others. The 'baron' managed to cajole a number of soon-to-be-important people to work for him too, including photographers Helmut Newton, Michael Roberts, Terence Donovan, Neil Kirk, Johnny Rozsa and paparazzo king Richard Young; fantastically fashionable illustrators Jean-Paul Goude and Connie Jude; and writers Nik Cohn (*Boulevard* published his seminal travel story '24 Hours on 42nd Street'), Craig Brown and Nicholas Coleridge. Now the president of Condé Nast International, Coleridge, who wrote book reviews for *Boulevard*, remembers the operation with understandable fondness. 'There was a very cool atmosphere in the office,' he said – which, naturally, was situated on Sloane Street, albeit above a pub. 'There were all these friends of Duggie Fields and Andrew Logan lolling about on black vinyl desks making phone calls to their friends.'

These magazines didn't last long, as there was yet to be the kind of critical mass to support them. They were too early. All were owned by entrepreneurs acutely aware of how easily new magazines (like new restaurants) haemorrhage cash, and the stark reality of 'vanity publishing' was compounded by the fact that many of these magazines were such odd sizes that, unable to fit them on to their shelves, newsagents simply put them on the floor.

Like these magazines, I was too early too. I turned up with my portfolio of St Martin's illustrations dressed in my black leather jacket, my bondage trousers, winkle-pickers and my Kensington Market T-shirt, and sat on a black leather sofa until the 'baron' came out to tell me that the magazine was closing down.

Boulevard managed just half a dozen issues, and though *Ritz* carried on well into the Eighties, the other magazines were gone by the time the New Romantics arrived, when mass elitism, lifestyle careers and the commercialisation of youth culture became the defining elements of the early-to-mid-Eighties. The underground went overground and, with the launch of *i-D*, *The Face* and *Blitz*, suddenly far more people had the opportunity and – apparently – the desire to be a 'trendy'. Suddenly everyone was media-genic. The big difference between the style magazines of the late Seventies and early Eighties was the fact that *Viz*, *Boulevard*, *Ritz* and *New Style* were all exclusive – they were preaching to the converted, and didn't appear remotely interested in adding to their flock. They were aimed at the 'Them' crowd, that hip, smart London set who all looked as though they were living inside a Roxy Music album cover. Art students, fashion designers, hairdressers and magazine journalists, they were the London equivalent of the Warhol New Yorkers – the women trying to look like Jerry Hall (even though most of them resembled Cruella de Vil), the men trying to pass themselves off as Bryan Ferry or Antony Price. If you picked up any of these glad-mags they'd be full of photographs of Andrew Logan, Justin de Villeneuve, Derek Jarman, Zandra Rhodes, Peter York or Keith from 'Smile', the celebrity hairdresser. The congregation had a restricted membership, which is why these magazines – great though they were – ultimately failed. Unlike *Nova*, the phenomenally influential Sixties women's magazine, which eventually closed in 1975, and whose formula many of these publications tried to emulate, *Viz*, *Boulevard* and the like were unable, or unwilling, to tap into public tastes. All sizzle, then, and no sausage.

Boulevard's closing-down party was a riotous affair, with enough champagne to sink the *Titanic*. One wag, a staff writer who was a little peeved that he had just been downsized, felt he owed the owners a parting gift. And so, as he left the office that night, walking away from the boulevard of broken dreams, he called the speaking clock in Los Angeles (something you were still able to do in those days) and left the receiver off the hook. It's not known when it was replaced, but one wonders if the bill was ever paid.

In a way *Ritz* was the real harbinger of change, and the magazine that made it possible for the launch of *i-D*, *The Face* and *Blitz*, and which really kick-started celebrity and style culture in the Eighties. In the early Seventies David Bailey was briefly the photographic consultant on a magazine called *The Image*, which was edited by David Litchfield. It focused on graphic design and photography, and featured the work of Elliot Erwitt, Andy Warhol, Horst, Richard Hamilton, Allan Jones, Peter Blake, William Burroughs and Don McCullin. The magazine was how Bailey met Litchfield, and although Litchfield didn't do a lot on the title, Bailey could tell that he was pretty good at what little he did do. Which was just as well, as Bailey wanted to start his own magazine. He was sick of working for other people, for *Vogue* and the *Sunday Times*, and wanted to do something for himself, wanted to do a magazine that he was totally proud of. And *Ritz* was the magazine he came up with, a stylish fashion and photography magazine that 'evoked the style of Fred Astaire'.

Bailey wanted it to be like a newspaper, but the more he developed it the more he thought what he really wanted to do was a cross between *Interview* and *Rolling Stone*, but very much for the British market. He'd been there at the birth of both magazines, and he thought a mix of the two would be perfect for London. He wanted *Ritz* to be artier than *Interview*, and wanted it to be more positive and less cynical. He wanted all the interviews to be strictly Q&A, 'without the journalist getting in the way', said Bailey. 'I certainly didn't envisage the magazine as being full of paparazzi pictures of chinless wonders running around ripping each other's bras off.'

Bailey & Litchfield's Ritz – that was the registered name – launched in December 1976 as a monthly. It featured everyone from Bianca Jagger and Manolo Blahnik to Oliver Reed and Sylvia Kristel. One of Bailey's favourite interviews was with Orson Welles, who only said, 'No.' Another was his interview with the Queen. Bailey said, 'Oh, hi.' And she smiled and said, 'Oh, hello.' Bailey also gave the paparazzo Richard Young his first break: 'He was originally hired to do the occasional party picture but became so good that he did all the paparazzi pictures in the magazine.'

Bailey was actually on the cover of their sixth-anniversary issue in 1982, but ironically this was one of the last times he was involved with the magazine. The last issue was in 1983, number seventy-eight, but by then he was long gone.

The reason *i-D*, *Blitz* and *The Face* worked was because they were inclusive: if you wanted in, then in you were – straight through the door, and turn left at the top of the stairs. I would end up as an editor at both *The Face* and *Arena*, the men's magazine that Nick Logan launched in 1986, but it was *i-D* where I started my career, in 1983, just three years after Terry Jones launched it.

The magazine started, naturally enough, with a wink, which is often the way with relationships, particularly ones that last. A wink, a smile, and the promise of a great new tomorrow. The original idea was a simple one, something Terry Jones hatched while still art director of British *Vogue*. Terry was at *Vogue* from 1972 to 1977, only leaving when it became evident that his colleagues didn't share his enthusiasm for the fresh and exciting new direction in street style that exploded in tandem with punk. So he left the magazine, eventually starting *i-D* in the summer of 1980. Initially looking like little but a punk fanzine, *i-D* was essentially an exercise in social documentation; a catalogue of photographs of 'real' people wearing 'real' clothes, what Terry liked to call 'straight-ups'. People on the street. In bars. In nightclubs. At home. And all of them on parade. And although in the

i-D staff, October 1983. Fashion editor Caryn Franklin, production editor Marion Moisy and Dylan Jones standing behind design anarchist Terry Jones, a man who had zero respect for the etiquette of the publishing business. Jones mixed punk with fashion and came up with *i-D*, the ultimate Situationists' tip-sheet.

thirty-five years since, the magazine has developed into an internationally renowned style magazine, full of fancy photographers and the very fanciest models, this 'straight-up' element has never been lost. Above all else, *i-D* was always about people.

When it launched, *i-D* didn't look like any other magazine on the shelves, and in many respects still doesn't. Turned on its side, the *i-D* logo resembles a wink and a smile, and every cover since the first issue has featured a winking, smiling face; a theme that has given the magazine an iconic identity as strong as that developed by *Playboy* in the Fifties (which always included a bunny silhouette somewhere on the cover). I can still remember where I was when I saw the first issue, in September 1980. I saw it on a friend's desk in the first-floor second-year graphics department of St Martin's School of Art in Long Acre, Covent Garden, where I was a student. Having long been an avid reader of *New Style*, *Viz*, *Midnight*, *Boulevard*, *Ritz*, etc., as well as their American counterparts (*Interview*,

Punk) – all of which focused on tightly knit groups of micro-celebrities – it was refreshing to find something which plugged right into British subculture, a heat-seeking style sheet which found room for every fledgling youth cult in the country – from punks, soul boys and New Romantics to psychobillies, rockers and penny-ante trustafarians. Along with *The Face*, which had launched a few months previously, *i-D* was suddenly the voice of a generation: a generation with no name.

Terry Jones felt that the best way to reflect the creativity he admired in street style was through 'immediacy', through visual imagery rather than just straight text, and so the magazine used typewriter-face print, ticker tape headlines and wild, often perverse graphics. And although this was a style born of necessity as much as any ideology, it gave the magazine an identity that it preserved for over three decades.

The magazine was always A4 in size (slightly thinner than most glossies), though in the early days it was landscape as opposed to portrait and opened – somewhat annoyingly – longways. The first issue was just forty pages, stuck together with three staples, and cost 50p. A bargain. 'Fashion magazine No. 1' it said on the cover, and that was all you really needed to know. Inside were several dozen 'straight-ups' of various upwardly and downwardly mobile exhibitionists: Cerith Wyn Evans, a St Martin's student, some fairly dodgy-looking Blitz Kids, a rockabilly or two, a goth and some Teddy boys from Brighton. A girl called Pennie, interviewed about what she was wearing, had this to say about her jumper: 'I got it from some shop in Oxford Street. I can't remember the name. I get so mesmerised when I shop along Oxford Street I never notice the names.' (For the first few issues Terry allowed photographers to shoot only two frames per person, so the 35 mm contact sheets became works of art in themselves, a sort of sartorial police file.) There were also a few fashion ads from Fiorucci, Robot and Swanky Modes. It even had a manifesto of sorts: '*i-D* is a Fashion/Style Magazine. Style isn't what but how you wear clothes. Fashion is the way you walk, talk, dance and prance. Through *i-D* ideas travel fast and free of the mainstream – so join us on the run!'

Jones was keen to reflect the fact that street style was a democratic, amorphous process. And *i-D* wasn't ever, if truth be told, anything like a barometer of style. Even though the magazine originally branded itself 'The Worldwide Manual of Style', it was never – has rarely been – prescriptive. Sensibly, Terry always believed that it's important to like the bad stuff too.

'I wanted to get the concept over that we don't lay down the rules about what you wear, the idea of "in-out" fashion,' he said at the time. He was never particularly keen on drive-by journalism, not interested in ring-fencing people in arbitrary social groups. For the quintessential style magazine this was ironic, seeing that the 'style' magazines and newspaper lifestyle sections that came in its wake seemed devoted to the reductive. *i-D* has been many things – irritating, infuriating, wilfully obscure, over-extravagant and often impossible to read – but it has rarely been without substance.

In a world that soon became awash with style magazines aimed at every different type of demographic, it was easy to forget that in 1980 magazines like *i-D* just didn't exist. *i-D* was the first street-fashion magazine, a pick 'n' mix grab-bag of punk fashion and DIY style, a pop-cultural sponge soaking up everything around it with inelegant haste. During a decade when the safety net of society was gradually folded away, *i-D* catalogued a culture of self-sufficiency, even if that culture was at times only sartorial. Sure, the Eighties were the decade when 'designer' became not just a prefix but also an adjective, but it was also the decade of unreconstructed, and often rabid, individualism.

The Eighties had a lot to live up to. If the Sixties had been a decade of confrontational happiness, and the post-punk Seventies full of agents of social change, the Eighties were crowded with a generation devoted to self-empowerment and self-improvement. It was a decade that couldn't wait to get ahead of itself. Reinvention became almost a prerequisite for success as soap stars became pop stars, pop stars became politicians and politicians became indistinguishable from their *Spitting Image* puppets. Everyone was a party catalyst, everybody a star. When Andy Warhol said that in the future everyone would be famous for fifteen minutes, he wasn't simply talking about New York in 1973; he was unwittingly describing London in 1985. A vortex of entrepreneurial hedonism, London hadn't swung so much since 1966.

And *i-D* was the first magazine to hold a mirror up to what it saw, exploiting the boom in youth culture and London's burgeoning reputation as a crucible of transient young talent. In a way the magazine made a genuine – if not always coherent – attempt to return control of the fashion world to those who actually inhabited it.

I have dozens of favourite *i-D* covers – Kirsten Owen photographed by Paolo Roversi from May 1988 and Leigh Bowery shot by Johnny Rozsa from May 1987 for starters – though coincidentally, the two I like best bookend my time at the magazine. The first is Nick Knight's photograph of Sade, which was produced at the tail end of 1983, not just because it was the first issue I worked on, but also because in one small wink it said more about the Eighties than a thousand editorials ever could. Striking a defiant pose and offering an immaculate statement of intent, Sade looked as though she was about to conquer the world (and eighteen months later she did). The other cover I love is the last one I worked on, the 'smiley' cover from December 1987, which incorporated the *i-D* wink as well as heralding the advent of acid house.

As he showed by giving Madonna her first magazine cover, Terry was always good at exploiting pop, but then during the first three or four years of the Eighties, all publications were. Pop music was vital in disseminating this new visual culture of fashion and arrogance, and the emergence of the new pop groups such as Duran Duran, Frankie Goes to Hollywood, the Eurythmics, Spandau Ballet and Culture Club – who, in a move away from the punk ethos (more like a volte-face, actually), began spending their vast royalty cheques in the designer boutiques along Bond Street and the King's Road – gave rise to a new-found tabloid interest in anything to do with pop.

Suddenly the red tops latched on to the idea that pop was fashionable again. The lives and loves of Boy George, Simon Le Bon, Annie Lennox, Holly Johnson and the Kemp brothers became front-page news. The pop stars believed their own publicity too, and many – particularly Duran Duran – began living the life of dilettantes and new-moneyed aristocrats, poncing about on boats and dating catwalk models. They had taken reinvention to its natural conclusion. Five years before their huge success, they had looked as though they were made of money even though their pockets were empty; now the good life was theirs for the taking. And they took it, with both hands. Greed was good, after all, and credit so easy to come by, while dreams and wishes seemed so easily obtainable. In a way success became democratised, and worlds that had once been available only to certain sets of people became accessible to, if not everyone, at least anyone with enough luck and tenacity.

The pop world wasn't just fashionable, it was sexy too, and the arrival of androgynous celebrities such as Boy George and Annie Lennox put a whole new spin on Swinging London (British pop was then such a potent export commodity that in 1983 more than a third of all American chart places were taken by British acts). Pop stars began hanging out with fashion designers and frequenting the many nightclubs that were springing up all over the capital; PR agencies were beginning to exploit this new-found confluence of art and commerce, and the high street began taking notice of all the new money.

As pop became big business, the tabloids began encouraging readers to phone in with stories about celebrities. Had they seen one misbehaving? Had they grown up with one? Consequently the features teams of the nationals became less averse to the telephonic ramblings of overexcited readers. One night at the *Daily Mirror*, one of the phones on the news desk rang. The night editor picked it up, only to find a very excited chap on the other end.

'Hello, is that the *Daily Mirror*? It is? Oh good. I just wanted to let you know that I've invented a time machine,' said the man.

'Aha, a time machine. I see . . .' said the night editor, with a heavy heart.

'Yes, it's a rather good time machine as it goes forward in time, backwards in time, and sideways in time. It really is the most amazing thing you've ever seen.'

'Well, that certainly does sound interesting. What would you like us to do about it? How about you bring it in to show us here at the paper?'

As pop became big business, so it became front page news, and the tabloids began encouraging readers to phone in with stories about celebrities. Had they seen one misbehaving? Had they grown up with one, slept with one?

This chap can't believe his luck, and stammers for a while before answering, in a typically breathless fashion, 'Yes, absolutely. When would you like me to bring it in?'

Just a split second before he quietly replaces the receiver, the night editor says, 'Yesterday.'

In the Sixties, when class divisions in society first began breaking down, if only in a narrowcast 'pop' way, the consumer aspects were largely confined to the female market: trendy women's magazines, trendy women's shops, trendy female icons. But in the Eighties it was different, and if the decade can be remembered for anything, it should be remembered as the decade in which post-industrial man finally became liberated. If women found their sexual liberation in the Sixties, men discovered their social mobility in the Eighties – as plain old consumers. That's right, by the mid-Eighties men were starting to consume like women.

By 2010, in the UK the men's market was roughly thirty years old. In 1980 you had Paul Smith, and you had a bit of Bond Street, and a bit of activity on the high street. And that was just about it. Then in the mid-Eighties along came Next, the emergence of a strong middle market, a generation of young men encouraged by youth culture and style magazines to start buying clothes with a vengeance, and you had the explosion of a money culture which encouraged men to consume in ways they had never done before. This was the age of the yuppie, when double-breasted suits became double-barrelled suits, and making money suddenly became sexy.

The generation of young men who began shopping like women in the Eighties were egged on in their task by the emergence of *i-D, The Face* and *Blitz*, magazines that acknowledged the fact that men were as interested in Martin Scorsese as they were in New Romantic nightclubs. We were the first generation of men to see images of ourselves reflected back at us in magazine pages . . . and these reflections helped turn us into consumers.

Almost overnight we stopped being defined by our jobs and started being defined by where and how we spent our money. Did we spend our wages in Marks & Spencer, or did we spend our salaries in Armani?

And so we started investing – in clothes, in interior design, in exotic travel, in lots of things that we bought in order to make ourselves feel better about our lives. Even if we didn't have proper jobs. Even if we were running up debt. This was the designer decade, a decade in which all men were encouraged to begin consuming in a way that women had done for years.

By the end of the decade, the lifestyle explosion had reached saturation point, with even street style morphing into its own designer reflection. Doc

Martens were no longer the boots of the disenfranchised but were worn by everyone from seventeen-year-old bricklayers to forty-five-year-old architects, from schoolgirls to ageing rock stars. Distressed leather jackets were just as likely to be found on the backs of advertising executives as they were on biker boys. People had done just about everything with their hair, with their clothes and with their bodies, piercing all the parts it is possible to skewer. As the American performer and comedian Sandra Bernhard said, there was not much more people could do to themselves 'unless they start wearing lumber'. Recycled nostalgia was now the thing, and in a postmodern age of arbitrary gesture and kitsch 'n' sink subculture, urban tribes were ten a penny.

By the end of the Eighties, everyone was a trendy of some description, comparatively speaking. Everyone was codified and hip to the modern world, while elitism was becoming increasingly fetishistic. Odd. Weird. Uncalled for. Why be wilfully different when you could consume with impunity? For many who came through the Eighties unscathed and successfully negotiated the perilous contours of the new face of consumerism and the free-market economy, life was good. Very, very good indeed. And many people – those living in the right postcodes, at least – saw how easy it was to become the people they had pretended to be all those years ago.

Sade were certainly those people, as they had escaped the clubs and hit the big time. When they walked out on to the Wembley stage on 13 July, they had to pinch themselves. Here was a band who had shot out of nowhere, and who seemingly only five minutes ago had been playing snotty little club gigs in Soho. For the band it was an incredibly important gig as it was so early in their career. They had only started to be on magazine covers during the last eighteen months, and the prospect of performing in front of so many people was daunting to say the least. Essentially they were only worried about their own performance. The likes of Status Quo, Queen and Elton John were used to playing stadiums, but not bands like Sade.

'To be honest I just remember being quite nervous and in hindsight I wish I'd spent more time there,' said the band's keyboard player Andrew Hale. 'We arrived, were shepherded in, amongst all these people backstage, and it was all a blur. I really wanted to see how amazing it was

One of the contrary things about Sade – and Sade was always a band – was their almost total ambivalence towards success, and no sooner had they conquered the world – one, two, three times – than they would run back home again.

but we were all swept up in it.'

They didn't allow themselves to get involved, however. Having only recently escaped clubland, they weren't about to compromise themselves by doing high-fives with Phil Collins or hanging out with Status Quo. They had an arrogance that had kept them in a bubble since they were signed by Epic Records in 1983. Although by the time they got to Wembley that day, they actually wanted to hang out with the more established bands. Inverted snobbery meant they kept themselves to themselves.

'We were honoured to be asked, although there was a discussion about whether or not it would be good for us to do it,' said Hale. 'There was a sort of arrogance about our generation, and we felt apart from these older rock people getting together and back-slapping. To be honest, I think I do have regrets about the Eighties, because I think we could have collaborated more, and maybe not been so stand-offish. We spent a lot of time avoiding each other, not necessarily socially, but I think this was actually self-defeating.'

They knew they were going to be good, though. 'We had "Is It A Crime?", which was a strong, anthemic song, and we knew it was perfect for Wembley. I think we were very confident about that song as it was so dynamic.'

And guess what? It worked. The whole set worked. The band may have behaved as though they were still playing in the dank, low-ceilinged room at Soho's Ronnie Scott's, yet the crowd lapped them up. They had no experience of playing stadiums, yet the Wembley video screens semaphored Sade's innate beauty. Sade used her arms – gesticulating wildly – opened her mouth wide when emphasising particular words, and shimmied like Eartha Kitt. They started, defiantly, with 'Why Can't We Live Together', their popular cover of the old Timmy Thomas hit from their *Diamond Life* album. Sade stood there in her thin white polo neck, her massive hoop earrings, her red-slashed lips, her black designer beaded bolero jacket and her matching slacks, looking for all the world like the world's most glamorous shop assistant. Some of the rest of the band wore suits, the kind that could have been worn to a job interview or the opening of Soho's latest club extravaganza. They were deliberately still, too, nodding nonchalantly, imperceptibly swaying in the breeze. They were, as Samuel Coleridge wrote, 'as idle as a painted ship upon a painted ocean'.

'I remember being in the pit for Sade, and thinking, "What a goddess", and thinking how great she looked,' said Bernard Doherty. 'She was so anti-rock 'n' roll, but she was one of the best performances of the day. The audience reaction was amazing – they love her.'

As they launched into 'Your Love Is King' the crowd roared, acknowledging the fact that many of them had spent every Friday night for the last six months listening to the song as they tucked into their Indian takeaway and sipped their Piat d'Or. Sade had been phenomenally successful, and it gave the crowd and those watching on TV some validation that they had made the right decision by buying their records. Lordy, they were on stage at Live Aid! The crowd roared again when the video screens showed her in close up, her humungous earrings looking as though they'd been excavated from Tutankhamen's tomb. Halfway through the song she slipped off her jacket and the crowd roared yet again, an isolated acknowledgement that Sade was indeed a woman, and that the incremental shedding of her clothes could only be a good thing. As soon as the jacket was off, we saw that her top was backless, injecting a little bit more sex appeal into the show, and into the day. There were so few women appearing at Live Aid, that its collective libido was insignificant; in this context Sade's appearance was positively libidinous.

'I'm beyond flagging,' she said later in the day, when she was interviewed by Mark Ellen for the BBC broadcast. 'It's been fairly nerve-wracking for everyone involved. It's such a massive thing, and it's a bit like school sports day, the feeling [backstage] behind the scenes. It's a great success.'

When Ellen asked her how it was to walk out on to the stage, he intimated that she must be used to it by now.

'Oh yes,' she replied, smiling. 'Every week we play in front of 80,000 people . . .'

Then, recovering, 'I'm always nervous when I go on stage, but I don't think I was more nervous today, because there was quite a lot of spirit, with everybody. It's been so big, so vast, that you can't comprehend it. Therefore it feels quite small in a way. The most impressive thing was everyone's spirit, all pulling together.'

SEVEN

**Sting and Phil Collins (with Branford Marsalis):
'Roxanne', 'Driven To Tears', 'Against All Odds (Take A Look
At Me Now)', 'Message In A Bottle', 'In The Air Tonight',
'Long Long Way To Go', 'Every Breath You Take'**

Howard Jones: 'Hide And Seek'

I have been perceived as an arrogant person, but I don't
see that. I think I have a lot of self-esteem. I'm successful,
I'm happy. I stand on my own two feet. I've always been
confident, and even when I wasn't I could pretend that I was.
I have always been able to mask my fears, which is what I
suppose was perceived as arrogance.

STING

The middle of the afternoon was so Eighties. What could sum up the
decade better than Phil Collins playing with Sting, supported by –
gasp, a jazzer, a real one! – Branford Marsalis, a genuine sprinkling of
cool. This was a veritable Radio 1 Roadshow, with lots of heartfelt emotion
and pained expressions. And they were all wearing white! Lordy! Looking
at them from way back in the stadium, they looked as though they'd just
stepped off the plane from Ibiza; no one would have been surprised if they

had taken off their espadrilles and shaken out the sand. That would have been a moment: two of the biggest rock stars in the world – and at the time there were few who could top them – giving each other an old-fashioned look as they recalled what they'd got up to on holiday.

Instead they ploughed through their hits, moving between them with ease. Jeez, they had had so many hits between them that they could have been there until the stadium closed for the night. Forget U2 and Dire Straits and Elton and Queen and Paul McCartney and all the others, we could have just stared at Sting and Phil bashing out their stuff till the sun went down. There were many in the crowd who would have been happy to see that, too. Maybe not my friend Robin, my girlfriend Kate or myself, although everyone seemed fairly up for it.

We shared a dislike of both of them, thinking them unreasonably smug. Looking back now, I think this was inverted snobbery more than anything else (we would all happily sing along to their records in the car), as we were possibly just twenty-four-year-olds being too cool for school. We had come to Live Aid because we knew it was going to be important, and because we would have been mad to have been anywhere else, and because we believed in it, although none of us had any interest in seeing Phil Collins or Sting.

There was something irrational about our dislike for them both, yet there it was, as large as life. There were no other Eighties pop stars who were as reviled as they were revered, no other pop stars who drew as much flak as they drew acclaim. Sting came across as a pretty boy trying to save the rain forest wherever he went – even if wherever he went didn't actually have one – while Collins just came across as a cab driver who got lucky, and who then wanted everyone to treat him as a deity. Neither perception is especially accurate, yet that's how many of us felt. They would forever be inextricably linked because of Live Aid, yet they were actually very different people, with Sting espousing humanitarian causes, and Collins trying to carve himself out a niche as an everyman.

The rise of politically motivated 'alternative comedy' in the early Eighties would become a phenomenon, and its ubiquity was as much of a talking point as the comedians themselves. Self-righteous Sting was often a target, a liberal who made rather more of his humanitarian angst than perhaps he should have. The British comedians had a huge influence abroad, too, especially in the US, where the likes of Bill Hicks and Sam Kinison would turn the barbed political comedy being pumped out by the Comic Strip into something far more aggressive. These comics in turn influenced the stand-up Denis Leary, who would soon turn against Sting in a major way. Leary's reactionary, high-octane humour, a flippant, quip-slinging tirade against liberals, rock music, environmentalists and the health police ('I represent angry, gun-toting, meat-eating people, OK!') was perfect for the likes of Sting.

'I think rock 'n' roll's taking itself a little too seriously,' Leary said. 'They made a two-hour movie about the Doors. Do we need this? I could sum it up for you in five seconds: I'm drunk, I'm nobody. I'm drunk, I'm famous. I'm drunk, I'm dead. They're just taking things too far. Guys in bands take themselves more seriously than the Pope. Railing against pretentiousness is organic, it's no great insight. Rock stars should know better. I only repeat on stage what other people say about Sting when they sit around watching him on TV. I'm not a fan of rock music per se. I liked rock music before there was video. I remember the first time I saw the Clash as clearly as I do performing on stage for the first time.'

In the gung-ho Eighties, mainstream American culture tended to be devoted to the young, a phenomenon exemplified in Hollywood and its satellite industries by the rise and subsequent demise of the Brat Pack. During the protracted decade of greed (as many saw it), if you couldn't aspire to wealth, then the next best thing was youth, and it was this hypocrisy that irritated Leary so much.

And Sting hated him almost as much as he hated Sting. In 1993, Sting would call Leary a cunt in an interview with *Rolling Stone*. He said, 'I saw Denis Leary deconstruct me on television. He said, "Sting singing about saving the fucking rainforest – he should save his fucking hair." I want to meet Denis Leary in about ten years. "Hey, Denis, how's it feel, you bald cunt."'

Sting was a difficult man to warm too, though. I interviewed him just a few years after Live Aid, and he gave the impression of a man who was still acting as though he'd just walked off the Wembley stage. On the wall in the ground-floor lavatory of his Highgate cottage there was a framed newspaper cartoon of two tired businessmen sitting mournfully at a bar. One is saying to the other: 'Oh, I'm pretty happy. I just wish my life was more like Sting's.'

At the time, who wouldn't? Here was a man who appeared to have everything: looks, talent, money, creative success, even – some would say – a conscience. But did he have respect? Though he was still enormously popular, he was also strangely reviled. He had become the man it was OK to hate, the pretentious rock star with an ego the size of Brazil.

At the time of Live Aid he had it all. He had already sold over 70 million albums (both with and without the Police), and was apparently worth north of £80 million. He was happily married to Trudie Styler, and had four children, including two from his previous relationship with Frances Tomelty. He was a committed, and very public, philanthropist, and had devoted a lot of time to the environmental pressure group The Rainforest Foundation, in which his wife had also been a driving force.

There was the property, too – houses in London, New York and LA. The trappings of success seemed to suit Sting perfectly. And why shouldn't they have had? Sometimes he had been his own worst enemy. In 1992, after twelve years, he finally married Styler, the actress turned film producer, daughter of a packer in a lampshade factory. She attended the service dressed in a £20,000 Versace gown, riding on a white charger led by her fiancé. Sting wore a Regency buck tailcoat nipped at the waist and cut away to reveal matching neckerchief – all designed by Versace. As an exercise in bad taste, it was exemplary.

Of course, he became a star in the age of presentation, and he took to this like a duck to water. After all, he was a pragmatist at heart: in the Police days, Sting had no qualms about dying his hair for a chewing-gum commercial.

But self-deprecation was not his forte: 'I have been perceived as an arrogant person, but I don't see that,' he told me. 'I think I have a lot of self-esteem. I'm successful, I'm happy. I stand on my own two feet. I've always been confident, and even when I wasn't I could pretend that I was. I have always been able to mask my fears, which is what I suppose was perceived as arrogance.'

And still was, I feared. Is this why we disliked him so? Was it simply envy, that particularly insidious English disease, or were we right to be annoyed by what appeared to us to be his ridiculous pomposity?

The man himself had heard it all before. 'I react to criticism pretty well. It used to annoy me and I used to write back to the journalist involved, but not any more. Once you've done one interview you've signed a pact with the devil, so you have to take what comes.'

So why was he so disliked? Well, it could be because he said things like this: 'Mistakes? Well, I don't think I've made any, do you? I suppose I might have done things which were perceived as mistakes by my critics – the odd movie, the odd shirt – but musically I really don't think I've made any. Can you think of one?'

According to Midge Ure, Sting had originally planned to do his Live Aid set with his full band. 'His musicians – who were all black – demanded payment before they went on stage. Sting told them to fuck off and promptly walked on stage with just a guitar, where he did an impromptu set opening with "Roxanne". Yet after the concert we were all lambasted for not having enough black artists on the bill. It became this anticolonial diatribe, "You whities, telling us poor black guys what to do." It was unfair but it happened. We couldn't get any black superstar to perform at either concert and it wasn't for lack of trying. We asked Prince, Stevie Wonder, Diana Ross and Michael Jackson, who were all otherwise engaged or not interested in doing it. As a result a wealth of American artists missed out on being part of Live Aid.'

He may have done the right thing before walking on stage, but to all of us in the cheap seats, he was still the arrogant king of pop. Sting walked on like he was making a cameo appearance in Michael Mann's *Miami Vice*, and a sense of brash entitlement that chimed perfectly with the yuppie notions of success that Sting appeared to embrace.

We even made a joke about it, Robin, Kate and me, saying how ridiculous it was that Sting looked the way he did, as though he'd just come off set, and had only recently been preening himself in front of the *Miami Vice* cameras. Every time he strummed a meaningful chord, perfectly captured a note or looked out enigmatically at the audience, we imagined him walking back on set, smiling at the continuity girl, quickly taking his shirt off, and waiting to be admired.

It was just too too perfect!

What I didn't realise – what none of us realised, obviously – was that his and Phil's duet 'Long Long Way To Go' was actually used in the series, in episode twenty-three of series two, to be precise, which was broadcast that very year. The song was also included on Collins's album, *No Jacket Required* and was one of three to be featured in the show, along with 'Take Me Home', which appeared in the premiere of the second season, and 'The Man With The Horn', which was rewritten for an episode in which Collins guest-starred as a con artist involved with cocaine distributors. At the time, embedding current pop songs in TV shows and movies was seen as the height of sophistication, but even then we thought it was a little bit self-aggrandising and rather naff. Much like the programme itself.

Miami Vice ran from 1984 to 1990, not only changing the way police detectives were portrayed on screen – Italian-casual clothes, sports cars and sexy boats, art deco buildings full of Memphis-style apartments (no 'earth tones' were ever allowed to be used by the art director) – but also using rock music, and rock stars in cameo (James Brown, Phil Collins, Miles Davis, the Power Station and dozens more), as a way of giving the stars of the show, Don Johnson and Philip Michael Thomas, a wash of cool. Visually, *Miami Vice* was one of the most influential television shows of the decade, and, by association, was often used as an example of how homogeneous traditional rock music had become.

Which is probably one of the many different reasons we didn't like it.

Everyone on the show seemed to wear T-shirts underneath unstructured Armani-style jackets, pastel linen trousers, sockless loafers and Ray-Ban Wayfarers (which experienced unprecedented growth after their exposure on the programme). Designer stubble was out in force, too, although, in a decade when provenance took on an unseemly importance, it's still not clear whether George Michael or Don Johnson got there first.

In certain respects Michael Mann can be held responsible for how much of the Eighties looked. His work was full of surface sheen, shiny flat surfaces, and the bright dynamic shades of aspiration. There was a rich 2D quality to it, almost as though each frame had started life as a spread in a fashion magazine, in *Harper's Bazaar*, *L'Uomo Vogue* or *Interview*. Movies were already being cut to imitate music videos, and many of the chase sequences in *Miami Vice* could have easily slipped on to MTV without anyone noticing. In fact, maybe they did. His establishing shots looked for all the world as though they were real-estate commercials, architectural tours of postmodern idylls. Those for whom the Eighties were little but a way of denigrating the great cultural strides of the Sixties and Seventies felt that this imagery was deliberately reductive, and while it is certainly true that what many in the image business were obsessed with at the time

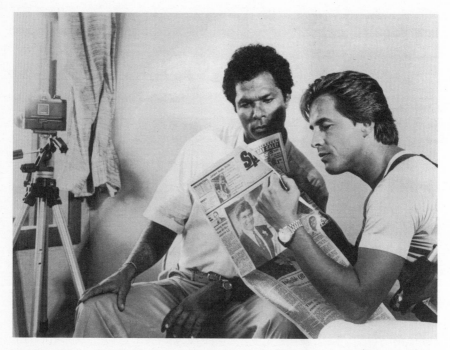

Miami Vice gave its stars, Don Johnson and Philip Michael Thomas, a wash of cool, incorporating unstructured Armani-style jackets, pastel linen trousers, sockless loafers and Ray-Ban Wayfarers (which experienced unprecedented growth after their exposure on the programme).

was rounding the sharp edges – metaphorical or otherwise – that had been before, what many forget is that technology had changed the quality of film beyond recognition, making the DNA of Eighties imagery completely at odds with anything made before it.

Mann's work, and the work of so many other directors at the time, needed good-looking, sullen heroes, part of a through-line that stretched from Clint Eastwood as the Man With No Name in the Sixties right through to Ryan Gosling in *Drive*, in 2011. Arnold Schwarzenegger could only have become a star in the Eighties, as the *Star Wars* generation was far more at ease with leading men being little but ciphers, or cartoons.

For instance, a film such as *Top Gun* – basically a long-form recruitment ad starring Tom Cruise in mirrored sunglasses – was quintessential Eighties fare, being largely a collection of brilliantly edited short, sharp shocks given a sexy, MTV patina. *Top Gun* was produced by Don Simpson and Jerry Bruckheimer, who were credited with the creation of the high-concept picture blockbuster, and for being the first producers to really understand and exploit the significance of MTV.

'MTV had made all British acts so internationally famous,' said Gary Kemp. 'Up until MTV started, the only kids making decent videos were the British kids, and it got just pipe-fed around the world. When I first went to New York in '81, it was just like a fashion vacuum, and when we went back in '83, everyone was wearing what we were wearing. And the leaders of all of this were definitely the British. That's why Live Aid was more influential than Live 8 as by the time of Live Aid, all the British acts were known around the world. Unlike Robbie Williams.'

The modern Hollywood blockbuster (those high-concept movies whose plots could be written on the back of a Marlboro packet; sometimes there was room for at least two on each side) was actually created halfway through the Seventies with films such as *Jaws* (1975), *Saturday Night Fever* (1977), *Star Wars* (1977) and *Alien* (1979) – famously known in high-concept terms as 'Jaws in Space'. These loud, flashy, simplistic, and highly storyboarded films became the template for the industry. If you look at *Flashdance* (1983) – with its high-density pop soundtrack and iconic 'freeze-frame' ending –

or *Beverly Hills Cop* (1984) – 'fish out of water' – *Top Gun* (1986) or *Days of Thunder* (1990) – er, stock car racing – you'll see high-concept movies with quick-cut editing, pop songs and sheen. Messages were simple and writ large, while nuance and ambiguity were banished to the cheap seats in the back of the stalls.

Just like *Miami Vice*.

If anyone personified the generic Eighties rock star it was Sting, a good-looking, rather imperious man with a glamorous day job. He took care of himself – a little too well for most people – and had started to take his top off at every available opportunity. The Police were initially laughed at by the music press, yet when they became the biggest group in the world thanks to a succession of amazingly well-crafted pop-reggae singles, they couldn't ignore them. It was only when Sting decided to go solo, around the time of Live Aid, that things started to go wrong. Largely because a lot of people found him a little too smug for his own good. Sting had a touch of the Noel Edmonds about him, even if he did write gloriously catchy songs. Oddly enough that didn't make much difference. After all, imagine how much you would have loathed Noel Edmonds if he had suddenly developed the talent to write something so clever and as life-affirming as 'Every Breath You Take'?

It was certainly Sting's signature song, and was liked even by those who tended to dismiss his work as anodyne and overcooked (a combination that was something of an achievement in itself). The single was one of the biggest hits of 1983, topping the UK singles chart for four weeks, and the *Billboard* Hot 100 singles chart for eight. Sting won 'Song of the Year' and the Police won 'Best Pop Performance by a Duo or Group with Vocal' at the Grammy Awards of 1984 for the song. It was ranked number eighty-four on the *Rolling Stone* list of the 500 Greatest Songs of All Time and number twenty-five on *Billboard*'s Hot 100 All-Time Top Songs. So popular is it that it is meant to generate between a quarter and a third of Sting's publishing income.

'I woke up in the middle of the night with that line ['Every breath you take, every move you make'] in my head, sat down at the piano and had written it in half an hour. The tune itself is generic, an aggregate of hundreds of others, but the words are interesting. It sounds like a comforting love song. I didn't realise at the time how sinister it is. I think I was thinking of Big Brother, surveillance and control.'

Sting likes to say that he thinks the song's ugly as it catalogues an obsession with a lost lover. 'People have misinterpreted it as being a gentle, little love song.'

Still, a signature song is a signature song, and even though it was barely two years old, Sting knew he would never write anything that resonates as much. Which is why he was determined to play it at Live Aid, solo or not.

He told *Playboy* the show was nothing less than an extraordinary event, a show that demanded big tunes. 'It sounds like a cliché, but it really was a wonderful day for rock 'n' roll,' he said. 'Even if no money got through, I think the symbol of goodwill and co-operation and togetherness was so important, it was useful in itself. Beyond that, however, we also raised so much money that I'm confident it will get through, which makes it that much more important. Everyone said it was our generation's Woodstock, and it was, but I think it was more important than Woodstock. It dealt with a wider range of things: we saw how the media can be used for good. We learned how much we can accomplish if we bypass the political process. In fact, we learned to hold the political process in some contempt, since governments have not been able to confront the issue of starvation. Yet here were people who got together, galvanised by Bob Geldof, and did something. We've always heard that rock 'n' roll could change the world. That's starting to mean something.'

He wasn't so concerned about the possibility of the money not ending up where it was supposed to, either.

'This is the most publicly accountable charity in history because of the high profile of everyone involved. Everyone is watching what will happen. Any of us can ask where the money has gone and will be answered in detail. If one penny is missing, we know who to hang.

'Before this experience, when British musicians got together, there was a lot of prejudice and fear of one another – all of that dissolved. The English rock scene has always been pretty gladiatorial: you all hate one another.

Unlike the US part of the Live Aid concert, all of us in England shared the same backstage area, so I was standing there with David Bowie and Freddie Mercury and, of course, Phil Collins, with whom I did a set, and all of us were sharing the same piece of sheet music – so this was very special.'

At the time he was also asked his impression of some of his Live Aid peers:

David Bowie: 'Most modern bands are facsimiles of Bowie. A lot of singers are imitators of Bowie.'

Mick Jagger: 'I like Mick. But knowing him, I find it hard to judge his work. My prejudices evaporate. And rock 'n' roll is too hard a lift for me to come down hard on people.'

Pete Townshend: 'Townshend shows us it's all right to grow up. There is dignity after rock 'n' roll.'

Paul McCartney: 'I worry about McCartney. I think he isn't sure what to do any more. There is fear of growing up in rock 'n' roll, of progressing, of experimenting, of incorporating what one has learned. McCartney is a genius in many ways, but I think he should push himself to do work that's more serious. His Beatles work was as important as Lennon's was – more important, in some cases – and he is one of the people in the world who could take more risks. If you have already accomplished a certain amount, you want to move ahead and break new ground. Another thing about McCartney: I thought his choice of song for Live Aid was a bit odd. He did "Let It Be" – but the whole point of the concert was to do something, to change things, to not let it be.'

Some would say that Sting was overly arrogant in criticising McCartney, especially as his own work tended to verge on the pretentious, but there were as many who agreed with him, and who liked the way Sting continually stuck his blond spikes above the parapet. Saliently, Sting knew the importance of Live Aid, and could see how it was going to change the music industry. 'It changed the entertainment world in a heartbeat,' he told me, when I interviewed him eight years after Live Aid. 'It basically raised the bar in terms of ambition. No longer was it OK just to make a generation-defining record, now there had to be a purpose to it. I can definitely see that it changed the way people made records.'

It certainly encouraged the music industry to look away from frail-looking synth duos and concentrate instead on the kind of rock acts who could carve themselves a proper stadium career. After Live Aid, no record company wanted another Nik Kershaw, or another Yazoo. They wanted another U2, another Sting.

Gary Kemp loved Sting, and loved his performance on the day. 'I remember watching Sting on stage at Live Aid and being brilliant. I remember his solo versions of "Every Breath You Take" and "Roxanne" being extraordinary. Everyone did a sharp intake of breath at his obvious talent. He wandered out there with no show, casually as you like and he pulled it off. He shone.'

Phil Collins shone too, at least according to those who liked Phil Collins. Which was a lot of people, as Sting's Live Aid brother-in-arms was slightly more tolerable to most people.

'Bob told me he really wanted Phil Collins to perform, and asked me to sort it out,' said Harvey Goldsmith. 'This was only two weeks before the show. He was being managed by my ex-business partner, Tony Smith, so I phoned Tony and I said, "Come on Tony, you've got to get Phil to do this." He phoned me back fifteen minutes later and he said, "Phil said he would do it, but . . ." and I said, "Go on . . ." and he said, "But he wants to do both shows. He wants to play Wembley *and* Philadelphia." So I said, "Ok done." It suddenly dawned on me, being a huge fan of Concorde myself, that we could use Concorde to fly between the two gigs. I loved it, used to live on it, and was fairly sure we could make it happen. I phoned up BA and I think it took ten minutes; I said we'd fill the plane up with press, and they loved the idea. They were trying to put pressure on the Americans to get better slots so they thought this would help.'

It was no surprise that Geldof had wanted Collins to perform; after all, this was a man who, since weaning himself off Genesis, for whom he had been drumming for a decade, and where he had successfully replaced Peter Gabriel as their front man in 1976, had racked up a simply extraordinary number of hits. Since 1981's 'In The Air Tonight' he had scored with 'I Missed Again', 'If Leaving Me Is Easy', 'Thru These Walls', 'You Can't Hurry Love', 'I Don't Care Anymore', 'Don't Let Him Steal Your Heart Away', 'Why Can't It Wait 'Til Morning', 'I Cannot Believe It's True', 'Against All Odds (Take a Look at Me Now)', 'Easy Lover' and 'Sussudio'. The man was a little bald hit factory, and a lot of people loved him for it.

He was also personally aggrieved that the press and many of his peers despised him so. He was once in the *Juke Box Jury* studio at the BBC and had just said that he quite liked the new (and very dreadful) Sigue Sigue Sputnik single. The singer Martin Degville – who had a pair of fishnet tights pulled tight over his face, trying hard to mix the aggression of punk with the fancy dress of the New Romantics – came up to Collins and said, bold as brass, 'God! We must have really got it wrong if you like us!'

Collins was flabbergasted, and started opening and closing his mouth like a goldfish.

'What's wrong with me?' he asked. 'I mean if Phil Collins likes it, it must be shit – right? Eh?'

'I went through a period where I apologised for being nice,' said Collins. 'But now I say what's wrong with being a decent human being? I don't particularly want to go around hitting people just to make me appear like everyone else.'

While he had had ridiculous worldwide success by aiming squarely at the mainstream, he hated being called a family entertainer, and hated it even more when people called him ugly.

'It's a cheap shot. I mean Joe Jackson – he's fucking ugly and no one has a go at him about it. Well, y'know, I look at him and I think well if I'm ugly, what the fuck is he? I was in Houston on tour five years ago and I read this article that said Phil Collins looks uncannily like Bob Hoskins . . . OK, fair enough, I suppose I do look a little like him. Now a couple of days later I read another article that went, "Phil Collins is the Danny DeVito of pop music" – right? I mean that's a little far out! I mean that's a little cruel!' Later he would say, 'I don't look like most sex gods. On my last tour I accumulated some amazing descriptions in reviews: stocky, balding, chubby, stout, urchin, elf, gnome! But I would never feel comfortable wiggling my bottom and dressing up in poncy clothes.'

As for Live Aid, 'Well, it was a matter of doing something or doing nothing,' he said, pointing out that the US concert was rather more rarefied than its British counterpart. 'On the other side of the Atlantic you had that "We Are The World" thing which was champagne and caviar and it was strange. Americans do things in a different way, but I'm sure that Quincy Jones's and Diana Ross's hearts are in the right place – it's just that the show had this um, ostentatious sheen to it. Backstage you could hear these stories of people telling Bill Graham, you get me on this bill or I'm afraid you're not going to get my tour – there wasn't that in this country, and it's very easy to be cynical about the whole thing. All I know is that I did it for the right reasons and so did a lot of other people.'

As soon as Collins left the Wembley stage he was whisked off to Noel Edmonds' helicopter, who piloted the chopper all the way to Heathrow, where the drummer caught Concorde – rerouted so it could fly over Wembley – to JFK airport, where he would then fly on to Philadelphia, to the JFK stadium. There he would provide backing for Eric Clapton, as well as the re-formed Led Zeppelin.

On the flight, he encountered Cher.

'All the baggage handlers came out to wave goodbye, then we took off in Concorde,' said Collins. 'Cher was on the flight, just heading back to the States. I'd never met her before so I went over and said hello – you know, "Hi, I bought 'I Got You Babe'!" – and she asked what was going on. I told her about Live Aid and she asked whether I could get her on. I told her to just turn up.'

He landed in New York, said his goodbyes to Cher and headed to Philadelphia. At the time he thought he was just playing with Jimmy Page and Robert Plant, but when he arrived he realised it was a full-on Zeppelin reunion, and that he would be playing drums alongside the Chic drummer, Tony Thompson. 'I'd always heard that individually these guys were great, but together there was this black cloud that appeared. I talked to Tony Thompson about playing with two drummers [something that Collins had

had great experience of, in both Brand X and Genesis] and I really got the impression that he didn't want me to be there. As soon as I got up on stage I could see it was going to be a weird one. Tony Thompson was just playing whatever he wanted. But then the essence of the day was about being there and doing the best you can, up to your neck in muck and bullets.'

By the time he'd finished Collins was bushed, and thinking he might collapse if he stayed for the finale, went back to his hotel in New York. He got there just in time to catch the end of the show on TV, and to see Cher on stage singing 'We Are The World'.

'She'd just turned up!'

Soon after Sting and Phil had gone, and at ten minutes to four, Howard Jones hopped on to the Wembley stage, playing his 1984 hit 'Hide And Seek', encouraging the crowd to sing along with the chorus. His set wasn't any kind of aesthetic triumph, and in effect was rather unremarkable, save for his ginger mullet and oversized jacket, which looked as though it had been made for a man at least twice his size. Howard Jones was as Eighties as glass bricks or shoulder pads. In fact that day his shoulder pads were so big you could be forgiven for thinking they were actually stuffed with glass bricks. Anyway, regardless of what he was wearing, he radiated mediocrity. During his performance we were all swallowing yawn after yawn after yawn, so boring was it. We swallowed because you really didn't feel as though you could openly mock poor old Howard as there were obviously so many people in the audience who were enjoying him, so who was to say they were wrong? But there it was, we swallowed. This was one of the few parts of the show that seemed genuinely embarrassing, and the only way to cope with it was by pretending it wasn't happening.

Compared to Howard Jones, Phil Collins almost looked like a pop star. Sure, he may have had a receding hairline and an almost comical scowl, but in a way he was already responsible for the soundtrack of the Eighties.

On both sides of the Atlantic.

Even though they hated to hear it, both Phil Collins and Sting knew that they somehow exemplified the yuppie culture of the Eighties. There was a point during the decade – roughly about 1984 – when it became unfashionable to care too much about culture. It's a terrifying thought in hindsight – in fact it was a terrifying thought then – but there was very much a feeling among those who had bought into elements of the fast-growing money culture that 'culture' per se was simply only content, there to be consumed in the same way as food or petrol, according to your income bracket. Taste didn't really come into it. In this culture, success was deemed to be more important than intent, as was the ability to surf the zeitgeist. And as Sting and Phil Collins were both successful, and both devoid of any nasty edges which may have alienated them from any part of their consumer database, they were perceived to be 'on-message' and devoured accordingly.

This was not the sort of culture that should have produced Live Aid; far from it in fact.

'Live Aid was a spaceship that landed in the middle of a culture that deemed greed to be good, where young people twigged that the purpose of life was to have a Porsche, wear red braces and work in the City, which was completely fine with me always, the loads-of-money characters who were emblematic of the Eighties,' said Bob Geldof. 'To be eighteen and have a fucking Porsche, to have the babes and the champagne – good on you, mate, but don't be a twat about it. There are other things. You're in the middle of the correction of Thatcherism where industrial society can no longer pertain, it just simply can't.'

Geldof's pet theory about the Seventies and Eighties has always been the links between punk rock and Thatcherism, and the fact that the punks were the result of the failure of the post-war collective consensus. To this extent he has often said that Johnny Rotten was simply Margaret Thatcher in drag.

'Without question, the Sex Pistols were the real deal, and for me the only real deal of punk,' said Geldof. 'This beautiful nihilism, this utter rejection of everything, Johnny's brilliant mind articulated that perfectly. People said it was a sneer, but it was so knowing, it was so funny, it was so brilliant apropos everything he said. You had a generation which was clearly saying there is no future, no future in England's dreaming, which Thatcher thought too. The Sex Pistols actually articulated something real, something that was actually going to affect the whole country, while all the Clash ever had was slogans. They were referring to a past politics that was no longer relevant. That's why I never got along with them and all their clichéd sloganising. I never got it. For me the Clash became everything they looked and sounded like with *London Calling*. But that took a while to get there. That's the great album, that's when they become, for me, the Clash.'

For Geldof, it was the Sex Pistols who mattered, or at least Johnny Rotten's take on the downfall of Britain's manufacturing base, and inability to stand up for itself in the world any more.

'All of this stew that happened was really a precursor of the Thatcher revolution, and they're quite right, it should have been exactly like that, because the job of an artist is to articulate what society is thinking and how it is feeling long before society knows that it's doing that. So when you hear it, that's it. When you heard 'Anarchy In The UK', you just went: fuck, that's exactly correct! All the noise, the lyrics, the laugh at the beginning, 'Right now,' with the laugh, the bitter laugh – it's all perfect. It was just so of its moment. That's the job of an artist, and even though the artists don't always consciously do that, on this occasion for me it prefigured this demand for change, this fucking, outright demand that something has to happen. You had all this bollocks with Jim Callaghan allowing the unions to wander in and out of Downing Street demanding ever more improbable things and threatening to shut the country down.

'There was a sense that things had to change, but no one expected it to come out of the right, and to be a woman with a fucking handbag. And why I say she's Johnny in drag is because she swiped at every institution that was there: her own party; the hierarchy; the monarchy; the unions, all of it was to be bashed. As for England, whether anyone likes it or not, the old industrialised nation had gone. Everyone understood that if you could get coal for 40p in Poland then there was no way we could subsidise it here. It's over. If South Koreans are making knives at fraction of what we're making them for, then I'm not going to buy a fucking knife from Sheffield when I can get a Korean one. It's over. And, dude, it's a tragedy what's happening in the villages, in the mining towns. But why are you striking so that your kid can go down a fucking hole, hit a rock face with a pickaxe when he should be going to college, which is why this whole edifice was created: to allow precisely that, a healthy child, educated, goes on to university and provides for the new economy.'

At the time, Geldof was on the TV chat-show circuit, and he used to continually bump into Arthur Scargill, a man he soon began to loathe. 'This guy was leading his people into oblivion. He was a genuine egomaniac, who didn't have his people's best interests at heart at all. He just liked being in front of the TV cameras. Deindustrialisation was all around him, yet he couldn't see it.' If Tony Blair's job would be to put a human face on the reality of economic transformation, it was Thatcher's to force open the door and push it through. Geldof saw at the time what it took many on the left decades to come to terms with – i.e. the inevitability of it all.

'It was a terribly politicised period, because we were in the middle of this revolution. Every single thing, if you remember, was politicised to the nth. There was not a pub conversation that wasn't politicised. We were all in this angry, cruel, bitter moment of politics, and it's not fair to visit it on one individual; it was going to happen one way or another. Of course there was great sympathy for those in the industrialised sector who were losing their jobs, but it was going to happen anyway. And if the left were really leading the charge, then how do you explain Thatcher's three landslide victories?'

It was into this environment that Geldof's spaceship landed, in a way offering an alternative to the market forces changing the economic and cultural shape of the country. 'It was all of us saying to ourselves, "We're not that." We're not all wearing red braces and driving Porsches with loads of money. We're not. There are other values that this planet has and that we hold dear as individuals. Completely by accident, we took the manhole cover off, and suddenly this other England erupted, this other Britain erupted.'

A Britain that was still nevertheless listening to Phil Collins, Sting and Howard Jones.

EIGHT

16:07

Bryan Ferry: 'Sensation', 'Boys And Girls', 'Slave To Love', 'Jealous Guy'

> There is an idea of a Patrick Bateman; some kind of abstraction. But there is no real me: only an entity, something illusory. And though I can hide my cold gaze, and you can shake my hand and feel flesh gripping yours and maybe you can even sense our lifestyles are probably comparable . . .
> I simply am not there.
> PATRICK BATEMAN IN *AMERICAN PSYCHO*

So, it was fourteen years since Roxy Music had revolutionised the industry with their ready-made retro-fit glam, and Bryan Ferry had just made a new record. *Boys and Girls*, it was called, and it wasn't half bad. If truth be told it was actually rather good. Where once Ferry had been lean, camp and (in the very early days) vaguely sinister, by 1985 he had been overtaken by a feeling of affluence, efficiency, comfort and calm. If the old Bryan Ferry was all teasing and foreplay, the new one was post-coital.

The phrase yacht-rock was once used to describe the self-satisfaction and the pretence of Steely Dan (whose music was as far away from Roxy's as Pluto is from the Sun), yet it could just as easily have been applied to the kind of music Ferry was making in the Eighties – smooth, slick, bereft of arch wordplay or anything approaching uncoiled fury.

Strangely, Ferry was completely uninterested in playing any shows to promote this new record, even though it was probably his best album for a decade, since 1975's Roxy Music album *Siren*, in fact (Ferry had finally achieved what he'd been trying to do since he started making solo records, namely making 'bedroom' music). A stickler for detail, he was far more interested in going back into the studio to record its follow-up. He had found his groove, and anyone who had worked with Ferry knew that he had a habit of losing it, usually because of appalling prevarication. So having found it again, he wasn't about to throw it away and go out on the road, where he would surely be pressured to rehash all the old Roxy Music material from the early Seventies, material he was proud of, but which hung around his neck like a medal he couldn't take off. During the late Seventies and early Eighties Ferry may have given the impression of succumbing to the inevitable pressures of the marketplace, but he was actually obsessed with the new, the mode, as he was when he started Roxy fourteen years earlier.

Bob Geldof was persistent, though, and had eventually convinced him to come out of hiding and play Live Aid. Ferry ended up forming a band with many of the session musicians he had been working with on *Boys And Girls*, including – notably – Pink Floyd's Dave Gilmour, giving his performance on the day even more credibility than usual. When he finally appeared on stage, his set was plagued by minor technical difficulties, which made Ferry look even more uneasy than he usually did, never being the most natural of performers.

'I have terrible memories of it all going wrong,' said Ferry. 'I'd put together an all-star band and the set was fraught with problems. We had David Gilmour on guitar and, poor David, his guitar wasn't working for the first couple of songs. With his first hit, the drummer put his stick through the drum skin. And then my microphone wasn't working, which for a singer is a bit of a handicap. A roadie ran on with another mic so then I was holding two mics taped together and I wasn't really sure which one to sing into. It was a great day though.'

By the time of Live Aid Ferry had been something of a style icon for nearly fifteen years. So cool was he when Roxy were in their first flush of success – 'Virginia Plain', 'Pyjamarama', 'Do The Strand' – that he became, almost overnight, a unique arbiter of style, so influential that fans would copy every little detail of his dress, whether he was trussed-up like a Fifties retro-future crooner, an American GI, or a tuxedo-clad lounge lizard. All were such fun things to pick from the dressing-up box. Marco Pirroni, the Adam and the Ants guitarist who had been bouncing around the Wembley stage a few hours earlier, was such a fan of Ferry when he was younger that he once used a magnifying glass to study a photo of him just to see what cigarettes he was smoking. 'Even the cigarettes were really good, because they were all white. It was an important statement,' he said.

It wasn't, not really, but what it was, was detail, which was what Ferry was all about. It was this fastidiousness that played against him, too, and critics mistook his fondness for archness for phoniness. Which was a shame, as it wasn't true. Still, he was considered such a part of the fabric of modern pop that he was invited up on to the Live Aid stage, and made a fair fist of it, especially when he sang 'Jealous Guy', the song he had recorded after John Lennon's assassination, and which had since become something of a hymn. Ferry and Lennon had hardly any history, although they did meet once, at Narita Airport in Tokyo in 1978, while Ferry was in Japan promoting his album *The Bride Stripped Bare*. Lennon came up to him in the departure lounge and told him that he had always been a great fan. A few years later Roxy Music were due to appear on a German TV show the day after Lennon's death, and rather than perform one of their own songs, Ferry elected to cover 'Jealous Guy' instead.

If you're being pernickety – which is what Ferry had built his career on – you could say that he looked too louche for the occasion, too detached, too cool; lounge lizards were OK after dark, but in front of 72,000 people who weren't especially interested in nuance, the supper-club lava-lamp sound of

Ferry was never going to work. But then what was he meant to do, reinvent his persona?

Ferry's languid stage presence was often captivating. The early Roxy records were beyond exciting, yet watching Ferry on stage these last few years had become something of an enervating experience. This was a deliberate strategy on his part, as he was remodelling himself as a modern-day crooner, and he had to force his audience to expect less of him. He always sang as though the effort of moving his mouth seemed disproportionate to the reward. He was sweet, though. I went to see him play the Palladium in London a couple of years after Live Aid, and after he did his rather stilted swaying-about on stage to one of his classic ballads, a couple of women who really should have known better rushed towards the stage, as if they were at a boy-band concert. Ferry visibly blushed, and said as much.

Ferry wasn't a natural choice for Live Aid, as he had steered away from agenda-driven projects in the past. He had always gone out of his way to avoid discussing politics, particularly as his lifestyle aspirations changed in the mid-Seventies to embrace all the things he had ironically nodded towards since the early days of Roxy. When he started to be photographed in three-piece Italian suits in the drawing rooms of Georgian houses in high-end London postcodes, the great-coated masses began to think that perhaps Ferry wasn't a card-carrying supporter of Harold Wilson or Jim Callaghan. Nevertheless, while many on the Wembley bill were some of the most apolitical acts of the era, they were all engaged in the most political act pop had ever attempted. For a social animal like Bryan Ferry to be involved, surely Live Aid had something all other benefit concerts didn't . . .

He sang four songs altogether, mainly recent ones – 'Sensation', 'Boys And Girls', 'Slave To Love' – as well as his by-now famous cover of 'Jealous Guy'. Perhaps he could have done some older hits, but no one really considered him to be a heritage act, least of all Ferry himself. He looked a little ungainly, as he was swirling around the stage carrying his two microphones, yet there was no mistaking his passion.

Ferry appeared to be more nervous backstage than he ought to have been, perhaps because there were so many of his peers there, and perhaps because of David Bowie. In the early Seventies, Ferry and Bowie had both been at the forefront of the glam movement, and it was perhaps felt that while Bowie had turned out to be the signature artist of the decade, Ferry was possibly guilty of unfulfilled promise.

Gary Kemp certainly remembers being underwhelmed. 'Bowie was the person who meant the most to me,' he said. 'I wasn't so keen on Bryan at that point in my life, and I wasn't really sure what he was up to. I didn't chat with him, as to be honest, maybe I had kind of grown out of him. I just wasn't quite into what he was doing. Early Bryan and Roxy Music were obviously good but I suppose my head was turned backstage by Bowie, the grand dame – David took all my attention. Plus, while there was a sense of camaraderie, I was really concentrating on my own performance.'

Ferry was all about grand seclusion – see the dismissive wave of the hand?! – which was the visual pop archetype that all the new Eighties bands were attempting to ape. Everyone from Visage and Spandau Ballet to Joy Division and Depeche Mode were trying to evoke the golden era of Ferry's glamorous if neurotic outsider, showing the world how intriguingly odd they were, like the anti-hero of J. P. Donleavy's *A Singular Man* (trying to appear uninterested yet obviously desperate for attention). Ultimately this was a pretentious exercise, as essentially what they were trying to do was make themselves appear more interesting, and more emotionally elaborate than they were. Much like Ferry, in fact.

In a small, difficult-to-get-into nightclub in the middle of Soho, this kind of attitude usually played very well; but not on a brightly lit stage in the middle of the afternoon on one of the hottest days of the year, and not when you're surrounded by 72,000 people who would probably prefer to listen to 'Radio Ga Ga' than 'Slave to Love'.

Ferry's very persona was considered decadent in the early Seventies – dressing up, transgender acolytes, and the idea of exclusivity, which was anathema to a generation only recently bred on peace, love and inclusivity

– but by the Eighties this was commonplace, so commonplace as to be considered conservative.*

Decadence was elsewhere, and not just in spirit. While Soho was experiencing something of a rebirth, contributing to the whole idea of a third iteration of Swinging London (the second had been the advent of punk in 1976), New York was also going through some changes, as was LA, and both were thought to epitomise, or at the very the least espouse, the new debauchery – sexually, financially, socially. London may have had the most exciting nightclubs in the world, but they were all start-ups, pop-ups, environments that were deliberately challenging, almost in an effort to keep people out. New York nightclubs were bigger, more commercial, more inclusive, more interested in showing off. Studio 54 made its name by turning people away, which appealed to the native New Yorker, as a door policy was like a glass ceiling: there to be broken.

Ferry loved it in New York. Some went there because its culture invented fame the size of the buildings. Ferry went in the hope that some of the fame would fall his way. He'd been in love with the city since he studied fine art in Newcastle in the mid-Sixties, and 'Virginia Plain', Roxy's first single, was a paean to the city, 'an inculcation of American pop imagery', according to Ferry's biographer Michael Bracewell. 'The American Dream, that's what the single was all about,' said Ferry. 'Dreaming of going to New York and living in an attic and painting. The whole Warhol set-up was fantastically attractive then . . . It's just a torrent of images. There's a reference to Baby Jane Holzer in there, who was part of the Warhol Factory, of course†.

---

* One critic summed up the Ferry lifestyle perfectly:
Interviewer: Happy birthday Bryan Ferry!
Bryan Ferry: Thank you.
Interviewer: How are you celebrating? Tuxedo, models, helicopters, Casablanca, models, being too damned suave, conversations about Picasso, models, making pained and passionate expressions while you croon, buying a new suit, models?
Bryan Ferry laughs before he's handed a cocktail and escorted on to a private jet by two models.

† Holzer, a central star of the Warhol coterie, had been famously profiled in *New York* magazine in 1964 by Tom Wolfe as 'The Girl of the Year'. This was also the year that Warhol had bought his first tape recorder.

.. It's about driving down the freeway, passing cigarette ads on vast billboards.' In terms of content and construction, the song was the musical equivalent of one of Richard Hamilton's early paintings. He may have been obsessed with Hollywood and the old notions of West Coast glamour, but he was equally obsessed about New York. At the time pop was absorbing all the great changes in technology, mass-production, media and domestic living, filtering this onslaught of information, and Ferry got it immediately. In New York Ferry hoped his fantasy would collide with reality, and for a while it did. 'Dance Away' had been a big hit for Roxy in 1979, and had briefly become a soundtrack to Studio 54. But he hadn't had a club hit there for years. *Boys And Girls* was a huge hit in the UK, reaching number one with ease. It also turned out to be Ferry's biggest US hit, too, selling half a million copies. The 12″ remix of 'Don't Stop The Dance' was one of the year's most popular records in Manhattan nightclubs – straight clubs, gay clubs, supper clubs, you name it. Reviews in the US press were mixed, but then Ferry had rarely been a critic's darling in the States. Words such as 'smooth', 'suave' and 'debonair' were used, and not always as compliments. Robert Christgau, who was the doyen of American rock critics at the time, called the record phoney: 'His voice thicker and more mucous, his tempos dragging despite all the fancy beats he's bought, he runs an ever steeper risk of turning into the romantic obsessive he's always played so zealously.'

Reviews didn't matter, though, as Ferry had finally broken America, something he'd been trying to do for nearly a decade and a half. Now he could go out in New York and hear his own records pumping out of car radios, wafting out of apartment blocks and, more importantly, filling dance floors. The success flattered him in another way, too, as in New York he was enjoying fame for the very first time, a new star enjoying a new career in a new town. The hot club at the time of *Boys And Girls* was Ian Schrager's and Steve Rubell's Palladium, down on East 14th Street, between Irving Place and 3rd Avenue. Where Danceteria, Area and Limelight (or Slimelight as it was almost immediately nicknamed) had been the real harbingers of change in New York City nightlife in the early Eighties, making downtown the centre of all things cool, the Palladium upped the ante by appealing to a bigger market, and a more fluid demographic, attempting to bring the 'voluntary apartheid' of uptown and downtown together. Originally a movie theatre and then a concert venue, Schrager and Rubell reopened it in 1985 as a nightclub, in the hope that they could recapture some of the magic of Studio 54 (in 1980 they had both been found guilty of tax evasion and sent to jail; released in 1981 and having already got into the hotel business, they were keen to find a club that would act as a cash cow). This they did: Palladium immediately became the club to be seen at, hanging out nonchalantly on the stairs, dancing in front of the huge banks of TV monitors, or hanging out in the infamous upstairs VIP den, the Michael Todd Room (it used to be the producer's personal screening room), its walls covered in a mural painted by Jean-Michel Basquiat. The Mike Todd Room was where Mick Jagger would celebrate his forty-second birthday two weeks after Live Aid. Elsewhere, Keith Haring had painted a backdrop for the dancefloor, Francesco Clemente had painted frescoes on the ceiling, and Kenny Scharf had customised the bathrooms. The Palladium was a big club, and was a world away from the dozens of flourishing little pop-ups in London. Even the VIP room held 700 people; it also had two further VIP rooms within it, 'as private as they were uncomfortable,' according to one regular, Anthony Haden-Guest. 'It may say something about these VIP rooms that they had acquired the in-house nicknames of Betty Ford Inpatients and Betty Ford Outpatients.'

'When you got to the Palladium, you felt you had arrived,' blogged one mid-Eighties patron, '80s Girl'. 'I worked an Azzedine Alaia fashion show there with steps reaching from the balcony down to the centre of the dance floor. Andy Warhol was talking to Simon Le Bon in the Mike Todd Room at the after-party . . . and I remember thinking there was no better place to be anywhere in the world at the moment. Pure over-the-top Eighties centre-of-the-universe magic. It was the Grand Central of clubs.' Sure, it was a postmodern gin palace, but the Palladium was also a statement. Rubell's and Schrager's policy had always been based on the 'build it and they will come' principle, and with the Palladium they excelled themselves. The DJs they employed were the very best in the city, in the country, who made sure they mixed the esoteric with the current, the popular with the arch. For a while, 'Don't Stop The Dance' could be heard there every night, not only testament to Ferry's unerring cool, but also a worthy addition to his 'disco canon' ('Love Is The Drug', 'Trash', 'Angel Eyes', etc.).

Nightclubs in Manhattan had to be bigger and better and smarter and faster and keener than any clubs in any other city. 'You make a lot of money in a big club,' said Steve Rubell at the time. 'This has become yuppie city. Wherever you go, [you see] these big barn-like restaurants. Everything's so BIG.' Everything was finely honed, even exclusivity. One briefly notorious downtown club, its name lost in the mists of SoHo, had – according to legend – half a dozen VIP rooms all inside each other, like Russian dolls. Having got into the first one you then had to negotiate yourself into the next, until you were in the very final room, which was big enough only for two people. What was inside the room? Two chairs, that's all. One hopes the club was actually called the Russian Doll, although it was gone so quickly no one can remember what it was called.

In the Seventies, if New York had been a book it would have been a tatty pulp paperback with dog-eared yellowing pages; in the Eighties it became a big, fat hardback, complete with a brash, colourful cover and a cellophane slip case. The city was still combating poverty, corruption and crime, but these were all elements that contributed to the city's mythic status, a First World city with Third World tendencies.

New York had always been mythic. Manhattan was the city of golden lights, of vertical dreams, the allegorical Gotham of comic-strip repute. Everything was bigger there: the restaurants, the banks, the cars, the corporate profiles. Girls were sexier, suits were wider, avarice more venal. Towards the middle of the Eighties there started to be more novels about New York, none of which appeared to be so removed from reality. Everything was writ large in New York, everything was drawn with broad brushstrokes, with its own shadows. The big books were advertised as such. Big. Brash. Aggressively ironic. New York was depicted as dark, dense, and the only place to make real money. Los Angeles may have been painted as colourful and vicious, with afternoons spent sodomising your assistant's girlfriend, perhaps dropping into a conference call halfway through, but New York was where the action was. Attitudes were determined by location: if you lived in New York you were avaricious, driven, full of corporate savvy. If you hailed from LA, you were genetically programmed to double-cross everyone you ever met, ideally just five minutes after you'd met them. New York, however, was the subject of all the big books.

And what big books they were: *Less Than Zero* by Brett Easton Ellis, *Money* by Martin Amis, *Slaves of New York* by Tama Janowitz, *Bright Lights, Big City* by Jay McInerney, Paul Auster's *New York Trilogy*, and the biggest New York book of them all, *The Bonfire of the Vanities* by Tom Wolfe. McInerney's book chronicled a fact checker for a highbrow glossy magazine whose cocaine-fuelled evenings were spent in yuppie nightclubs. Janowitz's characters were more bohemian, ricocheting between success and disappointment and the occasional flash of self-awareness.

While Susan Seidelman tried to capture the grungy, quirky nature of downtown in Madonna's first proper film, the romantic comedy *Desperately Seeking Susan*, others were attempting to celebrate this side of New York in print. Everyone and their nanny was trying their hand at the New York downtown novel, peppering their pages with brand names, 'funky' (read: English) dialogue and knowing references to East Village after-hours drinking dens, thinking they were punching the zeitgeist right where it hurt. But the real action was happening elsewhere, at opposite ends of the island, down on Wall Street, and way uptown on Madison Avenue, the conjoined worlds of boomtown sheen and opulence. Whereas McInerney, Easton Ellis and Janowitz were obsessed with getting dialogue and the vernacular on the page – their books were like reading screenplays – Wolfe's ambitions were bigger. He was trying to shrink the entire city into his book, every little bit of it. Published in 1987, *Bonfire* was originally conceived as a serial in the style of Charles Dickens, running in twenty-seven instalments in *Rolling Stone* three years earlier (Wolfe rewrote it completely for the published novel, changing the tense as well as some of the major characters).

Money and sex drove New York in the Eighties, not downtown nuance. Easton Ellis eventually realised this, as Patrick Bateman, the anti-hero

In Tom Wolfe's eyes, Live Aid didn't fit in with his idea of mass-market ambition, preferring to ignore the fact that Live Aid's global benevolence was another way for all of us to feel good about ourselves, which for many was status enough.

of his third novel, 1991's *American Pyscho*, was a banker, specifically a mergers and acquisitions specialist (which he facetiously referred to as 'murders and executions') at the fictional Wall Street investment firm of Pierce & Pierce – which was also Sherman McCoy's firm in *Bonfire*. Bateman was a serial killer, and along with Hannibal Lecter, the defining serial killer of the age, a man for whom rape, torture, necrophilia and cannibalism were as much a part of his life as fine Armani suits and the music of Phil Collins, Whitney Houston and Huey Lewis & the News. 'It's a brilliant satire of greed and the mindlessness of popular culture, of American life and of New York in the Eighties,' said Jay McInerney about his friend's book. 'It's a very thorough catalogue of the fixtures of urban existence in that era. It says that New Yorkers are so busy trying to get ahead that they don't even notice when people are being killed next door.' Norman Mailer initiated a very public spat with Easton Ellis by saying he wasn't a good enough writer to attempt such a satire, but the juxtaposition of designer brands and brutal violence worked enough for most.

The blurb for McInerney's third novel, 1988's *Story of My Life*, the tale of twenty-one-year-old world-weary Alison Poole, said all you needed to know about the city: 'In the late Eighties, New York has achieved an almost anarchic state of frenzy. Stockbrokers talk like artists, artists talk like stockbrokers, and everyone acts like there's no tomorrow. Each night is a new adventure, not infrequently catastrophic, from restaurants to clubs in a whirl of old boyfriends and new dilemmas.' This was a city consuming itself in reckless affluence, addicted to success and fuelled by neuroses. There were so many subterranean currents in New York, it was difficult to know where to look. What better places than nightclubs and restaurants? Harold Evans moved to the city in 1984, when his wife Tina Brown became the editor of *Vanity Fair*. 'Within a very short time, the New York vortex kicked in. When you're on the outer edges you can swim quite happily in cool waters, but as you get closer and get to know more people, you get sucked into a level of activity that is calculated to drive you crazy,' he said. 'It was very exciting – and very Eighties. People arrived in stretch limos. At the same time, I was astounded by the drug transactions I'd see on street corners, even in white-collar midtown, outside the New York Public Library. It was grim as hell, and all this alongside the intellectual excitement of media life and America being on top of the world.' Evans said it was like going to dinner with some wonderful person and looking underneath the table and finding mice droppings. 'It was an era of parties, and a great time for drugs and alcohol,' said *Rolling Stone* editor Jann Wenner, who moved to the city in the late Seventies. 'We felt more than welcomed. New York loves ambitious people – eats them up.'

Most writers new to the city – even those who lived there, but who had only recently chosen to tackle it in print – seemed intimidated by it. Manhattan was Gotham writ large, a grid city with hard dark edges and murderous shadows, and it had to be treated with respect. The New York nightlife was threatening to those who didn't know anything about it, although when I first went, in 1984, with a bunch of similarly hedonistic colleagues from *i-D*, I found it rather parochial. We did all the fancy places. Went to Danceteria (had a party there, actually), Area (a different theme every week), Limelight (the one in a church), and all the others, both grand and grim. But compared to the clubs in London, which were rougher, more glamorous, harder to get into, the New York versions seemed a little too pleased with themselves, as though by simply putting a velvet rope outside was enough to create intrigue.

Most New York writers were intimidated by the idea of exclusion, though, because exclusion was one of the defining characteristics of the city, and even those who considered themselves insiders were always worried that they might one day – soon, tomorrow – be cast out, to wander 1st Avenue with the rest of the wastrels. It was worse than ever in the Eighties, when the profile rise of Wall Street made money course around the city with more vigour, at least in the press. There were as many young bankers queuing up outside Limelight as there were club kids, as many hot-shot investment bankers as there were journalists from *Details*, *East Village Eye* or *Vanity Fair*.

And they were all so scared about not getting in, as scared as they were about not getting into Odeon, or the latest 'hot' restaurant to open that week. I was in New York a short while after Live Aid, and a restaurant way over in the East Village had become famous because they had held a private screening of the Philadelphia concert, giving away margaritas by the bucketload. It was impossible to get into, and as I was only in the city for two nights, didn't bother trying to get a table. When I told my New York friend Carol this she looked at me as though I'd just announced I was going to walk down Broadway with a traffic cone on my head.

'But it's the coolest restaurant in the city!' she said. 'Why wouldn't you want to go?'

I couldn't be bothered to get into an ideological argument with her over the insecurities of the native New Yorker, but I thought what I always did, which was that the place would probably be closed within six months, and no one would ever remember it. But for Carol and everyone like her – and everyone I knew in the city was like her – to not have been to the latest 'in' place was tantamount to social death.

New York in the mid-Eighties had an unhealthy obsession with status, and the only way to circumnavigate it was to ignore it, or to have so much status that it became meaningless.

Tom Wolfe could choose from either option, being arguably the most important American writer of the decade (which was extraordinary seeing that he had been up there in the Sixties and Seventies too). He wasn't scared by the city, he was enchanted by it.*

In his own way, Wolfe owned New York in the Eighties, especially towards the end of it, as he was then at the height of his powers. As soon as *The Bonfire of the Vanities* was published, he began being treated as society royalty. No one fucked with the dandy Tom Wolfe, not even those whose job was essentially fucking with people.

Manhattan was always an island, both culturally and politically, and the Eighties were no different. While the country may have embraced the uncomplicated old-school apple-pie popularism of Ronald Reagan – whose denunciations of communism chimed with those of Margaret Thatcher, and which made their 'special relationship' even more formidable – New York remained a liberal outpost, with a broadly Democrat mayor for the entire decade. Although he was a keen advocate of the death penalty, law and order and his citizens' right to a progressive and safe quality of life, Edward Koch was a liberal at heart, a liberal with the heart of a New Yorker. He was as passionate about his city as any native cab driver, which is why the city was so passionate about him: he served three terms (1 January 1978 – 31 December 1989), becoming something of a celebrity in the process.

His policy seemed to be Live and Let Grow, and it worked. Koch told the

---

* 'I end up doing a lot of window shopping,' he told *Arena*'s Gordon Burn in 1988, describing his relationship with the city. 'I love to go down Park Avenue and take in the Mercedes showroom, which Frank Lloyd Wright designed. It's a forerunner of the Guggenheim. There's also a fabulous bathroom showroom up in the forties.

'I can waste *days* in New York, just window shopping. It's just marvellous. Where I grew up, in Richmond, Virginia, the biggest event was the state fair that arrived for two weeks in September. Here, it's all year round. You have to keep your eyes open at all times.'

Wolfe had always loved the city, falling for the place as soon as he arrived. 'When I reached New York in the Sixties, I couldn't believe the scene I saw spread out before me,' he said. 'New York was pandemonium with a big grin on.' The city was a collection of 'statuspheres', and he was fascinated by the way people were finding new ways to make money. Advertising, film, nightlife, music, fashion, sports . . . he loved it all.

city to take pride in itself, to man up, and to take responsibility for itself. He was a big 'So what?' guy who tended to speak his mind, and consequently cultivated a huge fan base. He stopped the city going bust, and encouraged New Yorkers to have pride in themselves and in their city. He could be quite extraordinarily rude to people, but then as one of his friends said, when asked why Koch could be so dismissive: 'Ed has never lived with a woman, has never lived with a man, hasn't even lived with a dog, so he's never had to temper the way he behaves.' Which was exactly what New York wanted in a mayor.

Koch, however, was unable to deliver Live Aid. Because of the time difference, the US event had to take place on the Eastern Seaboard, and so New York was the obvious place to host it. Not only was it the most iconic city in the east, but it was serviced by three enormous airports (JFK, La Guardia and Newark, in New Jersey). Bob Geldof had talks with Koch, asking him to look into free policing and labour while pursuing Shea Stadium, home of the Mets and the site of the Beatles' 1964 debut US concert. But the city unions were so strong that this didn't work out. Geldof then tried for Giants Stadium across the river in New Jersey, but the NFL demanded that the New York Giants players be allowed to introduce the acts on stage in exchange for the use of it.

Washington DC's RKF Stadium was also considered, but Harvey Goldsmith soon ruled against it because of the location of the airport, the potential traffic problems and the not inconsiderable fact that he couldn't find a decent promoter in the area. There was briefly talk of looking at Boston before Goldsmith decided on Philadelphia – they had been gifted free labour and policing, he liked the promoter (Larry Magid), and the city had three airports. New York was already a distant memory.

'America was a nightmare, it was horrendous,' said Geldof, and with just three weeks to go before the show, the US promoter Bill Graham had stopped returning his phone calls. 'I was in a complete panic. I wouldn't show it, but I really did not sleep about America because we really weren't kept in touch. Harvey and I went there and it was a mess. When we went into the office, Bill Graham was rude, superior and very distracted.' Many felt that Graham was undermining the project behind Geldof's back, and that because it hadn't been initiated by him or anyone from his team, he was determined that it wasn't going to be a success.

He failed. Goldsmith sent Pete Smith, his number two, to Philadelphia to sort it out. Which he did, immediately, liaising with the TV stations, and mediating between Graham and Geldof. Between them, Smith, Goldsmith and Geldof snatched victory from the jaws of defeat, encouraging more bands to get involved in the Philadelphia show, successfully marginalising Bill Graham in the process. Many of the acts involved in the 'We Are The World' project had decided that the Philly show was too much of a British add-on for them to participate, although in the end Geldof managed to put a decent bill together.

There was actually a sense among some of the bands appearing in London that the Philadelphia gig was something of an afterthought, and that to be performing in Wembley was where you really wanted to be. U2 certainly didn't entertain playing Philadelphia, as for them, Live Aid was as much about supporting Bob Geldof as it was about the cause. Geldof had come calling, had made a big ask, and U2 had told him that they would be there for him, no matter what. And implicitly that meant performing in London. New York would have been more of a pull for the performers, as playing Philadelphia was a bit like playing in Coventry instead of London. There was nothing wrong with Coventry per se, but it wasn't London. And neither was Philadelphia.

This was not Bill Graham's first rodeo. As the US's foremost concert promoter, by 1985 Graham had already earned something of an extravagant and often comic reputation (kindly souls would say he had a 'charismatic but often difficult personality'), having grown up in the counter-cultural groundswell of San Francisco in the mid-Sixties. He started promoting gigs at the Fillmore West and Winterland before going on to manage Jefferson Airplane and move part of his operation to New York, operating the Fillmore East. For years he promoted the Rolling Stones, only to lose them on their comeback tour of 1989. 'Losing the Stones was like watching my favourite lover become a whore,' he said at the time. He had an ego that rivalled many of the acts he represented, and his behaviour during the lead-up to Live Aid was particularly challenging, confrontational even. Everything Goldsmith or Geldof said, he ignored. He'd pay lip service to whatever request they made, and then go to ground, not having done it. What was the phrase? 'Like teaching Hindu to a beagle.'

Afterwards Graham would obviously succeed in taking (demanding, actually) most of the credit, but by then it didn't matter. The show had been a success and it didn't really matter who was deemed to be responsible.

A decade earlier and Philadelphia would have made more sense. In the mid-Seventies the city was awash with soul, being the centre of the Philly scene, the proto-disco world of the O'Jays, Harold Melvin & the Blue Notes, the Three Degrees, Billy Paul and MFSB. The custodians of the Philly sound were the producers Kenny Gamble and Leon Huff, and they were responsible for most of the big Philly hits of the time, including 'Wake Up Everybody', 'Backstabbers', 'Me & Mrs Jones', 'I Love Music', 'When Will I See You Again', etc. Probably the only artists on the Live Aid bill who knew anything about the Philadelphia Sound were fellow Philadelphians Daryl Hall and John Oates, who made a virtue of their blue-eyed Philly soul roots. 'If you're from Philly, you can't escape it,' said John Oates. 'It's in the air, it's on the radio – it's a soulful place. If you live there you breathe it, and if you pay any attention and sense the feeling in the air, you're going to pick up black music.'

There was little that was funky about the giant Roman horseshoe of Philadelphia's JFK Stadium on 13 July, although the crowd was certainly on-message in terms of fashion. Look at the crowd in Philadelphia and they immediately look more fashionable than the crowd at Wembley, so consequently they look rather dated thirty years later. Even though it was a hot day you could see more than a smattering of men in stonewash denim and casual primary-coloured jackets with huge shoulder pads (why did everyone want to look like a linebacker?), and girls wearing oversized tops, leggings and leg warmers, fingerless gloves and miniskirts. They looked as though they had all turned up to audition for a John Hughes movie; and everyone wore a mullet (some with rat tails), regardless of their age or sex.

Originally called the Sesquicentennial Stadium and then the Philadelphia Municipal Stadium, like many other national landmarks – Idlewild Airport, for instance, in Queens – the stadium was rebranded after John F. Kennedy was assassinated in 1963. A few months after it had opened, over 120,000 people turned up to watch the heavyweight fight between Gene Tunney and Jack Dempsey on 23 September 1926. The stadium had been host to many important concerts before Live Aid, including the Supremes in 1965, the Beatles in 1966, Judy Garland in 1968, Peter Frampton in 1977, the Rolling Stones in 1978 (supported by Bob Marley) and The Who in 1982 (supported by the Clash). But nothing on the scale of Live Aid. It was somewhat ironic that Led Zeppelin played at Live Aid, as the JFK Stadium was one of those gigs the band had to cancel in 1978 due to the death of Robert Plant's five-year-old son Karac. The original band never played in the US again.

In 1985 Philadelphia was not just the largest city in Pennsylvania, but also the fifth largest city in the country, yet it never punched its weight. The city was yet to have its skyline cluttered by dozens of ugly, hastily erected, pastel-coloured Po-Mo skyscrapers, and so felt even less like an important East Coast town, and more like one of those New England towns whose only tourist attraction is an old Quaker barn or a broken bell of local significance (the Liberty Bell is here). You better believe it: Edgar Allan Poe once lived here. So starved was the city of attractions, that the steps outside the east entrance to the Philadelphia Museum of Art that Sylvester Stallone ran up in the first Rocky film had been officially designated as a location of genuine historical interest. Every year since the movie was released, 1976, tens of thousands of residents and visitors had made their way to the iconic 'Rocky Steps' to pay homage to Rocky's famous run. (In 2011, *Screen Junkies*, the TV and movie website, published their ranking of the ten most famous movie locations, and the steps had made number two.)

Still, Philadelphia had the gig, and New York didn't. By allowing itself to be bypassed by Live Aid, New York did itself a terrible disservice, retreating into the kind of arrogance that had previously stood it in such good stead. New York was cocky, top-of-the-food-chain cocky, and if Live Aid was an island in a sea of excess, then Manhattan in the mid-Eighties was an island fuelled by the very same. In a way this minimising of Live Aid made the city seem a little colder, a little more monolithic, the Gotham painted by Tim Burton in his 1989 *Batman*, or by Oliver Stone in 1987's *Wall Street*.

New York was made for an event like Live Aid, the kind of one-of-a-kind city that hosted the great and the good, the grand and the grandiose. News travelled fast on the streets of Manhattan, even before the days of mobile phones, twenty-four-hour rolling news stations, Twitter feeds and smartphones, when news passed on the street, from person to person, like a contagion. Live Aid would have spread through the city like that: 'Did you see what Madonna just did?' 'They say that Zeppelin were playing with Phil Collins!' 'Hey, Jack Nicholson's smoking a doobie on live TV and nobody's saying shit!'

But it wasn't to be. Philadelphia was what was going to be.

New York had been the birthplace of so much music. The street corners of Brooklyn, Harlem, Little Italy and the Bronx were the home of the finger-snapping doo-wop groups back in the very early days of rock 'n' roll; there was so much energy and vitality on the streets of New York in those days, it was inevitable that they would produce an art form that didn't need anything but the voice. More specifically, Broadway's Brill Building was where the modern pop song was hammered into submission by the likes of Carole King and Gerry Goffin, Burt Bacharach and Hal David, Tommy Boyce and Bobby Hart, Ellie Greenwich and Jeff Barry, Jerry Leiber and Mike Stoller, Barry Mann and Cynthia Weil and Neil Sedaka and Howard Greenfield. Then there was Greenwich Village, where Bob Dylan came to reinvent himself, and where the Velvet Underground invented everything else. A few years later, over on the Bowery, Richard Hell, Patti Smith and the Ramones would kick-start punk, helped along by a faltering New York Dolls and a nascent Deborah Harry. Manhattan was also where Chic would famously invent Upper East Side Disco, fusing the world of the nightclub with the wardrobe of *GQ*. In New York, the clubs spilled out on to the streets in such a way that the sidewalks became their own stage, their very own catwalk. The city was one giant auditorium, a musical set in *The Truman Show*, *West Side Story* on steroids. What a pity it couldn't get anywhere close to Live Aid.

In the Eighties, New York was still a talismanic city, still the vertical theatre of dreams. As it was continually changing – nightclubs opening and closing like venetian blinds – and in a constant state of renewal, it often felt like a place whose only reason for existing was so you could fail to conquer it. Manhattan's concrete honeycomb was such a treasury of aspiration it was as though it had a monopoly on ambition. In the Eighties New York was a city of superlatives, each one taller than the last. And while Walt Whitman once called it a 'mettlesome, mad, extravagant city', by 1985 Manhattan was so exaggerated, so excessive, it was almost beyond parody.

Almost, but not quite.

The Eighties were a decade made for New York, a decade drawn with very broad brushstrokes, where there were few shades of grey.

'In this steep and unkind city, downward mobility took extreme forms,' said Jonathan Raban. 'You could get rich quick, and you could get poor just as quick as you got rich. One week you'd be soaring over Manhattan in a tuxedo, martini in hand; the next, you could find yourself on Rikers Island, locked up in the company of Street People. New York fed greedily on these Icarian stories.'

New York was one of those cities where you could imagine everyone on the street waving their lighters in the air, holding a flame up to one and all for whatever they thought was the greater good. It was a city that prided itself on its ability to compete, and here compassion was as competitive as any other emotion. People knew the pulse of their city, knew everything about it. Get a New York cab in the mid-Eighties, and the driver would know everything there was to know about City Hall, would know anything worth knowing about the state of every new building creeping up into the sky. Some cabbies were so clued up they knew which bands were in town – Simple Minds, Duran Duran, Sade – and where they were recording. A few of them even knew who Bryan Ferry was. I remember one, a white guy in his thirties, trying to make conversation as a Roxy Music record came on the radio (probably 'Love Is The Drug'), asking whether the singer – 'Bryan, right?' – was English. 'He's the lounge lizard, right?' A pause.

'What's a lounge lizard?'

But if New York was the ultimate Eighties city then *The Bonfire of the Vanities* was the ultimate Eighties novel. Tom Wolfe's satire tells the tale of a Wall Street 'Master of the Universe', bond trader Sherman McCoy, a man who has it all — a smart Park Avenue apartment, a job that brings power, wealth and ridiculous prestige, a gorgeous wife, and an even more gorgeous mistress. But then one wrong turn makes it all go wrong, and McCoy spirals downward in a beautifully drawn fall from grace, a journey that takes him through labyrinthine social minefields. McCoy is involved in a car accident in the South Bronx, in which his mistress runs over and fatally injures a young black man. *Bonfire* charts the fall of the once-mighty Sherman, and the sequence of events that eventually result in his public disgrace, arraignment and trial.

Famed for his non-fiction, Wolfe had decided to write a novel as he felt most other contemporary writers had given up on it, notably most novelists. He wanted to write fiction that had the dirt and the humour of Dickens, the social arc of Thackeray, and the transparency of modern non-fiction, *his* non-fiction. He felt the modern novelist had got lost in magic realism, or symbolism or whatever. His Big Idea was a New York City panorama, a book about Wall Street and the criminal justice system, two mutually exclusive worlds.

As always, Wolfe was obsessed with the status of individuals within particular groups, as for him the psychological development of a person was utterly inseparable from the status that surrounded them. Christopher Hitchens may have called him shallow and affected ('He is simply, as was once said of the old German ruling establishment, blind in the right eye'), but Wolfe knew that people's wrapping was not something to be underestimated. New York was as much of a villain as anyone in the book, although Wolfe claimed there were no villains at all in *Bonfire*, not unless one considered the human condition to be villainous.

Having previously pronounced the modern novel dead, in the early Eighties Wolfe attempted to exhume it. Needing a proper deadline – he was prevaricating terribly – he decided to take another leaf out of Dickens' book, offering to write the book episodically for Jann Wenner's bi-weekly *Rolling Stone*. Armed with $200,000 he was soon up and running. And while the novel was seriously rewritten for its eventual publication, the *Rolling Stone* exercise at least gave him a framework to pursue.

He started work on the project in the early Seventies, or at least that's when he started talking about it, a book that would perform something of the same function as *Vanity Fair*, a book that presented a picture of ambition and status strife as he saw it in New York. His only quandary was whether or not to write it as a novel. 'Once I reach that decision the rest is purely technical,' he said, as it was all true, all based on proper reporting. He announced he was writing it at the very start of the Eighties, almost as though he were announcing a duel, so he couldn't back out. As if to prove that *Bonfire* could have easily turned out to be a non-fiction book (even though it was no *roman-à-clef*), the book had 2,343 exclamation marks, which was more than reminiscent of his hyperthyroid prose style. In Wolfe's world, the sidewalks of Manhattan were *littered* with exclamation marks.

Wolfe had the Eighties locked down before they even started. Interviewed on a TV chat show on New Year's Day in 1979, he was asked how he would describe the decade that was about to arrive. He predicted it would be called 'The Purple Decade', in the royal sense, as he thought it would become socially acceptable to be far more blatant in the pursuit of status than it ever had before. 'I turned out to be right,' he said, 'but my term was superseded by a better term, "Yuppie", which says the same thing. I wish I had thought of yuppie. It's a brilliant term.'

If pornography was the great vice of Seventies New York, 'plutocracy' – the graphic depiction of the acts of the rich – was the great vice of the city in the Eighties. And if *Playboy* and *Penthouse* were on the wane, all you had to do to take the temperature of the great town was to flick through *House & Garden, Architectural Digest, Town & Country, Art & Antiques, Connoisseur* or – Wolfe's favourite – *Millionaire*. New money was the lifeblood of the city in the Eighties, as was the brandishing of it. In the early part of the decade there was a pasta restaurant on 3rd Avenue way uptown. For a while it was 'this week's restaurant of the century', and it was so popular that they didn't bother taking reservations, and you just pitched up and hoped for the best. So you saw all these young investment bankers turning up in their chauffeur-driven town cars, marching in and asking for tables. Their names would be written down like everyone else's, but while they were waiting they would have drinks brought out to them in their limousines. It was instances such as this that piqued Wolfe's interest, and he delighted in them.

'Never in *Bonfire* did it cross my mind that I was writing satire,' said the author, perhaps a little disingenuously. 'Some things that strike people as mockery or hyperbole were, to me, instances of my barely being able to keep abreast of what was occurring.'

And *Bonfire* positively crackled with racial tension. 'If the city's going to be in the foreground, you can't duck the factor of ethnic hostility, which is so much a part of life in all our cities,' he said.

On publication, *Bonfire* was received by mixed reviews and vertical sales; Wolfe had a hit on his hands, even though some critics carped when they learned that the book almost won the National Book Critics Circle Award: 'That the bailiffs almost gave their bauble to Tom Wolfe's catalogue of shoes – electric-blue lizard pumps! snow-white Reeboks! bench-made half-brogued English New & Lingwoods! – is scary,' wrote *Newsday*'s John Leonard, a man for whom New York society probably still revolved around Upper West Side cocktail parties. New & Lingwood was Wolfe's big link with Bryan Ferry, two men who had circled each other like suitors, two men for whom the English upper classes were the very personification of sophistication. They both had their shirts made by New & Lingwood, as there was simply no one grander. Wolfe name-checked the brand on page 271: 'Sherman leaned forward and put his head down again. He found himself staring at the shiny tops of his New & Lingwood half-brogues.' The company was established in 1865 in Eton (at 118 High Street), becoming the official outfitters to the college, and in many cases fitting out five generations of the same family. That's why they both loved it so. Did any other store have so much class? There were vast leather-bound books full of personal measurements (Michael Caine, Roger Moore, various royals) and fabric swatches, while many customers would bring in their old shirts to have new collars and cuffs fitted. Oh my word!!!! Wolfe loved the old-school dandy connotations, and Ferry liked them too!!!!!

Wolfe was in his mid-fifties when he finished *Bonfire*, yet he had a handle on the city that escaped the generation of young hacks who had come in his wake. What the McInerneys and Janowitzes forgot was that stories remain the same, and that the status frenzy in the Manhattan of the early Eighties was not that much different to how it was in the Paris of the late nineteenth century or London in the Sixties. The protagonists were different, but the song remained the same. Wolfe's novel just happened to have come along at exactly the right time, because in terms of scale, contrast and sheer volume, there was nowhere like New York.

'To me the idea of writing a novel about this astonishing metropolis, a big novel, cramming as much of New York City between covers as you could, was the most tempting, the most challenging, and the most obvious, idea an American writer could possibly have,' Wolfe wrote afterwards. 'As I saw it, such a book should be a novel *of the city*, in the sense that Balzac and Zola had written novels *of Paris* and Dickens and Thackeray had written novels *of London*, with the city always in the foreground, exerting its relentless pressure on the souls of its inhabitants . . . American society today is no more or less chaotic, random, discontinuous, or absurd than Russian society or French society or British society a hundred years ago, no matter how convenient it might be for a writer to think so. It is merely more varied and complicated and harder to define.'

Wolfe had always put a lot of elbow grease into attacking the insecurities of Manhattan (always coming out on top, obviously), and with *Bonfire* he was doing this again, albeit through the veneer of fiction.

In the Eighties, Wolfe's world was a very deliberate world. His apartment, his family, his demeanour, his appearance – it all had order and borders. When you called his Upper East Side home, the maid announced, 'Tom Wolfe's residence?' in the most ridiculous approximation of grand old English resilience. In the modern age, there had been nobody better at dissecting the tricky games of status one-upmanship that underscored every socioeconomic group in the West, no writer more adept at bursting the bubbles of the wilfully modish. Which is why he walked it like he talked it. 'I realised early on that clothes are one of the few honest expressions people make about themselves,' he said, as though it were the most natural thing in the world.

In 'The Noonday Underground', Wolfe's piquant London letter from the mid-Sixties, he writes of a young mod called Larry Lynch, a fifteen-year-old who is better dressed than any man in the office: 'He has on a checked suit with a double-breasted waistcoat with a step collar on it and the jacket coming in at the waist, about like so, and lapels like this, and vents like this, and flaps about so, and trousers that come down close here and then flare out here, and a custom-made shirt that comes up like so at the neckband. Little things very few people would even know about, least of all these poor straight noses up here, who make four times his pay and they never had a suit in their lives that wasn't off the peg.'

At the time, Bryan Ferry was one of these boys, and he would regularly patronise lunchtime dances at the Majestic Ballroom or the Oxford Galleries Ballroom, both of which catered for the young Newcastle workforce, those office boys, students and shop assistants who would rather spend their lunchtimes dancing than eating.

At once both sympathetic and aloof – ever the perfect downstage voice – Wolfe always wrote as an outsider (it seems it's been just as important for him to be different as to be right), so it made perfect sense that whenever a fan discovered what Wolfe actually looked like, they discovered that – No, but, surely . . . it couldn't be, could it?! – he looked like an outsider too, or at least a man two steps removed from all the subcultural madness around him. He had a substitute personality.

A little like Bryan Ferry, in fact.

Perhaps predictably, Wolfe was no great fan of Live Aid, or any such venture that kept a person's social conscience in high profile. 'That's just Community Chest stuff,' he mocked, comparing it to the North American fund-raising organisations that collected money from local businesses and workers and distributed it to community projects. There were thousands of these organisations in the Fifties and Sixties, part of a nationwide charity circuit heavily promoted on syndicated radio stations (including the H. J. Heinz Company-sponsored *The Adventures of Ozzie and Harriet* and the Chevron-sponsored *Let George Do It* show).

Geldof actually agreed with him, in a way.

'Yes, that's exactly right, it was,' he said. 'But what was new, and where the romance was, was the shared experience. Exactly what you get with the Olympics. In Britain the Coronation was emotive because it was a shared national experience for the first time ever through television. The Americans have a similar thing with their flag. It's a shared, national, emotional experience, which is why they blub and put their hand on their heart. That was the difference. Suddenly the awareness that everyone was watching this, for the first time since we may have left Africa, humans spoke to each other again. It was a dialogue. You were asked to respond, it wasn't just a monologue telling you this. OK, what's your response now? I want to hear it. And we will focus that response in two ways, economically and politically, so that's what it was. That shared experience. The understanding that we were all talking together about something that shouldn't occur, it would be such a massive blow to the human corpus if we had let it continue, especially as we had all seen it on TV. I think that would have had intolerable consequences: great questioning of morality and society and all those things. I think it would have led to that. It didn't.'

In Wolfe's eyes, Live Aid didn't fit in with his idea of mass-market ambition, preferring to ignore the fact that Live Aid's global benevolence was another way for all of us to feel good about ourselves, which for many was status enough. The Eighties may have been the decade of greed, but Live Aid produced some of the most memorable images of the era, as well as some of the most enduring memories. Live Aid wasn't divisive, nor was it overtly political, yet it offered all of us a way to be involved in a global issue, one that made all of us feel good about ourselves as well as the cause.

For others, this status was suspect in the extreme, making Live Aid a bittersweet success: 'In a period where the very ethos of a planned, socialised and welfarised society is running down,' said the *New Socialist*, 'a happy story where an individual can be seen to put the world to rights is of tremendous ideological value. Value, that is, to an interest group which depends on fostering Victorian charity and free-market fantasies.'

Wolfe was always good at the sideways sneer, at saying the unsayable, especially where political correctness was concerned. In *Radical Chic and Mau-Mauing the Flak Catchers* he famously described the courting of the Black Panthers by the celebrity composer Leonard Bernstein at his chi-chi duplex apartment on Park Avenue, yet this was another example of Wolfe catching the wealthy trying to ingratiate themselves with those on the margins of society. With Live Aid, he was blindsided by the sheer force of numbers: the event was so popular, and gathered so much momentum that to criticise it from a philanthropic point of view would have simply been contrary. There was a sense of automaticity about Live Aid, so whenever anyone mentioned it, you automatically felt benign. Wolfe liked to say that Live Aid wasn't that important, but its very importance scared him away from discussing it. Live Aid wasn't a microcosm, it was a macrocosm, an event so big that the only way to critique it would have been to negate it. And even Tom Wolfe wasn't going to do that.

For Wolfe, Live Aid was terra incognita, as he didn't appear to understand it, principally as it didn't chime with the way in which he wanted to depict the decade. He had spent so long believing that Americans liked nothing better than wallowing in their own reflections, that he had forgotten that they were also capable of having a modicum of compassion, too, and that Live Aid wasn't an inconvenience, but rather something closer to a relief.

What happened in Philadelphia on 13 July was of a magnitude that it would take years to decode properly, a seemingly benign pop concert that affected the whole world. However, its effect on Philadelphia was almost instant, and in the space of a few hours, the sleepy East Coast city had increased its size on the map exponentially.

Ironically, the very last song ever played at the JFK Stadium would be 'Knockin' On Heaven's Door', as performed by the Grateful Dead on 7 July 1989. Six days after the show (which had been marred by many fans' disgust as the dilapidated state of the stairwells, gothic corridors and the rusty toilets; the utilities were laid out so badly it could take forty-five minutes to buy a beer), and on the exact fourth anniversary of Live Aid, the stadium was condemned by the then Mayor, Wilson Goode. It was finally demolished in 1992, having spent three years rotting in the south Philadelphia sun.

The Wells Fargo Center now stands on the site, host to the likes of Barbra Streisand, Rush, One Direction, Justin Bieber, Bob Dylan, Mark Knopfler, Carrie Underwood, Neil Young, The Who, the Trans-Siberian Orchestra, Kevin Hart, the Dave Matthews Band, Disney on Ice, Lady Gaga, Rihanna, Pink, and everyone else on the circuit.

NINE

16:38

Paul Young: 'Do They Know It's Christmas?'/'Come Back And Stay', 'That's The Way Love Is' (with Alison Moyet), 'Every Time You Go Away'

U2: 'Sunday Bloody Sunday', 'Bad' (with snippets of 'Satellite Of Love', 'Ruby Tuesday', 'Sympathy For The Devil' and 'Walk On The Wild Side')

Dire Straits: 'Money For Nothing' (with Sting), 'Sultans Of Swing'

Live Aid was the making of U2. Beforehand, most people didn't know who they were. U2 broke in America way before they broke in England so 13 July was the making of them. There were three or four classic moments in the show that will go down in history, and the U2 moment is one of them.

HARVEY GOLDSMITH

t's strange to consider it now, but in 1985 Luton-born Paul Young was set to be Britain's next Robert Palmer. At the very least. So much was expected of him that a lifelong career was thought to be something of a fait accompli. In 1985 Paul Young was as big as Adele was in 2011. His

1984 album *No Parlez* (on the cover of which Young wore an Antony Price leather suit, which at the time was the mark of any truly successful male British act) was CBS's most successful domestic release since the company had started its UK operation in 1965 (going on to sell an extraordinary 7 million copies). He was a white boy with a big voice singing blue-eyed black songs in a small way; there was nothing remotely edgy about his voice, yet it was sufficiently heartfelt to appeal to those who had previously bought soul records in large numbers. In the two years before Live Aid he had half a dozen hit singles, including 'Love Of The Common People' (helped somewhat by its inclusion in the John Hughes film *Sixteen Candles*), 'Wherever I Lay My Hat (That's My Home)' (the B-side of Marvin Gaye's 1969 hit 'Too Busy Thinking About My Baby', which were both originally recorded by the Temptations), 'Come Back And Stay', 'Every Time You Go Away' and 'Oh Girl'. At the 1985 Brit Awards, Young received the award for Best British Male. Young would of course soon be replaced in the nation's affections by Simply Red's Mick Hucknall, a man with an uglier face but a better voice, but 1985 was still his year. 'He's got the sort of looks of Paul McCartney, the sort of manners of Cliff Richard, moves like Tom Jones tangoing with P. J. Proby, and sounds like Marvin Gaye and Paul Rodgers in a Dusty Springfield soundalike contest,' said *Creem* magazine that year.

Nice guy, too.

'When we did Live Aid, I remember hearing nightmare stories about stars arguing about the running order on the American stage, but with the British lot it was, "Are we on next? Great,"' said Young. 'We had to get out of the dressing room to make way for Queen, and Brian May was saying, "Don't worry on account of us." It was all so polite and civil.'

He was diplomatic, too, even though some of his peers had been unkind to him, namely Boy George, who called him a Cornish pasty. 'I don't really like to air my views that much. Yeah, I come over as nice on a lot of things, because I don't go around slagging people off. I'm quite shy I suppose, though; I don't particularly like the attention that I get – apart from the time that I'm on stage, and that's the bit I enjoy, that's the reason I'm doing it now; and anything else that comes along with it I'll go along with, but that's as far as it goes.'

It's easy to forget now how big Paul Young was in the mid-Eighties. He was appealing to everyone from Golf GTI-driving young bachelors to teenage girls, and from suburban housewives to your local van driver. He was handsome enough, scrubbed up well, and he had one hell of a voice. Which didn't go unnoticed at Rod Stewart's record company. Towards the end of the decade, Rob Dickens, the executive who ran Stewart's label, Warner Bros, in the UK, had a meeting with the forty-four-year-old singer. The main topic of conversation was Stewart's fluctuating fortunes in the British singles chart, and how while he had been busy in the Eighties making American-sounding rock records, he had 'vacated' his rightful role, which according to Dickens was interpreting songs, taking material and making it his own. Trying to encourage Stewart to move back to this type of material, his opening gambit was, 'Why did you let Paul Young steal your audience?' Young had made a virtue of making old songs new – 'Wherever I Lay My Hat', 'Every Time You Go Away', etc. – reinterpreting them for an audience who didn't care where they came from, and didn't give a fig who had recorded them in the first place.

For a while it worked, as he was a Rod Stewart for the CD generation. He didn't have a rooster haircut, nor a succession of pneumatic, long-legged blondes, but he had the pipes.

Young was also spearheading the second British invasion of the North American charts. The week of 13 July, he was at number six in America with 'Every Time You Go Away', the Hall & Oates song. British acts were all over the US charts like a wet towel: Dead or Alive's 'You Spin Me Round' was at number twenty-six, Howard Jones's 'Things Can Only Get Better' was at number twenty-four, Depeche Mode's 'People Are People' was at number twenty-two, the Power Station's version of the T. Rex hit 'Get It On' was at number eighteen, Paul Hardcastle's '19' was at number sixteen, Sting's first single 'If You Love Somebody Set Them Free' was at number eleven, the Eurythmics' 'Would I Lie To You' was at number five, Phil Collins's 'Sussudio' was at number two, while Duran Duran were at number one with the James Bond song, 'A View To A Kill'. Tears For Fears actually had two songs in the top thirty, 'Everybody Wants To Rule The World' at number twenty-five and 'Shout' at number fourteen. They also had the number one US album, topping a chart full of Phil Collins, the Power Station, the Eurythmics, Wham!, Sting, Howard Jones, Dire Straits, Robert Plant, Supertramp, Sade and, of course, Paul Young. British pop was everywhere. The best-selling singles of the year in the States included four from the UK: 1. 'Careless Whisper' by Wham!, 'Separate Lives' by Phil Collins & Marilyn Martin, 'Money For Nothing' by Dire Straits and 'Everybody Wants To Rule The World' by Tears For Fears.

Some critics had questioned whether or not Young was a big enough live act to warrant inclusion on the Live Aid bill, but this was just petty sniping. Young was massive in the States, and also, as the PR Bernard Doherty said, 'Once Bob had said yes to someone like Nik Kershaw it was very difficult for him to say no to people like Paul Young.'

There were some predictably awful crimes against fashion at Live Aid, namely Midge Ure's and Tony Hadley's duster coats, as well as Paul Young's and Bono's mullets. Howard Jones had a mullet, as did Sting, and even Kiki Dee, although Rik Ocasek's was the very worst of all, as he looked as though he might be wearing a busby. One of the few people appearing at Live Aid not to wear a mullet was George Michael, and that's only because his haircut appears to have been copied from Princess Diana.

By the time U2 came on stage, after the Wembley crowd had been treated to live video footage of Bryan Adams shuffling through 'Summer Of '69' and 'Kids Wanna Rock', Robin, Kate and I were way in the back of the stadium, still on the pitch but about as far away from the stage as you could be and still be inside the walls. We had gone in search of beer and food, and it had taken us the best part of Paul Young's set to find them. When Jack Nicholson announced U2 from the stage in Philadelphia, crowds on both sides of the Atlantic started punching the air and making rock 'n' roll 'Whoops', although it has to be said that most of the whooping was in Pennsylvania, not Middlesex. The giant video screens may have told us that the band were on stage, but it wasn't immediately apparent which stage they were transmitting images from. At that moment Kate, perhaps suffering from too much sun and too little pampering, thought Bono, Edge et al. were performing in Philadelphia, and was only disabused of this fact when she saw that Bono had disappeared from view and had gone walkabout in the Wembley crowd.

We could see Bono, but the rest of U2 couldn't. Although this would turn out to be one of their most important performances, and the gig that really made them global stars, U2 only managed two songs. In the middle of 'Bad', Bono pulled a girl up from the crowd while the Edge played the guitar riff over and over again.

'Live Aid was at the end of *The Unforgettable Fire* tour,' said Paul McGuinness, the band's manager. 'And it turned out to be a very special day for U2.'

In more ways than one.

'Live Aid turned out to be one of the most important things U2 ever did, though we didn't realise it at the time,' said McGuinness. 'The whole Live Aid thing was a series of misjudgements, if you like, with me not completely comprehending it. I remember when Bob called me first about the single. I said to the band, "Geldof is putting a charity record together, or so he says. I don't think anything will come of it." And then a few weeks later I called them up and said, "Actually I've completely changed my mind about this. It's achieved not only critical mass but I think it's going to be an enormous phenomenon." So Bono and Adam went over for the session, although I think Bono found the line he was given to sing rather excruciating – "Thank God it's them, instead of you," – I think he found that a bit embarrassing. But we were all very happy to see Bob succeed.

'A few months later, despite the fact that Bob had said to me, "That'll be the end of it. There's no gig or anything," he called me and said, "Look, I know I said there would be no gig, but there is going to be a gig," and he gave me the date. I said, "OK, we'll be there. Just tell me what time we're on and how long we've got." People forget that this was in the days before you had these huge banks of videos at shows. There was very basic video reinforcement in Wembley, and in many ways that was the key to it. As

Bono understood, and I think as Freddie Mercury understood, Live Aid was actually a TV show.'

McGuinness denies that anyone from his organisation had called up Geldof the night before, threatening to pull out if the band didn't get a soundcheck.

'That's bollocks,' he said. 'No, I don't think so. God, I can't even remember if there was soundcheck, I suspect there wasn't for anyone. It certainly wasn't authorised by me or the band. We placed ourselves at Geldof's disposal, basically. I suppose the friendship between Bono and Bob started from that moment. They knew each other before Live Aid, but that was one of the landmarks and they are very close now.

'By 1985 I think U2's career was pretty firmly on track. By then we were starting to have number one albums all over Europe. We already had a reputation as a live act that exceeded the success we were having selling records. So we had already started to be successful. I suppose Live Aid also had a fundamental effect on Bono, in that shortly after that he went to Africa with [his wife] Ali and worked in a camp in Ethiopia. I think in the years following Live Aid the awareness that you can solve the world's problems by playing charity projects sunk in, not just for the members of U2 and myself but for everyone. The focus on Africa, which Bono has had ever since, certainly started then, and his life would have been totally different had that not occurred.'

'I was nervous about it, it was such a huge gig,' said drummer Larry Mullen Jr. 'People were queuing up to do it because of the exposure, they were talking about the amount of TV coverage and whatever. It was hard to convince some people that we were there for the right reasons.'

Bass player Adam Clayton was absolutely terrified as well as being exhilarated, principally because, like everyone else, the band only had fifteen minutes or so to make everything work, with no rehearsal and no soundcheck, something the band just weren't used to. 'The environment was a little out of control, there being numerous cameras around, and a lot of people generally in the backstage areas,' he said. 'So you were always exposed, always vulnerable. We were going on in daylight, which was not a great situation to be in, but we were underdogs at that stage and we had to make those fifteen minutes count, given that it was a bill filled with enormous talent and we just didn't want to get lost in that list.'

As for the Edge, he was completely freaked out, as just before the band were due on stage he had bumped into Muhammad Ali being photographed by David Bailey.

Before they went on, Bono had already had something of an extraordinary day, not least his encounter with Freddie Mercury, which in a way shows how rough around the edges U2 still were.

'People were very good to me,' said Bono. 'I was walking with Ali and Freddie Mercury pulled me aside and said, "Oh, Bono . . . Is it Bo-No or Bon-O?" I told him, "It's Bon-O." He said, "Come over here with me. We've all been talking, myself, Roger and Pete and David, and we all agree, there's no singers any more, everyone is shouting these days, but you're a singer." I was up against a wall and he put his hand on the wall and was talking to me like he was chatting up a chick. He had me laughing but I was shifting nervously at the same time, with Ali and myself exchanging glances. I thought, "Wow, this guy's really camp." I was telling somebody later and he said, "You're surprised? They're called Queen!" But I was really amazed. It hadn't dawned on me.

'David Bowie came over to me. And I was like, "David Bowie just came to talk to me!" And then we started walking together and I turned to ask him something, and I was wearing that ridiculous hat with the wide brim, and I nearly took his eye out. This is the Elvis of the UK! This is the man who, more than any other, set fire to my vivid imagination. If John Lennon lit the fuse for my political point of view as a performer, as an artist it was David Bowie. And to have a moment with this godlike genius and almost take his eye out with the brim of your hat, it wasn't a great result. Paul McCartney came over and said nice things to us. I couldn't believe it. So it was very important to go on and do well. But it was panic stations back there, changing sets every five minutes.'

'Backstage everyone was mixing with each other,' said McGuinness, 'although I suppose we were part of the new breed. We were certainly busier than a lot of the other groups – studio groups – because we had spent a lot of time on the road. In the early part of the Eighties we were constantly on the road. Every year, we would spend a few months in North America, whereas most breaking or wishing-to-break English acts tended to do very short American tours and then get fed up that they hadn't succeeded. In those days, the full effect of MTV was only beginning to filter through. In the mid-Eighties I seem to remember there were still markets in the US that did not have MTV, including Manhattan, believe it or not, for quite a few years. We all benefited enormously from MTV because we enjoyed making videos and the band had strong feelings about how to portray themselves on video. We would go to a market, a city in America where they had MTV, and we would be much bigger there than in a city which didn't have MTV. That was very palpable, very tangible. The relationship between media and bands was different there. There was nothing to correspond to the inkies, the British music papers like the *NME* and *Melody Maker*. People forget that in the early Eighties, *NME* was still selling a couple of hundred thousand copies a week. It's unimaginable. There was nothing like that in the States, and what there was instead was American radio. We were very friendly with the big critics on the *New York Times* and the *LA Times* and all the big city papers, but it was MTV that really worked its magic.'

'Jack Nicholson introduced us, [and] I could see an Irish flag flying,' said Larry Mullen Jr. 'I proudly said, "It's amazing, we're the only Irish band playing here today." Geldof was standing behind me and started to splutter. Of course, the Boomtown Rats had played earlier.'

The band were meant to play three songs – 'Sunday Bloody Sunday', 'Bad' and 'Pride', their big hit, the song they'd become known for. But then during 'Bad', Bono went out for a wander, and when he did, the band started to get jittery, and then they started to panic.

'Bad' was such an emotive song that it couldn't fail to stir the crowd. It certainly stirred Geldof, who went to sit next to Paul McGuinness backstage, to watch the band on a TV monitor. McGuinness was crying, and soon Geldof was too. Overcome with emotion, they hugged each other.

'I never liked you, you bastard,' said Geldof.

'I didn't much like you,' McGuinness laughed back.

Geldof had said earlier that he didn't want any members of the audience on stage, a rule that was made somewhat easier by the photographers' pen just in front of it. Not that Bono took any notice of it. What Geldof hadn't taken into account was the possibility of someone from the stage walking into the audience.

'Bono's dive into the crowd went a bit wrong because he had so much stuff to climb over to get to the front row,' said the Edge. 'It was a massive stadium show with multiple barriers between the stage and the floor that must have been twenty feet. We lost sight of him completely. He was gone for so long I started to think maybe he had decided to end the set early and was on his way to the dressing room. I was totally thrown, and I'm looking at Adam and Larry to see if they know what's going on and they're looking back at me with complete panic across their faces. Next thing I spot him way down below clambering over the last of the barriers to get to the people.

The moment when U2 turned onto the road that would lead them to global supremacy. 'We didn't do the hit because I'd gone AWOL to try and find a television moment and forgot about the song,' said Bono. 'The band were very, very upset – they nearly fired me.'

We're still playing away, giving it loads. So after he has a little cuddle with a girl down the front he starts to make his way back to the stage, which takes another five minutes. I'm just glad the cameras didn't show the rest of the band during the whole drama, because we must have looked like the Three Stooges up there: Curly, Larry and Moe.'

Paul McGuinness was having kittens, too: 'In the middle of the second song, "Bad", Bono completely disappeared from the sight of the band and indeed from mine,' he said. 'We had no idea where he'd gone, so they just kept playing along. What of course he was doing was that extraordinary interaction with the front row of the crowd, and with the girl at the front. When the set ended, we were all very emotional, as we didn't think it had gone well at all. We knew that there were a lot of U2 fans in the crowd, there were a lot of U2 banners and Irish flags, and there was a lot of support for U2. But we really didn't know it had gone well, in fact we all thought that Bono had fucked it up by departing from the plan. It really wasn't until two days later that I knew it had actually been a success, that along with Queen, U2 had stolen the show. It was only then that I realised how effective it had been, and how Bono's instincts were right all along. I was actually on holiday in the South of France and I remember going into a bookshop to pick up the English papers, as they arrived a day late. This is forty-eight hours after the event; I had finally stopped being depressed about it, because as far as I had been able to tell it was a huge opportunity that had been missed. Could I have been more wrong? It had an extraordinary effect on U2's career worldwide. I think all our records went into the top ten the following week. It really was one of the biggest things that ever happened to us.'

'We didn't do the hit because I'd gone AWOL to try and find a television moment and forgot about the song,' said Bono. 'The band were very, very upset – they nearly fired me.'

'I think it is fair to say there was a bit of a row afterwards,' said McGuinness.

Bono's depression continued for a few days. He went back to Ireland, going down to his wife's parents' house in Wexford. He was in a very dark mood, upset with himself for letting the band down so terribly, especially on such a momentous day. And then something strange happened. He met a sculptor called Seamus Furlong, a friend of Ali's family; he went to visit him, and immediately saw this huge new piece that Furlong was working on, depicting a figure in mid-air. It turned out that this thing was called 'The Leap', and was actually a representation of Bono at Live Aid.

'It's about the leap of faith,' the sculptor explained to Bono. 'That's you.'

'What are you taking about?' asked Bono.

'We saw you at Live Aid. You did a leap.'

'What do you mean?'

'Do you remember when you went into the crowd?'

'Oh, I remember all right. I've thought of little else for the last couple of days.'

'You were getting out of your skin. You weren't happy on the stage. You wanted something more. You made a leap of faith, you got something, you touched it. And I did this because I was inspired to.'

Two days later, Bono's growing realisation that Live Aid may not have been as bad as they all feared was confirmed by a call from McGuinness. 'You are not going to believe this,' he said, 'but everyone's raving about U2 on Live Aid. Radio stations and TV have been asking people what the highlights were, and a lot of them are picking U2.'

McGuinness thought they were mad as he was still convinced the gig had been a disaster, but who was to argue with public opinion? Wasn't that what Live Aid had been all about? 'That was the end of that particular tour and I went to the South of France the following day with my friend Michael Hamlyn, who used to produce all our videos. I really just thought what a great opportunity and what a big mess Bono had made of it. Then we went into Antibes to buy the English newspapers the next day and it was such a huge story and it seemed to have been popularly decreed that Bono and Freddie Mercury had stolen the show. It gradually dawned on me what had happened. All of U2's albums went back into the charts and their status took a huge jump. Nothing was really quite the same again now everyone knew who Bono was.'

Edge couldn't believe it, either: 'It really took us by surprise when people started talking about U2 as one of the noteworthy performances of the day.

I thought they were joking. I really thought we were crap. But looking back, as I did a week later, I started to see what it was. It was a sense of real, total jeopardy, which is always very exciting for a live event, and Bono's complete determination to make physical contact with the crowd and eventually getting there after two minutes of struggling over barriers. I think there was something about the amount of effort he had to put in to do it that somehow made it even more powerful.'

Bono's leap of faith, his journey, really meant something, and as well as carrying the emotion of the day, it made the enormity of the day, the project, quite personal. His instincts were right, as his small gesture became one of Live Aid's biggest

What could have been a Spinal Tap moment turned out to be the band's salvation. By the end of their set they had completely won the audience over, and by the following week all four U2 albums were back in the British charts. The story goes that in the days and weeks following Live Aid, thousands of people went into record shops all over the world asking for something by 'the singer that danced with the girl at Live Aid'. Within two years they were the biggest band in the world, with a classic album in the shape of *The Joshua Tree* about to make them rich.

U2 were always going to be the band to watch. Like a lot of people at Live Aid, I'd seen them play a few times already, but this was meant to be their big day, and they were the band that everyone appeared to be most interested in seeing. They were one of the only new acts on the bill who could play stadiums, as anyone who had seen their *Live At The Red Rocks: Under A Blood Red Sky* already knew. Recorded at the Red Rocks Amphitheatre in Colorado on the group's *War* tour, this was the band's first video release, and showed how determined they were to reinvent the stadium experience. There was a sense that you might be missing something if you didn't see U2 live, a feeling that good though their records were, they weren't a patch on the live experience. They were the band that Echo & the Bunnymen had threatened to be, the band Simple Minds desperately wanted to be, the band the Clash may have been had they stayed together. Ultimately, though, they were U2, and a very good thing they were too.

The nub was that U2 were always after the Big Mo, always interested in making music for stadiums, not pubs. They weren't interested in parlour tricks, they were interested in space travel, bouncing between the stars. So many bands at the time were obsessed with refining their manifesto that they forgot to cement the relationship with their audience, the most important relationship of all. The more crowded the marketplace became, the more groups had to really strive to make themselves noticed, which usually involved being increasingly narrow in their appeal. U2 did the opposite.

In a bid to become the best stadium band of all time, they tried to knock the ball out of the park with every key change, not just with each song. They understood scale, dimension and dynamics, understood that there had to be a redemptive aspect to what they did. In short, they had the kind of ambition that wasn't necessarily deemed to be cool in the post-punk world of early-Eighties Britain. The U2 world was a widescreen world, a 3D world. In their bid to become the best band of the decade, they took the passion of the Sixties and the dynamics of the Seventies and gave them both the surface smarts and the dynamism of the Eighties.

'Increasingly we try and record while we're on tour,' Bono said to me once. 'There is a word used in the studio – it should be pejorative, but it isn't. And that's "interesting". Edge always says, that's really interesting. I'll say, that's interesting. We sit around making music that's "interesting". The only music you won't play in front of 80,000 people, or 18,000 people, is interesting music. Because that's the only kind of music [our audience] don't want to hear. They want dramatic, melodramatic, angry, joyful, raw music. Just don't play fucking interesting music. No jazz funk, nothing odd, because people can't get into it.'

Live Aid conjured up that unique, unfocused passion of adolescence, a sense of inchoate longing, a vague evocation of general well-being. U2 epitomised that, even though they had yet to reveal fully the depth of their campaigning and activism. They weren't afraid to reference the historic bloodshed in their home country, always sure to present a non-partisan view (calling *War*, the album which contained one of their early signature records 'Sunday Bloody Sunday', 'the first non-political political record').

Their fourth album, *The Unforgettable Fire*, released in 1984, contained two tributes to Dr Martin Luther King, 'Pride (In The Name Of Love)' and 'MLK', proving that they were intent on using their music as a means of promoting social awareness. Bono would work on behalf of World Vision, Amnesty International, Sanctuary, Greenpeace, War Child and many other political organisations and pressure groups, and would become as closely associated with Africa as Geldof. His passion for humanitarian work had actually been inspired by a previous campaigning concert, the 1979 Secret Policeman's Ball, which was staged by John Cleese on behalf of Amnesty. 'It became a part of me,' said Bono. 'It sowed a seed.'

Essentially, the band looked as though they were keen to carry the legacy of campaigning, insurrectionist rock 'n' roll on their shoulders. They looked as though they were going to be difficult, obstinate and outspoken, all the things a rock group weren't meant to be in the Eighties. They looked suspiciously like insurgents, which is one of the reasons we all liked them so much. Bono would start to be lampooned regularly by the left and the right for his insistent meddling, with the *Guardian* acting suspicious, and the *Daily Mail* downright hostile, but this only made him more determined to use the band as a force for good.*

You could already see that at Live Aid, as although his performance was to some a solipsistic act of bravado, it also showed the world, in very broad brushstrokes, that here was a performer, a band, who weren't going to aimlessly jump around in search of audience response. They were going to demand it, on ideological as well as musical grounds. He was pro bono in both senses of the phrase, and so were we.

Interviewed after the show by the BBC's Paul Gambaccini, and asked whether or not Live Aid heralded a new era of responsibility for rock music,

---

* Bono would forever be pilloried for what many considered his pious nature. Usually, he took this criticism in good humour. After all, he had soon become something of an institution, a larger-than-life creation, admired and lampooned in equal measure. The 2012 *Viz* Christmas annual included an inane cartoon strip ('Bono Out Of U2: Short on arse, big on caring') that contained a Band Aid knock-off based on Bono's failure to buy his grandmother a Christmas present: 'Oh, there won't be chocs for Bono's nan this Christmas time, the only sweets she'll get is jellied fruits.'

Bono said, 'Well, I think rock 'n' roll music has shirked its responsibility for a long time. I don't know, I suppose it's a dual thing, isn't it, there's a private responsibility, and there's a public one. This is a public thing, and there's time for that. But it must also be private. So much of my, and other performers here, life is public. And I'm sure that Bruce Springsteen or Prince and other performers who aren't here today are generous in a private way as opposed to a public way. I think that this [Live Aid] was the time to be public about it. The thing that interests me about this, I don't know if this is the time or the place, but it's the government of this country's responsibility to look after our money, and it seems to be an either/or situation – either they invest in life, or they invest in death. For the cost of offensive defence budgets we could turn those deserts in Africa into fertile land. I hope today affects public opinion which will ultimately affect the policymakers.'

Watching U2 in her American hotel room, Joan Baez – who had never previously heard them – wrote down her amazement at what she was seeing. 'This young man . . . is expressing himself with such tenderness it is enough to break my heart. He calls to the audience. They call back . . . He is directing a choir. They are the choir . . . I can't recall ever having seen anything like it in my life . . . Out of the hours of Live Aid that I saw by the end of the day, the high point was witnessing the magic of U2. They moved me as nothing else moved me.'

That day, they seemed to move everyone, even those among us who thought they were performing in Philadelphia.

'I do think Live Aid was a little bit of a watershed for the new Eighties bands, as they all slightly suffered after that,' said Gary Kemp. 'In a way U2 was a Seventies band, but they stole the show. Bono stole the show. It was getting that girl up to dance, that was such a great moment. He's one of those few artists that can work an audience that big and thrives on an audience that big. I'm not a big fan but he can do that.'

'U2 arrived on the world stage that day and they haven't left it since,' said the PR Alan Edwards.

Live Aid was the first time that Bono had jumped down into the crowd, looking for a moment, or a person to save. Almost two years later I saw U2

play the Centrum Arena in Worcester, Massachusetts, just an hour's drive from
the centre of Boston (and where the band were staying at the Four Seasons,
their hotel of choice throughout the *Joshua Tree* tour). Halfway through their
set, Bono flung down his microphone and left the stage, walking up into
the seats at the back of the arena. The rest of the band continued playing,
acting as though nothing had happened, because by this point in their career,
this had become a nightly occurrence. Up above the stage, Bono mingled
with the crowd, laying his hands on them, embracing them and their flags,
which all had his name on them. Bono picked on one fazed individual and
held his arm aloft, much to the pleasure of the audience. He'd done it again,
becoming 'as one' with the crowd. Bono then hugged the boy (who in a
matter of seconds had become a Bostonian star in his own right), and headed
back down to the stage, where the band were patiently waiting for him.

'It's OK, I just keep playing when Bono does stuff like that,' said the
Edge when I mentioned this to him later the next day. 'He does seem to
have an amazing rapport with our audience. It's quite uncanny.'

'This symbolic bonding of performer and audience, music and people,
captured the mood,' said the band's first biographer, Eamon Dunphy. 'As it
was felt in Wembley Stadium – that unique atmosphere, part compassion,
part rock concert, part coming together of the young people of the world –
was by now a stupendous piece of showmanship conveyed to the millions
watching at home. Bono had taken the ultimate performing risk. It could
have seemed gimmicky, a gauche intrusion, a breach of the spirit of Live
Aid. But his animal instinct for an audience, for the occasion, had helped
him get it right.'

Inadvertently, Live Aid was also influential in the way it encouraged U2
as a band to look at the way they presented themselves on stage. During
the *Joshua Tree* tour they started becoming the all-terrain Range Rover of
modern rock, making the sort of music that Big Country would have given
all their right arms to be making (although at the time it appeared they had
given them to someone else); such was the influence of the band's imagery
that after the album's release in the spring of 1987 ('positive landscape
photography' orchestrated by the band's grumpy Dutch photographer,

Anton Corbijn, and what I liked to call the revenge of the gatefold sleeve), one in three videos on MTV appeared to have been shot in the desert. Yet they had found the visual support at Wembley sorely lacking, principally because it was so pedestrian.

The imagery at Wembley that day was finite, and the visuals that U2 would start to use in concert would be anything but. They had ambitions to play stadiums, but also knew that they needed to connect with their audiences in the same way they did in concert halls and arenas. 'You have to keep your feet on the ground,' Edge told me at the time. 'When most bands get as big as we are now they also start thinking that any old shit will be good enough, but U2 have worked too hard to get where we are to throw it all away.' They knew that they had to make the audience feel included, or else the band would just end up like the Rolling Stones, or any other band who had become too big to play anywhere smaller.

'The new stadium industry was just around the corner at that time,' said Paul McGuinness. 'We were playing arenas in 1985. We couldn't start to play stadiums in our own right until 1987 with the *Joshua Tree* tour, which started in arenas and then progressed into stadiums. Video reinforcement didn't become possible until the early Nineties, and again we were very much at the forefront of that with the Zoo TV production, but that technology was not really there in 1985. It was during the next few years, as the sound equipment and the video equipment and lighting generally became more sophisticated, that creative standards kept improving and more and more designers like Mark Fisher and Willie Williams got involved. The Pink Floyd productions were around about this time, too. The scale of the business became much bigger and much more interesting, creatively, for the artists themselves. Up until then, the stadium concept had been a pretty unsatisfactory experience – just a black hole at one end of the field and no chance of seeing anything unless you bought binoculars – not that different, really, to a festival. Festivals in those days were rare enough. There were a few of them in Europe and hardly any in America. I suppose the scale of the business started to multiply.

'Live Aid was the greatest compendium bill of all time. Plus, in the mid-Eighties the industry was just starting to enter what turned out to be the golden years of the industry. CDs were just launching, stage shows were getting more interesting, and we were starting to see the intertwining of movie culture and music culture. It was great seeing Jack Nicholson being the MC in Philadelphia – we were all very impressed that he introduced us playing in Wembley. That kind of made a point, I think, that the rock 'n' roll generation included actors as well as musicians, whereas a few years before you could not have imagined the Beatles and Frank Sinatra on the same stage as Bob Hope. There was definitely a feeling that the counter-culture had come of age and had built its own stars – they were all part of that, or so many of them were.

'Live Aid was the biggest rock 'n' roll television programme of all time, and a lot of people who would never have paid that much attention to music on television learnt a lot about it at that moment. I'm sure that's true. I've never sat down and watched it from beginning to end, so my impressions of it were really the highlights, from being there. It was very exciting to be part of it, although I couldn't quite shake off the feeling on the day that we'd blown it so I didn't enjoy it as much as I would have done if I thought we'd done well. For me, the defining image – when I eventually saw the television pictures – will always be Bono doing this remarkable performance in the crowd and I realised what everyone else had realised days before, and I finally twigged. Slow learner.'

And what about the drugs, all the coke that was backstage?

'Not in our dressing room,' said McGuinness, 'but I'm sure that's true!'

'I first went to Africa, to Ethiopia, to work in a feeding station following Live Aid – one summer that stayed with me for a lifetime,' said Bono. 'But I don't see Africa as a cause. To me, this whole thing is about justice. The fact that people die in Africa every day of AIDS, a preventable, treatable disease, for lack of drugs that we take for granted in Europe and America – that's about justice, not charity.'

In the years following Live Aid, Bono's work as a lobbyist and political irritant would often overshadow his work with U2, and while this occasionally annoyed his band mates, they knew that his extracurricular work only made him more charismatic as a performer and more relevant as a cultural leader.

'Bono has done incredible work with the debt cancellation and the AIDS problem in Africa, but we wince sometimes when we see him with politicians in the newspaper,' said the Edge. 'It's worth it, but sometimes you realise how some people are going, "Wanker!"'

'We've all asked him if this is something he can defend,' said Larry Mullen Jr, when discussing Bono's relationship with George W. Bush when he was president, 'and he's said, "I've been to Africa, I've seen people dying from starvation. I've been to AIDS hospitals and seen people dying from AIDS. If I have to have lunch with the devil himself to get people to help and do something, I'll do it." You can't really counter that.'

Dire Straits had the unenviable task of following U2, although there was the brief respite of the Beach Boys being beamed in from Philadelphia, working their way through their greatest hits. Mark Knopfler's outfit were a Seventies band and had little to do with the Eighties. Bankers loved them. Uncool people liked them. *Tremendously* uncool people. There was nothing remotely dangerous about them, there was no frisson, no edge. Can anyone who saw Live Aid seriously remember what they looked like? We knew Mark Knopfler tended to wear a headband, sweated a lot and was borderline bald, but the others in the band? They were who exactly? They were what exactly? Were they members of a pop band, a rock act, or simply session musicians, like the group of old musos who played on the Wombles records? They were so nondescript that I'm not even sure Knopfler knew what they looked like, and one of them was his brother.

The band actually looked a lot like a bunch of teachers, which is what both Mark Knopfler and Sting were, before they started slogging around the circuit in the punk years. They were also both actually rather traditional songwriters, and couldn't believe their luck that they had become part of the rock establishment in the space of only a few years. And now they were on stage at Live Aid together, two old teachers throwing their arms around the world.

They didn't half sell records, though. Between them, Dire Straits and Sting would go on to sell 240 million of the things, many of them in the Eighties.

When Sting sings the falsetto mantra 'I want my MTV' in 'Money For Nothing', the inference is only partially ironic. Mark Knopfler's paean was a perfect Eighties song as it was quintessentially postmodern, being a comment on the music industry from the perspective of a man working in a New York appliance store. Knopfler was shopping in the store when he overheard one of the assistants bemoaning his lot, and comparing it to the rock stars in the videos being played on the huge wall of TVs at the back of the shop, all of which were tuned to MTV. Knopfler said the man was dressed in a checked shirt, work boots, jeans and a baseball cap – just like he would be in the Steve Barron-directed Quantel Paintbox cartoon promo of the song – carrying all these boxes of microwaves and televisions and coming up with lines like 'Now look at them yo-yos, that ain't working . . . lemme tell you them guys ain't dumb', etc.

'I wrote the song when I was actually in the store,' said Knopfler. 'I borrowed a bit of paper and started to write the song down in the store. I wanted to use a lot of the language that the real guy actually used when I heard him, because it was more real.'

This was the Dire Straits song it was OK to like, even if you did hear it blasting out of far too many Golf GTIs driven by girls who looked like they worked for estate agents and boys who had obviously just started in the City. To those who thought they cared so much about pop that they had taken it upon themselves to protect the genre, Dire Straits were the unacceptable face of Big Rock, a neutered and mollycoddled version of Led Zeppelin fronted by a man wearing a towelling headband who by rights shouldn't have been a rock star in the first place. Many critics simply disliked them because they had had the audacity to support various punk bands during 1977, refusing to disguise the fact that they were a glorified pub-rock band. I remember seeing them support Slaughter and the Dogs and Talking Heads at the Roundhouse in 1977 or 1978, and thinking what a terrifically broad church this all was, although I could tell that the swarms of identikit punks around me thought they sounded like a country and western band. And so spat enthusiastically.

Nevertheless, *Brothers In Arms*, the album 'Money For Nothing' came from, released just two months before Live Aid, was the first CD to sell a million copies; in the following twenty-five years it would go on to sell nearly 30 million copies worldwide, and is currently the seventh best-selling album of all time in the UK. They toured it for two years, and it nearly broke them. They released only one further album, *On Every Street*, in 1991, which inevitably was treated as an anticlimax by press and public alike.

At Wembley, the band were keeping all eyes on the clocks around the stage, as they had to get back to Wembley Arena to play their own gig, in front of 12,000 people who no doubt wished they'd actually been in Wembley Stadium. After their slot, the band rushed backstage, and had to ask two policewomen to show them the way out so they could move their equipment out of the rear entrance. They told them they were in Dire Straits, although the women thought they were being literal, as neither had any idea who they were.

Their performance on the day was faultless, and at times the guitar interplay during their eleven-minute version of 'Sultans Of Swing' was so good it made them sound not unlike Eric Clapton's Derek and the Dominoes from the early Seventies – but what the hell were they doing smack, bang in the middle of the Eighties?

It hardly mattered, though, as the crowd loved them.

TEN

18:44

Queen: 'Bohemian Rhapsody'/'Radio Ga Ga', 'Hammer To Fall', 'Crazy Little Thing Called Love', 'We Will Rock You'/ 'We Are The Champions'

Tell the old faggot it's gonna be the biggest thing
that ever happened.

BOB GELDOF TRYING TO PERSUADE FREDDIE MERCURY TO PLAY LIVE AID

At six forty-four, and with the sun still blazing in the north London sky, the television comedians Mel Smith and Griff Rhys Jones ambled on to the Wembley stage, dressed inexpertly as policemen, before good-naturedly haranguing the crowd with some dodgy jokes ('I'm sorry but we have had a bit of a complaint about the noise . . . from a woman in Belgium') and then, Smith having removed his helmet and jammed it under his arm, and with some solemnity, introduced 'Her Majesty – Queen.'

'Mel Smith and Griff Rhys Jones were fabulous,' said the comedian David Walliams. 'They came out and immediately got two laughs. It isn't easy to do that, not in front of 70,000 people. It was brave enough for Bryan Ferry to whistle during "Jealous Guy", but coming on dressed as policemen was pretty brave too. It was quite anti-establishment, in its way, Live Aid, as there was a sense that Margaret Thatcher wasn't doing anything about the problem, so we were all going to do it ourselves. When Matt [Lucas] and I did Live 8, we were originally just going to go out and do exactly what Smith and Jones did, although we changed our minds just before we did it.'

I'm not sure exactly what we were expecting – after all, how exciting could Queen really be? Having never been a huge fan (I'm fairly certain I saw their free Hyde Park concert in 1976, but can remember nothing about it, not even the journey there and back), and never really understanding what all the fuss was about, I certainly didn't think this was going to be the greatest stadium performance of all time. But that's exactly what it was. With knobs on, with bells and whistles too. During World War Two, musical propaganda broadcasts were supposed to convince the Germans that we were patriotically more ardently motivated than they were, yet I don't know of anything that could be more rousing than Queen's performance of 'We Are The Champions' and 'We Will Rock You' that day in July 1985. Perhaps the atmosphere would have been more incendiary if Freddie and the gang had played 'Land Of Hope And Glory' as the Red Arrows flew by, but I doubt it, frankly.

They started in a familiar fashion, performing a perfectly reasonable version of 'Bohemian Rhapsody', with Freddie hunched over the piano, before cutting the song dead halfway through, and then launching off into a truncated selection of their greatest hits that had half the crowd singing along, while the other half (perhaps the previously unconvinced half, like me) were simply swept up in the dynamics, unable to do anything but stand there, slack-jawed, and stare in awe.

Mercury wielded a pale yellow Fender Telecaster and performed an onstage ballet with a BBC cameraman, proving that – ever the consummate performer, the quintessential showman, the irrepressible show-off – he could do macro and micro at the same time, using the grand gesture for those in the cheap seats way up at the back of the stadium, and adding nuance for television. Afterwards Mercury would be described as the supernova among a galaxy of stars at Live Aid, something the singer would no doubt have agreed with.

This wasn't a show that had been salted or tinkered with, this was a show that had been hauled into the pits, shunted up on hydraulics and had every part of it examined – the engine, the wheels, the undercarriage, the brakes, the lot. Fine-tuned to within an inch of its life, this was a show that had been thoroughly burnished, polished, and tested time and time again.

Time was the principal issue here, as the band were being asked to condense an entire career – which in Queen's case was an incredibly content-rich fourteen years – into a period of less than twenty minutes, including the walk on and off. The gaps between songs would become as important as the gaps themselves; even better, there shouldn't *be* any gaps.

It was a whirlwind of a performance, and, rather like the first four or five songs in a Bruce Springsteen show, which are designed to rush you out on to the highway, and then deliver you to a place where you will be entertained and toyed with for the next three hours, Queen's set was clinical not just in its attention to detail but also in the way that it was completely relentless. There would be no dissenting voices as there would be no time for them to be heard. Most bands don't get into their stride until they've been on stage for twenty minutes, while others are barely out of the dressing room, yet Queen squeezed in most of what they'd learned (the pyrotechnics, the light and shade, the bombast, the little screaming guitar tricks) and almost made it look easy.

This was theatre, and in this particular case, nothing was left to chance. The set had been rehearsed, including all the seemingly spontaneous moves, the audience call-and-response ('Day-O!'), everything. It didn't matter that some of the songs were ten years old, as that afternoon everything felt as fresh as a Wembley daisy.

'Queen had taken it very seriously, and properly rehearsed,' said Paul McGuinness. 'They had scripted exactly what they were going to do. They really were classic showmen and they could see the opportunity that was there and they seized it with both hands.'

So good was their performance that it's often made me think what Live Aid would have been like if everyone had done the same – truncated their career into twenty minutes – but then not everyone would have had the material or the tools. The Who could have done it, if there had been a little less rancour between them, and ten years previously they would have been the best band on the bill anyway (no contest). Elton's Red Piano show in Las Vegas years later hinted at what he could have done in just twenty minutes if he had chosen to do a dynamo-medley. Elvis could have done it too, if he had been with the Attractions, as for nine years (1977–1986) they were as good a live band as the E-Street Band (and in a rather striking way, quite similar). But the only band to touch Queen that day was U2, for whom Live Aid was almost a global coming-out ball.

This brevity had always been one of the appealing things about punk, a decade earlier, as not only did the new bands not want to perform long sets – in case they were compared to the dreaded behemoths of yore – but also they just didn't have the material. Many nights you'd go off and see groups who would run out of songs after half an hour and then start playing them all again, which split the crowd into those who relished the thought of hearing 'In The City' or 'Orgasm Addict' twice, and those who used this sign of weakness as an opportunity to scream abuse or hurl a glass at the stage (I'm fairly sure I saw Talking Heads once playing two incredibly long versions of 'Psycho Killer', their hero song, when they supported the Ramones at Friars in Aylesbury in early 1977, simply to fill out their set).

After Live Aid, so many stadium concerts would be viewed through the prism of Queen's performance at Wembley that day. What Live Aid encouraged was a move by traditional pop acts to try and conquer the stadium environment, through ego, greed, and the natural desire to play somewhere larger than they'd ever played before. Hence enormous tours by the likes of Madonna, Michael Jackson and Prince, only one of whom (the Purple Imp) stood any chance of conquering the crowd.

Watching Madonna and Michael Jackson in particular, you got the sense that their performances were more about them than the crowd, the people who had paid to come and pay homage. Queen always looked as though they were performing for the masses rather than just themselves; it was an act, a show, theatre (after all, didn't their album *A Night At The Opera* list the personnel as 'Cast'?). Madonna and Jackson were essentially dance acts who were being displayed on a huge 'rock' stage, whereas Queen's set at Live Aid was the perfect example of a large-scale rock group producing a bespoke 'club' performance.

Queen were properly amazing, and their performance was airtight. Freddie Mercury didn't *look* amazing, as he was dressed like anyone else who doesn't pay much attention to the way they dress, or at least he looked like anyone else at Wembley that day, which is probably more to the point. He was wearing a tight white vest, training shoes, a studded leather belt (with a smaller one on a bicep), and pale, tight-fitting jeans. He looked like, well, one of us, although I didn't consider myself to be one of us. Because if Freddie Mercury had been one of *us*, he would have been one of me, and would have been wearing a blue MA-1 flying jacket, slightly baggier silver-tab Levi's and a pair of Loake's loafers. And while I thought I looked cool, Freddie really was cool – he was just the coolest thing to ever jump out of the icebox, as his performance that day will be remembered as long as pop is remembered. Anyone wearing his clothes would have been easily mistaken for a boy racer who had parked his hot-hatch in the Wembley car park, but because of his physique and his cartoon moustache, he looked like a genetic clone.

His performance at Live Aid was as mesmerising and as important as any performance by Elvis Presley, and was as impressive as any performance there has ever been seen on the Wembley stage (including those by U2, Michael Jackson, Madonna, Bruce Springsteen and the Rolling Stones – certainly the Stones, who actually stopped being a decent live band in the mid-Seventies).

The group hadn't asked to open or close the show, and instead requested a slot around 6 p.m.; not just prime time in the UK, but, as the *Daily Telegraph* writer Peter Stanford pointed out, being five hours behind, perfect for the US audience, before there was any danger of viewers lapsing into big-band fatigue.

Dave Grohl of the Foo Fighters, who would later perform with Queen guitarist Brian May and drummer Roger Taylor, said, 'Queen smoked 'em. They just took everybody. They walked away being the greatest band you'd ever seen in your life, and it was unbelievable. And that's what made the band so great; that's why they should be recognised as one of the greatest rock bands of all time because they could connect with an audience.'

Spend too long watching programmes like *The X-Factor*, and you'll hear judges say how so-and-so 'smashed it', or 'owned it' or some such nonsense. That day, Queen *did* own the stage, completely. If Live Aid had finished after their turn, we all would have gone home happy.

Through their set, Mercury strutted around imperiously, cocksure, safe in the knowledge that whatever he does on stage was going to work. Watching it again (and there is a great upscaled and retouched 16:9 video with extraordinary audio on YouTube), it's quite chilling to see Mercury's handling of the crowd, and his apparently innate self-confidence. All through every song, he points to the gods, plays to the gallery, and exaggerates each gesture, making himself as large as can be, the perfect stadium showman. Mercury had been a fan of Liza Minnelli since the early Seventies, and her performances in *Cabaret* and *Liza With A Z* heavily influenced his stage antics. Camp. Theatrical. Throwing his head back, and demanding appreciation from the crowd. Beaming at the audience as though he were taking a curtain call, projecting himself to the very last row in the house, treating even the smallest venue as a sports arena. Small gestures writ large.

Following 'Radio Ga Ga', Mercury indulged himself by getting the crowd to repeat his vocal training pastiche – something he would always do at Queen concerts – and the Wembley crowd were with him all the way.

As someone remarked backstage, until Queen came on, it had all been a bit of a nice summer picnic. Queen may not have been talking much backstage – they had been on the verge of breaking up before Live Aid, so tensions between them were high – but they had come with a mission. For several years the band had been on the verge of going their separate ways (they certainly had no financial reason to work: in the 1982 *Guinness Book of Records*, they were listed as Britain's highest-paid company directors), and it would be Live Aid – the gig they didn't really want to do – that would make them come together again. In April 1986, there was an article in the *Sun* entitled 'How Live Aid Saved Our Queen'. And it was true.

While Brian May, Roger Taylor and bassist John Deacon were slightly fractious, Mercury remained upbeat.

'He sat holding court, in that perfectly camp but quite humble way of his,' said Bernard Doherty. 'He knew the power he had over people, but it didn't go to his head. If he'd been sitting outside a beach hut in Southend-on-Sea, he'd have taken people's breath away. He was a true star, with that indefinable quality. John Deacon I wasn't aware of, where was he? And I didn't see Brian May or Roger Taylor speak to each other all day. They were like a divorced couple at the same party.'

If there were differences, they were smart enough to put them aside and concentrate on the job in hand.

After six hours of what one critic called 'Euro wimp', Queen injected some electro-pizzaz into the show. 'Geldof called Live Aid a jukebox, so it seemed obvious to simply play the hits and get off,' said Brian May. 'The day was fabulous – people forget that element of [competition],' said John Deacon. 'It was a good morale booster for us too, because it showed us the strength of support we had in England, and it showed us what we had to offer as a band.' May agreed: 'I think Live Aid proved we didn't need backdrops or [the] cover of darkness.'

Mercury watched the first few hours of the show at his home in Kensington, before being driven up by limo around three o'clock, dressed in his 'high-clone' gear, complete with a silver amulet.

His friend David Wigg, from the *Daily Express*, was the only journalist allowed to join Mercury in his trailer as he prepared for the performance. Freddie said that he was looking forward to getting out there, and to doing his bit. He spoke fondly of the project, and expressed admiration for Bob Geldof, before admitting that he found some of the TV coverage of the Ethiopian plight hard to watch. To steady his nerves, he had a few vodka and tonics.

Earlier, when the band had been asked to meet the Prince and Princess of Wales, bass guitarist John Deacon was so shy he sent his roadie, Spider, to meet them instead. 'I thought I'd make a fool of myself [if I went],' he said.

When the thirty-eight-year-old Mercury jogged on to the stage after the Smith and Jones introduction, his biographer Mark Blake described him as looking like a ballet dancer running for a bus. Not that Mercury would ever be caught running for a bus. Mercury prowled around, parading himself for all to see, and immediately took possession of the stage. Jumpy, he was coursing with adrenaline. He stood, feet wide apart, and assumed ownership of everything and everyone in his sight line. He threw his head back, punched the air, and moved like a mad king. It was as though he were being directed by Ridley Scott or Martin Scorsese, so imperious did he look. Suddenly, for a moment, he was inside out, his hidden alter ego on display for all to see. Mercury stood there with his legs spread like a wrestler's, staring out into the crowd as though it were his own private army.

Halfway through the first section of 'Bo-Rap', the band launched into the synthesiser riff to 'Radio Ga Ga', which had been a massive hit for them the year before. The song's promo video had been inspired by the Twenties sci-fi epic *Metropolis* directed by Fritz Lang, and as the band careered into the first chorus, a large percentage of the crowd started mimicking a scene from the video, clapping their hands above their heads. 'I'd never seen anything like that in my life,' said Brian May later.

Few of us had.

'The band understood the idea that Live Aid was a global jukebox,' said Geldof. 'And that Freddie could ponce about in front of the whole world.' Geldof said they looked 'like the most unlikely rock band you could imagine'. But who cared? Live Aid belonged to Queen.

The video the crowd were aping had been directed by David Mallet using 500 extras, all recruited at short notice from the band's fan club. They were dressed identically, and told to clap their hands in sequence above their heads during the first chorus, something that would be copied by Queen concert-goers the world over, and would become the defining moment of Live Aid itself. So powerful was the image that as the band appeared on the screens at the JFK Stadium in Philadelphia, the entire crowd there started clapping over their heads as well, all 90,000 of them. Mercury had a fascinating power that even travelled all the way across the Atlantic.

'Radio Ga Ga' was written by drummer Roger Taylor, recorded in LA (a first for the band) and had been a huge hit when it was released in January 1984, only being kept off the number one slot by Frankie Goes to Hollywood's 'Relax'. A paean to the radio of yore, a lament at its present demise, and a rallying call for its future ('You had your time, you had the power, You've yet to have your finest hour'), 'Radio Ga Ga' initially sounded bland and glib, but on repeated plays – the damn thing was never off the radio, remarkably – started to become iconic.

Taylor's song (which was originally called 'Radio Ca Ca', after a lavatorial remark by his young son Felix, whose mother Dominique is French; Taylor is adamant that you can still hear the band singing 'Radio Ca Ca' in the background of the chorus) was a sideswipe, yet it was anthemic. It starts with a synthesiser bubbling away, before a drum machine comes in and turns the whole thing Germanic.

'It deals with how important radio used to be, historically speaking, before television, and how important it was to me as a kid,' said Taylor. 'It was the first place I heard rock 'n' roll. I used to hear a lot of Doris Day, but a few times each day I'd hear a Bill Haley record or an Elvis Presley song.' Lyrically the song follows the Buggles hit, 'Video Killed The Radio Star', and was therefore perfect for the increasingly self-referential MTV (for whom the song was not-so-secretly written). Mixing footage from *Metropolis* with concert footage and new film of the band, the video was quite haunting; the totalitarian *Nineteen Eighty-four* element – mechanical, meaningless, robotic – was a theme being used by many bands at the time, and as such says as much about the mid-Eighties as it does about the early days of radio.

Ironically, the iconic Live Aid moment wasn't even created by the band, as the double handclap in the first chorus was actually something invented by David Mallet and then reproduced on the record. How apt that the defining image of the Eighties was one created by a video director, an image created to accompany a record that pined for a better time, a time long since gone.

When Mercury saw all the hands in the audience start clapping above their heads, he was shocked. Exhilarated, but shocked. They had only ever performed in darkness – they didn't do festivals – so this was something of a novelty.

This was the moment that suddenly crystallised the day, and we all knew it. All of a sudden we were as one. As all those arms – our arms – rose as one, celebrating Queen's monochromatic, monotonous, melancholic anthem, the stadium felt somehow complete, actually alive. All over Wembley, all over the world, hands were clapping above heads, applauding the ironic nature of the gesture while also celebrating ourselves in a way. We were glad to be doing what we were doing, but we were even happier that we were all doing it together. It felt like the culmination of something that had started thirty years previously, a generational shift, and here we all were, in a stadium, in stadiums all over the world, in front of televisions all over the world, making a difference. Were we at a rally, or were we in a video? In essence we were at both. We felt the eyes of the world upon us, and we didn't want to be found wanting. Something in Queen's performance had crystallised not only the afternoon, but also the very idea of Live Aid itself. There was a heaving mass of humanity out here, genuflecting for the greater good. This was not just the pinch point of the afternoon, not just the pinch point of Live Aid, but in some ways the pinch point of the decade. It was almost as though we'd all been tattooed at once, as all of a sudden we were synchronised. Energised. Syncopated. Happy in the knowledge that we were doing something of worth . . . *contributing*. In the same way that all those counter-cultural events of the Sixties felt like harbingers of change as well as change itself, so Live Aid felt like the beginning of something, too. Standing there in the middle of Wembley on that sunny afternoon in 1985, you actually felt as though things were changing, that change *was* possible, regardless of what that might be. Whether it was political, societal, musical, sociological, whatever, here was a suggestion, a glimpse, that people en masse could be a force for change, for good. For a very brief time, you felt almost as though anything might be possible, almost as though giddy emotion and impassioned vocals really could move mountains, or shift borders, or do away with borders altogether. Whenever I think of that moment – that 'Radio Ga Ga' moment – I think of the lyrics from David Bowie's

'Memories Of A Free Festival': 'It was ragged and naïve. It was heaven.'

Gil Scott-Heron had famously said that the revolution will not be televised, but if you consider Live Aid to be a revolution, he was wrong. Media had brought the world together in a way not seen since the first moon landing, and arguably for a greater purpose. Neil Armstrong may have been stepping into space, into the great unknown, but Live Aid was trying to solve problems down here on Earth. A generation before David Cameron's much-derided 'Big Society', this was society rolling up to meet the state – activism and sweatbands with a disco beat, as the Pet Shop Boys might have put it.

Squint into the sun, and all you saw was a large mass of overly giddy Queen fans clapping their hands metronomically above their heads, but the moment seemed to signify so much more. If you allowed yourself to be truly swept along by emotion – which we did – it was easy to feel that the thirty-year history of post-war pop culture had all been leading up to this point, that the exuberance of the Fifties, compounded by the altruism of the Sixties, the cultural growth of the Seventies and the corporate professionalism of the Eighties had conspired to produce . . . well, this. Live Aid, a celebration of great pop orchestrated to help cure great ills.

This wasn't only about helping other people, as we were also indulging ourselves – by dint of our relationship with everyone else in the stadium, and with everyone else watching on TV.

While Freddie Mercury had managed to unite us all.

For a brief moment we all felt united in our glee, our sense of community, our sense of purpose. This was a World Cup moment, an Olympic highlight, a moon landing and a Wimbledon final all wrapped up in one. It was only a pop concert, yet those of us who were there felt our world tilt a little. There was a shudder, and all because of a double-handclap and a punch in the air from a thirty-eight-year-old man with a large San Franciscan moustache and a studded leather belt.

'This was not a Queen concert crowd,' said the band's biographer, Laura Jackson. 'Yet by the time they performed "We Are The Champions", the swaying forest of extended arms around the grounds and the sound of the massed voices singing along, provided an unforgettable display of unity. Queen were untouchable that day – a fact that, ego aside, few could dispute.'

Fellow performer Paul Young felt the same: 'I'd always liked Queen, but that was the night I said to myself, "These boys really are fantastic." The sound they managed to get was absolutely amazing. There was just the four of them on there, with none of their usual trappings, and they *still* blew everyone away. Freddie, too, proved to the whole watching world that evening just what a showman he was.'

Dave Hogan was one of only six people chosen as official Live Aid photographers, and so was allowed to wander most places backstage. 'It was obvious to everyone on the day that Freddie was the main man. [Although] no one realised how powerful he was until he went out there. At that point, we knew, this is it. I remember him launching into "Radio Ga Ga". It wasn't even dark, he was whipping up all this magic in daylight. That ocean of fans clapping and stamping together just sent shivers down your spine. For us it was heaven. This is the moment you want. He stole it. The day was full of fantastic moments – Bono leaping into the crowd, McCartney's first live performance since John Lennon was assassinated. But what I saw Freddie do that day took my breath away. He was engaged with every single person present. Total unison. Nobody has done that, before or since.'

'Queen were amazing, and I didn't even like them,' said Sade's Andrew Hale, who was hanging around after the band's performance. 'I remember watching them and just thinking how brilliant it was. I had no idea a stadium gig could look or sound like that.'

The broadcaster Paul Gambaccini remembered a frisson backstage as heads turned towards the TV monitors, like dogs hearing a whistle. This was a masterclass in audience stagecraft, and Mercury was giving a free lesson.

'Nobody remembers Spandau Ballet were at Live Aid, nobody remembers Adam Ant was at Live Aid, but everyone remembers Queen,' he said. 'Queen rehearsed. They got it down. They got the history of Queen into twenty minutes. They go out there, and they're doing it, and then fate intervenes in the form of a cameraman, the cameraman who gets up close to Freddie and Freddie starts this performance with the camera, and it was incredible.

'As their set unfolded, everyone thought the same thing: they're stealing the show. And they did.'

Queen's performance could not have been more different in scope, ambition or execution than U2's, as they kept to the script. Both, however, achieved the same effect, which was touching people. Bono's walk into the crowd, his touch, was all about human contact on a global stage, while Freddie's call-and-response, his pomp, his vigour, were tantamount to the same thing. Both performers were throwing their arms around the world.

Inexplicably, halfway through Queen's performance, in America MTV decided to cut away to commercials – seven of them: Camay soap; the Chevy Cavalier ('Live today's Chevy, with an interior that comforts your very soul'); Sun County wine cooler; Foot Locker ('When you've got your body going, we've got the shoes'); the Chevy Camaro; Pepsi (pitched by Lionel Richie); a General Electric cassette player ('The power of music: no one lets you experience it like General Electric); and English Leather men's cologne ('With its clean masculine scent').

In Britain we saw all of it, whether we were there or not.

'While it took me years to bring myself to be critical about anything I saw on 13 July 1985,' wrote music critic Pete Paphides, 'I clearly remember knowing within seconds of Freddie's first "DAAAAAAYO!" that Queen were about to win Live Aid. Only two moments that day truly managed to silence the John Motson in my adolescent head asking, "Is Pete about to undergo the defining experience of his life?" One of them was the Nuremberg-style double-clap on "Radio Ga Ga", with which I found myself joining in. The second was "We Are The Champions". Indeed, not only did Queen win Live Aid, but they rubbed everyone's noses in it with a song built around the age-old playground chant, "Nyer-nyer-nyer-nyer-nyer"! What a fantastically graceless thing to do.'

'For years afterwards people would ask for the "Sun goes down spot" at festivals,' said my friend Robin, 'as after Queen's performance at Live Aid, everyone wanted to appear at exactly that point. It became known as the twilight spot.' He had seen the band twice before, on the *Sheer Heart Attack* and *A Night At The Opera* tours, at Bristol's Colston Hall ('Bristol's premier concert venue'), but hadn't listened to them for years as they had become 'fantastically uncool'.

'I knew the band were going down well,' said Bernard Doherty, 'The crowd was going nuts. Everyone backstage stopped talking to watch them. That was bizarre. Never normally happens. Who came on before or after Queen? Hardly anyone remembers. What do I remember? That Freddie Mercury was the greatest performer on the day. Perhaps the greatest performer ever.'

After 'Hammer To Fall', Mercury hurriedly addressed the crowd. 'This song . . . ah . . . is dedicated to you beautiful people here tonight. That means all of you. Thank you for coming along and making this a great occasion.'

Queen's performance wasn't just perfectly judged, it was complete, almost like a perfectly judged meal. Watching it now on YouTube I'm fascinated by just how complete it is. Everyone that day was employed to produce a capsule performance, and instead of just getting up there and bashing out a couple of hits, Queen extensively rehearsed their performance at London's Shaw Theatre (with Spike Edney, who played additional guitar and keyboards at Wembley), and whittled their set down almost as though they were reducing a sauce.

Mercury knew what he was doing: 'We're just going to go on there and play,' he said beforehand. 'We're going to be doing our best songs. Basically you're not trying to put across your *new* material or anything. No, hit them with your best-known material.'

At the rehearsals they put clocks in front of the stage, to time their performance perfectly. They also made sure they were louder than anyone else.

Initially Queen had been unenthusiastic about appearing at Live Aid, but then Geldof had marched up to Mercury in a restaurant and told him that if he didn't do Live Aid, he was going to tell the world that it was Mercury who personally said no. In the end they were glad to do it, more than glad. Geldof initially approached the band through Edney, the Boomtown Rats' occasional keyboard player, who also played with Queen. He was in New

Zealand, as were the band, and he asked them on Geldof's behalf. To which they said, 'Why doesn't he ask us himself?'

So he did, and still they said no. They kept turning Geldof down as they didn't think it would actually happen. They continued to resist, even after Geldof had told them both Elton John and David Bowie had said yes (neither had at the time). But after a lot of toing and froing, they finally agreed.

'I had to just find Freddie's G-spot,' said Geldof. 'Roger Taylor was saying he'd do it, but he didn't think Fred would. The band were exhausted and they were really questioning their future as well. When I eventually got to speak to him I literally said to him, "Fred, why wouldn't you do it? This entire stage was built for you, practically. Darling, the world." That's literally what I said. I said that. He laughed and he said, "Oh, you have a point, Mr Geldof."'

'I don't think I'd be doing it out of guilt,' Mercury said. 'Even if I didn't do it the poverty would still be there. It's something that will always be there. We'll do all we can do to help because it's a wonderful thing. But as far as I'm concerned I'm doing it out of pride. It's something to be proud of – that I'm actually in with all the biggies – all the biggest stars – and that I can do something worthwhile. Yes, I'm proud more than anything.'

Queen hadn't been asked to contribute to the Band Aid single, perhaps as they were still surrounded by a lot of negative press regarding their series of concerts at the Sun City Super Bowl in Bophuthatswana a few months earlier, a serious error of judgement. Live Aid was also a way for them to assuage their guilt, and to do it in the most public way possible.

Having agreed to do it, Roger Taylor said, 'Of course it is a wonderful cause and will make a pot of money for that wonderful cause. But make no mistake. We're doing it for our own glory as well.

'Let's not lie, don't tell me there was one act there that wasn't aware that there would be more than a billion people watching.'

'Queen turned the day around,' said Harvey Goldsmith, when asked who put in the best performance that day. 'Everybody knew their records, everybody knew about their successes, everybody [in the industry] knew the problems [they'd been having] and everybody knew about what was going on. They were going through a bit of a funny period. They were having difficulties in America, and had kind of done everything they could do here and they were still reasonably on top of the pile. But they realised as Live Aid developed, that this was an opportunity. And they changed everything around with an amazing performance. Freddie was a consummate showman, and really worked hard to win over the 80,000 people there. The day had been relentless, and because of the circular, three-section stage, we were changing global acts round in under two minutes . . . The crowd had been bombarded. And Freddie came on and just took them somewhere else. He took advantage of the fact that there had been so many acts, and he knew he had to completely engage them. Hence the "Day-O" call-and-response. He thought he had to get them engaged and he engaged them in a way that nobody ever dreamed he could. And he was the moment, no question about it. It was one of his key moments of the whole event. Because he just took over the whole place.'

There are hundreds of websites devoted to Live Aid, many of which encourage those who were there, or who watched it on television, to share their memories. Cherie is one: 'What I remember most is sitting in front of [the] TV all day, afraid to move in case I missed something. I was sixteen years old, and a fan of just about every band there (England . . . not US) . . . The best performance, and I defy anyone to argue with this because I am simply unswayable on this point, was Queen. Having never seen Queen in concert, I didn't know what to expect. I was blown away. If I was asked to pick out three of the most memorable moments of my life, visually speaking, I would say watching the Space Shuttle explode (too horrible for words), watching the Berlin Wall fall (via CNN), and Queen performing "Radio Ga Ga", with the crowd's hands all moving in unison. I know this is a bizarre series of memories, but each has a place in my heart, and though I was not actually there for any of them, watching them live on TV made me feel part of history.'

While there were a couple of moments during the set which could have actually been filled with theatre, there's not much, seconds at most.

Everything about their twenty minutes was content, a fourteen-year career condensed into an assault so dynamic, so well executed, that it's no surprise that people still talk about it today, even those – especially those, in fact – who weren't there.

And it was Mercury's show. While the band were up there, wrapping their arms around their singer and making sure he didn't fall, it was really Freddie's show. I'd say three-quarters of the performance belonged to Freddie, and I don't think any of the others would take issue with that. The way he walks on to the stage and owns it immediately, well, I've seen so few performers do that, not without intimidating the audience, anyway. I've seen John Lydon do it, and Joe Strummer, and Jimmy Pursey come to that, or Mark E. Smith, but apart from Robbie Williams and Bono, I'm not sure I've ever seen a performer who treated the stage, and the people in front of it, with such studied casual regard and get away with it.

'I believe Freddie Mercury is the greatest rock 'n' roll showman to ever walk the stage,' said Gary Kemp. 'I saw them numerous times and they were kind of on their uppers at that point. What they got at Live Aid was that this was a moment just to sell your greatest hits and show yourselves to the stadium. Up until that point I'm not sure they were that successful a stadium band, and after Live Aid they were a stadium band, because everyone wanted to relive that experience with Queen.

'There's this music journalist, Neil McCormick, who wrote in the *Telegraph* that acts shouldn't play after a certain age and they should retire. Why? Fool. Look at Queen at Live Aid. If Chuck Berry played next week I'd probably go and see him. Same with the Stones.'

Even from the back of the stadium where I was standing at the time, with Kate and Robin, I was blown away. And I didn't even like Queen very much. Before Live Aid I found them bombastic, silly, off kilter, unnecessarily camp, and way too conservative for my tastes. Yet in the space of twenty minutes I was magically converted, almost as though I had experienced something religious. This was the era of the stadium, and although Bowie, the Stones and Zeppelin had owned arenas in the Seventies, the stadium gig demanded something else of the performer: the ability to talk directly to the back row. And Freddie Mercury had whatever it was innately, almost as though it were part of his DNA.

The people with this gift to talk to the gods was a very small club, one inhabited by Freddie Mercury, Elton John, Bruce Springsteen and U2. Hardly anyone else got close. The grand gesture, and the ability to play to a crowd of 100,000-plus people and treat them as friends, was something every entertainer lucky enough to draw big crowds had to contend with in the Eighties. In the second half of the decade I saw Madonna, Michael Jackson, Prince, Paul McCartney, Rod Stewart, George Michael and Dire Straits all try and conquer the stadium, and so few of them got away with it, taking glorified club tactics and amplifying them by treating the auditorium as a stage, bringing theatrics to a rock environment by relying on drama and costume. (It's something that's difficult to shake off, too, and if you ever see Elton perform in a smaller venue – at a sports arena in the US, say, or at a stately home in the UK – you'll see him make the same exaggerated gestures he'd make in a stadium, giving him a cartoon quality, and the impression that he is the master of all he surveys.)

The *New Yorker* writer Sasha Frere-Jones – who, unlike many of his peers, has a radar acquired from the very top shelf – has a word for it: 'squinting', the act of peering at a musician you fell in love with when you were much younger, to try to remind yourself why you found them so fascinating. 'The relationship grows through awkward phases,' he writes, 'nautical dress, orchestral arrangements, dodgy collections of poems. Along the way, you find yourself squinting to keep seeing what made you fall in love; you will need to pretend that the accordion and the Balkan song cycles are something else. (Fans of Bob Dylan have unusually deep creases.) In pop music, which is a worse deal for the ageing than painting and fiction are, there can be a fair amount of effort involved.'

And although Queen only really had a career that lasted twenty years, and whose oeuvre was crowded but not exactly perverse, their fans were always completely, totally forgiving. As they started out as a rather orthodox (if flashy) rock band, this was even more unusual, but as the band pinballed between theatrical ballads, disco and high-camp pop, their legions of admirers blithely followed along (honestly, if you liked 'Seven Seas of Rye', you weren't programmed to enjoy 'Killer Queen', not at all). The band got away with it as they wrote the sort of tunes you generally couldn't shake, even if you wanted to (and like I said, before Live Aid, I seriously wanted to). And as you continued to hear them, and as they worked their way into your subconscious, so they stayed there. Though Mercury tried to maintain some semblance of a private life, and went out of his way to avoid press, he could morph into the most theatrical of showmen, showing off his remarkable vocal range (four octaves, unparalleled in rock).

Their fans tended to be rather orthodox, too, and for a while appeared to be in some sort of collective denial concerning Freddy Mercury's sexuality. I always think of Freddie in the same way as the Robert De Niro character in the 2007 movie *Stardust*. De Niro plays a gay pirate called Captain Shakespeare, who tries to hide his sexuality from his crew. When he is eventually outed, his men give a collective shrug. 'We always knew you were a whoopsie,' says one.

In an era dominated by transgressive and camp imagery, a decade almost defined by 'gender bender' pop stars, and by images largely produced by a gay community that had never known so much power or influence, Mercury continued to be one of the most famous gay icons in the entertainment business. Mercury suggested coiled might, a big man, well built and fairly well cut, who often looked as though he had just stepped out of the confines of New York's West Village. Along with Elton John, by 1985 Mercury was probably the most famous 'non-heterosexual' in the music industry. Boy George, Frankie Goes to Hollywood's Holly Johnston and Marilyn were already in decline, Erasure's Andy Bell was rarely above the parapet, while George Michael, the Pet Shop Boys' Neil Tennant and REM's Michael Stipe were not officially 'out'. Morrissey had always made a big deal out of his so-called celibacy, while Jimmy Somerville (of Bronski Beat and the Communards) tended to make his sexuality a defining part of his proposition.

Not that Mercury discussed his sexuality. In fact he declined to talk about anything much. He didn't court the press in this way, and his private life was out of bounds. He was so publicity-shy that few people outside his circle had heard him talk. Everyone knew how Mick Jagger spoke, or Elton, or Bowie, but unless you went to Queen concerts, it was difficult to imagine how Mercury must sound when not singing. Mercury was an entertainer whose stage presence dominated Queen's stage shows. He didn't pontificate in the press, so why should they pontificate about him? He wasn't militant, didn't express any views about sexuality – his own, or other people's – and while his tendencies were one of the industry's great 'unspokens', it wasn't as though he were trying to disguise anything. Had we seen the way he dressed?

Ultimately, Queen's story, or at least Freddie Mercury's, is entwined with the way the band ended, and the way in which they suddenly stopped being Queen. Ultimately this would turn out to be a story about disease, one particular disease: AIDS. When Mercury died from AIDS in 1991, he became the most high-profile victim of the disease. Rumours about his health had been circulating since the end of the Eighties, and it soon became an open secret within the music industry that he had contracted the AIDS virus, and was actually seriously ill. 'I have a life to live,' he would say to friends in the years after the diagnosis. 'I just have less time to live it than everyone else.' He was diagnosed in 1987, although it was only towards the end of the decade that he started seriously deteriorating. At the very end, he was covered with lesions from the rare skin cancer Kaposi's Sarcoma, was too weak to stand, and was almost blind. Six and a half years after Live Aid, on 24 November 1991, Mercury finally died quietly at his home in Kensington, his management having sent out a press release the day before, officially saying he had the disease, to soften the blow for those fans of his who knew nothing about it (most of them, in fact). The release was only sanctioned when it was known that Mercury was on his way out ('I felt it correct to keep this information private in order to protect the privacy of those around me'). He was just forty-five.

'As soon as we realised Freddie was ill, we clustered around him like a protective shell,' said Brian May. 'We were lying to everyone, even our own families, because he didn't want the world intruding on his struggle.

He used to say, "I don't want people buying our fucking records out of sympathy." We all became very close. We grew up a lot.'

Because he couldn't perform, Mercury had been putting even more of an effort into recording, despite finding it tiring and stressful. 'It was tragic that that terrible disease should break up Freddie's career, because he was improving and improving as a singer and performer,' said Roger Taylor. 'It was just a terrible shame. He felt that he couldn't deliver what was expected of him.'

1985 had been the year of the first high-profile AIDS death, when, on 2 October, three months after Live Aid, Rock Hudson finally succumbed. It had been announced two weeks after Live Aid, on 25 July, that he was suffering from the disease, although as one of the most famous (and active) gay actors in Hollywood there had been rumours for years.

'I've always found it deeply ironic that after four years of gay men dying of AIDS, a turning point in Americans' perception of the disease was . . . a gay man dying of AIDS,' said Elton John. 'But Rock Hudson didn't fit prevailing stereotypes of homosexuality. He was the ladies' man who starred in *Pillow Talk* with Doris Day. He was a close friend of Ronald and Nancy Reagan. Rock became the "respectable" face of AIDS, and perhaps AIDS itself became a bit more respectable, a bit less vile, because he had it.'

Two weeks later Nicholas Eden, the gay MP and son of the late prime minister Anthony also died of the disease. He had served under Margaret Thatcher as both Undersecretary of State for Energy and Undersecretary of State for the Environment, and was the first semi-famous Brit to die from the virus.

At Live Aid, Freddie was in clover. We were all in clover, so enthralled we were unable to look at anything else but Mr Butch and his Three Henchmen. If we had been foolish enough to look away we would not only have missed something, we may – lost perhaps in our own little Greek myth – have been unable to look back at all. And that would have been unthinkable. So we looked straight ahead, and in a flash – Ha! Saviour of the universe! – Wembley went from warm Technicolor to vibrant dayglo (© Danny Baker). We were all in a state of complete awareness, at least I was.

I imagined everyone else was too, judging by the rapt expressions on their faces. The music shooting from the stage . . . The sun falling over the roof of the stadium . . . The energy being produced by over 70,000 complicit humans . . . Well, it all conspired to make us feel 'in the moment' – vital, supreme, connected. Mercury had a 72,000-piece human jigsaw in front of him, and he was going to solve it.

It was in 1985 that Dionne Warwick gathered some friends together to help her record the Burt Bacharach and Carole Bayer Sager song 'That's What Friends Are For', the proceeds from which were to be used to raise awareness about AIDS, and donated to the American Foundation for AIDS Research. The record, which featured Gladys Knight, Elton John and Stevie Wonder, raised over $3 million. 'You have to be granite not to want to help people with AIDS, because the devastation that it causes is so painful to see,' said Warwick. 'I am tired of hurting and it does hurt.'

It was Mercury's death, though, that really drew attention to the disease. It was a passing that affected so many people in the industry. 'By all rights, Freddie should have spent [his] final days concerned only with his own comfort,' said Elton John. 'But that wasn't who he was. He truly lived for others. Weeks after the funeral, I was still grieving. On Christmas Day, I learned that Freddie had left me one final testament to his selflessness. I was moping about when a friend unexpectedly showed up at my door and handed me something wrapped in a pillowcase. I opened it, and inside was a painting by one of my favourite artists, the British painter Henry Scott Tuke. And there was a note from Freddie. Years before, Freddie and I had developed pet names for each other, our drag-queen alter egos. I was Sharon, and he was Melina. Freddie's note read, 'Dear Sharon, thought you'd like this. Love, Melina. Happy Christmas.' I was overcome, forty-four years old at the time, crying like a child.'

If there was a disease of the decade, a disease that would go on to define the Eighties, then it was AIDS. The first US citizen died of an AIDS-related illness in 1981, when the biggest threat to mankind was still thought to be the bomb. The initial cases were a cluster of gay men and intravenous drug users with no known cause of impaired immunity showing symptoms of pneumocystis pneumonia, or PCP, a rare and opportunistic infection that was known to occur in people with compromised immune systems. Soon after, the victims would develop Kaposi's sarcoma, which would soon become the most obvious manifestation of the illness, a telltale sign that caused people to cross the street in fear.

As the disease spread, and the media followed suit, hysteria built up to such an extent that it was even reported by the British tabloids that you could catch the disease from toilet seats. Victims were deemed to be agents of their own misfortune, while the then chief constable of Greater Manchester Police, James Anderton, referred to victims as people 'swirling about in a human cesspit of their own making'. The press were generally insensitive, and specifically homophobic. Some papers reported that people were afraid gay plumbers might infect a cistern, or that you could catch AIDS from Communion wine, or indeed from sharing communal baths or dinner plates. One card player living in Memphis was even advised to wear rubber gloves when dealing at his own bridge club. In the early days it was even difficult finding a word for the 'gay plague': before it was officially dubbed 'AIDS' in the summer of 1982, it was often called 'Grid' (gay-related immune deficiency).

As there were beginning to be more and more cases in the UK, so the government decided to act, commissioning the TBWA agency to make a series of ads featuring a sonorous voice-over from John Hurt ('There is now a danger that has become a threat to us all, it is a dreadful disease and there is no known cure . . . the virus can be passed during sexual intercourse with an infected person . . . anyone can get it, man or woman') which would hopefully shake a nation into taking charge of its own sexual health. Between 1985 and 1993 the government allocated over £73 million to the development of the national AIDS public education campaign, at the time a staggering amount of public money.

The campaign was certainly effective, with new diagnoses of HIV, which were over 3,000 in 1985, dropping by a third in three years. But people continued to die, including many of my friends. The figures may have been improving, but towards the end of the Eighties, AIDS started to affect my life. The first person I knew to die of an AIDS-related illness – and no matter how many times we stopped ourselves mid-sentence, or loudly corrected ourselves afterwards, our friends were dying of AIDS – was Ray Petri, the great menswear stylist who, in a rather accidental way, was probably responsible for the birth of the men's magazine industry in Britain.

If the Sixties was the decade of the photographer, a decade when the likes of David Bailey, Terence Donovan and Brian Duffy revolutionised the fashion industry; and if the Seventies was the decade of the fashion designer, when Vivienne Westwood (in Britain), Halston (in the States) and Giorgio Armani (in Italy) all changed the way in which we dressed, becoming brands in the process; then the Eighties were the decade of the stylist, when magazine fashion editors suddenly became more important than the clothes they were working with, or the photographers they had chosen to shoot them. The eclectic nature of the Eighties meant there was more of a premium on the visual nature of just about everything, especially fashion, and the currency of the stylist soared.

In the pages of *The Face* and *i-D* from 1983 until his death in 1989, Petri's pictures became the very cutting edge of fashion, and he himself was at the centre of the so-called British 'street-style'. Petri's pictures pretty much had no respect for tradition. Here was the debut of ski- and cycling-wear as street chic, boxer shorts worn with Doc Martens, dayglo dungarees and cashmere tops, muscle-rippling boys in jewellery, wild-eyed girls in Crombie coats. He even famously put men in skirts, and then put one of them on the cover of *The Face*. Or at least convinced the editor Nick Logan to do so.

Perhaps Petri's most visible success was the surplus-store garment – the black nylon US Air Force flying jacket which he'd first seen in Paris, which not only became the most ubiquitous fashion item of the decade, but also replaced the leather jacket as a symbol of rebellion as it traversed the global fashion underground.

'I was in the Soho Brasserie in 1985,' said Robin Derrick, who worked with Petri at both *The Face* and *Arena* before going on to *Vogue*. 'Ray Petri came in, wearing the jacket, the polo neck, the whole look. Within three months it was the uniform of London. Then I went to work Milan in '87, and it was the uniform there.'

Unsurprisingly, it didn't take the rest of the world long to notice, and Petri was soon being courted from every district of the image business. Keen to acquire the force behind this new image school, captains of advertising and publishing began knocking on the door of his fashion house Buffalo, asking Ray to overhaul their corporate images, ad campaigns, television commercials, promotional videos and fashion shows. It didn't always work. In 1986, Petri was hired to style a video for David Bowie, who was keen to maximise the attention he'd received at Live Aid, directed by the ultra-hip Jean-Baptiste Mondino. Wembley had proved once and for all that he was a mainstream entertainer, and his next project would try and present him as a straightforward rock star. But he hadn't bargained on Ray Petri. The shoot took place in Los Angeles, on a huge sound stage. When Bowie came out of his dressing room, Petri took one look at him, shook his head and said, bold as brass, 'You can't wear that suit.' Bowie apparently had him thrown off the set, and he was only allowed back after much pleading by Mondino.

Petri was also one of the main forces behind the launch of *Arena*, in 1986, Britain's first general-interest magazine for men since the Sixties. Working often with the American photographer Norman Watson, it was in the pages of the early issues of *Arena* that he produced perhaps his finest work.

He was in Australia in 1988 when he realised he might have AIDS. He says he was sitting on Sydney's Bondi Beach when he felt a lump under his arm, and suddenly thought that this might be his last time in the sun. Like Freddie Mercury, Petri had been extremely active in the gay scene in New York in the early Eighties, and he suspected that it was here – where he was quite indulgent – that he caught the lethal virus. He went downhill quickly, the sallow blotches of Kaposi's covering his face. I remember the first time he walked into the *Arena* offices with the marks, and we were all visibly shocked. We couldn't pretend otherwise. There was Nick Logan, the art director Neville Brody, ad director Rod Sopp, and receptionist Chris, Nick's son. We all wished him well, asked if he was OK, of course we did, but his light was dim. We travelled to Paris together for the men's collections in the summer of 1989, and his face was covered with lesions. The reaction amongst his peers was fascinating – fascinating and disgusting. Some would come up and talk to Ray, asking him if he was OK, and others would recoil in horror, literally crossing the street or the catwalk to avoid him. I sat next to him for three days while he stoically bore this, and whenever someone did ask him how he was, his response was always the same: 'You know, some days are good, others less so, but I'm OK.'

It broke my heart to hear him, and see him like this, but Ray's was broken months before. Petri asked Jean-Baptiste Mondino to get him a fur-lined Helmut Lang jacket for the next men's shows in January, but by August he was confined to bed, drifting in and out of consciousness. He died soon afterwards, right up against the edge of the decade, and we – all of us in the image business – felt as though the Eighties were over. Petri had been there at the beginning, and he was nearly there at the end. He was a maverick whose outlet was the fashion plate. He was a creative artist in the purest sense – not so much a weathervane as the weather itself. His vision survives him in fashion pages, through the stylists and photographers inspired by his work, in chain-store rip-offs, and on the backs of hip young things all over the world. Dethroned by tragedy at the ridiculously young age of forty-one, he remains inviolate as one of the most influential forces in the fashion business. Which means you can still see him being ripped off in the pages of fashion magazines all over the place.

The second friend of mine to die from AIDS was Vaughan Toulouse, born Vaughan Cotillard in Jersey in 1959. Vaughan died in 1991, at the young age of thirty-three. A mainstay of the post-punk gig circuit in London – like Freddie Mercury, he was a huge fan of Marc Bolan – he briefly became a pop star before becoming embroiled in Eighties club culture, frequenting gay clubs such as Heaven – where Freddie Mercury occasionally visited, although he tended to do his serious clubbing in New York – while launching influential clubs of his own. A friend of Paul Weller, he was also part of the Style Council's miners' charity project the Council Collective, although he was the least earnest person you could ever hope to meet. He was initially going to dance with the Style Council at Live

Aid — I think they even rehearsed a number — but in the end it was deemed to be too sombre an event for such frivolity. It wasn't an awayday, after all, and even Weller understood that. And Toulouse was always someone who liked to treat everything as a jolly. The way that I will always remember Vaughan was when he was DJing at another *i-D* party at the ICA, in the Mall in London, playing 'Born To Lose' by Johnny Thunders and the Heartbreakers, singing his version of the chorus at the very top of his voice, 'Vaughan Toulouse, Vaughan Toulouse, baby I'm Vaughan Toulouse!' He was thrusting his hips and punching the air, just as Mercury had done at Live Aid. As an expression of self, of indulgence, and a celebration of Eighties reinvention, there is no better image.

Like Ray Petri and Freddie Mercury before him, Vaughan was cremated at the West London Crematorium on the Harrow Road, which was followed by a wake at the Wag Club, both of which were attended by Paul Weller. But any notion that death had somehow unified the afflicted didn't wash with Weller. Asked later about Mercury's contribution to the music industry, Weller spat: 'He said he wanted to bring ballet to the working classes. What a cunt.'

The number of people living with HIV would rise from around 8 million from the end of the Eighties to 34 million by the end of 2010, although the overall growth of the epidemic has stabilised in recent years. The annual number of new HIV infections has steadily declined and due to the significant increase in people receiving antiretroviral therapy, the number of AIDS-related deaths has also dropped.

As for myself, I really thought this was the beginning of a deluge, and — knowing many, many gay men — assumed I'd be going to crematoriums and wakes for the foreseeable future. I thought the creative industries were going to be decimated, and that a generation of young men would be swept away by the big disease with a little name. Of course, this did happen to a certain extent. Haoui Montaug, a close friend of mine from New York, would soon die from the disease in his top-floor apartment next to the CBGB music club on the Bowery. I didn't go to another AIDS-related cremation for a decade, and it was almost as though we — the friends of those we knew who had died – had had a warning shot (in our case, three) across the bows, alerting us to the fact that this was a disease that was going to affect everyone in one way or another.

Death is always an unwanted accomplice, but it seemed to be everywhere. In London, New York, Barcelona, all over the place, AIDS was cutting a swathe through society, with photographers, club owners, fashion designers, stylists, musicians and writers all being cruelly struck down in their prime. It was almost as if any man involved in the image business was being penalised for having the audacity to dream. Some would say that they were being punished for having an extravagant gay lifestyle, although in some respects they were one and the same. The iconic New York club entrepreneur Steve Rubell succumbed, as did the fashion designer Franco Moschino. And on 26 December 2002, at the tender age of fifty, the celebrity photographer Herb Ritts died of complications from pneumonia. 'Herb was HIV-positive,' said his publicist, 'but this particular pneumonia was not PCP. But at the end of the day, his immune system was compromised.'

Ritts photographed many of the stars at Live Aid, including Elton John, David Bowie, Bob Dylan, George Michael, Paul McCartney, Sting, Mick Jagger, Madonna, Bruce Springsteen, Jack Nicholson, Michael Hutchence and Tina Turner, and in that respect could be legitimately called the one photographer who had the closest relationship with the performers that day. Sure, David Bailey and Brian Aris both had their makeshift studios backstage at Wembley, but in Bailey's own words these pictures were snapshots, grabbed on the day. Ritts had an important tangential relationship with Live Aid, as he had a fundamental influence over the way in which its stars projected themselves during the Eighties (like Mercury, Ritts was a control freak). It's a pity that Ritts never photographed Phyllis Diller, the grotesque American comedienne. 'My photographs do me an injustice,' she once said, 'they look just like me.' With Ritts she could have looked like anyone at all.

In a way, this was what the Eighties were all about, looking like anyone you wanted to. Which is why there were so many new industries that grew up to cater for this. There may have been stylists and photographers and

Richard Gere with his friend Herb Ritts, who photographed many of the stars at Live Aid, including Elton John, David Bowie, Bob Dylan, George Michael, Paul McCartney, Sting, Mick Jagger, Madonna, Bruce Springsteen, Jack Nicholson, Michael Hutchence and Tina Turner, and in that respect can be legitimately called the photographer who had the closest relationship with the performers that day.

fashion designers and nightclub hosts before the Eighties arrived, but this was the decade that made them important, as so many people professed to need them. We all thought we deserved to be better dressed, to look better than we ought to, and to be swept past the velvet rope on our way to the VVIP room. Ray Petri became a star in the Eighties because the decade was ripe for him, and much the same can be said about Haoui Montaug, Vaughan Toulouse, Franco Moschino and Herb Ritts, come to that.

In April 2003, *Poz*, a monthly magazine chronicling the lives of those affected by HIV and AIDS, ran a profile of Ritts by Degen Pener ('Putting on the Ritts'), one of the first to discuss the cause of his death openly: 'When famed photographer Herb Ritts died suddenly at fifty, the media never mentioned the A-word, let alone his heroic battle against blindness. Gay critics cried cover-up. Even his friends were upset. This is the real story they say Ritts wanted told . . .' The piece quoted friends and colleagues who were upset that AIDS was not mentioned in any of the obituaries, and wondered whether those protecting his image were trying to push the real reason for his death back in the closet.

Others just mourned their friend. Cindy Crawford, whom Ritts once shot for *Vanity Fair* shaving an in-drag k. d. lang, said: 'Herb wasn't about living life untruthfully. But I don't think he had a responsibility to be a poster child. He obviously didn't want to be in that position.'

Ritts was described by friends and family as a sweet, quiet man, said Pener, and an intensely private one. He said that they strongly denied, though, that Ritts had something to hide. Openly lesbian singer k. d. lang herself said: '[Having HIV] wasn't something Herb was really public about, but it had nothing to do with being ashamed.'

His reluctance to admit his illness said more about his fears about press intrusion than any latent homophobia. After all, it wasn't as though homosexuality was unheard of in the fashion industry, and admitting he was gay would hardly have hurt his business. Like many fashion photographers, like many actors or musicians, it was generally assumed that he was gay, and what of it? What Ritts was more than aware of, and what Freddie Mercury was more than aware of, was the way in which the

Haoui Montaug was the greatest doorman of the Eighties, the gatekeeper at Danceteria, the Palladium, and most of the big New York clubs of the decade. He prided himself with being able to create the perfect social mix, always careful to keep a lot of the uptown mob on the wrong side of the velvet rope.

media would have invaded his life had he admitted he was ill. Mercury always knew that as soon as he admitted he had AIDS, the British tabloids would have used this as an excuse to pester everyone and anyone the star had ever met, had dinner with, or slept with. He was using his silence as a way to protect his family and friends as much as himself, which is ironic considering that in other respects the Eighties had turned out to be a fairly benign decade as far as sexuality was concerned. In 1988 the Conservatives may have introduced Section 28 (also known as Clause 28), demonising homosexuality by passing a bill that outlawed the promotion of it, but culturally the decade appeared to espouse creativity in the gay community more than ever before.

Freddie Mercury was never a standard-bearer for the gay community, or indeed for his own sexuality. But far from being an abnegation of duty, he simply didn't feel part of the discussion. Far from disguising his predilections, instead he decided not to articulate them. Which, it turned out, was dignified in the extreme. During a decade in which it was deemed expedient to exploit one's feminine side (this was a generation, we must remember, which had seen David Bowie do exactly this over a decade ago), Mercury just got on with the job in hand, which appeared to be nothing more convoluted than entertaining the troops in the most effective way possible.

Queen's twenty-minute appearance at Live Aid was one of the most captivating performances of the decade, and in 2005 Channel 4 voted it the greatest gig of all time. It was also great television. Seen by 2 billion people, they stole the show, and completely revitalised their career. In the weeks following the event, all of Queen's albums tumbled back into the charts. (Queen's *Greatest Hits* is still the UK's biggest-selling album.)

'I remember a huge rush of adrenaline as I went on stage and a massive roar from the crowd,' said Brian May. 'And then all of us just pitching in. Looking back, I think we were all a bit overexcited, and I remember coming off and thinking it was very scrappy. But there was a lot of very good energy too. Freddie was our secret weapon. He was able to reach out to everybody in that stadium effortlessly, and I think it was really his night.'

Of course it was. It was his day, too. All of it.

Whenever anyone ever questions how tolerant the Eighties actually were, at least compared to the last decade before the West's cultural revolution, the Fifties, I always think how different Live Aid would have been if, instead of an overtly gay Freddie Mercury leading Queen through an exultant 'Radio Ga Ga' in 1985, we were treated to an overly camp Elvis Presley grinding his way through a libidinous version of 'That's All Right' in 1955, and then exposed to the media furore that would have inevitably followed it.

'Son, that gal you're foolin' with,
'She ain't no good for you . . .'

On 13 July Queen's stadium dynamics actually transcended the occasion, and the lightness and the deftness of their offer was all on display for anyone who cared to want it. Having spent over a decade finessing their act, they had developed the ability to protect whatever elements of their sound that needed to be small, while maximising the rest, and spreading it around in widescreen, Technicolor fashion. You heard it on the records, if you were that way inclined. With operatic power chords, bombast and filigree, Queen redrew the parameters of where rock was meant to sit. It was loud but cartoonish, heartfelt but fiction, black but mostly white. It was easy to like Queen, apparently, even if you didn't really like rock music. Their music seemed to do what rock music was meant to do, with all the extravagant bits, the funny bits, and the obviously serious bits at the piano, while Mercury had turned into just about the most generic rock star in the genre's short history (even though it would have actually been difficult for him to have been any more idiosyncratic). But what Queen did more than anything, and more than anyone else, was to paint their picture on a bigger screen than anyone else; if they were going to go down fighting they were going to do it while skywriting.

Like many others, their Live Aid performance took me back to those records, not just to hear again the things I'd taken great delight in ignoring, but also to discover what I'd missed. And there was quite a lot. However, at a time when club culture was producing such an abundance of content, and when dance records seemed to redefine the genre three or four times a week, every week, it felt somewhat decadent to spend time with Queen's records, a little wrong, almost as though having middlebrow taste was tantamount to having a penchant for hardcore pornography. Please don't tell!

In broad brushstrokes you could see that, like many Seventies bands, they were basing a lot of what they were trying to do on what the Beatles had done when the members of Queen were growing up. Yet they mixed in the sort of theatrics that would have been alien to the Fab Four, that would have been alien to any group in the Sixties, even those who prided themselves on their stage shows. Queen mixed their orthodox melodic pop with their hard rock tunes and deliberately attempted Thirties-style vampy songs, the sort of carnival and music-hall stuff that had won the Beatles favour with the mums and the dads (the 'lurking schmaltzy' stuff that John Lennon hated so much): where the Beatles had 'When I'm Sixty Four', so Queen had 'Lazing On A Sunday Afternoon' (complete with megaphone vocals). If anyone could carry off a straw boater and a blazer, it was Freddie. If anyone could steer a rock crowd away from beer-drenched dance halls towards manicured lawns and a glass of Pimm's, it was Freddie. There was a *Carry On* strain to Queen (they were *so* Kenny Everett), an old-fashioned, unthreatening type of camp that few had attempted with such success.

Mercury wanted Queen to be 'the Cecil B. DeMille of rock', and in this respect there was no one else in the running. Bowie had cornered cool, Zeppelin and The Who had conquered what we all understood to be mainstream hard rock, so in order to make themselves noticed, Queen had to turn everything else up to eleven. We first knew Queen weren't your solid bog-standard rock band when they released 'Killer Queen' as a single in 1974. It was all very well having something like this on an album, but releasing it as a single (albeit as part of a double-A side) could have been a risk; it was calculated and it worked, magnificently, helping define the band even before 'Bohemian Rhapsody' (the six-minute mega-single with 180 overdubs and a vocal section that took seventy hours to record).

So elaborate was their fourth album, *A Night At The Opera* (taking its name from the Marx Brothers film – announcing yet again that they weren't taking themselves too seriously), released in November 1975, that it soon became known as the most expensive album ever recorded. What I didn't know until doing due diligence was that many of the guitar parts on the album were initially played on piano by Mercury, to demonstrate to May exactly how they needed to be played on guitar. '*A Night At The Opera* featured every sound from a tuba to a comb,' said Mercury. 'Nothing is out of bounds.'

They could muck about with their sound, too. When the Stones went disco, it looked expedient, no matter how much everyone loved 'Miss You'. When Queen started layering their records with Chic-style bass lines and drum machines, it simply looked as though they were cleverly adapting to the marketplace. They were so populist that they could veer from rockabilly to pomp and records like 'I Want To Be Free', complete with comic transvestite video (even though this dented their popularity in the US). How many other supergroups could do the same?

As Mercury figure-skated to his inevitable, oh-so-dramatic halt – 'Ta-dah!' – all around us in the crowd there were exultant hugs, fists punching the air, and so many people mouthing 'Wow', their palms upturned as if to say, 'Follow that!' Not that anyone could. Not even on the day of days. While the whole country – ha, the whole world! – found itself carried along on a glutinous tide of happiness, inside the stadium we were all still smiling at each other, our nerves still jangling, our ears humming. Robin and I instinctively put our arms around each other. It was a boy thing. Queen. Jesus, who knew? Were they always this good? I think we then went off for beer. I don't remember any of us drinking so much; not only was it too hot, it just didn't seem appropriate.

'I was right at the back of the stadium in one of the far towers when they came on,' said Bernard Doherty, 'and I couldn't believe how good they were, and how strong the audience reaction was. It was almost as if the crowd had decided they were going to have a good time regardless.'

As Queen left the stage after rocking Wembley's foundations with 'We Will Rock You' and 'We Are The Champions', I wondered why I hadn't been a Queen fan all my life, and felt rather embarrassed that I had treated them with such disdain. Like the other 71,999 people in the stadium on 13 July, and the 1.9 billion TV audience, I was completely won over. Their performance not only gave them a new lease of life, but they completely altered how many people viewed them. Their performance has since been voted by more than sixty artists, journalists and music industry executives as the greatest live performance in rock (Jimi Hendrix's appearance at Woodstock in August 1969 came second, followed by the Sex Pistols' gig at Manchester Free Trade Hall in June 1976). And with good reason. 'Though I am more jazz-funk orientated,' said the chap who uploaded the YouTube clip of Queen at Live Aid, 'I do agree this is the best live gig in rock history, ever.'

This would prove to the very best of the band's 704 performances. Queen played only twenty-seven more times with Freddie Mercury; their final gig turned out to be the performance at Knebworth on 9 August 1986. They would never top Live Aid.

On reaching his trailer, Mercury shouted, 'Thank God that's over,' and promptly downed a double vodka.

Reaction to Queen's performance was predictable. In the stadium, the crowd was completely floored, as were the other acts, especially those who had yet to appear: Elton John rushed into their trailer afterwards, screaming that they had stolen the show.

'Queen were absolutely the best band of the day,' said Geldof, in summation. 'They played the best, had the best sound, used their time to the full. They understood the idea exactly, that it was a global jukebox. They just went and smashed one hit after another. It was the perfect stage for Freddie: the whole world. And he could ponce about on stage doing "We Are The Champions". How perfect could it get?'

Next up was David Bowie, but how could he be anything other than anticlimactic? Seven-twenty should have been the perfect time for him to grab the audience, but Freddie Mercury's extraordinary performance made it impossible. Bowie stood no chance, appearing as though he had pre-recorded the emotion as well as the music. In truth, he felt a little queasy.

ELEVEN

19:22

David Bowie: 'TVC 15', 'Rebel Rebel', 'Modern Love', 'Heroes'

**The Who: 'My Generation'/'Pinball Wizard',
'Love, Reign O'er Me', 'Won't Get Fooled Again'**

I watched The Who from the side of the stage and it was
obvious they weren't getting on very well with each other.
Sparks were flying – it was actually quite exciting.

BRIAN MAY

'A s soon as Bowie said he was in, it all started to roll,' said Bernard
Doherty. 'When Bowie said he'd do it, everyone said they'd do
it.'

By securing David Bowie, Geldof had raised the bar of the entire event.
Bowie was gold standard, top drawer, the toppermost of the toppermost.

Bernard Doherty was not only handling the publicity for Live Aid, he
was, along with Alan Edwards, also looking after David Bowie. 'It's always
a little nerve-wracking when you are looking after your artist and doing two
jobs at once,' he said. 'In my case, that day, I was doing about eighteen jobs.
There wasn't much love lost between David and Elton – they'd obviously
fallen out. The one musician David was genuinely pleased to see was Freddie
[Mercury]. They really were delighted to be together again. They stood

279

chatting, as if they'd only seen each other yesterday. The affection between them was tangible. David was wearing an amazing blue suit, and looked incredibly sharp and healthy. Just before David went on, Freddie winked at him and said, "If I didn't know you better, dear, I'd have to eat you." No wonder David went out on stage with such a big smile on his face.'

There was the obvious rivalry, though, and although they were friends, each wanted to outdo the other. And while Bowie may have been smiling, he was worried inside. Like everyone else at Wembley that day, he knew Queen had stolen the show, and he was a little queasy.

Bowie and Mercury had worked together just a few years previously, when they had recorded the 'Under Pressure' single in Montreux in 1981, and they got to see each other's foibles and predilections at close quarters. Bowie was living there, Queen were recording there, and it was suggested by a mutual colleague (the producer David Richards) that they meet. This resulted in a new composition, kick-started by John Deacon's bass line, and then accessorised by both Bowie and Mercury. Bowie originally called the song 'People On Streets', but then settled on the slightly more abstract 'Under Pressure'.

'[Bowie] was quite difficult to work with,' said May, 'because it was the meeting of two different methods of working. It was stimulating but, at the same time, almost impossible to resolve. We're very pig-headed and set in our ways and Mr Bowie is too. In fact he's probably as pigheaded as the four of us put together. After "Under Pressure" was done, there were continual disagreements about how it should be put out or if it should even be put out at all. David wanted to redo the whole thing.'

Nevertheless, all this was meaningless now, as Queen had just delivered an earth-shattering experience, while Bowie was appearing with a scratch band he'd only put together a few days earlier, especially for the show.

Bowie had originally intended doing something far more adventurous than just simply performing, which is why he hadn't put a band together earlier. He had originally intended to perform a transatlantic duet with Mick Jagger, exploiting the half-second time delay between Wembley and Philadelphia by performing a reggae song. Their respective management teams organised a conference call that resulted in both megastars singing in harmony down the telephone line with Bob Geldof.

'I sang Bob Marley's "One Love" as an example,' said Geldof. 'Jagger and Bowie joined in. I sang, "One love, one heart, let's get together and feel all right." Then Bowie sang it. Then Jagger. Then together. Verna [Live Aid's technical director] was somewhere in America listening to Bowie and Jagger crackling down the phone at him.' He said later he was too shocked to run off and get a tape and record it for himself. 'It seemed unbelievable to me that I was sitting in a room with these two rock greats, working out a song, making suggestions to them, singing with them. *Singing* with them. Fuck me! It was so odd hearing their two familiar voices together in that tiny room. Jagger was tilted back on his chair. Bowie sat beside me on the sofa. I started "One love, one heart," Jagger and Bowie harmonised on the last line, then David began in his low voice "One love", and Jagger in a great blues shout repeated "One love", then Bowie deep and sad "One heart", Jagger like an old black woman "One heart" and then joyously together "Let's get together and feel all right."'

After several attempts at working out a way to make it work, they eventually decided that this wasn't going to happen, and so went off to a nightclub together and spent the evening trying to outdo each other on the dance floor. This gave them the idea of recording a cover of 'Dancing In The Street', to be broadcast at the event and released as a single.

'At one point I was going to be doing my part in Britain, and Jagger was going to be doing his part over there in the States,' said Bowie. 'But we couldn't find anyone who was convinced that we could actually sing at the same time and make it work. So we abandoned that idea.'

The next idea involved a rocket ship, as Bowie wanted one of them to be inside a NASA Space Shuttle, doing a duet with the other on Earth. 'I actually made a call to NASA,' said Harvey Goldsmith. 'I asked them if they had a spare rocket that we could send Mick Jagger up in. I could tell they were thinking, "Who is this nutcase?"' (A similar idea was realised during U2's 360 tour in 2010, with a video link-up with the International Space

Station, with crew member Mark Kelly reciting the lyrics to 'Beautiful Day', before the band launched into it on stage.)

In the end they decided on an old-fashioned video, camping their way through a rather average version of the Motown classic by Martha and the Vandellas (the song that had inspired the Stones classic 'Street Fighting Man'), and helping it to number one. Jagger and Bowie recorded 'Dancing In The Street' in London a few weeks before Wembley, and if the record turned out to be rather anodyne, it was certainly triumphantly upbeat (with Jagger exaggerating the professional cockney singing voice that both Bowie and he had made their own: 'Cawlin' awl aroun' the world . . .').

The producer Clive Langer was working on Bowie's 'Absolute Beginners' at Abbey Road when the singer asked if he wouldn't mind doing a charity single when they'd finished the backing track. 'Mick will be coming down,' he said. 'Mick came into the studio and was twiddling his arms around and everything and we knocked the backing track down,' said Langer. 'We recorded most of it. I think they did the horns in America and somebody else mixed it. It was nice of David to put our names on it because it was really produced by a lot of people.' The drummer on the track, Neil Conti, said, 'It was a huge ego trip for Mick, he kept trying to upstage David.' As soon as they'd finished the recording, they both rushed down to Docklands to film the video for the song, where Bowie and Jagger proceeded to perform some of the worst dance moves ever committed to videotape.

The recording left a sour taste in at least one person's mouth. 'Jagger came off as the nicest guy in the world, asking about everyone's families, et cetera, doing all that meeting-the-troops stuff,' said the drummer on the session, Neil Conti. 'Then when I ran into him a couple of weeks later it was as though we'd never met. "Hi, Mick," I said. Not a flicker. He literally turned on his heel and left.'

Their duet wasn't ever going to be included on any greatest hits collection, yet the fact that they had recorded it meant more than the quality of the record itself. The record was almost incidental. It was the spirit of the thing that mattered.

'There is a general assumption that it was easy for bands to do it,' said

Geldof. 'It wasn't. Do you know how many times these people are asked to support things? Mick Jagger, for example, in the face of opposition from his own band, had to interrupt recording, come to England, rehearse and record a song with Bowie (who had to finish filming and put a band together and rehearse himself), choreograph and make a video, fly to America to rehearse with a new band, contact Tina Turner, rehearse a routine with her, then do the show. It meant weeks of work for free, and considerable inconvenience.

'As well as Simple Minds and the Pretenders, Billy Ocean and Duran Duran flew to America with their equipment. They found rehearsal rooms, played for fifteen minutes, then flew home without charging a penny. Paul Young, Spandau Ballet and U2 flew in from everywhere. Bands paid for rehearsals and trucking, moving their stuff from coast to coast, cancelling lucrative concerts because this was where they wanted to be.'

Bowie had flown in earlier in the day on a helicopter owned by the TV presenter Noel Edmonds, who had kindly agreed to shuttle people from the Battersea Heliport to London Transport's cricket ground, about 400 yards from Wembley Stadium. 'On the day it was the climax of their cricket tournament, and they wouldn't abandon their game for us so the umpires had whistles and when they saw a helicopter coming they blew the whistles and cleared the field for us to land,' said Edmonds. 'I seem to remember that David Bowie's management said he only flew in a blue helicopter – that's blue on the inside – and we managed to find one. I was killing time with him at Battersea before he flew in and I said, "Look at the inside of this helicopter!" He looked at me as if I were mad. He didn't give a shit what colour the helicopter was.'

Bowie wore a suit he'd worn on the *Young Americans* tour, a decade earlier, showing his band the waist size, amazed he could still get into it, and wanting to share his delight. 'Bowie had wheeled out a suit from his younger days and was delighted to explain to me how well it still fitted,' said Pete Townshend. The band was practically new, having only played together three times previously, which is one of the reasons Bowie's set was so flat. Thomas Dolby was playing keyboards, and was one of the few band members to enjoy it: 'To my astonishment, I felt like I was on a magic-carpet ride. These songs were like our teenage anthems – my fingers just wafted along.'

'What I thought was interesting was the way the hierarchy fell into place almost immediately,' said Gary Kemp. 'I had a particular moment when I arrived, when I saw my hero, David Bowie, at the bar wearing this beautiful suit. I made an approach, but he was talking to someone and I didn't quite get the connection that I would have liked to have got, so I rather secretly gathered myself and crawled away. I think a lot of us felt that we were in the room with our betters. And the Seventies generation had never been better than they were that day, so I think a lot of the younger boys felt very much in their place.'

Bowie's best performance was when he came back on to the stage after 'Heroes' and introduced the Canadian Broadcasting Corporation video of

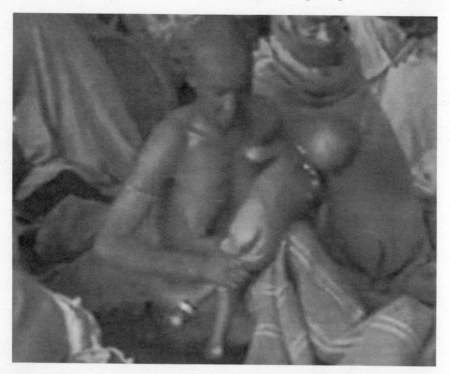

When Bob Geldof showed David Bowie the video that had been edited to work with 'Drive' by the Cars, Bowie said he wanted to cut a song from his set in order to show it. This moment is one of the three or four that people will always remember about Live Aid, and can still produce tears.

'Drive'. 'God bless you, you're the heroes of this concert. Lest we forget while we're here, I'd like to introduce a video made by CBC Television. The subject speaks for itself. Thank you, goodnight. Please send your money in.'

He had made one of the most magnanimous gestures of the day by allowing one of his songs to be replaced by a video. He had decided at the last minute to drop 'Five Years' in order for there to be enough time to show a specially made video to accompany 'Drive' by the Cars. The video had everyone in the stadium, and everyone at home, on the verge of tears, and was responsible for a massive spike in donations. Edited by CBC engineer Colin Dean, the film showed images of people who were starving, diseased and – perhaps even – dying as a result of the famine, the majority of them children. Dean explained that he had been listening to the song and, only semi-seriously, wondered whether it may fit the video he had to cut together, yet soon he found himself mirroring images to lines in the song. The effect was devastating. 'As it was broadcast – and simultaneously played on the stadium's big screens – the bouyant, bouncing festival atmosphere in Wembley was cut to pieces,' said one journalist. 'It was a sudden, unequivocal reminder to the revellers what the day was really all about, just as it proved to be for all those watching at home.'

'Bowie and Bob were in my office and I had one of those pop-up televisions,' said Harvey Goldsmith. 'And we literally had a pile of videos and we were chucking them in, looking for suitable material to play at Wembley. That piece popped up, with the song already on it' – "Who's gonna drive you home tonight . . ." – 'and we all looked at it and welled up. And Dave immediately said, "Take one of my numbers off and put that up instead." That was another iconic part of the day.'

'I showed that film to David at Harvey Goldsmith's about 7.30 at night,' said Geldof. 'Let's remember for a minute that Bowie is an absolute god. I got to know him when I was a kid. I hitch-hiked to see him in Belgium on the *Station To Station* tour, told him I was in a band and showed him pictures of the Rats. I blagged backstage and he was so nice. Don't forget he launched Band Aid [by wearing] this lame T-shirt, Feed the World, looked like a doofus. But he's the sweetest man. You just never think about David Bowie like that.

'We showed him the film, famine footage cut to the Cars song "Drive". He sat there in tears and said, "Right, I'm giving up a song." I said, "Hang on . . ." I didn't want David Bowie giving up a fucking song. I mean, hello? But of course he was right. That was the moment that people said, "Fuck everything, take whatever you want from me."'

Bowie was in floods of tears after his performance, blown over by the sheer force of emotion from the crowd. 'He was crying his eyes out,' said Bernard Doherty. 'He couldn't cope with the enormity of it all, which was astonishing. This was David Bowie!'

'There was a sense of drama about the day, as the whole thing felt innovative, groundbreaking, fundamentally important, as though we all knew we wouldn't ever be at something like this again,' Alan Edwards said. 'I remember watching Bowie, and while he certainly wasn't overawed, you could tell that he was carefully watching people. It was one of those days. You wanted to look around and remember things, as you knew it was a special day. There was a healthy competitive spirit backstage, although you also felt that everyone was involved for the common good. Every five minutes there was another surprise. Phil Collins getting on an aeroplane and playing in Philadelphia. I suppose it seems commonplace now, but as soon as that happened – and as soon as it happened everyone in the stadium knew about it – you knew you were a part of a truly global event.

'There was a sense of oneness, a feeling that the crowd and the performers were somehow all in it together. For one day. We all felt as though we were right at the centre of the universe. This was before all the big global events, before the idea of global summits, or big charity events, or colossal fund-raisers. The G8 had started back in 1975 with the Group of Six, hosted by France with the UK, Germany, Italy, Japan and the States, but it didn't have the resonance it would have after Live Aid. It fused politics and pop together, and made both seem far more important than they had been in the past, or at least gave both a different media perspective. Politics was immediately made popular in a way that appealed to a younger set of people, and pop was suddenly front-page news in a way it had never been before. In hindsight, none of the big events of the last twenty or thirty years would have happened without the ambition of Live Aid. Woodstock didn't have any politics, it was a just a big festival. Live Aid really meant something.'

Then it was time for three-quarters of The Who. I had seen the band's comeback gig at the Rainbow in Finsbury Park in May 1979, just eight months after Keith Moon, their original drummer, had died at the age of thirty-two, and it was a complicated affair. On the one hand the audience was rejoicing in the fact that the band were carrying on, and thrilled that they sounded almost as good as they once did; but on the other, that was the problem: they were never going to sound better than they did, only slightly worse. They were almost as good as they once were, and while this was just about good enough for all of us in the Rainbow that night, it was never going to be good enough for posterity.

The thing I remember most from Finsbury Park was staring at Kenney Jones, the old Faces drummer who had been chosen to replace Moon – a similar gig to the one Ronnie Wood had once been offered in the Rolling Stones (around this time Jones appeared to add an extra 'e' to his first name, possibly thinking that Kenney made him sound more exotic; it didn't). When Moon had died, Phil Collins had called to offer his services, but was rebuffed, and even though Daltrey wasn't a fan of Kenney Jones, and wanted someone more expressive, Townshend plumped for the former Faces drummer. It was almost as if the Faces were a sort of mobile rock 'n' roll hospital, dispensing band members to supergroups whenever one of them decided to leave or slip off the mortal coil. But the Stones only needed Wood in the way that they'd needed Mick Taylor – to fill out the sound, come up with an occasional riff and stay out of the way. In the end Wood would turn out to be far more important than anyone thought when he was hired, yet Kenney Jones had proper big boots to fill, one of the biggest pairs ever made (a bit like the ones Elton John wore in Ken Russell's atrocious film version of The Who's rock opera, *Tommy*).

Townshend later said he enjoyed the Rainbow concert, yet all I kept thinking about was the ghost of Keith Moon. Dressed in a Nazi outfit and a leotard.

Keith Moon wasn't 25 per cent of The Who, but more like 35, even 40 per cent. He wasn't just a drummer, he was a flailing lunatic who happened to have taken up hitting things for a living, one of the few drummers whose style had a real personality of its own, one that was often more dynamic and more appealing than the sound it was meant to be containing. Never was there a man less like a metronome, and never was there a man less likely to fill Keith Moon's boots than Kenney Jones. Even though he'd been with the band for six years, on and off, he looked mildly apprehensive at Live Aid, scared to make a mistake, scared to attempt some clever fill that might not work, scared in a way he looked scared the first time I'd seen him play with the band, back in Finsbury Park.*

At the Rainbow I remember watching Pete Townshend shouting at Jones when he got things wrong, impatiently carrying on as if he was somehow hoping that Moon would suddenly appear behind him, bashing the living daylights out of his Premier tom-toms. Townshend's anger was always the salient emotion that propelled the band on stage, which is why the comeback gig was so good: he was genuinely angry and he wanted you (us) and Jones to bloody well know about it.

For years I had one of Keith Moon's drumsticks, thrown into the audience at a Rainbow gig in 1975. It moved everywhere with me, from bedsit to flat to – oh, damn, where did it go? I'd kept it as it was always the drums that I liked the most about The Who, the drums which first appealed to me, the drums that I thought made the band sound so wild, so anarchic, the drums

---

* The Sex Pistols were actually a carbon copy of The Who. In the mid-Seventies, Malcolm McLaren showed up at Track, the record company run by Chris Stamp and Kit Lambert, The Who's management team. He wanted to know how they had made The Who so big. So, according to Townshend, Stamp said, 'Well, we went out to this club and found the four ugliest guys we could find – they were idiots, they were cunts and they couldn't play – and then we added our panache and gave them a decent name, dressed them up nicely, and that was it.' And McLaren went, 'Got it!' And that was the Sex Pistols.

that filled me with such an urgent sense of immortality. If you listen closely (and in truth you don't have to listen that closely) to the drums on *Who's Next*, it's not only 'Baba O'Reilly', 'Bargain' or 'Won't Get Fooled Again' that sound so important, it's the weaker songs too, 'My Wife', 'Going Mobile' and 'Getting In Tune'. Take away Moon's feverish bashing and the songs sound almost ordinary. On some songs, you can even imagine Moon sitting down, picking up his sticks and starting to drum away on his own little journey, obviously never completely oblivious to what was going on around him, but knowing he could make it to the end without needing to turn himself into a human metronome. '6.34? Sure, I'll set off now and see you at the end.' Moon's magic was actually gold dust, adding a sparkle and at least an extra 40 per cent to every record he ever played on.

Pete Townshend wrote generation-defining songs, sung by someone who had no problem singing them, yet – like no other band before or since – The Who were defined by their drummer. Keith Moon's style was so idiosyncratic, so brutal, and so surreal, that it became impossible to imagine the band without him. Which is why it was so difficult for them when Moon died, and why their frenzied noise was never the same again.

The best way to understand The Who's very particular dynamic was to read James Wood, writing in the *New Yorker* in 2010: 'The Who had extraordinary rhythmic vitality, and it died when Keith Moon died, thirty-two years ago. Pete Townshend's hard, tense suspended chords seem to scour the air around them; Roger Daltrey's singing was a young man's fighting swagger, an incitement to some kind of crime; John Entwistle's incessantly mobile bass playing was like someone running away from the scene of the crime; and Keith Moon's drumming, in its inspired vandalism, was the crime itself. Most rock drummers, even very good and inventive ones, are timekeepers. There is a space for a fill or a roll at the end of a musical phrase, but the beat has primacy over the curlicues. Keith Moon ripped all this up.'

They were 'the anti-Beatles', according to their ex-manager, Kit Lambert.

We loved the power chords (how easy it was to drown in the aural pyrotechnics of 'The Kids Are Alright', 'Substitute', 'Pinball Wizard', '5.15', 'How Many Friends' and all the rest), we loved Townshend's stripped-down ballads ('Blue, Red and Grey', 'Too Much Of Anything', 'They Are All In Love', etc.), we loved the studied belligerence of the microphone-flailing Daltrey, and we loved the way John Entwistle used to walk on stage as though he were looking for his dog. But most of all we loved the mad man on the riser, eagerly creating harmony from chaos.

In 1965, twenty years before The Who ambled on to the Live Aid stage at Wembley, a young reporter asked Pete Townshend how he prepared himself mentally for The Who's thunderous and debilitating live performances. Townshend, always aware of drama, replied, 'Pretend you're in a war.'

On 13 July, he wouldn't have any choice.

Critics liked to say that Daltrey spent most of the band's career making Townshend's personal neurosis acceptable to the record-buying public – conflict was Townshend's middle name. The problem was, it was also Roger Daltrey's – but by 1985 that public knew the animal, and they liked it. Good God, they were legends! Sixties survivors! Formerly the greatest rock 'n' roll band in the world!

By the time of Live Aid, The Who were no more, and their future was largely behind them. Band infighting had become too much, while Townshend was more interested in his solo work. But the idea of a one-off show was intriguing, especially for such a good cause. Townshend had called up Geldof out of interest, but initially only to perform solo. It was Geldof who announced at the press conference that The Who were reuniting especially for Live Aid, causing both Townshend and Roger Daltrey to get on the phone to Geldof immediately and tell him how opposed they were to the idea, and how much they still vehemently disliked each other.

However, after a while they had no choice. When Geldof felt that the band might pull out, in Townshend's words 'he took the gloves off': 'If The Who appear we know we will get an additional million pounds of revenue,' said Geldof. 'Every pound we make will save a life. Do the fucking maths. And do the fucking show.'

Townshend prevaricated, but then he also prevaricated about playing at Woodstock, and had to be forced by the band's management to perform. Afterwards he understood that Woodstock came to represent a revolution for musicians and music lovers, as well as becoming a model for what music gatherings could be, but he still thought the experience was a 'crock of shit'.

Townshend had only recently recovered from a period of intense drinking. 'He collapsed one night in the toilet at Club For Heroes,' said Gary Kemp. 'In fact, he was at Steve Strange's house one night. And Steve Norman [the Spandau Ballet saxophonist] said to him, "Pete, I adore you, why are you doing this to yourself?" And years later I saw Pete and he said, "Your mate Steve said things to me that really made me think I better do something about it."'

Live Aid was the first time I'd seen them since the 1979 Rainbow gig, and as the band had broken up three years previously, it was something of a novelty to see them up there on the Wembley stage. It would be unfair to say they were simply going through the motions, but they weren't the force they'd been ten years previously, when they were without question the best live band in the world. The choice of songs could have been better, as could Kenney Jones's choice of attire: honestly, would Keith Moon have been seen sporting a pale blue cap-sleeved T-shirt? He wouldn't have been seen dead in one, let alone alive. On the day they took too long to get started (there was a problem with John Entwistle's bass), wiping nearly two minutes off their set, while due to a technical problem some of their performance wasn't even broadcast.

Daltrey no longer had the corkscrew perm or the tasselled shawl that became such a defining aspect of their stage shows, but he still had the voice. Townshend meanwhile still threw perfect Who shapes, while John Entwistle still stood statue-still, his fingers 'flying like a stenographer's, the notes a machine-gun chatter' (© Pete Townshend).

The highlight was actually the introduction in Philadelphia by Jack Nicholson. Of course they redeemed themselves by playing a blistering version of 'Won't Get Fooled Again', but then they'd been playing this song in their sleep for the last fourteen years, and it had immediately become their centrepiece. Townshend executed a few near-perfect windmills — a trick he had actually stolen from Keith Richards, after he'd seen him limbering up in this way, swinging his arms back and forth, when The

Who supported the Stones in London at the end of 1963 – and by doing so almost redeemed the band's performance. It was always an exhilarating song to hear live, and while they had played better versions (there were a couple of clunkers, including Townshend coming in with the last verse far too soon), it was certainly good enough to fool the crowd.

It wasn't good enough to fool Townshend though, who was extremely unhappy about the band's performance. As always, he cared about what The Who meant, and what they continued to mean. 'When I quit The Who in 1982, I didn't really quit because I was sick of the road; what I felt was that I couldn't serve . . . I hesitate to even call it a "band",' he said. 'I couldn't serve the brand any more. The brand being not so much Pepsi – so there's The Who and Pepsi as brands – it's the brand as something that includes the fans. As a writer, I felt that I couldn't use the band to reach the fans any more, so I quit for a while.'

Townshend and Roger Daltrey had made a habit of falling out with each other; sometimes before they went on stage, sometimes after they'd just come off, and were bickering in the dressing room, and often halfway through their set, much to the delight of their fans.

'If Roger and I were close we would not be successful,' said Townshend. 'We respect each other absolutely, and cherish each other. I would say that we love each other. But playing golf and having lunch is not for us, because we are so different, have different needs and passions. But on stage we share a commitment to our audience, and that is all Who fans need to worry about.'

The band would be resurrected time and time again over the years, even surviving Entwistle's death in Las Vegas in 2002, and remarkably the noise they make today is (architecturally, at least) not so different from the noise they made in their heyday in the Seventies, but it is a fraction of what it was.

Perhaps the only good thing to come out of the band's performance at Wembley was their acknowledgement that, having been so bad, they would have to get back together and do it properly. 'As for our performance, The Who were out of practice and should probably have left it to Queen and George Michael, who stole the show,' said Townshend. Still, this was The Who, talkin' about pan-generation.

But even if The Who weren't on the best of terms, everyone else appeared to making an effort to get on with each other. Townshend wandered around backstage, sensing a growing feeling of community. 'The press was flocking mainly to the young black singer Sade, whose sultry beauty was intoxicating,' he said. He talked to Bono, 'who was never afraid of waxing lyrical at such times. We all felt proud to be there.' David Bailey took Townshend's picture as soon as he came offstage, a photograph that ended up on the wall of Le Caprice, the fashionable London restaurant, where it remains to this day.

Bono remembers standing beside Pete Townshend just before The Who went on, asking him if he ever got nervous. He gave Bono an incredulous look, stared at him for a while and said, 'Nervous? Nervous about playing live, in front of people? I'll be nervous when I meet God. But nervous in front of you or anyone else out there? Never!' This outburst made Bono feel like an apprentice, although U2's set was certainly more accomplished than The Who's that day, by quite a considerable margin.

Many people backstage had some sort of relationship, having worked or played together at some point during their careers. Townshend was on particularly good terms with Sting, as the former Police singer had starred in Franc Roddam's 1979 film adaptation of The Who album *Quadrophenia*, which also stared Phil Daniels as Jimmy the Mod. Townshend's original choice for the Daniels role was the Sex Pistols singer Johnny Rotten, but he had turned the part down. Townshend, who called Rotten a 'fucking diamond' and 'so smart', revealed that a heavy drinking session with Roddam may have been to blame for Rotten's decision not to appear in the film. 'I knew [Rotten] as he'd been using my studio in [London], but unfortunately we went out with the director,' Townshend said. 'Johnny Rotten liked to drink and so did I, and we went out and got [drunk] and I drove my car the wrong way around a roundabout. We went to [a club in London] together and I got stopped by the police and they hauled us [in].'

This sounds like the sort of behaviour that would have been meat and potatoes to Rotten, yet Townshend feared he may have started worrying about the ability of Roddam and himself to pull the project together.

'I really wanted him,' said Townshend. 'I don't know how good he would have been, but he's very, very intense. He could have been good.'

Townshend knew Elton, and was certainly on better terms with him than Bowie, as Bowie and Elton hadn't seen eye to eye for years. Bowie and Townshend had known each other since the Sixties. They had first met when Bowie's new band, The Lower Third, opened for The Who in Bournemouth on 4 March 1965. Townshend watched their soundcheck and heard them rush through a song – 'You've Got A Habit Of Leaving' – that to his ears sounded a little too like a pantomime version of a Who song, complete with choppy windmill chords. He then berated Bowie for copying him.*

Bowie never stopped monitoring Townshend, however. *The Rise And Fall Of Ziggy Stardust And The Spiders From Mars* was heavily influenced by The Who's concept album *Tommy*, and he recorded two Townshend songs for his 1973 *Pin-Ups* album ('I Can't Explain' and 'Anyway, Anyhow, Anywhere'). In 1979 Bowie also asked the guitarist to contribute some work to his *Scary Monsters* album, which was being produced by long-term Bowie cohort Tony Visconti. According to the producer, Townshend turned up in a 'foul, laconic' mood before pouring himself some red wine ('There's no such thing as white wine!' he had snapped when Visconti offered him a choice). '[Townshend] asked what we wanted him to do on this track,' said Visconti. 'David looked at me kind of puzzled and said, "Chords". Townshend asked, "What kind of chords?" I think both David and I were a little afraid to state the obvious but I finally offered, "Er, Pete Townshend chords." Townshend shrugged, "Oh, windmills," and did a perfect windmill on his guitar.'

The ironic thing about both performances was the fact that while neither was exemplary, they resonated so much with the crowd. Millions of people watched Bowie and The Who and were reminded how much they liked rock music in the first place. Bowie might have just had a massive hit with his *Let's Dance* album, but The Who hadn't had a proper hit in years. Yet here they were, large and in charge, on the Wembley stage looking for all

---

* Bowie re-recorded 'You've Got A Habit Of Leaving' thirty-five-years later for his un-released album *Toy*, and eventually released it as a B side to his 'Slow Burn' single in 2002.

the world like the rock gods they had been ten, twenty years previously. The nuances may have changed, and their drummer may have moved on, but they were still The Who, still one of the greatest rock bands in the world.

Had we forgotten that? Perhaps we had.

'At the time there was still a rivalry between the old guard and the new guard,' said Mark Ellen, who as well as helping present Live Aid was also the editor of *Smash Hits* and *Q* during the Eighties. 'The Pink Floyds and the Roxy Musics and the Phil Collinses were enormously unpopular and much derided by the generation led by Paul Weller and people like that, as they seemed to be energetic and aggressive and emblematic of something young and new. So that was the first tension resolved by Live Aid. The second tension was the one between pop music and rock music, which was also resolved that day. Although they didn't sit there and denounce each other publicly, there was a huge division developing between Spandau Ballet and Duran Duran and all those people who were completely different from the rock 'n' roll guard, the Status Quos of this world. There was also the huge divide between British pop and American rock 'n' roll, as we were very resistant in this country to the likes of George Thorogood and the Destroyers.

'So those three things were changed, and quite radically, by the arrival of Live Aid. Because at Live Aid, and it's a terrible cliché of level playing fields, effectively groups played for the same amount of time, which was democratically elected. It didn't really matter also what time of day they came on, it could be mid-afternoon and you could still feel that they were all almost headliners.

'To see those groups, that mix of groups, changed people's minds slightly about the divisions within rock music. Up till then people were a little bit more segregated in the way that they saw things. But at Wembley people just sort of relaxed about it, it was all part of some same universe and it was OK to like something from another generation.'*

---

* The Who appeared at the closing ceremony of the 2012 Olympics, along with Madness, the Pet Shop Boys, One Direction, George Michael, Emeli Sandé and many others. 'It was like Stella Street backstage,' said Suggs from Madness. 'The Spice Girls were practising their singing and we could hear Pete Townshend going, "Shuuuuuut up! Someone feed them, for God's sake!"'

In a decade supposedly obsessed with cool and surface and fashionability, on 13 July, none of this seemed to make much sense. Not even David Bowie seemed to make much sense. Bowie had for such a long time been the bastion of cool that cool was deemed to be the benchmark of success. But all of a sudden, being cool didn't seem to mean too much. Queen weren't cool, Live Aid wasn't cool, half the people – more! – on this bill weren't cool, yet the whole day seemed part of a different agenda. Live Aid appeared to be so much bigger than the sum of its parts, and whether it was Phil Collins or Sting or indeed any member of the peloton, popularity for a moment took precedence over cool. And we didn't question it for a minute. Exclusivity, that elusive quest, the goal the image business had been striving for since the beginning of the decade, well, it just seemed a bit silly now. So many of us had spent the first five years of the decade rushing to get away from everyone else, pushing ourselves onwards, upwards, mobilising ourselves simply to escape our past, often without a passing thought as to why we were doing it . . . And now? Well . . . This silly pop concert had very quickly made us remember how good shared experiences could be.

Three years later this shift became manifest, at least where London club culture was concerned. Walk into a West End nightclub in the spring of 1988 and you would have been shocked by the change in clientele; gone were the nervy, sniffy, overdressed regulars, as overnight they had been replaced by slightly younger young men wearing billowing T-shirts, baggy trousers and bandanas, dancing as one, inexpertly moving to a new, slightly fluid, trippy dance sound, acid house, that couldn't have been more different to the sniffy, insular dance music that preceded it. The Ecstasy generation appeared almost overnight, almost as one, demanding to be taken seriously, and completely uninterested in anything that had been before. I remember walking into the Astoria one night, having spent the evening in the Groucho Club, expecting another grown-up cocktail party, another collection of velvet-rope professionals who had spent their lives in places like this. Instead we found a nightclub with an empty bar – everyone was drinking water on the dance floor, having already taken more than their fair share of Ecstasy – and a heaving mass of sweaty white cotton. We were

i-D

love
hate
push
y-ft
kiss
wipe
misc
find
pet-
bcup
dcup
-vpl
noft
s-ex
stop
home
h-rt

sexsense

Madonna and *i-D,* two more icons of the decade. *i-D* was the ultimate street fashion
bible, an esoteric and occasionally anarchic tip-sheet; while Madonna (here, on her
first British magazine cover) was as famous and almost as divisive as Margaret Thatcher.
Mark Lebon, *i-D,* Sexsense Issue, Apr 1984

THE RACE AGAINST TIME

Sport Aid was one of the many brilliant spin-offs from Live Aid, an event that kept the brand moving, as well as continuing to raise more funds for the charity

Bob Dylan's shambolic performance was one of the most notorious elements of the Philadelphia Live Aid concert, a segment that was completely overshadowed by Mick Jagger's perfectly judged duet with Tina Turner

Ray Petri was one of the greatest stylists of his generation, a man who inadvertently kick-started the men's magazine boom in Britain, while dressing some of the most important stars of the decade. He died of an AIDS-related illness in 1989 Ray Petri photographed by Jamie Morgan © 1980

Watching Michael Jackson try and conquer a stadium was an odd experience as you got the sense that his performance was more about him than the crowd, the people who had paid to come and pay homage. It was an exercise in ego more than anything...

THE FACE REVIEW OF

1985

A LOT CAN HAPPEN TO A GIRL
IN A YEAR. THIS IS THE GIRL.
THIS IS THE YEAR . . .

1 9 8 5

Last December, THE FACE told a pop singer named Madonna that she was a lot like Marilyn Monroe. "I know," she replied. It was a charming conceit. In a year in which celebrities seemed to have the power to feed the world, she was playing with dynamite . . .

Decades don't normally develop their abiding themes until half way through, although by 1985 the Eighties had already been fairly defined. However no one knew just how important 1985 would turn out to be

Comic Relief is one of the projects that arose directly from the remnants of Live Aid. Since its launch from a refugee camp in Sudan on Christmas Day in 1985 the charity, founded by Richard Curtis and Jane Tewson, has raised over £800m and has been at work in over 70 countries around the world, and formed the Comic Relief Committee, which included many well-known British comedians. Footage courtesy of Comic Relief and Fulwell73

Timed to coincide with the 20th anniversary of Live Aid, Live 8 was a string of benefit concerts that took place on July 2nd 2005, in the G8 states and South Africa. They were also timed to precede the G8 conference and summit held at the Gleneagles Hotel in Scotland that year

What perfect synergy for the fashion industry, a home-grown international cause that it could embrace, celebrate and add value to without looking exploitational. It was a match made in the glass-walled boardroom of a PR agency, and why on earth not?

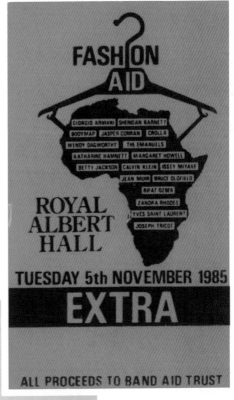

FASHION AID

GIORGIO ARMANI | SHERIDAN BARNETT
BODYMAP | JASPER CONRAN | CROLLA
WENDY DAGWORTHY | THE EMANUELS
KATHARINE HAMNETT | MARGARET HOWELL
BETTY JACKSON | CALVIN KLEIN | ISSEY MIYAKE
JEAN MUIR | BRUCE OLDFIELD
RIFAT OZBEK
ZANDRA RHODES
YVES SAINT LAURENT
JOSEPH TRICOT

ROYAL ALBERT HALL

TUESDAY 5th NOVEMBER 1985

EXTRA

ALL PROCEEDS TO BAND AID TRUST

The changing nature of celebrity culture was partly responsible for the global attention paid to the death of Princess Diana, as she was the first glamour icon to die in the full glare of twenty-four-hour media, although we felt as though we were far closer to her life and her world than was true...

In 1987, the Zeitgeist moved again, this time to the dancefloor, as the club scene turned almost overnight from an exclusive world to an inclusive world, an environment where Acid House ruled the car parks and nightclubs of the UK. Terry Jones, *i-D*, The Happy Issue, Jan 1988

David Cameron and Steve Hilton's 'Big Society' had its roots in Live Aid – a bold if ill-thought-out initiative to empower local people and communities while taking power away from politicians, that nevertheless helped detoxify and reposition the Conservatives as a more compassionate organisation only in our mid-to-late twenties and already we felt old. The world had moved on, and it hadn't bothered to tell us. Clubs soon got bigger, moved out into fields in order to have enough room to put all the punters in, and everyone was welcome. Guest lists became a thing of the past, as everyone became a trendy. This was the second Summer of Love, the genuine coming of age of a new subcultural movement, and egalitarianism writ large. These didn't look like the kind of people who were going to worry about where their next Tizio lamp was coming from. The aspirations of the early Eighties suddenly looked very old-fashioned indeed.

'Before Live Aid certain people like Van Morrison and Rod Stewart or whatever were considered to be super-antiquated and surplus to requirements,' said Mark Ellen. 'But when they saw Live Aid they saw a lot of bands that they hadn't heard of and they quite liked them. Also, people thought, "I'd forgotten about all these bands, I'd forgotten that Dave Gilmour existed, I'd forgotten about Queen, I'd forgotten about David Bowie and I saw them and they were wonderful and actually the stadium experience looks very pleasant." Like it might be a worthwhile venture to go to see people in places like that.'

The Who would eventually get over their differences and re-form, while David Bowie would manage to lose his mojo before finding it again before he retired. And although Bowie and every member of The Who would have mixed emotions about their appearance at Live Aid, they all went home relatively happy.

Live Aid documentary producer Jill Sinclair was also producing a Christmas special that day for *The Tube*, the Channel 4 early-evening pop show. 'The interviews were more like a gossip between old friends – what was it like and so on. In a break Paula [Yates] and I sat down and tried to figure out some questions that would spark a different response. We came up with a list including, "What are you going to do [right] now?" The first person we thought we'd try it on was David Bowie. I grabbed him and she asked the new question. He looked at her, then straight into the camera and said, 'I'm going to go home, and I'm going to have a really good fuck."

TWELVE

20:50

**Elton John: 'I'm Still Standing', 'Bennie And The Jets',
'Rocket Man', 'Don't Go Breaking My Heart' (with Kiki Dee),
'Don't Let The Sun Go Down On Me' (with George Michael),
'Can I Get A Witness'**

No one ever talks about the music any more. It's partly my
own fault because I've become a larger-than-life person, but
it's all about the hair, the glasses, the houses, the lawsuits, the
marriage, the divorce, the this, the that. People say I never do
anything small, and I suppose I don't.

ELTON JOHN

My girlfriend Kate had waited all day for Elton. She had initially
been looking forward to the likes of the Style Council, Sade and
Bryan Ferry, but, like many others out on the Wembley grass,
she'd found them to be a huge disappointment. In her eyes, the new broom
wasn't sweeping clean at all. A couple of hours earlier she had been blown
away by Queen – she wasn't a fan and didn't really understand why they had
been so impressive – but she'd always been an Elton fan, and her expectations
were high. When she was nine, pretty much the only record she played at
home – in Bushey, not far from where Elton grew up, in Pinner, in north-
west London – was *Goodbye Yellow Brick Road*. Her father, Doug Flett, was

a songwriter (I'd actually bought our Live Aid tickets from him), and had written 'The Fair's Moving On' for Elvis Presley, 'Fallen Angel' for Frankie Valli, 'Save Me' for Clodagh Rodgers, 'Power To All Our Friends' for Cliff Richard, 'By The Devil (I Was Tempted)' for Blue Mink, 'Lady Put The Light Out' for Joe Cocker, etc. He also wrote the wonderful 'I Can't Tell The Bottom From The Top' for the Hollies in 1970, on which Elton had played keyboards (Elton had also played piano on their previous hit, 'He Ain't Heavy, He's My Brother'). At the time, Elton was a jobbing session musician, and as well as playing on other people's records, he also recorded over a dozen songs for various 'covers' albums ('Come And Get It', 'Spirit In The Sky', 'Lady D'Arbanville', 'Signed Sealed Delivered', etc.), one of which was 'I Can't Tell The Bottom From The Top'.

'Back in the early days I supplemented my meagre earnings from Dick James Music by playing on sessions – paid in cash!' said Elton. 'My speciality then was backing vocals – I'm on Tom Jones's "Daughter Of Darkness", "Back Home" by the England World Cup Squad and even some of the Barron Knights stuff. Fucking hilarious they were. I worked on that Here Come The Olympics spoof ["An Olympic Record"] they did at Abbey Road. In wanders [Paul] McCartney – he was in Studio 2 and thought he'd pop in and see what the peasants were up to. Me and Bernie Taupin just froze and made some mumbling noises and he said a few things, then sat down and started to play the piano, told us it was the latest thing the band had finished and it was "Hey Jude". Blew my fucking head apart.

'I also used to do all those *Top of the Pops* cover records too – I'm quite a good mimic so I could adapt my voice to whatever act it was. Singing lead on "Saved By The Bell" by Robin Gibb, I had to sing in this dreadful warble and I couldn't get it so I ended up actually manually warbling my throat. I do a pretty good Leon Russell impression too.'

It wasn't just Kate who had been looking forward to seeing Elton, as both Robin and I were fairly keen too. Back in Bristol Robin had been a huge fan of *Goodbye Yellow Brick Road*, while I was looking forward to finally seeing Elton play Wembley, something I'd missed out on ten years earlier, having decided at the last minute not to go and see him play *Captain Fantastic And The Brown Dirt Cowboy* there in June 1975.

During 1985, Kate, Robin and myself tended to go everywhere together, and thought we would forever. We lived in each other's pockets. We went to clubs together, went to parties together, went on holiday together. We even spent Christmas together. The previous Christmas, Kate and I had gone to Robin's parents' house in Clifton in Bristol on Boxing Day and had stayed there until we all went back to work (Kate and I were at *i-D*, Robin *The Face*). That year, one of Robin's grandmothers was staying, and, at the age of eighty-two, she was already having some trouble grasping reality. We had spent the day after Boxing Day mostly watching television, and in particular a snooker tournament, which for some reason had caused Robin's granny much anxiety.

'They shouldn't be using those sticks you know,' she said, to no one in particular, as she clutched her handbag a little too tightly. 'They'll end up hitting each other. I've always thought snooker is a very dangerous game.'

Kathryn Flett and Robin Derrick in the *i-D* office in 1985, a month before Live Aid. For years afterwards, Derrick would talk about Live Aid as though he were riffing on the St Crispin's Day speech from Henry V, in which the king rallies his troops before the battle of Agincourt.

After an especially long lunch, she fell asleep for a few hours – still clutching her handbag – and woke up halfway through *Ben Hur*. At the moment when spears started to be thrown, she turned to Robin and said, 'I told you snooker was a dangerous game.'

On the Tube to Wembley we had been laughing about this, and wondering what she would make of Live Aid as she watched it on television.

'In a way everyone else on the bill was a support act for Elton and Queen,' Kate said, thinking back to 13 July. 'I remember walking up Wembley Way towards the stadium, and trying not to look excited about the fact that we were going in. You have to remember that before it happened, Live Aid wasn't actually very cool, and although we were all excited about going, and secretly thought that it was going to be great, we sort of had to pretend to be blasé about it. It was ridiculous but it was true. I was looking forward to Elvis Costello and the Style Council and some of the younger bands.' But at the end of the day – literally – it was all about Elton and Queen.

'U2 were obviously magnificent, but then we expected them to be. I think I'd had too much to drink by this stage as I watched them on the screens and was convinced that they were playing in Philadelphia. I think this may have been because Jack Nicholson actually introduced them in Philadelphia, but there we are. The surprise was Queen, who were so infinitely better than practically everyone who had been on before them. The whole "Radio Ga Ga" moment looked a bit fascist, but it was still extraordinary. I could play "Bohemian Rhapsody" on the piano, but there was no way I was ever going to play it in public. That's how I felt about them.'

Elton, though, Elton was different.

For years afterwards, Robin would talk about Live Aid as though he were riffing on the St Crispin's Day speech from Henry V, in which the king rallies his troops before the Battle of Agincourt – Act IV Scene III. (It is so called because 25 October – the day of the battle – is the feast day of saints Crispin and Crispinian.) 'From this day to the ending of the world, But we in it shall be remember'd; We few, we happy few, we band of brothers; For he to-day that sheds his blood with me Shall be my brother; be he ne'er so vile, This day shall gentle his condition: And gentlemen in England now a-bed Shall think themselves accursed they were not here, And hold their manhoods cheap whiles any speaks That fought with us upon Saint Crispin's day.' Who went with us to Live Aid . . .

'It was one of those days when you wanted to be with everyone else,' said Robin. 'There was a VIP area, and you could buy tickets for £100 to be in it, but I remember all of us wanted to be with everyone else. We spent our lives being on guest lists, and being ushered into VIP areas, but none of that seemed appropriate for Live Aid. This was a day for the shared experience. We had all been given permission to be mainstream. It was like being at an FA Cup Final, and we weren't really there for the music, for the entertainment, we were there for something bigger. This wasn't about seeing Jimi Hendrix playing "The Star Spangled Banner", this was no artistic critique of capitalism . . .

'Queen were obviously amazing, although I can't remember many of the bands we saw. I don't remember seeing Howard Jones or Nik Kershaw, and nobody was really interested in Phil Collins getting on Concorde. It just seemed like a gimmick – this was also before the days of energy conservation; there was no dichotomy about the waste of fuel. The Boomtown Rats were obviously batting outside their comfort zone, as were a couple of others. I was interested in the big acts, like Paul McCartney and Elton John. By the time Elton came on we were all in the zone, and by the time the whole day had spun out, we all really believed in it. Live Aid was the most un-cynical, un-ironic, un-snide event of them all. It was nothing like the Eighties at all in fact. We put on the Woodstock glow, and we all bought the T-shirt.'

This wasn't a rock crowd, this was a Wembley crowd, and the people here were probably no different from the ones a few hundred yards away waiting to see Dire Straits in the Arena. These looked like the same kind of people who would soon come and see Michael Jackson or Madonna here, in the same way that the audiences at a Broadway or West End matinee performance always look the same, regardless of what they've come to see.

Throughout the latter part of the twentieth century, postmodernist historians increasingly championed the value of the experiences of ordinary people, as though being on the receiving end of history, rather than being its architect, was somehow more valid; well, if that really is the case, then Live Aid was the most postmodern event of all time, a spectacle driven completely by those who watched it. After all, without its audience, Live Aid would just have been a couple of concerts in empty stadiums. At Live Aid, a tree fell in the forest and everyone saw it.

Because the scale of the event had dominated the pre-publicity, just being involved made you feel part of it, whether you were there, whether you were watching on television, or whether you were listening to the radio broadcast in the back of someone's car. The content was almost interchangeable, and if the US finale had involved a duet – or duel – between Bruce Springsteen and Michael Jackson, then so be it; if the denouement of Wembley had involved Boy George and Rod Stewart camping it up, then wouldn't that have been dandy? It wouldn't really have made any difference, as that day the audience was as important as the performers. This was one of the reasons why those performers were so discombobulated backstage; not only did many of them not grasp the scale of the event until afterwards, but they weren't altogether sure how much of the main event they were contributing to. There was no point asking their managers or their vassals or their sidekicks or girlfriends, as none of them had ever been to a Live Aid concert before. Had anyone?

The images from Live Aid are finite. This was before the era of mobile phones, when everyone would demand their own personal record of events as a matter of course, when whipping out your iPhone made it possible for you to take as many frames per minute as you wished, so we all got our own Zapruder film, our own digital photo gallery. The pictures we remember from Live Aid are unlikely to be replaced by others, as what we saw was what we got. The pictures supplied by the Velcro strip of photographers who lined the front of the stage, and the stills from the BBC coverage – that's it. There was such a cavalcade of celebrity backstage that it seems a crime of sorts that there wasn't more of a record of it; oh to be able to find an audio snippet online somewhere of Rock Star A idly chatting to Rock Star B before passing over the coke.

The crowd wasn't how I remembered a festival crowd to be. A festival crowd was pungent, reeking of a mixture of Red Leb, sweat and patchouli, of stale pale ale and cigarette smoke. The Live Aid crowd all looked like they'd come straight from home, maybe having picked up a cellophane-wrapped egg sandwich in the local Esso station. They looked completely normal. There wasn't even an abundance of denim. Whenever I had gone to festivals in the Seventies – or indeed the first Womad festival in 1982 – blue seemed to be the defining colour of nature. Not brown or green, but a dirty sea of denim. Here, everyone looked as though they'd popped out to buy a new shirt, not really knowing or indeed caring where they'd bought it from. No one went to Live Aid trying to make a sartorial statement; they'd gone to Live Aid to see Elton John.

Live Aid was already nine hours old by the time he came on stage, and it had been one hell of a sweltering day. Most people in the crowd were sunburnt, many on just one side of their face. Both Robin and I were wearing MA-1 flying jackets, Lonsdale baseball caps and shorts, while Kate (she thinks) wore a white parachute-silk boiler suit by Katharine Hamnett and an English Eccentrics blouson. We were all soaked through, as it was impossible to hide from the sun. The only respite involved plastic pints of sticky beer, which were used to wash down the burgers, chips and ice cream. By the time Elton came on, we'd almost had enough.

'After a while the acts had become a bit "meh", as the crowd started to greet everyone with a sense of indifference,' said Kate. 'The day was actually punctuated with boredom, so the good acts really stood out. There was also a slight sense that the whole thing might actually be a lot better on television, not that we wanted to admit it. We didn't care about Phil Collins and the Concorde gimmick, didn't care about the likes of Howard Jones, and I really wanted the thing to get a move on. You had a feeling that if Elton turned up then it would be amazing, and when it happened it really was. The set slowly built up, until it felt like a genuine stadium moment. I can't even remember what he played, but I know that it worked. Suddenly the stadium came alive again, which it hadn't since Queen. He had this intergenerational gift of appealing to everyone. First he brought Kiki Dee on to sing "Don't Go Breaking My Heart", and then there was George [who Kate had actually known back in Bushey]. As soon as he brought George Michael on, he owned the place. It was a meeting of two worlds, and they met perfectly.'

The old guard had taken possession of the stadium. George Michael may have been singing on stage, but he was being driven by Elton. All those who were a little too cool for school – and that included some of us in the audience as well as some of those on stage – felt a little silly, as the goodwill engendered by the likes of Elton John and Queen had enveloped the stadium like a Christo shroud.

'As soon as Elton started playing I remember thinking that I was really glad I wasn't in Philadelphia,' said Kate. 'It suddenly felt very special to be there, along with 70,000 other people. I don't remember seeing a single other person we knew that day, but it didn't matter. The whole thing about Live Aid was that it weirdly wasn't of its time. In the Eighties, pop was flashy, it was 2D, whereas Live Aid harked back to a better time, a more benevolent time. It was amazing to think that pop music could be a catalyst for something so special. Live Aid came from a place of great sincerity.'

Elton had last been at Wembley the previous summer, to watch his beloved Watford play a resurgent Everton in the FA Cup Final. On the day Watford lost 2–0, while Elton shed a tear and said it was 'the biggest day of my life'. But today would be bigger.

Elton John and George Michael were the only performers not to make the journey from Battersea Heliport, as the chopper came to Elton's house in Windsor to pick them up, landing on the lawn (Michael having arrived earlier by car). They hadn't rehearsed the song they were going to perform – 'Don't Let The Sun Go Down On Me'– and so Michael spent the journey to Wembley learning the lyrics.

Elton had built a little house backstage, complete with an artificial lawn, and he encouraged everyone to come and hang out there. Here, pop stars of every vintage lolled about watching their peers on TV, behind miniature thickets of plastic beer glasses. It was like a circus. George Michael spent a lot of time there, seemingly unaffected by nerves. He was still in his early twenties, and about to perform an unrehearsed song to the largest audience in the entertainment industry's history, and he appeared to be completely unfazed.

As he was introduced by Billy Connolly as 'a friend of mine from planet Windsor', Elton bounded on to the Wembley stage, dressed approximately as a Cossack. Like Queen, Elton had decided to make his show a brilliant composite: 'I'm Still Standing', 'Bennie And The Jets' and 'Rocket Man', a song which was the cue for mass arm swaying in the crowd. He had initially decided to perform 'Dancing In The Street' with Kiki Dee, but when he heard that Bowie and Jagger had beaten him to it, he considered 'Don't Go Breaking My Heart' instead, before second-guessing himself. 'So there we were, trying desperately to think of something new and different,' said Kiki Dee, 'while George [Michael] insisted: "Do something the public wants to hear." In the end, he persuaded us to stick to [it].'

When Elton introduced George Michael, it provided one of the day's most poignant gear changes. This was truly a marriage made in heaven. Not only did Elton look supremely clever by embracing Michael – the latest new kid on the block – but the Wham! singer had already nailed his colours to the mast by admitting a fondness for Elton's music, much to the annoyance of the music press, who were still trying to banish him to the past. Earlier in the year, Elton had presented Michael with an Ivor Novello award for Best Songwriter (for 'Careless Whisper'), calling him the 'Paul McCartney of his generation'. They had met six months earlier, in France, and had immediately hit it off. Both had had similar childhoods, feeling overweight, unattractive, and sexually confused, and both used costume and stagecraft to disguise their shyness. Their paths would keep crossing after Live Aid, and almost exactly a year later, on the same stage, Elton would make an appearance at 'The Final', Wham!'s farewell performance, singing 'Candle In The Wind' and 'I'm Your Man'.

Where chart sensations are concerned, it's always easy to dismiss all that went before them, difficult to imagine any one pop phenomenon being able to inspire the same kind of national – if not quite global – loyalty. With pop it's always Year Zero. Think of Take That, Bros, Culture Club or T. Rex and we automatically think of bargain basements full of discarded copies of 'Back For Good', 'I Owe You Nothing', 'Karma Chameleon' or 'Jeepster'.

As built-in obsolescence always seems to be the order of the day, apart from Take That (who have a bizarre and yet fascinating hold on the nation's throat) it is unlikely that a greatest hits collection by any of the aforementioned teen dreams would stand much chance of making it to number one in the UK any more. Yet Wham! were always different, and while they never had the kind of long-term Queen Mother appeal of Take That, during the rashly extravagant Eighties George Michael and Andrew Ridgeley were treated by press and public alike as minor royalty. Maybe there were some who actually thought they *were* minor royalty. Their records were insanely popular, and although *NME* critics dismissed them as formulaic pop, they were anything but: our radios rattled to the sub-Motown sound of 'Wham Rap' (number eight, January 1983), 'Wake Me Up Before You Go Go' (number one, May 1984), 'Freedom' (number one, October 1984) and the rest. Wham!'s controlled exuberance epitomised everything that is good about pop, and though they were in the charts for just four years, from 'Young Guns (Go For It)' (number three, October 1982) to 'The Edge Of Heaven' (number one, June 1986), during that time they hardly made a duff record.

The late Seventies and early Eighties were not exactly giddy times in Britain, yet out of the recession came dozens of smart young pop groups willing to dance while London, Coventry or Sheffield burned. None was smarter than George Michael's Wham! They were part of the biggest British pop explosion since the mid-Sixties, as Frankie Goes to Hollywood, Culture Club, Duran Duran and Spandau Ballet broke the American charts, paving the way for such unlikely glamour kids as the Thompson Twins and the Eurythmics. When we think of a Wham! song, we tend to think of a rose-tinted illusory past. And we rather like it. George's 'Careless Whisper' (number one, August 1984) sounds like our past, even if it had nothing to do with it. The duo also had the perfect pop divorce: George being granted ascension to the very top of the pop hierarchy, Andrew fading from view like a GTI-driving Garbo.

I first saw Wham! in July 1983 at the launch of their debut LP *Fantastic* (such confidence!), in a small suite of offices just behind Fulham Broadway Tube station in London. While dozens of sneering music journalists and record-company bigwigs stood about, working at being brilliant, the two twenty-year-old soul boys, dressed in Hawaiian shirts, cutaway jeans and deck shoes, jived together on the dance floor, jitterbugging along to their own version of the Miracles' 'Love Machine'. Rarely had I seen two men enjoying themselves so much. To be dancing to one of their own records! At their own party! In front of other people!

Suburban boys with West End aspirations — second-generation immigrants, Andrew's father is Italian/Egyptian, while George (real name Georgios Panayiotou) is half Greek — they were high street through and through: their white T-shirts and socks came from Marks & Spencer, their blue jeans from Woodhouse. They hailed from Bushey in Hertfordshire, in the heart of the disco belt. For years they danced themselves stupid at the New Penny in Watford High Street, moving on to the Camden Palace as soon as it opened in the spring of 1982, immersing themselves in London's holier-than-thou nightlife. To west London sybarites they looked oddly naïve in their quasi-naff clothes and floppy fringes, yet anyone with eyes in their head and loafers on their feet could tell that they had a very spangly future ahead of them.

After they became famous they still went out dancing, and it was not unusual to see Andrew on display at the Limelight or George down at the infamous Taboo. For about eighteen months 'Everything She Wants' (number two, December 1984) was the hippest record to be seen dancing to, and George could often be seen doing just that, right in front of the DJ booth. Even at 3 a.m. in the bowels of some sweaty West End nightclub, he looked as though he'd just stepped off the plane from Ibiza: tandoori tan, summer whites, designer stubble (something the singer invented) and perfect Princess Diana hair. He was always serious about his hair: 'Some days I made the covers of the tabloids. Some days Princess Di made the covers of the tabloids,' he said. 'Some days I think they just got mixed up.'

George was less home-boy than homely boy. If he was the suburban sonneteer, happy in his bedroom writing tear-jerkers, then Andrew was the quintessential party animal, the Liam Gallagher of his day, unable to leave a party without a bottle of Moët in one hand and a bottle blonde in the other.

It was Andrew who realised George's pop ambitions, Andrew who acted the extrovert to George's shy loner. George might have written the songs – in four years Andrew only gained three co-writing credits, for 'Wham! Rap (Enjoy What You Do)', 'Club Tropicana' (number four, July 1983) and 'Careless Whisper') – yet it was his partner who looked the part when they sang them. Andrew's image was crystallised on the 12″ version of 'I'm Your Man' (number one, November 1985): a racing car is heard careering through a plate-glass window, followed by the sound of its driver cackling with laughter as he asks, 'Where's the bar.'

The boys were managed for a time by Sixties impresario Simon Napier-Bell, but it was always George who had the vision thing, even at school. There was nothing haphazard about this affair, and Wham!'s career seemed organised with staggering efficiency. Their songs were hardly arch (unlike, say, the Pet Shop Boys), but even to the untrained ear one instinctively knew the people behind them weren't stupid. Not only were they perfect fodder for twelve-year-old girls, they also had a superior ironic quality: whether you were an art student or an estate agent, you knew they were cool.

It all ended in the most spectacular, and – for a pop group – impressively orchestrated manner. Displaying unusual sagacity for a twenty-two-year-old, Georgios decided the clock was nearing midnight, and that Cinderella really ought to go home. Ziggy Stardust-style, he broke up the band to go solo, organising one last showbiz gesture, the final farewell triumph at Wembley Stadium in the scorching summer of 1986.

One got the feeling that Andrew could have carried on forever, but for George there were only so many shuttlecocks he could put down his tennis shorts. Andrew gradually disappeared, moving to Cornwall and dropping out. George decided he wanted to be a sex god, then he changed his mind (changing the name of his second album *Bare* to the slightly more off-putting *Listen Without Prejudice Vol. 1*), then he started smoking a lot of weed, hanging out in public lavatories, crashing cars and generally making a nuisance of himself.

George jumped around the stage like an animated glove puppet, the piano player's dummy, for tonight he was Elton's *ami necessaire*. Live Aid was a big day for him, although Andrew Ridgeley wasn't really in the loop. He had raised funds backstage, and sang backing vocals, but to all intents and purposes, this was a solo outing for George, the first of many.

'The Live Aid thing was fantastic because the emotion behind it was genuine – at least on the English side of things,' Michael told Tony Parsons. 'There was lots of talk about the squabbles that were going on over in Philadelphia but over here the British bands were too nervous to push themselves up front, they didn't argue over their spots and it went really well.

'I was aware that after Live Aid I was seen in some quarters as . . . a solo act. I was nervous as hell. It was the first time I had ever sung in front of an indifferent audience because every one I had sung in front of before had been mine – or ours. The miners' benefit [at which Wham! had played the previous September, at the Royal Festival Hall] wasn't an indifferent audience – that was hostile. But that was OK – I did the miners' benefit because that was what I believed in and I knew what we could expect from the audience. So I was angered by it, but I wasn't surprised. But with the Live Aid audience I knew that I would be judged differently. More than anything, it showed that people wanted me – quite unfairly – to do stuff on my own so that they could admit to liking me. Everybody raved about my performance, which I honestly thought was very average. Everybody said – God, he showed that he can really sing, but I thought it was nothing special. The interpretation I did of "Don't Let The Sun Go Down On Me" was very close to what Elton had done and I was out of tune for the first couple of verses. I actually sing a lot better than that on my records and I don't see why everyone should suddenly like me because I am up there with musicians twice my age and I am taking myself away from my friend. I didn't understand why that should be suddenly credible.

'Live Aid was good for me but people's reaction kind of annoyed me. It irritated me.'

It would turn out to be a good year for George, and by Christmas his voice could be heard on four records in the top twenty: Wham!'s 'I'm Your Man', the re-released 'Last Christmas' and Band Aid's 'Do They Know It's Christmas?', as well as Elton John's 'Nikita'.

Elton was on something of a roll too, and he hadn't been so popular since the mid-Seventies. He had survived the hair transplants, the unlikely marriage to studio engineer Renate Blauel in 1984 – 'You may still be standing,' Rod Stewart's wedding telegram read, 'but we're all on the fucking floor!' – and appalling press intrusion. But by Live Aid he was well and truly back. The 'comeback' record, or at least the one that immediately made him relevant for an Eighties audience, was 1983's *Too Low For Zero*, which contained the mammoth hits 'I'm Still Standing' and 'I Guess That's Why They Call It The Blues'. This was his first album since 1976's *Blue Moves* exclusively to feature lyrics by his long-term partner Bernie Taupin, and it showed. He followed this with *Breaking Hearts* in July 1984, which included 'Passengers' and 'Sad Songs (Say So Much)', and was the album he was still promoting throughout much of 1985. Four months after Live Aid he released *Ice On Fire,* his nineteenth studio album, and the first since *Blue Moves* to be produced by his old producer Gus Dudgeon (as well as 'Nikita' it included 'Wrap Her Up', which also featured George Michael). By the time of Live Aid, and at the age of thirty-eight, he was already a national institution, and had already had enough careers for six people.

Britain in the Eighties had been called Fantasy Island by some, an age of bogusness, artifice and self-delusion. 'In Britain, little remains that does not wear the cosmetic disguise of something else, considered happier, more desirable or glamorous,' said Philip Norman. Pastiche was ripe, as the emerging lifestyle culture determined that in order to be successful, entertainment had to be like stuff that had been before, but only slightly *less.* Elton may have worn some ridiculous outfits – coming on stage dressed as a duck, or Minnie Mouse – but he was never a parody. Only Elton could do what Elton did, which is why he was a true original. You could easily call Wham! a parody, but never Elton.

There was another true original in the stadium that day, a twenty-four-year-old Sloane from Sandringham, Diana Frances Spencer. Prince Charles, at the old-before-his-time age of thirty-six, may have worn a navy blue suit to Live Aid, and then referred to it as 'some pop concert jamboree my wife made me go to', but for Princess Diana this was almost a coming-out party, four long years after their wedding. Here was a Sloane Ranger with a taste for pop – she adored George Michael and Duran Duran – and who wore John Galliano. A royal whose causes weren't typical of someone in her position – the victims of AIDS and landmines. A royal who found a role by transforming herself into what Alastair Campbell would one day brand her, the People's Princess.

Geldof had buttonholed the pair at a Dire Straits concert ten days beforehand, corralling and almost begging the royal couple to attend. 'I thought it would be important for them to come because at that time it was glamorous, there was excitement around their relationship, and they represented the country,' said Geldof.

When Diana died in 1997 we streamed into London to mourn her at the rate of 6,000 an hour. The gates to Kensington Palace became the biggest floral tribute the city had ever seen, and I lost count of the unlikely people I knew who were making the pilgrimage. Like Live Aid, they wanted to go because they wanted to show they cared, with everyone else who felt the same way. As Tina Brown put it in her book on Diana, 'The diversity of the crowd, as much as its numbers, was what made it a miracle: young, old, black, white, South Asian and East Asian, in shorts and saris and denim and pinstripes and baseball caps and hijabs. The death of an aristocratic girl who became a princess but refused to let palace walls enclose her had somehow triggered a historic celebration of inclusion.'

For sure this was in part due to the changing political nature of Britain at that moment, as we had recently embraced a new 'inclusive' Labour leader after nearly two decades of Tory rule, but the outpouring of grief when Diana died had its roots in Live Aid, when a nation – all nations – came together to show their compassion. Celebrity culture had something to do with it too, as she was the first glamour icon to die in the full glare of twenty-four-hour media, although we felt as though we were far closer to her life and her world than we did about anyone else caught in the headlines. As with Live Aid, her death, and the grieving that followed, was almost a participatory exercise.

'Live Aid sparked an appetite for people to want those communal moments again,' said Mark Ellen. 'They are very rare, and when they happen they tend to mean a lot to people. When Princess Diana died, I was as fascinated as everyone else in the way it affected people. I wasn't a big admirer of hers, but I still went along to the funeral with my kids. There was a general desire to feel the same way at the same time as everyone else, and I know on the face of it Princess Diana and Live Aid don't have much in common, but they absolutely do. Diana's death had a very complicated political frame around it. I remember taking a photograph of the coffin going under the tree we were standing by, and all the people around me started tutting, because at that point everyone thought that she had been killed by photographers. And as I looked like a photographer, quite possibly a paparazzi, I was treated as one of the enemy, as one of them. That's how hot-headed people were at the time, as she meant so much to people.'

Attending Princess Diana's funeral, or watching it on television, resonated with Live Aid in the same way, because of the sense of community. I've always thought this was the same reason why so many people buy copies of the *Radio Times* at Christmas. Television listings have been free for years, yet people want the connection, want to relate, and so buy the *Radio Times*. We might all have strands of ourselves that we tease out to define ourselves, yet many of us want to connect with each other far more than we like to let on.

'For a few days Hyde Park became like a festival,' said Ellen. 'You're not allowed to camp in Hyde Park, but there were so many people who wanted to come to Kensington Gardens and pay their respects that the police couldn't do anything about it. So many people came down to London just to be part of this extraordinary event. No one could stop them camping, so in a way it was a bit like a free rock festival, like Glastonbury in the middle of London. The whole idea of buying a tent and going to a rock festival is absolutely mandatory for an eighteen-year-old, and all of this had tremendous echoes of Live Aid. Echoes of rock music culture bringing together people on such a mass scale, either as a kind of worship, or just togetherness.'

Diana was already the People's Princess, as by the time she died she had spent over a decade reaching out to those on the margins. Among the

SUNDAY Mirror SPECIAL EDITION

August 31, 1997   60p

DIANA DEAD

Dodi killed too in Paris pile-up

By Millicent Brown

PRINCESS Diana and her lover Dodi Fayed were killed early today in an horrific car crash in Paris.

Shocked eyewitnesses told how the inside of their limo was "full of blood" after the smash in a road tunnel, and how Dodi had been unsuccessfully given heart massage.

First reports said the couple's car could have been speeding to get away from pursuing paparazzi photographers who were trying to get pictures of them. The tragic couple had

Turn to Page 2

DEAD: Diana

When Diana died in 1997, people streamed into London to mourn her at the rate of 6,000 an hour. Like Live Aid, they wanted to go because they wanted to show they cared – 'the diversity of the crowd, as much as its numbers, was what made it a miracle: young, old, black, white, South Asian and East Asian, in shorts and saris and denim and pinstripes and baseball caps and hijabs.'

most notable of her causes were those that worked with AIDS. She would both comfort the patients and strive to get across the message that they should not be treated as pariahs. In 1991 she not only became the patron of the National Aids Trust, but on a highly public visit with the wife of the

314

American president, Barbara Bush, to the AIDS ward of the Middlesex Hospital, she actually hugged a patient. The image bounced around the world faster than the disease itself. Her gesture emphasised her words in a speech she had made shortly beforehand: 'HIV does not make people dangerous to know, so you can shake their hands and give them a hug – heaven knows, they need it. What's more, you can share their homes, their workplaces, and their playgrounds and toys.'

'When it came to the AIDS epidemic, like Elizabeth [Taylor], Diana was among the first global figures to speak out,' said Elton John. 'She did more than that, in fact. She reached out, quite literally, to those living with HIV/AIDS. In 1987, Diana opened the first hospital AIDS ward in Britain. Reports of her shaking hands with AIDS patients raced around the globe, and a big deal was made of the fact that she was not wearing gloves. At the time, many were still frightened to have any contact whatsoever with someone living with HIV/AIDS. Diana, with a simple yet profoundly human gesture, helped to ease the hysteria and correct the harmful misinformation surrounding the disease.

'In the years that followed, Diana continued to raise awareness about the AIDS crisis, and pictures of her touching and interacting with HIV-positive people went a long way to calm irrational fears that continued to persist. In fact, she never stopped championing those living with HIV/AIDS. In 1997, just before her tragic death, Diana and I had been in discussion about her taking on an active role with my foundation as global ambassador for our work. She met with my staff, and we were thrilled at the prospect of working together. Had she not been taken from us so soon, I know she would have continued to greatly impact the fight against AIDS.'

The princess also campaigned on behalf of leprosy sufferers, which was first demonstrated during an official visit to Indonesia with Prince Charles in 1989. She had asked to visit the Sitanela Leprosy Hospital, where she pointedly shook hands with a large number of patients, many of whom were children. The following year, during a tour of Nigeria, she visited a leper hospital and a leper colony. Diana subsequently became the patron of the Leprosy Mission in Britain. At the time she also became a patron of

Relate – which had been launched in 1987 as an updated version of the National Marriage Guidance Council – and Turning Point, the alcohol, drug and mental illness counselling organisation. In a speech for Turning Point in 1990 she said, 'It takes professionalism to convince a doubting public that it should accept back into its midst many of those diagnosed as psychotics, neurotics and other sufferers who Victorian communities decided should be kept out of sight in the safety of mental institutions.'

She made many visits for the charity, to centres looking after sufferers, and to institutions such as Rampton and Broadmoor. She was extremely public about these visits, as she was about her AIDS work. She wasn't trying to draw attention to herself, but rather to those she was visiting.

'Nothing gives me more pleasure now than being able to love and help those in our society who are vulnerable,' she said, without a hint of irony. 'If I can contribute a little something, then I am more than happy.' The fairy-tale princess who had once been considered a royal 'problem' earned her stripes by taking on everyone else's problems.

She persisted in bypassing routine, which is how she came to actively support so many causes. Leslie Rudd, who ran Turning Point at the time, said, 'We're not a charismatic cause in the public eye. Children and animals obviously come before us, along with cancer and heart disease. The issues to do with mental health are always at the bottom of any list. We wrote to her because we needed to increase the public's appreciation and sympathy – not a word I like to use. People are responsible for their own decisions, and I like to keep pity out of it. As a patron, she's given us a higher profile and publicity for issues in relation to helping people with drink and drugs. We don't use her for fund-raising; we have an ethical understanding about that.'

Elton's relationship with Diana was a real one. Duran Duran may have been her favourite band, but when she finally met Elton, a friendship actually developed quite quickly. 'Your Song' was – perhaps predictably – her favourite of his compositions, and Elton would say that the line 'Yours are the sweetest eyes' always reminded him of her.

'I think her greatest physical attribute was those eyes,' he said. 'They flirted with you; they were sorrowful and they were laughing. She had those beautiful eyes. I got to know her quite well and, of course, we had something in common. We were both bulimic for a start and we both had marriages that failed and we were both extremely interested in AIDS. You could talk about those and other issues with her in a way that you probably couldn't with any other member of the Royal Family. That's why she was such a special person.'

In 1996 Elton and Diana briefly fell out over a charity event that he had organised, and which she had originally agreed to attend before pulling out – 'I wasn't too happy and I let her know that. And she wrote me a very terse letter' – but they were reunited by the death of mutual friend Gianni Versace. In 2001 I asked Elton how he felt about playing at her funeral. 'Once I decided to do it, I had to make sure I pulled it off. It would've been horrible to go there and do it, and be a complete and utter flop. I don't really remember much about it because I was concentrating so hard. I didn't perform "Candle In The Wind" for a couple of years, but I think it's a bit precious of me not to do it, so I do it from time to time.' When it was released as a single, Keith Richards rather uncharitably said that Elton was only capable of writing songs for dead blondes, and so he retorted by calling him 'a monkey with arthritis'. Elton has had feuds with many people over the years, not least Madonna and David Bowie, who he was keen to avoid backstage at Live Aid.

Apparently Bowie had originally thought that Elton's 'Rocket Man' had ripped off 'Space Oddity', and he subsequently called him the Liberace of rock, a 'token queen'. 'I was so gutted because David and I used to be very good friends,' said Elton. 'It was at the point where I wasn't ready to come out, so I didn't speak to him for about twenty years. I had been very friendly with David up to that point. I'd hang out with him and [his wife] Angie in Covent Garden, and we were always having dinner together. It hardened me, and I was quite angry about it, and quite bewildered by it. I don't think David and I spoke for a long time after that. We made amends when we did the Freddie Mercury memorial concert at Wembley [in 1992]. I just didn't see why he said it. I thought it was unnecessary, but you know we all say things, listen I've said things.'

Elton and Freddie had been old friends for years, and whenever they met, they would float the idea of some ridiculous duet they should perform together. They were forever turning up at each other's concerts with a view to causing havoc on stage. Along with Rod Stewart they even toyed with the idea of forming a spoof supergroup. 'The name we had in mind was Nose, Teeth & Hair, a tribute to each of our most remarked-upon physical attributes,' said Stewart. 'The general idea was that we could appear as the Beverley Sisters. Somehow this project never came to anything, which is contemporary music's deep and abiding loss.'

Rod Stewart wasn't at Live Aid either – there was a diary clash – but you just know that if he had been, a hundred footballs would have been kicked into the crowd, a thousand tartan scarves would have been brandished as soon as he'd played 'Sailing' (and how could he not play it?), and 72,000 hands would have punched the air (maybe twice as many!) when he launched into 'Maggie May'.

Both Princess Diana and Paula Yates were the big silent-screen stars of Live Aid, two iconic blondes who had individually held sway over the decade in their own particular way. Diana had used her demure, coy, insistent eyes to transfix the media, while Paula had used her innate sexuality, flirting with anyone and anything that came in her sight line, especially roaming TV cameras.

'I do remember thinking what an extraordinary pairing Diana and Paula Yates were on the day,' said Gary Kemp. 'Paula was really the queen of our particular pop royal family, and in a way, Charles and Diana and Bob and Paula were sort of like the Superman Bizarro world of the royal family.'

Both were enigmatic in their own way, and both were the subject of wild sexual speculation: as the presenter of the afternoon pop TV show *The Tube*, Yates was rumoured to regularly bestow sexual favours on the (male) guests, while the erroneous list of Diana's alleged suitors would have filled a phone book. Both were unlucky in love, both doomed to die in ignominious circumstances.

Yates had met Bob Geldof in the early days of punk, as the Boomtown Rats were just starting to get attention in 1976. They married ten years later, the year after Live Aid, in Las Vegas. Duran Duran's Simon Le Bon was Geldof's best man. The year before she had met INXS's flamboyant lead singer Michael Hutchence on *The Tube*, and was reportedly asked to leave him alone by the band's road manager when she walked up to him and said, 'I'm going to have that boy.' It was to be an explosive partnership, as an affair subsequently ensued, eventually causing Yates to leave Geldof in 1995, divorcing him in 1996.

Hutchence already had a terrible reputation in the industry, partying as though it had just been made legal. Not that there was anything very legal about the partying. As a friend of mine who spent a lot of time with him said, he drank and took drugs in a robustly Australian way: never take a half when half a dozen were available. Heroin, cocaine, Ecstasy, and all points in between and beyond. During the acid house craze he had a strobe light and a smoke machine in his dressing room. 'I was an idiot, but a lovable idiot.' Cigarettes would regularly fall from his mouth as he failed to grip them with his lips, and when he walked into a room, drinks would fall over like skittles. He was doing what all nascent rock stars do: paaarty. Hard, with conviction, and with no thought as to what tomorrow might bring. In spite of this, INXS became the embodiment of a new pop culture, one which has been turned into an art form by MTV: be everywhere at once!

If anything, Yates had an even bigger personality than Hutchence did, and when they decided to go public with their affair he was in the middle of a profound personality crisis. Perhaps predictably, they both descended into a co-dependent drug spiral. Hutchence collapsed in full view of the world media. 'Whereas before he would glide into a room as if on celestial castors,' wrote *GQ*'s Adrian Deevoy, 'he now hobbled bow-legged like a cowboy who had been abruptly estranged from his horse.' And Hutchence couldn't handle it, hanging himself in a Sydney hotel room in November 1997, just three months after Princess Diana died in the Pont de l'Alma tunnel in Paris. He hanged himself with his own belt. At the age of thirty-seven.

On 17 September 2000, her daughter Pixie's tenth birthday, Yates was found dead at her London home of an accidental heroin overdose. She was just forty-one. The coroner ruled that it was not suicide, but rather the result of 'foolish and incautious' behaviour. Her funeral took place in the picturesque church of St Mary Magdalene, in Davington near Faversham in Kent, which adjoins the country mansion the Priory, where she and Geldof had lived before separating in 1995. Guests included Annie Lennox, Paul Young, Rupert Everett, Paul Gambaccini, Yasmin Le Bon, Jasper Conran and Bono, who sang 'Blue Skies' accompanied by Jools Holland on the piano.

'Live Aid? I just wish I could remember more than I can. But that's because I had a bloody good time,' said Elton. 'All I remember is that I wore a silly hat and Queen stole the show. End of story.'

End of story.

THIRTEEN

21:48

**Freddie Mercury and Brian May:
'Is This The World We Created?'**

Paul McCartney: 'Let It Be'

Band Aid: 'Do They Know It's Christmas?'

It's hard to say if it was the best gig of all time, as George
Harrison's concert for Bangladesh was something of a
groundbreaker in this department. And that all came
together by accident as well, as it happens.
HARVEY GOLDSMITH

As a small-scale coda to their performance earlier in the day, after
Elton John, Freddie Mercury and Brian May came out and
played a stripped-down version of a song inspired by watching
a documentary on television about poverty in Africa, from their 1984
album *The Works*. They were on and off the stage almost before anyone had
noticed, and then it was time for the grand reveal, Paul McCartney himself,
a real live Beatle.

It was crucial that there was at least one surviving member of the Beatles
at Wembley – Geldof felt that having a genuine rock icon from the British

music industry would give it greater legitimacy in the eyes of the political leaders whose opinions he was trying to shape – and Paul McCartney was the obvious choice. While he hadn't performed live since the assassination of John Lennon five years earlier, it was felt that if anything could drag him back on to a stage, then this was it. He was also the quintessential 'elder statesman' of the music industry, and the event potentially could have been marginalised had he not appeared. The show had already lost Springsteen – even though it had never really had him in the first place – so it couldn't afford to lose a Beatle. Not this Beatle, anyway.

'The idea of there being no representative of what had been the greatest band in pop music seemed unthinkable,' said Bob Geldof, 'so I wrote to Paul McCartney at home and asked if he would sing "Let It Be"; Beatles music for some reason evokes a more emotional response than any other, [and] "Let It Be" is like a hymn to faded dreams. I asked him if he would do it at the end of the show. "If you do, the world will cry," I wrote. I knew he must get a hundred requests to do things, but I really felt that the programme would not be complete without him there. I was not writing to Paul McCartney the man, I said, but to *Paul McCartney* the phenomenon. If he played, millions would watch who would not otherwise watch. That would mean money would come in which would not otherwise come in. If he felt he really couldn't do it, there would be no pressure, but if he did, it would be the crowning glory to the enterprise. As I sealed the letter, I knew I could do no more.'

When he finally agreed to take part, McCartney said that it was 'the management' – his children – that persuaded him. Geldof had bagged his lion. Soon after, Geldof apparently had a call from McCartney's office, the gist of which was this: 'No one here minds if you want to call George and Ringo.' Oh really, so a full-scale Beatles reunion then? But Geldof's call to George Harrison was slightly less than productive ('He didn't ask me to sing on it ten years ago, why does he want me now?'), and so the idea was initially parked.

Then Harrison's office started making encouraging noises, and the 'reunion' was back on again.

'There was an idea of getting Julian Lennon to join the three remaining Beatles on stage, and there was a huge discussion between Paul, Ringo and George,' said Harvey Goldsmith. 'The press were desperate for stories about Live Aid, and obviously the Beatles getting together again was the biggest story of all. But someone from the camp leaked it, and as soon as it was leaked, Paul, George and Ringo killed the idea. But there was definitely a discussion about making it happen. The press was feeling out for stories, as they were now totally obsessed with pop, with the music industry. Culture Club, Wham!, Duran Duran. They were obsessed with the glitz and the glam. This was perhaps the only disappointing thing about Live Aid, the fact that we almost had a genuine Beatles reunion. But then you knew that wasn't part of the deal.'

When McCartney finally came on stage, and sat down at the piano that Elton had just left behind, 72,000 people suddenly got goosebumps. And when he started playing the opening chords of 'Let It Be' those same 72,000 people realised that this was the first time they'd heard a Beatles song sung by an actual Beatle. I'd certainly never seen a real live Beatle before, and neither had Robin or Kate.

Just before he'd come on stage, a rumour suddenly started that the Beatles were going to perform. Someone in the Royal Box had caught a glimpse of Paul McCartney backstage, and so a whispering campaign began, a rumour that spread all the way round the stadium. Apparently someone had seen George Harrison, while someone else had seen Ringo Starr. It was like the last day of the football season, when two crucial matches are being played at the same time, and someone hears on the radio that a goal has been scored at the other match, and the word spreads like wildfire. But in the end all we had was McCartney, although he was certainly good enough. He was a real live Beatle!

There had been a short burst of rain just before McCartney was due on stage, no doubt an indignant riposte to George Michael singing 'Don't Let The Sun Go Down On Me' shortly before. It only lasted for ten minutes, and while some in the crowd enjoyed it – those down the front would later say that 13 July was the hottest day they'd ever known – the rain played havoc with the electrics. So much so that as soon as McCartney started to play 'Let It Be', he found his microphone wasn't working. Well, he didn't know at all, it was us, the crowd, who knew. He hadn't played live in over five years, not since his arrest in Japan in January 1980, and then when he does, at the biggest concert ever produced, his microphone dies on him. McCartney said that through his headphones he could hear the crew running around backstage like crazy, and so he knew something was wrong, but he didn't exactly know what. He didn't know if it was a TV feed, or if there had been an accident, or whether or not he was singing out of tune. But he knew something was up. He told himself to be professional and not to worry about it, as the techies were bound to fix it soon, but not before the crowd started singing the song for him. After all, everyone knew the words to 'Let It Be', so why shouldn't we enact the biggest karaoke singalong of all time? We completely drowned out what little sound from McCartney could be heard during this part of his performance.

'I felt very strange,' said McCartney. 'It was very loosely organised and I turned up not knowing quite what was expected of me, other than that I had to do "Let It Be". So I sat down at the piano, looked around for a cue to go, and there was just one roadie, and I looked at him for a signal. I started and the monitor was off and I thought, no sweat, this is BBC, this is world television, someone's bound to have a feed, it's just that my monitor's off.

'Then I wondered if the audience could hear because I knew some of the words of "Let It Be" were kind of relevant to what we were doing. Anyway, I thought, this is OK, they can hear me, they're singing along. I just had to keep going, so it was very embarrassing. The terrible thing was that in the middle I heard the roadies come through on the monitor, shouting, "No, this plug doesn't go here!" I thought, hello, we have problems. The worst moment was watching it on telly later.

'The event itself was so great, but it wasn't for my ego. It was for people who are dying and it raised over £50 million, and so it was like having been at the battle of Agincourt. It's something you'll tell your grandchildren about. I know Paul Simon slightly regrets that he didn't do it. He was asked, but he had other things to do. I very nearly didn't do it; Bob just badgered me into it.

'It galvanised the nation.'

He later said he'd thought about changing the lyrics to 'There will be some feedback, let it be.'

Sensing there was a problem, Harvey Goldsmith instructed Geldof to rush on stage with David Bowie, Alison Moyet and Pete Townshend, to help out with the vocals, by which time the microphone was working. 'Apparently as our figures appeared out of the shadows, there was a huge roar in the Philadelphia stadium because the *New York Post* had been spreading the rumour that the Beatles were to re-form long before I had even spoken to George,' said Geldof. 'But for me there was legend enough in the reality. The line-up on stage was McCartney, Bowie, Townshend – and Geldof. It was like the fulfilment of some crazy schoolboy dream.'

Townshend tried to distract McCartney by tickling him, adding some levity to the situation, but by then McCartney had completely won over the crowd.

It's odd to think about this these days, when the thought of Paul McCartney being the finale – the hero product – of any major charity event or awards ceremony is rather commonplace, almost a fait accompli, but McCartney's appearance at Live Aid was actually something of an anointment. It was obviously a coup – a novelty – getting a real live Beatle to perform in public, although it flattered McCartney as much as the event itself. He had spent much of the Seventies being underappreciated, treated as John Lennon's bantamweight sparring partner (I think it's fair to say that there had always been more John people than Paul people), but since Lennon's death in 1980, things had changed. Lennon's reputation grew and grew – as it always does with the recently deceased – but so did McCartney's.

Lennon became untouchable, immortal. His myth could be flattered in perpetuity because he was no longer with us. McCartney, meanwhile, previously had to be content with growing old, happy, and saggy around the middle, not least metaphorically. However, after 1980, people started to get protective.

McCartney's first records after leaving the Beatles were slight affairs, brimming with melody if not meaning. After years of wanting more and more and more and more, McCartney suddenly wanted less. Furious that Lennon and George Harrison had allowed legendary producer Phil Spector to remix his beloved 'The Long And Winding Road' on *Let It Be* (layering it with a wash of James Last-style strings), McCartney released his first solo album – *McCartney* – three weeks before it in the spring of 1970, hoping to steal its thunder. At the time the album was considered a disappointment – the makeshift quality and conspicuously handmade nature of his early work annoyed those who were acclimatised to sophisticated Beatles product – though in hindsight, its almost scatter-shot celebration of 'home, family, love', as McCartney called it, seems remarkably tender and unequivocally sincere.

Critics like to say that McCartney's career is analogous to Orson Welles's, who started out with *Citizen Kane* and ending up doing sherry commercials. (The same could be said of Francis Ford Coppola. I overheard him in the Carlyle Hotel in New York a few years ago, telling an admirer, 'I've had my brushes with creativity. I used to make films to make art; now I make films to make wine.')

But McCartney carried on regardless, releasing album-after-single-after-album of home-grown paeans to love and marriage. If the most evocative pop music resembles westerns – epic, grandiose, an assault on the senses – then McCartney's early records were more like home movies, with the same bad editing, half-hearted ideas, and 'little moments' that often mean little to those uninvolved with the subject. They did, however, overflow with charm. His songs are often little more than doodles, but as the late, great *New Yorker* cartoonist Saul Steinberg once said, 'The doodle is the brooding of the human hand.' And, in McCartney's case, the human heart.

McCartney saw himself as a variety artist, a music-hall tinker able to knock off a ballad as well as a sweaty R&B workout; an all-round entertainer firmly rooted in the tradition of the music hall and early American rock 'n' roll. Always a staunch traditionalist, the man responsible for some of the most far-reaching and influential music ever recorded has, in the following years, often seemed tyrannically nostalgic for the early days of pop – his neon-garlanded world little but a giant replica of a jukebox.

To paint him as pop's first real slacker is a mistake, though, as his extraordinary sequence of solo albums proves. When he formed the lamentable Wings at the end of 1971, he again put his head above the parapet, and so risked constant comparison with his 'previous group'. McCartney wanted success. Badly. And during the Seventies he turned Wings into a stadium-filling supergroup, releasing seven albums, from the sublime (*Band On The Run,* 1973) to the ridiculous (*Back To The Egg,* 1979) via the merely ordinary (*Venus And Mars,* 1975). And though this was almost beyond the call of duty, for some it was never going to be enough.

After Lennon's death, McCartney's records may not have exactly been treated with any less disdain by the critics (they had obviously always sold in large numbers, even the terribly mawkish ones), but his public perception started to change, something which Live Aid sealed.

After 13 July 1985, almost overnight, McCartney was suddenly a national treasure, a Queen Mother-type character, to be treated with care instead of caution. And while his problems with the PA might have been an embarrassment, it actually helped endear him to the crowd, and to the watching billions at home. From here on in, McCartney became the default 'get', the grand finale to everything from the Grammys to the Super Bowl. We almost expected him, as to not have him somehow cast doubt over the whole proceedings; I mean, what kind of awards ceremony is this if Macca isn't here? Honestly!

He had all but disowned the quirky, flimsier material he recorded in the early Seventies too, and whenever he was hauled out he would perform a Beatles classic, one of *his* Beatles classics, and so we got used to hearing the hymnal strains of 'Hey Jude', 'Let It Be' or, occasionally, 'The Long And Winding Road'. 'Ram On' was nowhere to be seen, or heard.

By the time of the opening ceremony of the 2012 Olympic Games in London, this had become something of a joke. A week after his rather lacklustre performance (a week in which phone-in shows had been incessantly calling time on his public appearances), *Private Eye* offered this Olympic tidbit: 'There was a shock for Gladys Baxter of Stevenage on Saturday when she opened her fridge and Paul McCartney started playing "Hey Jude" in the sitting room. "Like London 2012 this was another opening ceremony I just couldn't miss," said the old man singing that bloody song. "Over the coming week I'm going to be at the opening of a can of beans in Stevenage and the opening of a bank account in Uttoxeter." "Na na na na, etc.," he added. Paul McCartney is 104.'

A few days later, a viral email started doing the rounds. 'Sir Paul McCartney's HEY JUDE-O-GRAMS. You name the event, and Sir Paul McCartney will sing "Hey Jude" at the end of it (sometimes even if you don't want him to). Available for weddings, bar mitzvahs, opening ceremonies, opening supermarkets, royal weddings, royal bar mitzvahs, etc . . . Free sense of crushing inevitability.'

I was at the opening ceremony, and actually thought McCartney's performance was fine, although it very much punctured the evening, and as soon as he started to play, a sizeable chunk of the crowd got up to go, hoping to make a quick getaway before the rest of the stadium emptied. The problem was, everyone in the audience had the same idea.

At Wembley, twenty-seven years earlier, as McCartney drew his performance to a close, out of the blue, Paul McCartney and Pete Townshend hoisted Geldof up on to their shoulders and paraded him in front of the crowd. It was Townshend's idea, a way for all of us to thank him for what he'd done.

'I couldn't believe the Pete Townshend moment,' said Geldof. 'Here was Townshend, really one of my heroes, who told me as a kid how to be intelligent and individual and rock 'n' roll, whilst being part of a band. A man who was honest and self-lacerating to a fault, which is why you believe the songs, which is why they were so good. Pete had written to me asking why he should do the gig – it was all letters back then, no mobile phone calls in the middle of the night. He really wanted to know where all the money was going to go, and whether or not it was going to be worthwhile him getting involved. And then there was Paul McCartney doing the same. All these guys. George Harrison called me and said, "You know, you've got to watch out for the lawyers, Bob." I said: I know that, George. I've got rid of them, I think. Everyone stuck their nose in. Every generation of rock. People forget Miles Davis was at Live Aid, playing in Holland. He actually rang me and berated me for being a racist. Whatever, Miles. All I knew was that I was fucking talking to Miles Davis in my house in Chelsea! Miles was with me in spirit on the Wembley stage, along with Bowie and Macca.'

Oddly enough, McCartney's performance somehow made the earlier part of the day – the part occupied by the likes of the Spandau Ballets, the Sades, the Style Councils and the Paul Youngs – seem somewhat old-fashioned, almost as though the decade had been defined and then completed (abolished, even) on the same day. All of a sudden our Beatle moment made the surface smarts of the Eighties bands appear a little trite, and if Adam Ant had ushered in the Eighties by literally dressing up punk, McCartney's finale swept him from the building as though he were a cartoon ghost, floating back to the sweaty Soho basement clubs of the late Seventies. If Adam Ant's performance had already been responsible for killing his own career, McCartney's performance killed everything else it supposedly stood for. Here was a forty-three-year-old man who didn't feel the need to put on make-up and jodhpurs or dabble with synthesisers in order to appeal to his fan base. What we were reminded of on 13 July 1985 was the fact that McCartney's fan base – Live Aid's fan base, actually – was everyone, everybody, all the time. There wasn't anyone who didn't like McCartney, or so it felt at that moment. The style decade was never going to be robust enough to stretch to the full ten years, and one could say that it actually ended in July 1985. Killed by a Beatle in a few short minutes.

Suddenly, dressing up as a dandy highwayman looked fantastically inconsequential.

Geldof's day, our day, was almost over. But before it was, there was just time for the finale, starting right back at the beginning, which is where everyone came in. It was six minutes to ten, and from the wings came every performer who had been on stage that day, moving to the front to sing 'Do They Know It's Christmas?', with David Bowie standing in for Paul Young (who had retired early, although luckily unhurt), and Bob Geldof filling in for Boy George, who wasn't there in the first place. 'It might be a bit of a cock-up,' said Geldof to the crowd. 'But if you're going to cock up it's best to do it with 2 billion people watching.'

'It was organised chaos!' said Bernard Doherty. 'I had to go and photocopy "Do They Know It's Christmas?" because Bob suddenly realised that half the acts didn't know the words.'

'At the end, when everyone went on stage to sing the final song, if there was a barometer that registered people's ambition, you'd never get a better one than that,' said Gary Kemp. 'It wasn't like, "All right, can you queue up? We've got Bono here, we've got Elton next." It was people just gathering. We all knew we had to get on the stage at some point, and if you look at the TV footage, the ones who gravitate to the middle, towards Bob, they are the most ambitious and now the most successful.

'So Bono was not really happening at the time, but he got himself right in the front. He made sure he was right up front, bang in the middle. Tony [Hadley], disappointingly, didn't make it in time. I often wonder if that says something about him, as by rights he should have been right at the front. We were all in awe of Freddie and Macca, so we would kind of stand back and let them get slightly in front of us. It's interesting: Bono was a nobody who made sure he squeezed right up there. As it gets to the outer edges, it's the people who are less and less, I wouldn't say ambitious, but have a lower sense of self-worth, and it was very scruffy. It was a very scruffy moment.

'Sting was handing out the lyrics, and he really looked like the head boy at that point. It just felt like school and everyone gets into the status quo – some down the front, some at the back of the bus. Within bands, there were people who would rather be at the back of the bus, and people who kind of wanted to be the head boy's friend, probably like me.

'We were all desperately practising the song, and it was all really very ad hoc. There was no sense of a stage manager hanging out, or the kind of slickness that I'm sure you'd see nowadays because it was designed by people who did rock 'n' roll, and the TV people just kind of set up camp and filmed it. There wasn't the sense that TV were running it, like I imagine it would be today.'

Someone said the finale should have been painted by Peter Blake, as it was almost as impressive a line-up as the *Sgt Pepper* cover. Looking at their bodies on the giant video screens flanking the stage – George Michael's billowing yellow shirt! Freddie Mercury's white trousers! Andrew Ridgeley's tartan! – they all looked like Guy Peellaert cut-outs, with a vast bank of *Close Encounters*-style lights behind them. Many were punching their arms in the air, emphasising the universal gesture of good-time rebellion. There were weary smiles from left to right and from front to back, with only a few performers jostling for position in front of the cameras. Everyone was either too tired, or too overawed. The feeling backstage was uncharacteristically benign, too. 'The atmosphere on the day was great,' said David Bailey, who had yet to pack up and go. 'At one point towards the end of the day I got a tap on my shoulder and spun round. Suddenly there was a big tongue down my throat! It was Freddie Mercury.'

What a day. Not only had Geldof managed to corral most of the world's major pop acts into playing together, he had booked a few bands which, at the time, didn't even exist: he had convinced the surviving members of Led Zeppelin to play their first gig together since the 1980 death of drummer John Bonham, while also managing to coax the remaining members of The Who and the original line-up of Black Sabbath out of retirement. And the day was actually only halfway through.

The Wembley concert ended exactly two minutes late, which was some achievement in itself (you could see the time on the clock positioned right above Elton's piano).

We of course stayed until the very end. This was unusual for a gig at Wembley, as you always wanted to leave early and try and get ahead of the queue. The Underground was always overflowing, you always had to wait ages for a Tube, and so you tended to rush out of the stadium and up Wembley Way in order to try and get home before Christmas. Tonight, though, like everyone else, we stayed until the bitter end. Who would want to miss this, for the sake of an early night and a quicker ride home? So we saw it all through, heard the final chords, and all the whoops and the hollers and the cheers from the crowd, and began filing out of the stadium, along with everyone else. We were tired, euphoric, drained and exhilarated in equal measure. It had been the day of days, one of the best, one to be cherished, remembered, filed away for safe keeping.

Today we had participated in a display of communal adoration, one that had more to do with the idea of the event rather than the acts themselves. We had all come to see all of those on stage, from Status Quo and Elton John through to Sade and the Style Council, of course. But we had also come to see ourselves. We wanted to be heard, to be counted, to be together.

And today we had been.

There was already a sense that this grand event had equalled England's 1966 World Cup win, or maybe even the 1953 Coronation.

The Tube station looked like one of the taxi ranks at Delhi airport – the old one, pre-gentrification – as it was surrounded by tens of thousands of people. These were happy, smiling, resigned people, though, and there was very little pushing and shoving. Everyone was brimming, full up. I'd been to see England play football matches at Wembley, and the crowds afterwards made your heart sink: vile, obese racists, whose chosen form of expression was to chant, incoherently, while peeing in someone's front garden, their ursine white bellies overflowing in front of their shorts. And although the Live Aid crowd was not exactly the crowd you may have found at Glyndebourne or Glastonbury, or one of the more soporific free festivals of the early Seventies, they were perfectly prepared to wait their turn for the trains, and think about the amazing day they'd just had. Various different groups involuntarily started singing snippets from 'Do They Know It's Christmas?', until everyone was singing together, the more ambitious singers role-playing, pretending to be Bono, Sting or Paul Young, some even daring to jump around like Freddie Mercury or Pete Townshend.

'As we left the stadium all you could hear is people singing "Do They Know It's Christmas?" at the top of their voices,' said Robin. 'It turned into a terrace chant, as that's all you could hear for an hour afterwards, repeated ad nauseam. I remember as we walked back to the Tube thinking that it seemed ridiculous to be singing about Christmas in July, but then that was part of the fun.'

The song continued, unvarying in the busy night.

We strap-hung all the way back to Brixton, where Kate and I said farewell to Robin, and watched him climb Brixton Hill as we scooted round to Railton Road, and our first-floor housing association flat, where we made tea and climbed into bed to watch the rest of the American show. It was kind of weird that it was still going on, and it was strange to think that just an hour or so previously we had been part of it, the whole thing, but then we already knew that we'd be part of it forever.

Lying in bed that night, watching the Philadelphia concert kick into life, I had the sensation that maybe this day was never going to end, that maybe this might turn out to be one of those feelings that never ends, an epiphany in perfect harmony with everything and everyone around it, some mad exponential soliloquy going on forever and ever and ever, chorus after chorus after chorus.

After today, would life ever be the same again? Would pop? Would philanthropy, come to that? Had we really started a period of public endowment? In a way, Live Aid memorialised itself, and was its own celebration, its own cultural watershed, its own epitaph. As an example of Eighties largesse, it would set the standard for the celebrity fund-raiser, and would influence every other major charity concert that came in its wake.

It had certainly made us feel good about ourselves. Uniting the long-lost rock community, luxuriating in an act of Christian charity, people gave and received a rare moment of satellite-linked fellowship.

'Live Aid worked because it was an urgent, emotive, simple, single-issue event aimed at achieving immediate, tangible results,' wrote the *Daily Telegraph* many years later. 'It had an uncomplicated spirit of universal charity that corresponds with the ethos of popular music, and it was run with a haphazard, devil-may-care approach that tapped into rock's favoured anti-establishment pose.'

It had the patina of rebellion, of not caring, but then caring too much. 'Live Aid evoked a sense of manning the barricades, not preaching from a podium. Maybe (when you take away the sentimentality of nostalgic recollection) Live Aid really wasn't such a great concert. But it didn't need to be. It worked because it risked failure for a genuinely humanitarian cause, and people responded to that sense of risk . . . It really was a pioneering moment, a revelation of the global village, presaging the connected world to come. 2 billion people took part in Live Aid. It worked because we wanted it to.'

'We bought cheeseburgers at Euston and ate them on the train to Birmingham,' wrote the critic Pete Paphides, who had been at the show, and who was only in his teens at the time. 'My dad picked me up. "Did you see us on the telly?" I asked. "We were in the middle of the pitch and Annette had a colourful golf umbrella." No they hadn't, but everyone was talking about how Bob Geldof had said "Fuck" live on air. The revolution had been televised.'

Some BBC employees were still working, as were the road crew, breaking everything down before the massive clean-up in the morning. Mark Ellen's last link was at 3.30, and by the time he got home it was light.

As for the stars, those who didn't go home headed off to Legends in Old Burlington Street, where Bob and Harvey were hosting the official after-party.

Some decided to drive. 'I got stuck driving through the streets of Wembley with all the audience squished up around the car, walking home or back to the Tube,' said Midge Ure. 'People were throwing open their doors and having parties. It was like Hogmanay in Glasgow. People were inviting complete strangers in off the street. This is London, that just doesn't happen. But it happened that night.'

Geldof arrived later than he should have, and was reduced to hitching a ride outside the stadium. Hilariously, when he was eventually picked up, the driver could only take him to Archway, where Geldof had to pick up a minicab.

Legends had recently become cool again, and had started to host some of the capital's more interesting parties. It was still being let out on a nightly basis, for pop-ups, but it had also become an oasis of calm for those

British pop stars who could no longer just turn up at a club in the hope of being left alone. Legends would soon lose this status to the Groucho, who were even better at keeping out Joe Public; clubs like Legends were always approaching but never reaching some axis of perfect exclusivity, so a members' club made perfect sense. But at the moment it was still being patronised by the likes of Duran Duran, Culture Club, Spandau Ballet and David Bowie, the sort of pop stars who wanted to be noticed but also wanted to be left alone. Boys tended to wear *Miami Vice* linen, and girls wore a Princess Diana flick. And everyone drank Tequila Slammers.

'I crawled down there at around 1 a.m. I suppose,' said Harvey Goldsmith. 'Bob and I were just completely shagged out. It was a really nice buzz. All I really wanted to do was go to bed, but it was just so fantastic being there with everyone, because at that point we were watching the American show, and everybody was in such a great mood and I didn't want to spoil the party.

But I just wanted to go to bed and go to sleep and so did Bob, as he was in terrible pain because of his back.'

At Legends, most people were giddy with excitement, astonished that the day had gone off without a major hitch, their bodies combusting with a mixture of adrenaline and alcohol. Geldof sat around and swore at the television coverage of the Philadelphia gig, asking, 'Who the fuck are these people? Get them off!' This went on for most of the night. 'He was

Harvey Goldsmith conducted Live Aid as though he were organising the Olympics. It was extraordinarily debilitating, as tiring as much as it was heroic. 'Afterwards all I really wanted to do was go to bed, but it was just so fantastic being there with everyone. I didn't want to spoil the party.'

particularly rude when Bob Dylan came on,' said Doherty.

Legends was a bubble of euphoria, most people in the condition that F. Scott Fitzgerald used to call 'pleasantly jingled'. Well, as pleasantly jingled as anyone could be with Bob Geldof swearing at a large television set. The club was the bonkers green room of rock 'n' roll history, a micro end to a macro day. There was no official guest list as such, though it would have been slightly surreal for any punter to pop their head round the door, under the porte cochère, to see such a bandwidth of celebrity.

Gary Farrow went home after Legends and watched the first hour that he'd recorded on his VCR. 'It was like watching a recording of a Cup Final when your team have won. The goals look better on TV, but you can't replicate the atmosphere of actually being there.'

Like many who didn't make it to Legends, Paul McGuinness went back to the Mayfair Hotel, which was quite the rock 'n' roll hotel at the time, and where a lot of the Live Aid acts were staying – 'Basically it was a lot of people letting off steam, and it was quite a party' – and spent the early hours watching the US concert on a television in the corner of the bar. 'I suppose my perception of what was going on in America was a little hazy. There was quite a lot of activity in the bar.'

'I went out and got all the papers and then went back to Legends and just threw them on the table,' said Bernard Doherty. 'It was then that we all realised what an amazing day Live Aid had been, because we suddenly saw it through other people's eyes. We knew then that it had been a proper global event.

'It was Live Aid that convinced the Fleet Street papers that pop could sell papers. So they all immediately hired showbiz editors.'

Live Aid finally brought pop music from the entertainment pages to the front pages, as before the event pop was firmly in the domain of the music press. It was only after Live Aid that the press realised that music could sell papers in the way they had hoped it would with Culture Club and Duran Duran three years earlier.

'I remember going down to Legends and drinking at the bar with John Hurt,' said Gary Kemp. 'Other than that it's just a blur.' For him it was a day of contemplation: 'I spoke a lot to Pete Townshend that day and Sting as I'm the kind of a guy who likes to be in, and I admire people who are older than me so I was much more involved. Thinking about it now, we'd had our time, in a way, that British invasion of new acts, those New Romantic acts. In a way Live Aid saw the rise of Queen and Clapton and Collins – all of the old, established acts really came back after that. Because they had the legacy.'

Bono had gone home immediately, still thinking he'd blown U2's show. He turned on the TV just in time to watch Bob Dylan walk out on to the Philadelphia stage with Keith Richards and Ronnie Wood. These were three people he hugely admired, with Dylan being the lightning rod in Bono's spiritual quest as a musician, 'and they all looked like they were out of it. They were mumbling all kinds of stuff. It was the end of a very long day and I just saw my hero as a man, as a frail, vulnerable fellah who had quite obviously bitten off more than he could chew in the hours coming up to the performance. I felt very sad, because of all the prophetic utterances out of that mouth, all the references to scripture in his versification, his ability to take it on the nose from the critics, to stand up and say simple, proud, upright things. And here he was, just looking confused, addled.

'I thought, "I hope he's OK." I worried for his health. I didn't know what he was doing but I knew he was close to some kind of edge. He didn't fall off; in fact, after a few stray comments about American farmers he catalysed Farm Aid, but something really disturbed me. There was just myself and Ali in the room and I got out of bed and down on my knees. It was a very real moment, the end of a very long day.'

Bono had had a good day, not that he knew it yet. But he soon would. 'U2 established themselves as a global band that day,' said Howard Jones. 'And Queen established themselves as probably the best band of all time.'

'I'm not sure there are any misconceptions about Live Aid because nobody really had a conception of what it was, including us,' said Harvey Goldsmith. 'So we were to some extent stabbing in the dark. We were reinventing the wheel as it went wrong. Our aspiration for this event was raising a million pounds. Which at the time was a huge amount of money.

The night before the show, at some time around two o'clock in the morning, I remember Bob and I had our penultimate conversation of the night. We both said, "I reckon we could raise £5 million," and we'd go, "Wouldn't that be amazing." That was it, that was our goal. Little did any of us realise just how much would come in.'

As Geldof had mentioned during the concert, the Republic of Ireland gave the most donations per capita, despite being in the throes of a serious economic recession at the time. The single largest donation came from the ruling family of Dubai, pledging £1 million.

'The real of star of Live Aid was the audience,' said Gary Kemp. 'When you're talking about that day, about what it meant, about who was good and who wasn't, well, it's the audience. It was for them. There hasn't been an equal to that since Woodstock. The whole idea that a concert was a gathering that just so happened to have bands play; bands that maybe slightly represented their feelings on the bigger stage, that all died in the early Seventies because the rock 'n' roll stars scurried off to Switzerland and we got glam rock as a substitute. We got a sense of an elevated theatre that was happening and it had very little to do with the audience.

'I always thought that this feeling they had in the Sixties, I would never experience in my lifetime. I'd always been a bit disappointed about it. I think everyone in the audience that day felt equal to the bands on stage, and I think everyone around the world did. And I think this was why it was such a key moment in history. Plus, Live Aid was right at the apex of the decade.'

According to some, Live Aid was the inevitable cultural commodification of rock 'n' roll, strengthened by corporate involvement and global advertising. According to Michael Bracewell, 'the protesting gene within English popular culture seemed to be not so much silenced as coaxed into partial tokenism'. At least even he acknowledged that the power and influence of corporate rock meant it was easier to put it to good use, especially where telethon philanthropy was concerned.

Some days after Live Aid, Geldof got up late. He was dozing, worried that even though the papers seemed to say that the event had been a total success, the actual fund-raising might have been a failure. Wanting to clear his mind, around lunchtime he went for a walk. 'I started walking down the King's Road and I saw all these queues outside banks, and at first didn't twig what was going on. I asked a few people what they were doing, and they said they were all queuing up to put Live Aid money into the accounts. I thought it was fucking amazing.'

Backstage, at the end of one of the most extraordinary days in the history of rock, a random stagehand came up to Geldof and asked, 'Is that it?' It became the title of Geldof's autobiography.

FOURTEEN

From the outside at least (and probably unfairly) these shows were presented like a magical panacea, a chance for pampered pop stars to demonstrate that they care without marshalling the kind of political will to produce real change. Live Aid gave pop stars instant validation. Now they weren't just musicians, they were philanthropists. And it can't have hurt that a well-received appearance for charity generally boosts their own sales at the same time.

DAILY TELEGRAPH

Bernard Watson: 'All I Really Want To Do'

Joan Baez: 'Amazing Grace'/'We Are The World'

The Hooters: 'And We Danced', 'All You Zombies'

Four Tops: 'Shake Me, Wake Me (When It's Over)', 'Bernadette', 'It's The Same Old Song', 'Reach Out I'll Be There', 'I Can't Help Myself (Sugar Pie, Honey Bunch)'

Billy Ocean: 'Caribbean Queen', 'Loverboy'

Black Sabbath: 'Children Of The Grave', 'Iron Man', 'Paranoid'

Run-DMC: 'Jam Master Jay', 'King Of Rock'

Rick Springfield: 'Love Somebody', 'State Of The Heart', 'Human Touch'

REO Speedwagon: 'Can't Fight This Feeling', 'Roll With The Changes'

Crosby, Stills & Nash: 'Southern Cross', 'Teach Your Children', 'Suite: Judy Blue Eyes'

Judas Priest: 'Living After Midnight', 'The Green Manalishi (With The Two-Pronged Crown)', 'You've Got Another Thing Comin''

Bryan Adams: 'Kids Wanna Rock', 'Summer Of '69', 'Tears Are Not Enough', 'Cuts Like A Knife'

The Beach Boys: 'California Girls', 'Help Me, Rhonda', 'Wouldn't It Be Nice', 'Good Vibrations', 'Surfin' USA'

George Thorogood and the Destroyers: 'Who Do You Love' (with Bo Diddley), 'The Sky Is Crying', 'Madison Blues' (with Albert Collins)

Simple Minds: 'Ghost Dancing', 'Don't You (Forget About Me)', 'Promised You A Miracle'

The Pretenders: 'Time The Avenger', 'Message Of Love', 'Stop Your Sobbing', 'Back On The Chain Gang', 'Middle Of The Road'

Santana and Pat Metheny: 'Brotherhood', 'Primera Invasion', 'Open Invitation', 'By The Pool'/'Right Now'

Ashford & Simpson: 'Solid', 'Reach Out And Touch (Somebody's Hand)' (with Teddy Pendergrass)

Madonna: 'Holiday', 'Into The Groove', 'Love Makes The World Go Round'

Tom Petty and the Heartbreakers: 'American Girl', 'The Waiting', 'Rebels', 'Refugee'

Kenny Loggins: 'Footloose'

The Cars: 'You Might Think', 'Drive', 'Just What I Needed', 'Heartbeat City'

Neil Young: 'Sugar Mountain', 'The Needle And The Damage Done', 'Helpless', 'Nothing Is Perfect (In God's Perfect Plan)', 'Powderfinger'

Power Station: 'Murderess', 'Get It On'

Thompson Twins: 'Hold Me Now', 'Revolution' (with Madonna, Steve Stevens and Nile Rodgers)

Eric Clapton (with Phil Collins): 'White Room', 'She's Waiting', 'Layla'

Phil Collins: 'Against All Odds (Take A Look At Me Now)', 'In The Air Tonight'

Led Zeppelin: 'Rock And Roll', 'Whole Lotta Love', 'Stairway To Heaven'

Crosby, Stills, Nash & Young: 'Only Love Can Break Your Heart', 'Daylight Again'/'Find The Cost of Freedom'

Duran Duran: 'A View To A Kill', 'Union Of The Snake', 'Save A Prayer', 'The Reflex'

Patti LaBelle: 'New Attitude', 'Imagine', 'Forever Young', 'Stir It Up', 'Over The Rainbow', 'Why Can't I Get It Over'

Hall & Oates: 'Out Of Touch', 'Maneater', 'Get Ready' (with Eddie Kendricks), 'Ain't Too Proud To Beg' (with David Ruffin), 'The Way You Do The Things You Do', 'My Girl' (with Eddie Kendricks and David Ruffin)

Mick Jagger (with Hall & Oates/Eddie Kendricks/David Ruffin): 'Lonely At The Top', 'Just Another Night', 'Miss You', 'State Of Shock'/'It's Only Rock 'n' Roll (But I Like It)' (with Tina Turner)

Bob Dylan (with Keith Richards and Ronnie Wood): 'Ballad Of Hollis Brown', 'When The Ship Comes In', 'Blowin' In The Wind'

USA For Africa: 'We Are The World'

By mid-morning the American Telegraph Company reported that the toll-free telephone line it had set up to receive pledges, 1-800-LIVE AID, was overloaded. The 1,126 circuits allocated were simply getting more traffic than they could handle.

NEW YORK TIMES

'Who the fuck are the Hooters?' asked Ozzy Osbourne backstage, of his fellow performers, and there was not exactly a queue of people waiting to help him. The list of artists performing at the JFK Stadium on 13 July was far more eclectic than the Wembley version, to put it mildly. On the one hand you had serious heritage acts such as a re-formed Led Zeppelin, Neil Young, Eric Clapton, Bob Dylan, and various members of the Rolling Stones, while on the other there were leading examples of the new vanguard, including Madonna, Duran Duran and Run-DMC. However, there were also the likes of Billy Ocean, Patti LaBelle, Rick Springfield and Judas Priest.

Joan Baez officially opened the Philadelphia show, as the promoter Bill Graham was convinced this would set the right tone. 'We've plugged her into the next generation of kids,' he said. 'The ones who love U2. Jack Nicholson introduced Joan Baez as a singer whose voice was always heard when there was a just cause that needed a song. Joan said, "Good morning, children of the Eighties, this is your Woodstock and it's long overdue." She sang "Amazing

Jack Nicholson and Bette Midler: according to Daryl Hall, Nicholson was passing joints around backstage, getting some into the right mood for appearing in front of the largest television audience there had ever been. Everyone had smiles on their faces, whether they had partaken or not.

Grace" and we were in business. The day had officially begun.'

Baez was not without condescension, however, and insisted on quickly saying the words before she sang them, in the hope that the crowd might sing along. As the song was so famous, and was already entrenched in the national psyche, this was a bit like Bob Dylan doing the same with 'Blowin' In The Wind'.

In terms of global exposure, this was a big day, and there was incessant haggling over time slots, unlike at Wembley, where people mostly did as they were asked to. Madonna was originally scheduled to appear quite late on the bill in Philadelphia, but by July she had already established a firm foothold in the States, so her manager Freddy DeMann made sure she secured an earlier slot, so she could be seen by all the millions in Europe. She almost looked as though she were performing at a school concert, but then she was young and raw. She had recently made headlines as some old racy photographs of her were due to be published in *Playboy*, which may have been one of the reasons she came bounding on to the ninety-five-degree stage in Philadelphia dressed in a classic Eighties pantsuit complete with enormous shoulder pads. Someone called from the crowd, 'Take it off.' To which she replied, not unreasonably, and without missing a beat, 'I ain't taking shit off today.' Immediately, the JFK Stadium part of Live Aid belonged to Madonna.

'The Americans saw Live Aid clearly as just a rock event and still talk about it as one of the great rock gigs,' said Geldof. 'It's not a political event in their eyes, and never was. To them it's like Woodstock or Monterey, a great rock festival, the biggest of the Eighties. But for them it was never political. Of course they see it as one of those significant generational things that indicate a shift in what music does and what it says, how it articulates a moment. But it's still a rock gig. For me, Live Aid was the most political gig of them all.'

In some ways backstage in Philadelphia was no different from Wembley. Bob Dylan was hugging Keith Richards and Robert Plant, Bryan Adams was hugging Jimmy Page, and apparently Eric Clapton was hugging himself as there was nobody left. At one point, one of the backstage trailers contained these seven people: Eric Clapton, Robert Plant, Phil Collins, Ronnie Wood, Jimmy Page, Keith Richards and Bob Dylan, all trying to help Robert Plant scribble down the words to 'Stairway To Heaven' (a song he hadn't sung for so long he'd forgotten exactly how it went). According to Daryl Hall, Jack Nicholson was passing joints around. Madonna and Sean Penn were inseparable, fondling each other in full view of anyone in their vicinity. 'She's so in love she's radiating it,' said Seymour Stein, the president of Sire, her record label. (There were tales that she demanded to have the backstage area cleared when she went to the lavatory, but you only have to squint at this story for a while to see that it almost certainly couldn't be true.)

'It was bedlam backstage,' said Bryan Adams. 'I remember I walked up the stairs to the stage and Yoko Ono passed me. When I got to the top of the stairs someone said that I was to start after the gentleman introduced me. That gentleman was Jack Nicholson.'

Nile Rodgers said being backstage at Live Aid was like seeing a walking collection of *Rolling Stone* covers – Led Zeppelin, Eric Clapton, Mick

Jagger, Phil Collins, Lionel Richie, Joan Baez, Bob Dylan, Ashford &
Simpson, Tom Petty, Hall & Oates, Teddy Pendergrass, Duran Duran,
Keith Richards, Jack Nicholson, Madonna. And wasn't that Rupert Everett
over there babysitting Jade Jagger? This was a rock 'n' roll rogues' gallery.
Moments before he went on stage with Black Sabbath, the band's manager
Don Arden issued Ozzy with a complex lawsuit. Sharon Osbourne, Ozzy's
pregnant wife and manager, and Arden's daughter, said the lawsuit was 'of a
baseless and nuisance nature'.

Eric Clapton had been on tour with Roger Waters when he got a phone
call from Pete Townshend urging him to get involved. Clapton then told
Waters to cancel a show in Las Vegas so he could make it.

'Landing in Philadelphia the day before, one couldn't help but get swept
up in the atmosphere,' said Clapton. 'The place was just buzzing. The
moment we landed, you could feel music everywhere. We checked into
the Four Seasons Hotel, every room of which was filled with musicians. It
was Music City, and like most people I was awake most of the night before
the concert. I couldn't sleep with nerves. We were due to go on stage in the
evening, and I sat watching the performances of the other acts on the TV
during most of the day, which was probably a psychological mistake, as
seeing all these great artists giving their best made me a hundred times more
psyched up than for a regular gig. How could I ever match the performance
of a band like the Four Tops, with their fantastic big Motown orchestra
combined with all their energy?'

By the time Clapton got to the stadium, he was in such a state of nerves
that he was tongue-tied, and couldn't talk to anyone. It was also boiling hot,
and he and his whole band felt faint. Clapton was even close to passing out.
The tunnel, which everyone had to walk through from the dressing room
to the stage, was crowded – too crowded – with security, which unnerved
the guitarist no end. His mood wasn't helped by finding out that his guitar
amps were completely different to the ones his team had asked for.

'To say the whole band was jumpy would be an understatement,' said
Clapton. 'As I climbed on stage, I luckily saw the reassuring presence of my
old mentor, Ahmet Ertegun [founder of Atlantic Records], standing in the

wings, smiling broadly at me and giving me a big thumbs-up sign.'

The show got off to a shaky start when Clapton got an electric shock the first time his lips brushed the microphone, meaning he spent his entire set worried it would happen again. The band whizzed through 'White Room', 'She's Waiting' (from his *Behind The Sun* album) and 'Layla', and then they were off.

'Phil Collins came on, followed by Led Zeppelin, then Crosby, Stills, Nash & Young. After that, I remember very little, other than being herded back on stage at the end to join in the finale, singing "We Are The World". I think I was just in a state of shock.'

He wasn't the only one. 'I was stressed out about doing Live Aid. I hadn't talked to [Sabbath guitarist Tony Iommi] for years, so it wasn't exactly the most comfortable of situations,' said Ozzy Osbourne. 'Then the organisers put us between Billy Ocean and the Four fucking Tops . . . At ten o'clock in the morning. I don't know what they were thinking. People kept telling us that they needed more black acts in the show, so maybe they thought *we* were black – like when we played Philadelphia on our first American tour.'

For Ozzy it was a day of contradictions. 'On the one hand, doing Live Aid was brilliant: it was for a great cause, and no one can play those old Black Sabbath songs like me, Tony, Geezer and Bill. But on the other hand, it was all a bit embarrassing. For a start, I was still grossly overweight – on the video, I'm the size of a planet. Also, in the six years since I'd left the band, I'd become a celebrity in America, whereas Black Sabbath had been going in the other direction. So I got preferential treatment, even though I hadn't asked for it. It was just stupid little things, like I got a Live Aid jacket and they didn't. But it still felt awkward. And I didn't handle it with much grace, because my coked-up rock-star ego was out of control. Deep down, a part of me wanted to say to them, "You fired me and now I don't need you, so fuck you." Looking back now, all I can think is, why was I like that? Why did I have to be such a dickhead? But the gig went smoothly enough. We just checked in to the hotel, met up at the soundcheck, ran through the set list, got up there, did the songs and fucked off home.'

Live Aid was the perfect opportunity for comebacks and for bands to re-form. There had obviously been the rumours about the remaining Beatles getting together and even talk that Pink Floyd and the Faces might both re-form. A Rolling Stones reunion was off and on, but such was the acrimony between Mick Jagger and Keith Richards that Jagger ended up performing with Tina Turner while Richards and Ron Wood disastrously backed Bob Dylan. Geldof said getting The Who to play was 'rather like getting one man's four ex-wives together'. But, big though Live Aid was proving to be, some legacies and personal estrangements proved to be even bigger.

From the outset, Geldof had wanted Led Zeppelin to perform. It had been exactly five years and one week since their last live performance, and since the death of original drummer John Bonham in 1980, the band had officially been on hold. They had kept a deliberately low profile, and were considered to be rock dinosaurs from another era. Their back catalogue wasn't being marketed, bands like Def Leppard and the Cult were active and hip, and liking Zeppelin was considered to be seriously uncool.

'American rock radio just played the shit out of Zeppelin, to the point where it was almost embarrassing to like them,' said former White Stripes leader and Zeppelin aficionado Jack White, 'because it was too obvious. They kind of represented so much in that realm, because of punk rock destroying prog rock and all the big regular rock. It was almost like you were more likely to have a statue of Led Zeppelin in your house than to actually mention them in conversation.'

Yet Geldof wanted them on the bill. They had been one of the biggest bands of the Seventies, both in Britain and the States, and Geldof knew that getting them together again would fuel interest in the show. Jimmy Page also wanted to do it as, after years of serious drug abuse, he wanted to prove to himself and everyone else that he was still a fully functioning rock god, and that Zeppelin remained worthy of all their acclaim. And so they decided to perform, using Chic drummer Tony Thompson as a stand-in for Bonham.

Phil Carlo was the tour manager on the last Zeppelin tour, and Page's right-hand man for most of the Eighties. 'We rehearsed [for Live Aid] at a place called the Warehouse in Philadelphia. We had a break in rehearsing and Robert [Plant] announced that he didn't want to do "Stairway". Jimmy said to me, "I fucking knew this would happen. We've just got to play this game all fucking afternoon until we get up tomorrow morning and he'll announce that he'll do it. It's just a fucking game and he's a fucking old tart." [Apparently Plant would do the same thing before the Atlantic Records Fortieth Anniversary Concert in 1988, resulting in yet more arguments between him and Page.] So at Live Aid I'm sat with Robert watching Queen on a TV and he goes, "Fucking hell! We've go to try and top that.'"

In the end they did play the song, although it didn't work. When it was announced that Phil Collins was going to play at Wembley and then take Concorde to play in Philadelphia, the band thought it would be a great idea for Collins to play with them as well (one of the principal reasons being that Bonham always sounded as though he had four arms anyway, and was deemed to be irreplaceable).

'Live Aid was pretty shambolic,' said Jimmy Page. 'We came together and rehearsed with a drummer we'd never met before and then we were joined by Phil Collins, who we'd never played with before.' Thompson apparently didn't want to share the stage with Collins, while the latter's microphones had to be turned off during 'Stairway To Heaven' as he simply didn't know how to play it. He had been given tapes to listen to and been told what the band were going to do, yet couldn't grasp it. Afterwards he apologised, saying he didn't realise how complicated Zeppelin's music was to play. 'The two drummers proved that . . . Well, you know, that's why Led Zeppelin didn't carry on,' said Plant.

'I landed in New York, said my goobyes to Cher [who he'd met on the flight and convinced to turn up and perform] and headed to the stadium in Philadelphia,' said Phil Collins. 'When I got there I discovered that it wasn't so much me playing with my mates Jimmy Page and Robert Plant, but a Zeppelin reunion. I'd always heard that individually these guys were great, but together there was this black cloud that appeared. I talked to Tony Thompson about playing with two drummers – something I'd done quite a lot – and I really got the impression that he didn't want me to be there. As soon as I got up on stage I could see it was going to be a weird one.

Thompson was just playing whatever he wanted. But then the essence of the day was about being there and doing the best you can, up to your neck in muck and bullets.'

Before they were due to go on, Jimmy Page asked Collins how the drum parts to 'Stairway To Heaven' actually went, and as Collins tried to explain what he thought was the correct answer (demonstrating air snare with his arms), Page started shouting 'No, no, no!' Afterwards the band would accuse Collins of just 'bashing away aimlessly'.

This certainly wasn't any kind of denouement for Zeppelin, more of a missed opportunity. The band would reach some sort of closure with their Ahmet Ertegun Tribute Concert at the O2 Arena in London on 10 December 2007, with Jason Bonham taking his father's place on drums. It was an extraordinary performance, and if you closed your eyes the music sounded exactly as it had done thirty years previously, yet if you opened them and glanced up at the huge video screens you saw not the lithe twentysomethings who had made the noise in the first place, but rather the world's oldest-looking men. In fact they looked like the Ents in Peter Jackson's *Lord of the Rings*. 20 million people had applied for tickets for the show, and Page wanted the band to reunite for a proper tour. When Plant bowed out (actually he had never bowed in), Page considered offering the job to a replacement singer (including Aerosmith's Steven Tyler) before quietly dropping the idea. The success of the 2007 show proved that at Live Aid Zeppelin hadn't been trampled by their legacy, only hampered by a lack of rehearsal, and perhaps a lack of purpose. Perhaps they weren't really sure why they were doing it, and while Page certainly saw the gig as an opportunity to resuscitate the band (something he was desperate to do), Plant saw it merely as a day out.

Would Zeppelin have been any better if they had performed at Wembley? Perhaps. After Band Aid, and Live Aid, there was always a tertiary feeling about 'We Are The World' and the Philadelphia concert. Band Aid was a British response to a British-mediated news story, about the problems of a continent rarely discussed by US TV networks. For many of the entertainers who were initially intrigued by the notion of a US version of 'Do They Know It's Christmas?', it was a run-of-the-mill charity record with the accompanying PR benefits. 'We Are The World' always had more of a mainstream, Hollywood aspect to it, as did the Philadelphia gig. This was a charity being driven by an Irishman living in London, raising funds for a part of Africa that most US citizens were hardly aware of, let alone the US entertainment industry. One didn't get the sense that the Philadelphia concert was as micro-managed as the Wembley gig, or indeed was imbued with the same macro ambitions.

In Britain, even before it had happened, you felt that Live Aid was going to mean something, whereas in the States it seemed like it was going to be little more than a day out. A walk in the park. That big charity thing happening down in Philly.

It would be easy to say that the JFK concert was insufficiently imagined, but on paper the bill looked rather formidable. Yet, oddly, it also seemed a little old-fashioned, and while it was the pre-punk watershed acts who had largely shined in London, Philadelphia's greatest achievement was one of spectacle rather than content.

Writing in *Rolling Stone*, Pete Hamill said, 'I often think that this is a particularly anaesthetised generation of young Americans, devoid of history or memory. I might be wrong, of course, and I hope I am. But these young people certainly don't believe, as millions did in the Sixties, that rock 'n' roll could be a redemptive moral force, an agent of radical change. For them, rock 'n' roll is not something fresh, original, special; it's the mainstream of American music. These are, after all, the first Americans whose parents grew up with rock 'n' roll.

'But as they listened to this music, I wondered whether this enormous event would change them in any permanent way. How can you watch Mick Jagger and Tina Turner luxuriate in the brazen, humorous sexuality of "State Of Shock" and think that Ronald Reagan has anything to say to you? How can you choose Madonna as a role model, cheering as she acts out her part as America's most cheerful tart, and then turn to Nancy Reagan for wisdom? I don't think you can undergo such an experience and be quite the same again.'

So much of the Wembley concert had felt painfully temporary, as though most of the acts were just passing through – it would have been difficult to have started scheduling a bill for Live Aid '87, say, and still have the likes of the Thompson Twins, Alison Moyet, Adam Ant and Spandau Ballet on speed dial. Yet the US concert somehow felt more considered, even if the performances were largely quite uneventful.

The London leg eventually became so full that Geldof asked various acts if they wouldn't mind playing in Philadelphia instead, which is how the Pretenders, Simple Minds and the Thompson Twins ended up on the JFK bill. Graham wasn't happy about it, but there wasn't a lot he could do about it, apart from complain, of course.

'Bill Graham was completely autonomous, and was always at loggerheads with Harvey,' said Bernard Doherty. 'He was so argumentative, and was always pushing for more American acts. He tried to take ownership of the whole thing. He hated all the Nik Kershaw acts who were on the bill as they meant nothing in America.'

When Bob Geldof told Graham he'd managed to secure Charles and Diana, the promoter thought long and hard about how he could top it. He said to himself, 'Who is fucking royalty in this country?' It wasn't the president or the vice president, it was baseball stars, football stars, movie stars. Over breakfast one morning in the Philadelphia hotel where he was staying, he started making a list of who might fit the bill, and after a short while came up with two stars who would work, two Marlboro Men who would be as good as royalty: Clint Eastwood and Jack Nicholson.

Graham had known Nicholson since he was an usher at a Jerry McGovern benefit that the promoter had organised in 1972, and had kept in touch (who wouldn't have kept in touch with Jack Nicholson?). He called an intermediary, to see if he might be able to place a call directly to Nicholson, and having got caught in the rain on the Jersey Turnpike, and unable to find a phone box, finally got through to him, ten minutes late. When he explained what it was exactly he wanted him to do – introduce the show – Nicholson said, 'So you want *me* to be fuckin' royalty?'

Graham eventually convinced him to get involved, and when he put the phone down, he was on 'Cloud Fucking Eleven! I ran back through the pouring rain to the car and I said, "We got fuckin' *royalty*! We got

Jack. Fuck the prince and the princess. We got *Jack*!" I felt great. Then we drove to New York and had this great rehearsal with Mick [Jagger] and Tina [Turner].' At the time Graham was obsessed with Nicholson's most recent film, *Prizzi's Honor*, and especially the line he says when he's lying in bed with Kathleen Turner. She says, 'He was such a great man, my husband.' And Nicholson says, 'If he was so fuckin' great, how come he's so fuckin' dead?' Graham loved the line so much that he asked Nicholson to say it when they had congratulated each other after the show was over.

The Neil Young and CSNY performance was the result of a 'bumble-fuck reunion' according to Neil Young biographer Jimmy McDonough: '[He] was plagued by monitor problems . . . unveiling a new song called "Nothing Is Perfect". This plodding, turgid, overripe "message" song possessed one great couplet – '"But nothing is perfect in God's perfect plan/Look in the shadows to see" – but there was nothing subtle about it.' Elsewhere, Tom Petty added 'American Girl' at the last minute when he realised that they would be the first act to play the American half of the concert. In London, the screen had kept cutting back to the JFK Stadium, so every now and then we would be treated to shots of Madonna or the Beach Boys going through their moves. As soon as the Wembley show ended, at 10.02 p.m. GMT, it was time for Americans to take over, which Tom Petty kick-started with some panache. Later, Teddy Pendergrass would make his first public appearance since his near-fatal car accident in 1982 which paralysed him; and while they were hardly noticed at the time, Run-DMC were the only rap group invited to participate in Live Aid, something they referenced in their 1986 crossover hit 'My Adidas': 'My Adidas walk through concert doors and roam all over coliseum floors/I stepped on stage, at Live Aid/All the people played and the *poor* got paid . . .' In Philadelphia, *everyone* got paid. While the cost of the Wembley show was just $250,000, Philadelphia cost over $3.5 million, principally because so many of the technical and support staff expected to be paid.

In the US, Live Aid was broadcast on ABC and on MTV, whose VJs hosted the event. The presenters didn't exactly cover themselves in glory, however, and they were panned for their woeful performances. '[Critic]

Kurt Loder called us airheads in *Rolling Stone*,' said one of the VJs, Alan Hunter, who had joined the channel at launch, in 1981. 'That was a little mean, but he was not far off.'

Television viewers were no less obsessive than they were in Britain. At that time, the blogger Shlomo Schwartzbergl was working in a video rental outlet located in a department store in downtown Toronto, fortuitously right in front of all the televisions. When he showed up for work that Saturday morning of 13 July 1985, he made sure all the TV sets in the department were tuned to the live broadcast of the concerts and also that they were turned up loud. 'I would have to say the highlight of the American show was Page, Plant, Jones and Collins,' said another blogger, called Michael. 'When they played "Stairway To Heaven", people were crying all around me (myself included). It truly was an emotional show. I think a lot of others thought we were going to change things. Guess we were wrong. Famine exists on this planet today like at no other time in history. Well, I'm thirty-one now (wow). I have my Live Aid ticket stub framed and proudly hung on the wall. Shows like that come around only once in each generation. I would tell any younger folks to say hell with their job or school that day when theirs comes around. It will give them memories to last a lifetime. I'm not some kind of Eighties nut or anything, I just have fond memories of past glories.' Amber, from San Antonio in Texas, blogged: 'Was there anywhere Live Aid wasn't broadcast? I was sixteen years old, living in Guam, that small island in the Pacific (my father was in the US Air Force stationed there). Although I was thousands of miles away from most places, I felt that the young people of the world were somehow connected for those twenty-four hours. It's the closest thing to world harmony I've ever experienced.'

This was a long way from the international perception of Live Aid as a political event. If the US networks censored some of the content, in the Eastern bloc the concert was deemed to be positively subversive. A Bulgarian friend of mine, Spas Roussev, was working for the cultural festivals organisation in Sofia at the time, and along with some friends he rigged up an enormous aerial on top of the apartment building of their rock-star friend George Minchev in order to beam the programme in from the more liberal Yugoslavian TV (it was banned in Bulgaria). This DIY piracy and the fact that they actually managed to see the broadcast were political acts in themselves.

'We were so, so excited by the prospect of watching the show,' said Spas. 'We watched every minute of the British concert, along with everything we could see from the American one. The reception wasn't especially good, and for a lot of the time we could only see a black fuzz on the screen. What was important was the noise, hearing it, hearing all the names, hearing the music, knowing we were part of it. When we heard "Neil Young" being announced it sent shivers. There was the Boomtown Rats, Phil Collins . . . It was so special just to hear those names . . . To see Sting and Dire Straits, to hear "Money For Nothing", honestly, you have absolutely no idea how powerful it was, and how much it meant to us.'

Just to hear those names, names that meant so much, names that, if not immediately associated with the counter-culture of the Sixties and Seventies (and Nik Kershaw and Lionel Richie were hardly Jimi Hendrix or Richie Havens), were all part of the lineage, the pop pantheon of alternative entertainment. To those in the East, behind the Iron Curtain, this was an extraordinarily heady mix.

'This was forbidden, as was most Western music and Western culture,' said Spas. 'In those days, if restaurants or nightclubs played Western music, there were strict restrictions outlined by the Ministry of Culture regarding the percentages of what you could play. For instance you might have to play 60 per cent local music, 10 per cent Russian, and 30 per cent Western, which is all we really wanted to hear. In those days we had to rely on stewardesses smuggling in records from abroad. So the nightclubs were terrible.'

The only time that decent Western music was televised was on the Saturday night before Easter Sunday, when the government wanted to encourage as many young people as possible to stay away from church. Hollywood musicals would be screened, and Tom Jones concerts. There was no political upside to screening Live Aid, and so it was ignored.

'We were all encouraged to be very competitive in Bulgaria, and so it was a shock to see all these pop stars getting together to help other people.

We had always been told that rock musicians were selfish, subversive, self-obsessed people, and it was a revelation to see them all coming together in this way, essentially to help other people. We were continually told that they were a bad influence, yet it was all lies. Here they were, getting together to help another country. You have no idea how shocking that was to us behind the Iron Curtain.'

For Spas, the through line of this narrative went all the way to the closing ceremony of the Beijing Olympics in 2008, when Jimmy Page started playing 'Whole Lotta Love' with only Boris Johnson and a red Routemaster Bus for company.

'I cried when I saw that because for me it meant freedom, and having the freedom to express your culture. It was one bus, one person, one song, and I knew what it meant. It meant, we are the best, and we're allowed to shout about it. It was an incredibly strong message. The only other time I've cried for similar reasons was when we went to see our daughter's end-of-term performance at her English school. That year they sang "Let It Be" and "Here Comes The Sun", two songs that we wouldn't have been able to sing in Bulgaria when I was young. And it meant so much to both me and my wife. But all these emotions all somehow go back to Live Aid, where we heard for the first time all this great music being performed for good, for other people.'

Four years later, Spas's life would change, when hyperbole turned out to be understatement, then commonplace. Political metamorphosis was everywhere. In Prague's Wenceslas Square in November, one man interviewed for a British newspaper spoke words that were echoed by millions of his countrymen, and throughout the region: 'The main thing is, we have broken the chains.' Communism in the East had been crushed before collapsing.

'None of us involved in it had any idea how huge Live Aid was going to be,' said Mark Ellen. 'We didn't have any idea it would work, the great panic was that in those days, those clunky, analogue days, it was not absolutely guaranteed that you could fix on the scenes like Neil Armstrong on the moon. Somebody was trying to feed in, from all over the world, different scenes and using very different media . . . I remember when Philadelphia came on stream, there was a tension in the gallery as to whether these pictures would crackle into life at all but it was a long time ago, it was 1985. And it worked!'

But what if Live Aid had never happened? Would the world have been any different? The weather certainly played its part, and the event would have been very different seen through a filter of drizzle. In 2009 *The Word* magazine ran a 'What If?' feature, including *What If . . . David Frost hadn't accidentally invented alternative comedy?* (he becomes an MP instead), *What If . . . Steve Jobs had never returned to Apple?* (download services peter out as punters prefer the Sony DVD Walkman), *What If . . . The Edge had chosen God over Bono?* (Echo and the Bunnymen become the biggest group in the world), and *What If . . . It had rained at Live Aid?*: 'The concert at Wembley Stadium on 13 July 1985 begins in warm sunshine but by the late afternoon, during Paul Young's set, clouds gather and a downpour as U2 take the stage means Bono doesn't go among the audience. Showers persist in the evening. By the time Queen take to the stage much of the audience has retreated to the stands or drifted off to the Tube. Looking at the dispiriting pictures from a control room at Television Centre, Michael Grade restricts coverage to BBC2. The TV audience accordingly withers to a million people. BBC's "appreciation index" research indicates that the only people watching were *Whistle Test* viewers. A *Daily Mail* survey in the week following indicates that most people would definitely not attend an outdoor rock event and Michael Eavis abandons plans to buy the adjoining farm and extend Glastonbury. The Who, Eric Clapton, Queen, Paul McCartney and Bob Dylan quietly retire in the early Nineties. U2 are doing quite well, even supporting the Alarm at Madison Square Garden, but there is no boom for stadium-rock bands. By 2003, Bob Geldof is running an arts centre in Dublin where his daughters Clodagh, Colleen and Caitlin are beginning to make themselves known on the Irish party scene.'

So much for Wembley, there were obviously some tense moments at JFK. 'Duran had broken up and there was a rift,' said John Taylor. 'Andy Taylor and I were touring with Power Station in America, and Simon and Nick were working on the Arcadia album. We met in Philadelphia and did several days of rehearsal, and it was not a friendly or happy situation. The only time we were able to get in the same space together was when we did the photo for the programme. Live Aid was the last time the band played together for a few years.'

The original idea was for Simon Le Bon, Nick Rhodes and Roger Taylor to do Arcadia in London, then fly to Philadelphia to perform with the Power Station, but logistics again sent this idea tumbling. The Duran set was memorable for Simon Le Bon's off-key falsetto note that he hit during 'A View To A Kill', a blunder that echoed throughout the media as 'The Bum Note Heard Round The World'. The singer later said it was the most embarrassing moment of his career.

There were hiccups everywhere. 'That show was mayhem,' said Tom Bailey from the Thompson Twins. 'We were announced, the curtains went up, and as I walked towards the mic stand, I realised my guitar cable wasn't long enough to get there. It was a shambles.

'On the bus back to the hotel, I sat next to a corpse who turned out to be David Crosby. He looked white as a sheet and he was unconscious. It was a bit like the final scene in *Midnight Cowboy*.

'There was a huge party afterwards, but I went back to the hotel with Nile Rodgers and we played Scrabble. Nile was very good at Scrabble.'

Mick Jagger and Keith Richards were famously in dispute at the time, as in Richards' eyes his writing partner was spending too much time on his solo career. 'For much of the summer, the 800-pound gorilla in the room was Live Aid,' said Stones insider Bill German. 'When the Stones left Paris at the end of June, they agreed they wouldn't go near it. If their recording sessions [for *Dirty Work*] told them anything, it was that they were not functioning as a unit. Why go in front of the world – a billion TV viewers – and pretend otherwise.

'Furthermore, the Stones did not trust the charity itself. Live Aid was the feel-good concert of the decade, and the Stones didn't question the motives of anyone participating. But they did question the realities on the ground. Would the food and the money get to the famine victims? Or would it be intercepted by Ethiopian warlords and corrupt government officials? The Stones sincerely debated the point, and their concerns would later prove warranted. Lastly, the Stones, as a group, were never big on public displays of charity. They did a benefit for Nicaraguan earthquake victims in 1973, but had otherwise steered clear.'

So the Stones declined, saying they were 'no longer a band', but Jagger was determined to plough his own furrow at the time, and was intrigued by the offer to perform. So when Bill Graham had offered Jagger the penultimate slot at 9 p.m., right before Bob Dylan (as his biographer said, the one figure ranked above him in the rock pantheon), he grabbed it. But then on the night Keith Richards would turn out to have the last laugh. Two days before the Philadelphia show, Bob Dylan dropped by Ron Wood's house on New York's West 78th Street, and asked him if he was busy at the weekend, 'mumbling something about "playing this gig" on Saturday'. Wood said he'd be happy to play as long as he could ask Keith too, and so in a matter of hours Richards was suddenly topping the bill at Live Aid. Much to Jagger's irritation.

'I rang Keith and started to explain, "I'm here with Bob Dylan," when Keith blurted out, "Bob who? Fuck you,"' said Wood. But he turned up two hours later. When Keith turned up, Dylan just thought he was making a social call, so the two Stones ended up backing Dylan by default rather than design.

But although Richards had now leapfrogged his partner, Jagger's performance was in a different league. It was actually quite sparkling, and in his billowing shirt and his smart new trainers and with his twisted smile Jagger managed to completely seduce the crowd (as well as managing to tear Tina Turner's dress off theatrically, which, according to Jagger biographer Philip Norman, revived whispers of a long-ago affair between them). By chance, Geldof had managed to mate Mick Jagger's lips with Tina Turner's hips in front of millions. It was his first live appearance since the *Tattoo You* tour, his first official solo performance without the Stones, and was perceived to be a huge success.

Jagger had read in *Rolling Stone* that Turner liked his new single 'State Of Shock', and so invited her to sing with him at Live Aid. They rehearsed the performance for exactly an hour: 'Come on, it's not about perfection,' said Turner, just before going on stage, 'it's about having a good time and being with the people, and that's what we're doing. We might mess up a few lines, but we're here.' She then went on to pledge her support for the cause, and – in a genuinely heartfelt manner – explained that she and her band had cancelled a gig in Newfoundland to be in Philadelphia, and that world hunger wasn't anything to be treated lightly. 'These people are in desperation, and that's why I'm here.'

Bob Dylan's performance with Richards and Wood, however, showed that Live Aid would not be the salvation of those involved in the ancient art of weaving. Dylan once said that a songwriter doesn't care about what's truthful, 'What he cares about is what should've happened.' Well, his performance at Live Aid should never have happened.

'Some artists' work speaks for itself, some artists' work speaks for a generation,' said Jack Nicholson, introducing the final act. 'It's my deep personal pleasure to present to you, one of America's great voices of freedom . . . It can only be one man, the transcendent Bob Dylan!' In the end, the introduction was more memorable than the performance.

Dylan, Keith Richards and Ron Wood had spent the previous afternoon drinking and jamming, without any great success. Drunk they may have been, but they were no closer to being ready to play the biggest concert of their lives. While working their way through various bottles of booze, they discussed former Rolling Stones guitarist Mick Taylor's technique.

'There are some really great songs on that record,' said Dylan, referring to Taylor's first album. 'I'm not sure it's even in print any more.'

'They're not that great when you're trying to play them,' countered Richards, slurring. 'Mick Taylor's a very nice guy but he's very hard to get to know, at least he was when I knew him. I never see him any more, maybe once a year, maybe once every three years sometimes now. I imagine it was a problem for him as he was coming in for Brian [Jones].'

'He always had a problem going on stage even when he was in his first band, the Gods,' said Wood. 'He used to ask me to go on for him, so I used to do his set and then ours.'

They start playing 'Ballad of Hollis Brown', although it's immediately apparent that neither Richards nor Wood really know how the song goes, and as Dylan appears to be playing an apparently unique version of the song itself — something he would begin to do every night on stage until even his backing band had no idea what song he was playing, even when the vocals came in — there was no reason why they *should* know what's going on. At one point Richards says that he'll probably just hang on for an extra half a bar like John Lee Hooker, and take it from there.

Wood then says self-deprecatingly that one thing he should not attempt to do is solo during the song, at which point Dylan says, 'Yes, that wouldn't be a good idea,' just in case Wood was expecting another response.

Obviously frustrated by the way things are going, Dylan says, 'One of the joys of playing by yourself is never ever having to rehearse.'

They then send out for more vodka, rum and Jack Daniels ('Half-pints?' asks a gofer. 'No, pints I think,' says Dylan) along with several packets of Marlboros. They continue jamming, but it only gets worse. This goes on for a while until Dylan says he has to 'split', and they then spend twenty minutes deciding on the various ways they're going to get to the stadium, accompanied by whom and in how many cars. At one point Wood suggests that they should all 'roll' in the same car — Dylan's, as it has a tape recorder — so they can learn the songs. But then where was Patti going to sit, and Marlon, and Jo, and all the others? It's strange to think that this happened three years after *Spinal Tap*, as the conversation could have been a blueprint for the film. As they go their separate ways, Dylan says that they shouldn't bother taking the tape they've just made with them, as he's played 'Blowin' In The Wind' so many different ways that it wouldn't be indicative of how it was going to sound in Philadelphia. This would turn out to be the understatement of understatements. Then Richards asks what time they're meant to be 'hitting the boards', and after he is told that it's going to be 10.30 p.m., Dylan contradicts them by saying it's 11.30 p.m. Thus prompting another five minutes of garbled, drunken nonsense. When Wood says, 'At least we haven't got a band to worry about, as it's only us!' you can see where it all went wrong, because the following day we would see that they really hadn't appeared to worry about anything.

As soon as Dylan has left, Wood and Richards start worrying about what they've achieved during their rehearsal. 'Don't worry,' says Keith. 'At least we've got the rhythm.'

Mick Jagger had flown down from New York the day before on a private jet with Hall & Oates, who were going to back him. But Richards, Dylan and Wood chose to drive down on the day of the concert, only stopping at a Howard Johnson's on the Jersey Turnpike for a pee.

They continued jamming when they arrived, in a trailer in the stadium, not that it made any difference, as their performance was a shambles. Neither Richards nor Wood could hear anything through their monitors, and Dylan broke a string on his acoustic guitar. When this happened, Wood gallantly took off his own guitar and gave it to Dylan, and so was left standing on stage guitarless. After nonchalantly shrugging to the audience, he started playing air guitar, swinging his arm in wide circles, as a homage to Pete Townshend (a stagehand eventually brought him a replacement). It was obvious that not only did Richards and Wood not know how to play Dylan's first song, 'The Ballad Of Hollis Brown', but also that they were in no condition to play it anyway (ludicrously they were both smoking cigarettes like teenage hoodlums suddenly stuck in front of a local TV camera). To compound the embarrassment, behind them Lionel Richie could be seen practising the show's finale performance of 'We Are The World' (along with Peter, Paul and Mary who were meant to have joined Bob Dylan for 'Blowin' In The Wind').

'Their performance was pathetic,' said Paul McGuinness. 'God, that was awful, laughable, so disappointing. The other thing I remember, of course, was Mick Jagger and Tina Turner, which was brilliant. That was a star turn. They had figured it out in rehearsal, treating it like a huge worldwide event, and they got it right. The contrast with poor old Keith was dreadful.'

'There was a huge problem with the mics,' said Richards in his defence. 'No one knew Bob was gonna come on with an acoustic guitar, and all we could hear is people in the background tuning up and getting ready for the big finale. "Shut the fuck up!" You know, Bob Dylan's coming on to close the show and nobody knows he's on. He was bashing about on an acoustic guitar in front of 90,000 people and nobody could hear a thing, let alone us. And there's Ronnie and me, the schmucks trying to keep it together. No one's going to hear three fucking acoustic guitars in front of 90,000 people, never! It was very hard, man, I mean we could have walked off. As a matter of fact some great things came out of that gig, I mean, you should have heard the rehearsals . . . We had to do it as Dylan asked us to. He actually said, are you coming down to Philly for this Tom Petty thing or are you going to watch it on TV? I'm still glad we did it though. Bob and I have a lot of things in common, and even though we don't see each other very often, we like playing together. Ronnie is an avid Dylan fan, but he doesn't know the early stuff, but I knew it all as I grew up on his stuff in art school. Woody knew everything from *Blonde On Blonde* . . . So when Bob pulls out these three early songs, it was like, OK! But if you could have heard it, it would have [sounded] great. If you listen carefully you can hear Ronnie playing some vicious steel, if you could just get your fucking ears down. Following twenty-four hours of heavy, amplified Sassenach rock 'n' roll . . . it was an interlude, right, and it was better than selling ice cream.

'We were just waiting for the guy to bring the blindfold and the last cigarette. Shoot me, I wanna be back in the car! We just held the fort and did our bit. We were waiting for the fucking firing squad. But it's OK, nobody was getting paid for it. It wasn't my fault no one could hear it. All I could hear was ambience. It was all in a good cause and it worked out. I loved it and I'm glad I was on it . . . as I had [originally] no intention of being on it. As soon as we'd finished, the next thing I saw was Harry Belafonte walking up to me. I thought, what a strange place to be. So I tried to slink out as gracefully as possible. I don't think it came across badly, it just would have been better if you could have heard it. You had an arbitrary acoustic guitar, and one with a broken string. It wasn't that bad, and all we were trying to do was cover the ground as best we could. I was just Bob's guitar player. You know, we were only trying to feed people, we weren't trying to prove anything. But I enjoyed it actually, it was a right laugh. Hats off to Bob, and everyone else involved. There are only so many Mozarts, and if you're a musician you just do what you do for a short period of time and then pass it on. If you've just turned one person on in your life then you've done your job. You've passed it on.'

Interviewed a few months after the show, Richards was asked if something like Live Aid could ever happen again, to which he replied, 'It depends how hungry they are.'

Looking back nearly thirty years later, Harvey Goldsmith wouldn't change a thing. 'Some of the American stuff didn't make any sense in Britain, but it did to America. There wasn't the same kind of vibe in America as there was here at all, which was a bit weird actually. I mean I had to send two of my guys over because the Americans didn't really get it. We had to take the whole thing over and put a show together. And when they realised two or three days before how big it was, then they got in and took it over. But I wouldn't have changed any of the US show either.'

Oddly, it was only when Madonna took to the stage in Philly that Goldsmith realised what they had achieved, and that Live Aid was actually a lot bigger than anyone had anticipated, including both himself and Geldof.

'When Madonna came on the screen, via satellite, this was the first time that America and England were together. It had never happened before. I mean to me the day was a bit of a blur, as we were just [pushing] people on and pulling them off. I was worrying about everything, even things I had almost no control over, like what was happening in America. I wanted to make sure that this Phil Collins thing didn't fuck up, but there was little I could do. There were just so many things going through my mind. But when those satellite pictures of Madonna went up I thought, "Wow, OK, now look at what we've done."'

Pete Hamill summed it up thus: 'Yes: the paying audience in Philadelphia was overwhelmingly white, middle class and docile, as was the crowd at Wembley Stadium in London. Yes: the Live Aid concerts did not feature enough black, Latin or Caribbean artists. Yes: the live television coverage was often ragged, haranguing and downright ignorant. Yes: some performers walked through it, while others were under-rehearsed or over the hill. But granting all of these cavils, we are left with what I think is an incontrovertible fact: the Live Aid show was the single greatest one-day event in the more than thirty-year history of rock 'n' roll.'

FIFTEEN

'How long will Pepperland last?'

'As long as people nod and smile to each other,' said the major. 'And think about the next person. All you need is love. Now, may we finish our quartet?'

When, at noon, the lord mayor's quartet finished, there would be another concert. To celebrate the close of one pleasant day and the beginning of another, the one and only Pepperland band would play.

YELLOW SUBMARINE

By the time the TV satellites had been turned off, over £50 million had been pledged to Band Aid's Ethiopian fund. But even though the *Daily Mail* the following day declared it 'Rock's Finest Hour', the sniping began almost immediately. The *New Musical Express* were especially negative, firstly because they found the idea of aid rather patronising, and secondly because of the content, as most of the acts appearing were anathema to the paper's left-leaning, shoe-gazing sensibility. They also hated the fact that there weren't any black groups on the bill. The left were generally opposed to the project, principally because of the 'justified self-righteousness' of the performers themselves (Michael Buerk in the *Observer*). The left felt that the wrong people were waving the flag for poverty, and that the world would be a much better place if fund-raising were left to those they approved of (in the *NME*'s case, the eccentric, the arch, the critically anointed and the socially adrift). Spandau Ballet, for instance, were called 'hideously nouveau bourgeois'. For the *NME*, if you were British and arrogant enough to want to be a pop star then you also had to be a keen and vocal supporter of the miners' strike. If you weren't, or if you had no passion for left-wing politics, then in their eyes you were already an outcast. Which is why it was so hypocritical when they castigated those supporting Live Aid.

Almost immediately there were cries that those on the bill were using the event for their own devices, almost as though the performers were expected to be munificent without actually performing. The worldwide audience for Live Aid was going to be close to 1.5 billion they said – an incomprehensibly huge number and obviously a great marketing opportunity. For the audience this was charity on a different scale, an epic scale; as Peter York said, there was an intense and lasting sensation of having bought into the charity business in a way they'd never done before. 'As a rule, *giving* tends to be a quiet, even furtive affair – *just between me and my conscience, thank you*. The cheque goes in the pre-addressed envelope and disappears, or the coin goes in the box and maybe you get a paper sticker for your lapel; but it's a small transaction with a small reward.'

Pet Shop Boy Neil Tennant once wrote in a bracing essay on the power of hatred: 'I retain the old-fashioned belief that pop music is meant to be a challenge to society as well as an affirmation of it. And so I consider it my duty to hate things . . . to hate a lot of things is tantamount to really caring about others.'

Geldof maintains that Live Aid was not a cultural event, but solely a political lobby, 'entirely empirical. It turned out, much to my dismay, that it had a greater romantic resonance than I had anticipated. I wanted an organisational continuum and I wanted a political lobby to elevate what I thought was a serious global issue: poverty. More than half the world lives on less than $2 a day and the economic logic of that with the globalisation that was just beginning – and Live Aid was an avatar of that by using the international language that was not English, but rock 'n' roll – and you could suggest an idea of change. Not articulate it, but suggest it.'

Which is what a lot of people felt about Live Aid, opposing the very idea of it for subjective, snobbish reasons as well as liberal, ideological ones. Critics such as the *Guardian*'s Dorian Lynskey accused the event of being so uncontroversial that if they chose to, everyone could appease their consciences without the slightest risk of ruffling feathers. Apparently the inherent folly of 'stadium protest' was just overblown and self-congratulatory. Although even Geldof himself would fluctuate between pride and disappointment at what he had achieved, and would often try and negate the event. 'We've used the spurious glamour of pop music to draw attention to a situation, and we've overloaded the thing with symbolism to make it reach people. But people get bored easily. People may have been profoundly affected by the Live Aid day – some were shattered by it – but that does not translate into a massive change in consciousness.'

In an article in the American music magazine *Spin* in July 1986, exactly a year after Live Aid, Robert Keating expressed grave misgivings about the Band Aid Trust's ability to distribute the donated money adequately. The article was based in part on evidence supplied by Dr Claude Malhuret, from the relief agency Médecins Sans Frontières, who said that the single obstacle to feeding the famine victims in Ethiopia was the Marxist government, which had confiscated much of the food and was using it to feed its army, as leverage with political opponents or to trade for arms from the Russians. Malhuret compared Ethiopia with Germany in 1939 or Kampuchea in 1977. 'The situation is so bad,' he said, 'that no one should collaborate. We must denounce it.'

Geldof's response was unequivocal: 'If the Médecins Sans Frontières story is an attempt to discredit us, make us appear naïve or at best irresponsible, it is a matter of public record that this cannot possibly be the case. On the other hand, by our own operational status in the field, we are free to pursue such a course of action without hindering the flow of money to the agencies and through them to the people most in need. And even MSF must agree that sometimes we get results simply because we have money. Unlike MSF, we have done this from the start. I said as early as January 1985 that I will shake hands with the Devil on my left and on my right to get to the people we are meant to help.'

Many thought that Geldof would draw a line under his music career after Live Aid, but he says nothing was further from his mind. However, he was now one of the most famous men in the world, with a public profile that he found difficult to come to terms with.

'I knew that some people would think that going back to music was a little bit silly. After all, I was now St Bob and it was diminishing to go back to music. In fact, it's the very opposite. That was it. They, the great they, didn't want me to go back. They wanted me to be this figure that they'd put values upon that I may not necessarily have held. I'd moved suddenly from having been in a declining rock 'n' roll band into being this figure that could be debated. When they heard I was making a solo record, they said, for fuck's sake, how pathetic.'

The level of fame that Live Aid brought him at first totally freaked him out. When he brought out his first solo album, *Deep In The Heart Of Nowhere*, in 1986, it was the third item on *News at Ten*. 'I was very confused about myself. I only made money through music, so what did they expect my job to be? That's what I wanted to do, that's what I could do. I've done this other thing. I'll still do it because I promised I would because the political views are so huge, you'd be an idiot to not seize it. But what I do is play tunes. You might not like them, dude, but it's what I do. I was fucked. So I had to change course entirely from where I thought I was heading.

'It was the type of fame, not the fame itself that I hated. It's not normal to walk down a street and have a pile of people stuffing fivers in your pocket. Or old ladies coming up, standing stock-still in front of you, reaching out to touch you tentatively and then bursting into tears. That's not normal. It's normal if you're a member of One Direction to do precisely that, but it's not for a grown man. It's extremely limiting. The cult of personality is deeply disturbing, as it's an abhorrent type of politics. And it's seriously damaging to the personality. In my way, I had to deconstruct it, while at the same time being criticised by anyone who had a newspaper column.'

He is still criticised today. In 2009 the BBC aired a radio documentary on the World Service suggesting that funds from Band Aid had been diverted to Eritrean 'rebels'. This obviously infuriated Geldof, who claimed they had done 'appalling' damage to his cause. Speaking in Nairobi, he condemned the documentary as soon as it was broadcast, saying it had not 'a shred of evidence'. It took the BBC over a year to apologise.

However, Africa is creeping towards fulfilment, and while it still struggles with famine, disease, poverty, drought, AIDS, corruption and civil war, self-assertion and investment are changing the continent's profile. 'It is not the role of the media to sell a rebranded version of Africa, any more than it was right to paint it as the heart of darkness in the past,' wrote the *Observer* in 2012. Although its income per capita was still among the lowest in the world, in 2011 Ethiopia grew by 7.5 per cent, and was the world's tenth-largest producer of livestock. And as China became the continent's biggest trading partner, with bilateral trade standing at around $160 billion, so they funded a $200 million African Union headquarters in Addis Ababa, a symbol of 'deepening relations'. Remarkably, in 2012, CDC, the UK's development finance arm, announced a £50 million investment in the private equity fund backed by Geldof that focuses on Africa. 8 Miles – named after the shortest distance between Europe and Africa – has been promoted by Geldof, Kofi Annan, the former UN Secretary General, and sponsored by CLSA, the Asian brokerage and investment group. It invests in consumer-driven businesses and service providers with strong growth prospects.

Live Aid spawned a new generation of giving. It woke people up in a way that no event of this kind had ever done before. Not only was it done on a global scale, but the technological advances of the age had made the Woodstock spirit come to life in a completely new way. Comic Relief wouldn't have happened without Live Aid, and neither would the Amnesty International concerts have grown in the way they did.

Fund-raising had never had such a fillip, and while Queen and U2 might have been the most obvious beneficiaries of the day – Freddie Mercury instigating what can only be described as a resurrection, and Bono rubber-stamping his persona on 2 billion nascent U2 fans – the entire charitable sector was given a massive shot in the arm.

'Before Live Aid, rock 'n' roll was still to a degree a miscreant mongrel art form,' said the writer and broadcaster Stuart Maconie. 'After it, it became the centre of the global entertainment nexus. Before Live Aid vexed issues of international trade and aid, of intervention and colonialism, were regarded as the province of diplomats, economists, politicians and aid agencies. After it, it became the remit of Madonna, Bono, Brangelina and Becks. Live Aid changed everything. But it's not Africa that changed. It's us.'

And he was right.

Live Aid was something else again, a spectacle which you were part of, complete with tears, laughs, and the feeling of being part of a staggering global event. Peter York said this was the Eighties' way of self-projection, and in a way he was right, as we were all presenting ourselves as caring, thoughtful participants, just as the stars were presenting themselves as caring, thoughtful performers.

The Eighties were all about promotion, projection, said York, and he wasn't all that wrong. 'We were starting to sell ourselves in a way we'd never even dreamt of before. We sold ourselves professionally – marketing ourselves. People became known for always, say, using a specific shade of lipstick; or [wearing] Doc Martens all the time; or tweed suits – these little tics of appearance, these tiny individuations, which at another time would have been no more than personal affectations, became our own tiny *logos*.'

In November 1969, John Lennon was asked to sum up the Sixties. 'Nothing happened,' he said, 'except that we all dressed up.' It sounded strikingly apposite at the time, yet the same thing could have been said at the end of the Seventies, and especially at the end of the Eighties. Yet it was only the Eighties that gave birth to Live Aid, only the Eighties where all that dressing up seemed to have achieved anything.

'What it really did was show that in the absence of a great national football team, or any great sporting prowess, that Britain could excel at something,' said Gary Farrow. 'It was like hosting the Olympics.'

'There was massive industrial change going on,' said Tony Blair, who at the time was the Shadow Treasury spokesman, 'and the community I represented up in County Durham was basically losing all its old coal and steel industries, and so Live Aid was a big moment of change in the country.'

Oddly enough, Michael Buerk, the BBC journalist whose early TV reports were the catalyst for the formation of Band Aid and Live Aid, found the whole thing rather distasteful. But as he was Michael Buerk, and as he was largely responsible for the project anyway, he was sanctified enough to get away with what he had to say.

'Pop stars are egotistical,' he announced, as though this were news. 'They're also rich beyond the dreams of the normal, let alone the destitute – but they are not indifferent.'

And yet he knew that the event had not only worked, it had also been boosted by the zeitgeist. 'Britain was five years into the Margaret Thatcher era; Ronald Reagan had been in the White House for nearly four years,' he said. 'Everywhere, the notions of a corporate state and welfare socialism, the consensus politics of the post-war world, were in retreat. But even those who believe this was long overdue, by definition the majority of those who voted in the elections, seemed to be uneasy about it. Market-driven individualism might work better with the grain of human nature, it might make most of us more prosperous, but it sometimes made us feel selfish. There *was* something obscene about us piling up mountains of food we could not eat while millions of others starved to death, a few hours' flying time away.'

According to one of the *NME*'s suitably polemical columnists, Don Watson, this was the key to the event. 'If Nik Kershaw is to exist is it not best that he should put his dubious talents to some use that is beneficial to humanity? Well yes, but there's still something sick about the juxtaposition of the preening culture of British pop, so concerned as it is with Third World notions of movie-star glamour, with sights of swelling stomachs and wasted homes. It's one step away from an eat-in for Ethiopia.'

Not really.

In the Eighties, people stopped buying the *NME* for the same reasons they stopped voting Labour, as both had become too strident, too socialist, and way too dogmatic. And neither organisation would have had it any other way. In the Eighties the *NME* went from being a paper read by a quarter of a million people to one whose influence was negligible, and whose place was about to be taken by *Q* magazine (which launched in 1986, a year after Live Aid), a publication much less concerned with its readers' political persuasions. Some would see *Q*'s attitude as an abnegation of responsibility, as though counter-cultural seams and left-leaning sensibilities were prerequisites for pop. But the Eighties weren't really like that; Live Aid was how the Eighties manifested themselves in terms of the sociopolitical. *Q* was launched as its publishers felt that the *NME* wasn't catering for its readers as much as it once did, and that the mainstream rock consumer might be looking for a slightly less strident guide to their musical tastes. *Q*'s first few issues had the likes of U2, Elton John, Simply Red and Paul McCartney on its cover, while exploring the careers of everyone from Paul Simon to ZZ Top. It was a magazine aimed at the album devotee, one who perhaps was being persuaded to replace all his vinyl with these newfangled CD things which the record companies were pushing.

In *The Uncyclopedia of Rock*, published in 1987, Angus Deayton, Jeremy Pascall and Geoffrey Perkins had their own tasteless dig at Live Aid: 'At the almost worthwhile BPI Awards [soon to become the Brits], after Paul Young had picked up the Best Male Singer Award for his outstanding performance on every single groove of the one record he had released that year, Bob Geldof received a special award for his Band Aid single. His speech caused a furore when he claimed the situation was worse than the concentration camps of Nazi Germany. Unfortunately, those listening were not aware that he was not referring to the Ethiopian famine, but to the awards ceremony itself.'

Live Aid had proved to be fertile ground for comedians, and was ripe for satire. Even some of those involved in it took against it. 'Musically, Live Aid was to be entirely predictable and boring,' said the DJ Andy Kershaw, who had helped present the programme for the BBC. 'As they were wheeled out – or, rather bullied by Geldof into playing – it became clear that this was another parade of the same old rock aristocracy in a concert for Africa, organised by someone who, while advertising concern for, and sympathy with, the continent didn't see fit to celebrate or dignify the place by including on the Live Aid bill a single African performer. There were, meanwhile, hundreds of guitarists in the beer halls of Zimbabwe or Zaire, and dozens of others dotted along the Niger, who could wipe the floor with Eric Clapton.' Kershaw would go on to accuse Geldof of encouraging cultural apartheid, an example of the presenter's enduring ability to bite the hand that feeds him.

Live Aid soon became unmistakably more about television than it was about anything else. Even those in the stadium spent most of the day watching the two huge video screens flanking the stage. This grated with some, as the epic nature of the stars' presentation meant that those performing got a 'relief conscience massage'. The likes of the *NME* even found the use of the Cars' 'Drive' beyond the pale. "These pictures speak for themselves," said David Bowie, introducing them. And yet they weren't allowed to – tragic though these pictures were, there was something genuinely pornographic about ladling over them the thick syrup of a pop song soundtrack,' wrote Don Watson. 'To the American viewer, idly flipping through the channels, it must have looked like the most sensationalist pop video ever made.'

The left's impression was that this was a media event dedicated to old-fashioned Tory wet values of care and compassion. And therefore a bad thing.

Live Aid was the world's first proper global cultural event, and as such, was owned by anyone who cared to own it. Yet many felt that they couldn't endorse it, simply because they couldn't control it. The moon landing was probably the world's first global television event, but at the time we were too busy being impressed by technology – and what it could do – to acknowledge it as a truly global moment. Given that it had only taken sixty-six years from the Wright brothers making the first controlled, powered and sustained flight in 1903 to the 1969 moon landing, this was hardly surprising.

Live Aid was something else again, as it was the result of subjective content rather than technology. With subjectivity came opinion, not all of it positive.

'I [actually] didn't see Live Aid,' said Michael Buerk. 'I knew it was happening, but South African television didn't carry it. South Africa was the story of the day with townships in flames and riots. On the day of Live Aid I was actually being teargassed by the police.

'The money raised, however, would have saved about 1–2 million lives. Live Aid made a terrific difference. But actually, the key thing it did, which utterly dwarfed Band Aid and Live Aid, was to force a change of policy in the EU and particularly in the UK and America. The public opinion that they mobilised and represented was what counted.'

Didn't it just.

'A little girl who used to live next door to me a few years ago told me that she had learned about us in history,' said Midge Ure. 'She said she had been reading about it all and my name had come up. That's just weird. I think the legacy of Live Aid is not just the fact that there are people alive today who wouldn't have been alive, but I think young people's perspective of charity has changed. Twenty years ago charity was something the Women's Institute did. All of a sudden their heroes are up there saying, "I'm involved."'

Gary Kemp had his own thoughts. 'I think Live Aid was a genuine response from the populace,' he said. 'In Britain, Thatcher had run roughshod over the miners, she'd really done what she felt was right, but not necessarily what the general public felt was right. Obviously we all felt great about the fact that we'd finally made her drop the VAT on the Band Aid record,* but up until that point, politics was only a tick in the box every four years, and not everyone got what they wanted. Live Aid gave everyone the opportunity to do something above and beyond government and make a political change internationally with their postal orders, their chequebooks, their piggy banks and credit cards and whatever. What came out of Live Aid was a sense of people power that was so strong that it's carried on and on and on to Red Nose Days and everything else in the area of television and fund-raising and charitable concerts.

'Without Live Aid I still think the second Summer of Love would have

---

* When Geldof was trying to get Thatcher to waive the VAT on the money accrued by Live Aid, he twice cycled round to her Chelsea flat. 'She never offered me anything other than whisky. I'd ask for some water in it and she'd shuffle off to the kitchen and pour it from the tap.'

happened in '87, which blew all the bands away and we got DJ culture. But I don't think there would have been as many of the charitable events that we see today. As far as Ethiopia is concerned, maybe it did make a change where people were at least feeling that they could make a difference.

'I think in the Sixties, people dropped out and they just ignored the establishment but complained about it elsewhere. In the Seventies, you think of it as being about punk, about being outside of the establishment and trying to kick the doors in and shouting a lot and being very angry. Both of those kind of failed. I think our generation really felt like we could change things from within by being the new establishment: selling records, being commercial, involving yourselves politically and trying to make a change, in a way. And ironically all of this was from a generation that was meant to be up its own arse, shallow, callous and not caring.

'It gave the general public a sense of power that they've never really let go of, and they demand more and more. I think it was also the start of our cynicism towards government, the banks. The state.'

In the aftermath, and for a long while afterwards – in reality, I would say, right up until the swagger of Britpop made rock music quasi-dangerous and semi-palatable again, and when personality became paramount once more – projects that came with a cause attached, or which were deemed to be supremely worthy, tended to leapfrog those which weren't, at least in terms of cultural resonance and critical appreciation. Even though he was part of the day's cavalcade, George Michael's emergence as a solo performer after Wham! was considered to be just that and only that, while Paul Simon's *Graceland* project (featuring Ladysmith Black Mambazo) was lambasted for being naïve and insensitive to the South African apartheid struggle, and therefore demonised. Mere pop was trivialised after Live Aid, seen as just that: pop without purpose. In the years that followed, Michael Jackson, Madonna and Prince would all come through London with the sort of spectacles that had tabloid editors salivating; yet without any *raison d'être* other than 'admire and consume', spectacles were all they were (even the extraordinary concerts Prince performed in the round at Wembley Arena in 1988, which were undoubtedly some of the best British concerts of the

Eighties). The Final, Wham!'s last ever concert, in the summer of 1986, and again taking place at a sun-drenched Wembley Stadium, felt like one big British prom party, a Gang Show for kids, with two pop puppets performing all in white at one end. There was no cause, no drama, no significant narrative arc other than the public bowing out of a phenomenally successful pop duo (it perhaps says something about my relationship with the event that one of the few things I can recall about it was the fact that I was wearing a white cotton Katharine Hamnett suit; how very Eighties).* Expediency, which had always been the norm in pop, was suddenly frowned upon. Altruism became as relevant as talent, socially more so. Aid became the big business, as did causes. All sorts of causes. From Farm Aid to the Nelson Mandela concert organised by Jerry Dammers, 'event pop' drove the culture from within. Even grunge, which was largely a genre based around apathy, can be traced back to Live Aid culture, as it was devoid of self-aggrandisement. The members of Nirvana were never going to throw their arms around the world, but they could at least spend an afternoon disparaging those whose prime motivation seemed only to be their ability to monetise their success.

The Nelson Mandela Seventieth Birthday Tribute was staged on 11 June 1988, again at Wembley, and broadcast to sixty-seven countries and an audience of 600 million (although in the US, the Fox network heavily censored the political aspects of the show). It was the brainchild of Jerry Dammers, whose band the Special AKA had released the single 'Free Nelson Mandela' in 1984, and founded the Artists Against Apartheid organisation the following year. The concert was designed to raise awareness of the imprisonment of the ANC leader, kick-starting the movement that eventually led to his release in 1990. (There were various political complications with the politics, not least those involving Whitney Houston, who was contracted to make advertisements for Coca-Cola, and who performed in front of a black backdrop instead of the usual picture of Nelson Mandela. Apparently

---

* To commemorate the gig, Elton John sent the pair a yellow Robin Reliant, a replica of the same three-wheeler seen in the TV series *Only Fools and Horses*, with 'George and Andrew' written across the windscreen and a pair of fluffy dice hanging from the rear-view mirror. It was still backstage when Bon Jovi played there two months later.

007 **WEMBLEY**

** Enter by: NORTH OR SOUTH **

A.L.E. LTD.

PROUDLY PRESENT

PRINCE

LOVESEXY '88
7:30PM PROMPT

PLEASE NOTE THERE IS NO SUPPORT ACT
Wednesday 03 August 1988 07:30 pm

As soon as the impact of Live Aid was felt – which was immediately – every act suddenly wanted to play stadiums, including Prince, Madonna and Michael Jackson. Live Aid had proved once and for all that pop was now such a part of mainstream popular culture that it was now part and parcel of the entertainment industry. It WAS the entertainment industry.

this was nothing to do with censorship but was the result of an electricity generator failing. Such was the diversity of the acts on the bill that Jerry Dammers was worried the message would be diffused. I had a drink with him a few days before the show and he was moaning about the possibility of having to sing 'Free Nelson Mandela' with Bryan Adams.)

The presenter of the BBC broadcast of the concert, Robin Denselow, called it 'the biggest and most spectacular pop-political event of all time, a more political version of Live Aid with the aim of raising consciousness rather than just money'. Just three short years since Live Aid, and already the idea of simply fund-raising was being downgraded, compared to the lofty idealism implicit in 'raising consciousness'. Music wasn't just a force for change, it was now implicitly a force for good.

'Aid' entered the vernacular as the suffix of choice for any fund-raising event. It has stayed in the vernacular, too, moving in and out of irony like an unwieldy car on the motorway (South Park's 'Chef Aid', for instance, from 1998). Animal Aid. Tree Aid. Muslim Aid. Football Aid. Asylum Aid. Gift Aid. In 1986, the heavy metal band Dio spearheaded Hear 'n' Aid, a hard-rock supergroup (Judas Priest, Iron Maiden, Blue Oyster Cult, Motley Crue, etc.) whose single 'Stars' was recorded in order to raise funds for African famine relief.

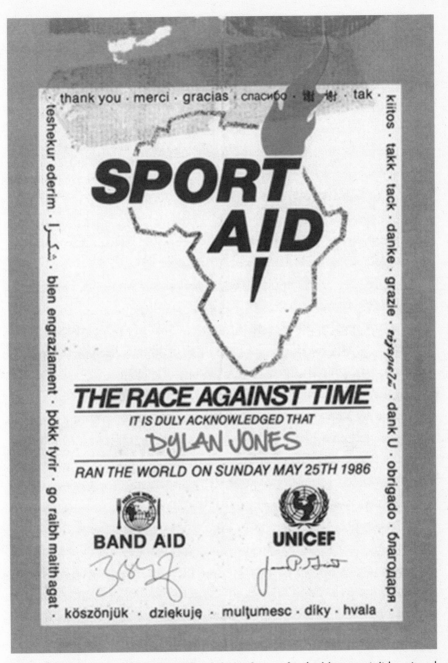

'Aid' entered the vernacular as the suffix of choice for any fund-raising event. It has stayed in the vernacular, too, moving in and out of irony like an unwieldy car on the motorway. Animal Aid. Tree Aid. Muslim Aid. Football Aid. Asylum Aid. Gift Aid. Hear 'n' Aid.

Then there was Sport Aid, another Geldof initiative, that took place ten months after Live Aid, on Sunday 25 May 1986. At 3 p.m. GMT, 20 million sponsored runners in 274 cities in 89 countries ran, jogged or walked (and in my case all three) ten kilometres. As we ran round London's Hyde Park (I remember insisting I wear my navy MA-1 flying jacket – 'for the silhouette' – much to my girlfriend's frustration), huge speaker stacks pumped out Tears For Fears' 'Everybody Wants To Run The World', a remixed version of their mammoth hit 'Everybody Wants To Rule The World'. The band were due to appear on the Philadelphia bill but had gone on holiday instead, incurring the rage of Geldof. 'He gave us so much gip for not turning up,' said the band's leader, Roland Orzabal. This was their way of apologising, and they donated the proceeds to the Band Aid charity (even though the band's original version had been a hit only a year before, the remixed version reached the UK top five).

Farm Aid started as a one-off benefit concert on 22 September 1985, in front of 80,000 people at the University of Illinois Memorial Stadium in Champaign, Illinois, held to raise money for US family farmers. The concert was organised by Willie Nelson, John Mellencamp and Neil Young, spurred on by Bob Dylan's (at the time unhelpful) comments at Live Aid that he hoped some of the money generated by the US event would help American farmers in danger of losing their farms through mortgage debt. That first concert featured performances from Dylan, Roy Orbison, Billy Joel and B. B. King and raised nearly $10 million.

Mellencamp and Nelson almost immediately became politically active, and brought family farmers before Congress to testify about the state of non-corporate farming in America. This brought about the Agricultural Credit Act (to help save family farms from foreclosure), which was passed by Congress in 1987. Farm Aid itself became an annual event, featuring a variety of country, blues and rock stars, often accompanied by one of Neil Young's rambling speeches about the environment.

One of the many tangential Ethiopian projects immediately resulting from Live Aid was Fashion Aid, a ridiculously glitzy designer fund-raiser that took place at the Royal Albert Hall in London in November 1985. 5,000 people filled the auditorium for what was billed as an evening of spectacle and glamour featuring eighteen of the world's top fashion designers and a host of 'superstars'. Twenty-five-year-old fashion designer (and godfather of Geldof's and Paula Yates' daughter Fifi Trixibelle) Jasper Conran led the charge, corralling the likes of Katharine Hamnett, Yves Saint Laurent, Anthony Price, Giorgio Armani, Zandra Rhodes, Calvin Klein, Body Map, Scott Crolla, Issey Miyake and the Emanuels (who four years earlier had designed Princess Diana's wedding dress). The 'superstars' included Margaret Thatcher, Boy George, Princess Michael of Kent, Jerry Hall, Grace Jones, Tina Turner, the newsreader Selina Scott, Madness, Freddie Mercury, the Eurythmics' Annie Lennox and Dave Stewart, Paul King (the lead singer of a fairly dismal 'designer oik' band, King, who had designs on following Queen and Prince into their subject's hearts), Spandau Ballet's Steve Norman, and many more, and it was publicised by Lynne Franks, who, several years later, would become the basis for the Edina character in Jennifer Saunders' *Absolutely Fabulous*.* What perfect synergy for the fashion industry, a home-grown international cause that it could embrace, celebrate and add value to without looking exploitational. It was a match made in the glass-walled boardroom of a PR agency, and why on earth not? Fashion Aid displayed a passion for compassion at a time when charity had hit the media sweet spot.

Each of the eighteen designers was given fifteen minutes for their catwalk presentation; along with about twenty other 'volunteers' (journos,

---

* I happened to be at Lynne Franks' house in West London's Maida Vale one Saturday night towards the end of the Eighties. We were celebrating Guy Fawkes Night, and had just been up to Primrose Hill to look at the fireworks. We then spent most of the rest of the night, and the early hours of Sunday morning, downstairs in Lynne's kitchen, listening to extremely loud reggae with various journalists, fashion designers, architects, photographers, PRs and celebrities, including . . . Well, actually that could get me into a lot of trouble, so I'd better not say. My memory might be playing tricks on me, but as well as vast quantities of alcohol, I'm fairly sure slightly less legal intoxicants were consumed, mainly of the herbal variety. There were around twenty of us, and we were very, very stoned. The air was a fug. Anyway, around eleven o'clock, Lynne's teenage children quietly came in from the cinema, walking down the metal stairs, just as they appear in the basement kitchen in *Ab Fab*. The children took one look at the carnage surrounding their mother, and promptly took themselves off to bed for some Ovaltine, a good book and an early night. They were real-life Saffies.

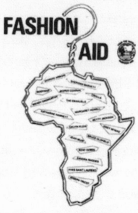

FASHION AID

THE DIRECTORS OF THE GROUCHO CLUB

AND

HMV

INVITE YOU TO A CELEBRATION OF THE FASHION SPECTACULAR OF THE YEAR!

BANGERS AND MASH

11PM

THE GROUCHO CLUB - 45 DEAN ST. SOHO W1

ADMISSION BY
INVITATION ONLY

LYNNE FRANKS P.R.
01. 836 7076.

WINE GENEROUSLY DONATED BY BERKMAN WINE CELLARS AND CORNEY AND BARROW.

One of the many tangential Ethiopian projects immediately resulting from Live Aid was Fashion Aid, a ridiculously glitzy designer fund-raiser that took place at the Royal Albert Hall in London in November 1985. It was daahling: Jasper Conran, Grace Jones, Lynne Franks, Giorgio Armani, Calvin Klein, Katharine Hamnett, Yves Saint Laurent and all.

nightclubs runners, DJs, etc.), I was asked to be in Katharine Hamnett's section, which involved parading down the runway wearing little but a smirk, an orange smock and an MA-1 flying jacket turned inside out. For the life of me I can't recall why, but I remember I was holding a Roman torch of some description. I had also recently had my head shaved, so in hindsight must have looked like a dayglo Buddhist fashion victim. Apart from feeling ridiculous, the only other thing I remember is looking out into the audience and seeing Peter York (who can lay claim to leaving his own mark on the decade by writing not only *Style Wars* but also *The Official Sloane Ranger Handbook* with Ann Barr, two of the most influential books of the early Eighties) slip into his seat. The look (and smile) on his face openly semaphored the following: 'I am so glad I am sitting here in the audience watching you up there rather than the other way round.' I couldn't disagree with him, although obviously the only reason I (and everyone else that night) was up there was because It Was A Good Cause. Just like everything else at the time.

Then there was Ferry Aid's 'Let It Be', the Stock, Aitken & Waterman charity single in support of the 1987 Zeebrugge Ferry disaster, in which 193 people were killed when the Townsend Thoresen ship *Herald of Free Enterprise* capsized (the bow doors had been left open). Some *Sun* readers had been on board, winners of an offer in the paper, and so the paper set up a disaster fund and announced a charity record. It featured Paul McCartney, Kate Bush, Boy George, Frankie Goes to Hollywood, Suzi Quatro, Mark Knopfler, Bonnie Tyler and a host of others stars, on various A, B and C lists. (Stock, Aitken & Waterman would also chart with a newly recorded version of 'Ferry Cross The Mersey' following the Hillsborough disaster in 1989; a few months later they were responsible for Band Aid II, a fairly sorry re-recording of 'Do They Know It's Christmas?' featuring Bananarama, Jason Donovan, Kylie Minogue, Cliff Richard and Wet Wet Wet.)

Whenever a new 'hero' concert was planned – for the purposes of ameliorating equality, raising awareness, or simply fund-raising – some PR would say 'This is going to be bigger than Live Aid'. It was almost as though they had to, as though it were part of the contract. There was even something called Visual Aid at the Royal Academy. According to some, Geldof was lobbied by the press to dress up for the launch as Tony Hancock in *The Rebel*, in a smock and beret, carrying an artist's easel.

Live Aid was influential in other, more fundamental, more pervasive ways too. For a generation of fledgling politicians, it was patently obvious what Live Aid had managed to harness, at least emotionally, and for many it acted as blueprint for the future, or at least one to reference. Tony Blair had watched Live Aid, and it painted for him a picture of what a new Britain could potentially be like under a new kind of government. Here was a Britain that had rejected Michael Foot, was in the process of rejecting Neil Kinnock, and yet was prepared to endorse – nay, enthusiastically pursue – a fund-raising event the like of which had never been seen anywhere in the world. Here was a glimpse of what a new Britain could be, a New Labour Britain perhaps.* Blair never forgot Live Aid (or at least never forgot the effect it had on ordinary people), and it became a memory that would eventually result in his Commission for Africa, as well as the orchestrated pressure on G8 leaders to sign up to African priorities during the summit of 2005.

Blair declared 2005 the 'Year of Africa', and his Commission, co-chaired by Ethiopia's prime minister, Meles Zenawi, pledged to raise $50 billion a year on the international markets, which Blair made the centrepiece of Britain's presidency of the G8. The leaders also agreed to write off $40 billion of debt and pledged to double aid to Africa to $50 billion by 2010 (although these figures have yet to be reached).

'I have said on many occasions that I believe Africa is a scar on the conscience of the world,' he said, 'and I think it is right that we continue to treat this as an absolute priority over the coming years.'

In 2005, Blair's chancellor Gordon Brown pledged to waive bills for staging Live 8, in a move equivalent to writing off £500,000 in VAT. In

---

* On 14 November 1985, Blair asked his first question in the House of Commons regarding Sub-Saharan Africa, asking the then Chancellor of the Exchequer, Ian Stewart, how much British banks received by way of debt and interest repayments from countries in the area. Four days later he asked it again. He would also go on to found the Band Aid cross-party parliamentary committee.

advance of the G8 that year he said he hoped he could secure a 'big decision' that would transform the 'lives of millions' of Africans blighted by poverty and debt. He branded his proposals for Africa a 'modern Marshall Plan', a reference to the US-inspired initiative to rebuild Europe in the wake of World War Two.

'This is not a time for timidity nor a time to fear reaching too high,' Brown said, as he set out his G8 plans to reporters in Edinburgh. The G8 talks were 'our chance to reverse the fortunes of a continent and our opportunity to transform the lives of millions'.

Today we are governed by politicians who define themselves as the Live Aid generation, and British Prime Minister David Cameron – who watched Live Aid on his parents' television in Berkshire while on his gap year – has said that the memory of watching Live Aid, and the way it made him feel, made him realise how important releasing foreign aid is. 'I remember where I was when I watched Live Aid, and it had a huge effect on me,' said Cameron. 'Of course we all liked watching the groups, but it was remarkable to see so many people involved in such a gigantic act of charity. I couldn't believe the way in which it galvanised everyone. Everybody saw it, and if they didn't then they knew they'd missed something. It was all anyone could talk about for weeks afterwards. It was also an unusually apolitical event.'

Unlike many of the other G8 leaders, Cameron pledged to raise domestic aid spending to 0.7 per cent of national income, saying he wouldn't renege on aid promises made at Gleneagles in 2005 by his predecessor. 'Of course it's difficult when we're making difficult decisions at home,' he said. 'But I don't think that 0.7 per cent of our gross national income is too high a price to pay for trying to save lives.' Challenged by the *Daily Mail* about the wisdom of this, he responded, 'If we don't invest in them before they get broken we end up with the terrorism and the crime and the mass migration. If we had put a fraction of what we are spending now in Afghanistan on military equipment into that country as aid and development when it had a chance of making its own future, wouldn't that have been a better decision?

'Most people in this country want Britain to stand for something in the world and be something in the world. What enables us to do that is not just the incredible military hardware we have, not just the incredible bravery of our armed services personnel, not just the brilliance of our Foreign Office and our Civil Service and our soft power. It is also actually the fact that when it comes to the big crises, whether hurricanes or earthquakes or tsunamis or pandemics, that Britain is there with a substantial aid budget to meet and match those problems and keep our promises at the same time.'

I spent a year writing a book with David Cameron not long after he became the leader of the Conservative Party in 2005, and he went out of his way to show that Live Aid was exactly the kind of event that he was fond of emulating, or at least referencing. His former advisor Steve Hilton also talked about Live Aid, as for him it was a way to steer people towards one of their big ideas at the time, the Big Society (the bold if ill-thought-out initiative to empower local people and communities while taking power away from politicians), an idea that while it never took off, initially helped detoxify and reposition the Conservatives as a more compassionate organisation (it remains part of the legislative programme of the Conservative–Liberal Democrat Coalition Agreement, although one suspects that's all it will ever be).

'For years we have been at the forefront of the poverty-fighting agenda,' said Cameron in the *Wall Street Journal*. 'The world's greatest aid agencies – we've got them. Live Aid and Live 8 – we made them. And Britain's leadership on aid is still needed when preventable diseases like malaria, pneumonia and diarrhoea kill almost 7 million children every year. It is still needed when we face an acute hunger crisis, compounded by rising food prices, that leaves 165 million children in the world without the nutrition to grow to their full potential.'

It is extraordinary to think how different a place Britain is from what it was in 1985. To have a Conservative government espouse the virtues of foreign aid, over and above other G8 countries, including the US, remains anathema to many backbench Tories. Yet aid – particularly aid to Africa – has become such an intrinsic part of foreign policy (Blair's foreign policy) that it would be impossible to dismantle the agreements. In fact in some respects something as emotive as the recalibration of the NHS or the police force is probably an easier ask.

Geldof is very careful to say that the Eighties would have been no different had Live Aid not happened – he has been punched too often by hubris – yet he knows this isn't true.

'I think politically it had a huge effect, to the point now that all parties agree with that agenda that was put forward that day. Despite our powerless economic circumstances, this country magnificently will live up to its political commitment, which only became tangible as a political commitment a few years after as 0.7 per cent of the national economy. It's an immense achievement and has bought this country great political credibility.

'It had an effect. Certainly. And you can harness that and point it to a political end, so that so many generations were affected. David Cameron and George Osborne watched it. Blair and Brown were deeply affected by it, politically. They've written about it. They were trying to work out how to sell Labour, as all the old Labour ideas were so old hat. As Live Aid ramped up, I think they watched it rather like how people watched the Obama campaign. Blair immediately got the social emotive effect and Brown was trying to work out how to make it happen. I've talked to both of them about this and they saw this as being the real Britain that they wanted to speak to. So when Blair came to power, it was a shoo-in for me to go and talk to him as prime minister.'

Like Danny Boyle's Olympics opening ceremony, Live Aid was a corrective, and in the same way that using Johnny Rotten as an icon of Great British culture as an antidote to all the pomp and majesty that usually surrounds these events, so Live Aid had been a way to correct a world that was in danger of veering too much to the right. Both Live Aid and the 2012 Olympics were great unifiers, events that made being British feel very correct. Both events evoked a massive emotional outpouring and a sense of togetherness that felt perfectly appropriate.

Looking at Live Aid, the Tories saw individualism, the individual deciding to do things in a political way. The liberals saw community and activism, so everyone could take and pick and choose whatever they wanted from it. 'I was on the cover of *Marxism Today*, and I was on the cover of the *Spectator*,' said Geldof. 'Live Aid could be all things to all people.'

Twenty years after Live Aid, Geldof did what he had sworn never to do, which was try and repeat the exercise, in the form of Live 8, the even more ambitious, although perhaps less successful, series of concerts he organised in the summer of 2005. However, Live 8 actually had its roots in another humanitarian project, Jubilee 2000, this one spearheaded by Bono. This initiative was officially launched at the 1999 Brit Awards, which, as usual, was a great night for autograph hounds. For the second year running the Brits — the biggest event in the pop calendar — were held at the London Arena, an aerodrome-sized barn only a skip away from the Millennium Dome. Collected together were the record industry's great and good. David Bowie (complete with new David Beckham-style hair), Stevie Wonder, Texas's Sharleen Spiteri, Goldie, girl group All Saints, plus all the important industry executives and a smattering of Labour politicians Mo Mowlam, Chris Smith and Paul Boateng included. Although the public was, as usual, penned in the back, the Sony Music table was inundated with visitors — music-biz types seeking the autograph of a star guest, Ross Kemp, who played the monosyllabic brute Grant Mitchell in BBC1's soap *EastEnders*.

The real star of the evening was Muhammad Ali, drafted in as a PR initiative by Bono to speak on behalf of Jubilee 2000, the pop humanitarian cause *du jour*. Bono's impassioned speech was certainly heartfelt, although a lot of the audience were more interested in catching a glimpse of the boxing legend in the flesh, a broken man for sure, suffering terribly from Parkinson's disease, but a legend all the same.

Ali had been jetted in by PolyGram, U2's record label, at Bono's request, to create awareness of the charity, which was itself trying to create awareness of the scale of Third World debt. A coalition of ninety organisations in Britain, including Oxfam, Friends of the Earth, Christian Aid, Comic Relief and the TUC, the movement had sister organisations in fifty other countries. Through this kind of publicity they were aiming to celebrate the millennium by persuading world leaders to cancel the unpayable debts of some of the world's poorest countries. According to the United Nations, if these debts were cancelled the lives of 7 million children could be saved each year in Africa alone.

Yet again, the pop industry was on a mission to save the world. Encouraged by Bono, Jubilee 2000 encouraged musicians to put a slogan – 'Drop the Debt' – on to CD packaging and to display lobbying material at concerts. Although unlike Live Aid, Jubilee 2000 was greeted with less than enthusiastic noises by the record companies. The industry saw Band Aid not only as an original solution to a genuine problem, but also as a great way to expose artists to a worldwide audience. The consensus on Jubilee 2000 seemed to be that it was something of a waste of time. The feeling among many music-business bigwigs was that John Kennedy, who was then the chairman and chief executive of Universal Music UK (the parent company that owned PolyGram) had been railroaded into giving the scheme his support lest he risk offending U2, his biggest act.

That year the Brit Awards were broadcast by the ITV network, which was not exactly jumping up and down at the prospect of giving up two minutes of valuable airtime to a political soliloquy, during which millions of viewers could potentially switch channels. Claudia Rosencrantz, then the network's controller of entertainment, even wrote a letter to Guy Freeman, who was directing the Brits for Malcolm Gerrie's Initial production company, asking him to make sure the segment was worthy of inclusion.

Although some thought Ali's appearance was a mite unnecessary and possibly exploitative, the fact that he was there at all made the programme worth watching: he was still an inspirational figure and his reception far exceeded that of any other guest, including the main attraction, the Eurythmics, who won an award for their outstanding contribution to the industry. Ali's performance was memorable, as was Bono's, but the industry seemed to doubt that the campaign had 'legs'. PolyGram was being bullish in its support, as were people such as Paul Conroy, then president of Virgin Records and head of the Brits committee, yet almost none of the dozen or so record company executives were prepared to go on record expressing their support. Some, like EMI, offered a guarded, corporate response –

'EMI supports this in principle and we're writing to all our artists to give them the opportunity to participate,' said a company spokeswoman – but most were willing to be quoted only off the record.

'The campaign has come out of the blue for a lot of people in the business,' said Ajax Scott, editor of *Music Week*, the industry's bible. 'For it to mean anything the organisation behind it will really have to put some effort into making it work. It's not the kind of thing that can be allowed to fizzle, it needs constant attention. Which is why there might be some resistance.'

Perhaps they felt that this particular humanitarian exercise was doomed to failure. There was a sense that although the case for radical action against debt seemed compelling, the reality of the situation was somewhat cloudier than the picture painted by Jubilee 2000. So many African countries had volatile or discredited leadership that acts like this were causing concern at governmental levels as well as record company ones. If countries such as Nigeria and Zimbabwe were suddenly relieved of their debt burden – reasoned one Whitehall mandarin – there was no guarantee that any more money would find its way into the hands of its citizens, while a debt write-off for Sudan, for instance, could have actually helped to fund its escalating civil war. It was thought that unless the deals were heavily encumbered by conditional guarantees, such generosity could be little more than meaningless.

To their credit, Jubilee 2000's response addressed these concerns. It said it wanted to see 'decisions about spending priorities in developing countries made in partnership with people represented by civil society and elected representatives of people's groups. These groups can work to monitor governments and officials and expose corruption and ensure that funds diverted from debt repayment are spent effectively on improving health care and education. This process will open up Third World governments and help foster democracy and respect for human rights.'

Enthusiasm for the project was a little more positive by 2005. Like Live Aid, Live 8 was also similarly born out of a mounting sense of desperation. Having revisited Ethiopia, Geldof found the people still starving. 'That really did my head in and it made me understand that we must deal with the structures of poverty and not just the symptoms, like AIDS, corruption and hunger,' he told *Sunday Times* and *GQ* journalist Robert Sandall. So he pestered Tony Blair to produce a report, *The Commission for Africa*, which was then distributed to all the G8 leaders, and promptly ignored. 'I'd spent a fucking year persuading the PM to put his neck on the line and there's this report gathering dust! Fuck off! That's why I did Live 8. It was time to bring on the boys and girls with guitars. It was a big ask, but geezers had to be told.'

The rest is, of course, more history. In one week in July in 2005, over a thousand artists in nine cities played concerts drawing attention to the cause, encouraging the cancellation of debt and an increase in aid. Geldof told Sandall that his most treasured memory happened in Edinburgh after he and Bono ('he feels like my little brother') met Richard Branson. Branson had just arrived at the G8 with a plane full of American children seeking to remind George Bush that there was a world beyond the White House lawn. 'It took Geldof back to the last time the three of them had been together, in a Dublin basement bar thirty years earlier. "There was me on stage with the Rats, Bono in the audience and Richard was there trying to sign us. And here we all were again. And I just thought, this is weird . . ."'

Held on 2 July that year, almost twenty years to the day since Live Aid, Live 8 was designed to draw attention to the G8 conference and summit being held at the Gleneagles Hotel in Scotland four days later.

'With the UK about to begin a six-month stint as president of the European Union, as well as being chair of the upcoming G8 summit of world leaders in Gleneagles, it seemed there was a unique opportunity to make this G8 the one that changes everything,' said Bono. 'Tony Blair and Gordon Brown had taken these issues very seriously and they were in charge of the agenda.'

There was a real sense of momentum surrounding the build-up to the G8, with campaigners all over the world gearing up for it. The scriptwriter and film-maker Richard Curtis had joined forces with various NGOs and coined the phrase 'Make Poverty History'.

But as the summit approached, Bono knew they needed to create a sense of occasion if they were to have any hope of achieving anything. What they really needed was a concert, a big one. Bob Geldof had continued to say that there wouldn't be a twentieth anniversary of Live Aid, but Bono kept haranguing him to change his mind. He was relentless, and eventually wore Geldof down. Six weeks before the G8, he had finally relented, having come up with the idea of using 'Live 8' (as he had christened it) as a global lobbying event, with television events in each of the G8 countries, to try and force the G8 members to properly consider writing down African debt.

The concert in London's Hyde Park was the main event, although there were a string of other concerts taking place in the G8 states as well as in South Africa. Geldof again spearheaded the concert, which was organised in order to encourage the members of the G8 summit to reduce Third World debt substantially, and to support the aims of the UK's Make Poverty History campaign and the Global Call for Action Against Poverty. And to a certain extent, it worked, as on 7 July, the G8 leaders – led in this case by Tony Blair – pledged to double 2004 levels of aid to poor nations from $25 billion to $50 billion by the year 2010, with at least half of the money going to Africa.

'There is no doubt in my mind that the agreements of Gleneagles are two of the four legs upon which African growth has been built,' Geldof said later. 'It was followed by massive Chinese investment and the unprecedented effect of connectivity as the largest mobile phone market in the world took off.'

This investment helped transform health and education all over the continent, helping send 46 million children to school, in a part of the world where half the population is still under the age of eighteen. In the four years to 2009, Ethiopia experienced higher growth than China, while seven of the fastest-growing economies in the world are African, and 70 per cent of Africans live in countries that have enjoyed an average growth of more than 4 per cent since 2002. At Live Aid, Geldof was at pains to point out that a pound from Halifax or Hull could help people in Harare, directly, and it worked. 'That relationship [gave] people a tangible connection,' he said. He knows that he was partly responsible for the 'toxic' image of Africa, forever preserved in aspic, of a continent at war with itself, that needed investment and aid or else it would not survive. 'But it was necessary at the time.'

Wanting to close the circle, and to make up for his embarrassment at Live Aid, Geldof approached Paul McCartney, although the response was the same as last time. McCartney prevaricated before tentatively saying yes. 'The thing is, you get an offer you can't refuse, really,' McCartney said. 'It's Geldof, number one, so that's one of the reasons it's hard to refuse. He just rang up and explained the idea, which attracted me. Then he said, "We'd like you to open with U2, singing 'It was twenty years ago today.'" Sold! Kerching! You don't want to get clever – just do a few hits and pull "Helter Skelter" out of the bag as a surprise. But yeah, a lot of people came up to me and said, "*You* shouldn't have been the guy to do that. There's a lot of younger bands who should have been doing that."'

McCartney vetoed the idea of U2 and him wearing Sgt Pepper suits, though. 'Bono had a jacket ready which was a sort of modern, darkish take on the Pepper costumes, but I said, "We're going to have live horns, what about them wearing the costumes?" The lyrics work: "Lemme introduce to you/The band you've known for all these years/Sgt Pepper's Lonely Hearts Club Band!" Enter band. So we've done the nod to the era and the costume, and U2 can do the rest of their set without a funny outfit. Bono said, "Yeah, I hear you," and that was the way it went.'

They had one rehearsal the day before, to which McCartney brought his own group, just in case U2 didn't know how to play the song. But they knew it. The original idea was to try and replicate the album cover with real people – Bill Gates, Steve Jobs, Nelson Mandela, Madonna, Robbie Williams, etc. – but this was scaled right back to a video element.

No one knew the brass parts, not even McCartney, so George Martin was tracked down in Canada, and was dispatched to a record store to buy the CD. He wrote down the parts and then faxed them over just in time for the rehearsal.

Harvey Goldsmith said they had the same problem with Live 8 as they did with Live Aid in terms of finding big black acts that were interested or available to play. 'I've had a lot of experience putting together shows like this, especially with all the Prince's Trust events, and it never gets any easier, as you're always juggling. But we were disappointed that it wasn't easier to get some of the acts we wanted. All the trustees met in July the year before and discussed what we might be able to do to celebrate the event, as there was bound to be pressure from broadcasters who would want to repeat Live Aid in some form. We didn't want to do another show, unless of course the pressure came from outside, from the bands. Then the whole G8 thing came together and then we started getting calls from the likes of Paul McCartney, Elton and U2. We had a dozen of the biggest acts in the world that wanted to do it, and so we went for it.

'U2, Paul McCartney, and all these bands were ringing Bob up, ringing me up, yelling at me and saying, "What are you doing? You've got to do something!" It got to the point where there were literally twelve of the top acts [in the world] saying you've got to do a concert. Then Bob came into the office and I said, "This is insanity, we have to do it."'

'Such a ludicrous Islington argument,' Geldof said in response to the criticisms about the lack of black or African artists on the bill. 'Young Africans want to see Eminem and 50 Cent. Not even having Mandela on stage there made a difference.'

For some it was a disappointment, 'I thought it was a bit of an anticlimax, to be honest,' said Elton John. 'The thought behind it was fantastic, but Hyde Park is a charisma-free zone. There was no sense of occasion and from a musical point of view, I didn't think there were too many highlights.' His own performance wasn't his best, and while it may have looked good on paper – a duet with Babyshambles singer Pete Doherty on the T. Rex song 'Children Of The Revolution', the reality was rather more shambolic. One of Elton's band said that before they went on, he got stoned just by standing next to Doherty.

Also appearing at Live 8 was Birhan Woldu, who became one of the world's most recognisable faces when her skeletal image was included in the CBC film that accompanied the Cars' 'Drive' was shown at Wembley twenty years earlier. When she walked out on stage at Hyde Park, the billions watching hadn't seen an image of her since 1985.

I spent a lot of the day backstage, milling among the performers and the guests, and soaking up the air of expectation. This was a sequel and everyone knew it, and while theoretically the content looked better than Live Aid – Paul McCartney performing with U2, Robbie Williams, Madonna, an historic once-in-a-lifetime performance by Pink Floyd – there was a somewhat inevitable sense of anticlimax. The day had already been hampered by the weather – it was overcast – although everyone was willing it to be more memorable than it eventually turned out to be. Everyone was backstage at some point during the day, although for some reason the following images have stuck in my mind: David and Victoria Beckham sitting like celebrity royalty, receiving people (including me) in one of the hospitality tents; Richard Curtis, who helped organise the day, looking supremely flustered; and Mariah Carey's phalanx of bodyguards, who appeared to accompany her everywhere (although I think she was allowed to go to the mobile loos by herself).*

We left halfway through Pink Floyd's performance to pick up our kids, who had been left with friends for the day, but as we live just a couple of hundred yards north of Hyde Park, we spent the rest of their set watching it on TV and listening to the strains of 'Wish You Were Here' pouring through our open windows.

Live 8 was such a huge event, which involved such a huge amount of work, that when it was all over, Geldof collapsed, just like he'd done on 13 July, twenty years earlier. 'I felt weird and dislocated after Gleneagles. My mate texted me while I was there: "Be careful of the void." I watched the choppers overhead going "foo-foo-foo" as Putin took off and then I just walked away into a small copse and blubbed. Not sobs, just tears. Because it was over, finally.'

Geldof said that in some respects there was no great correlation between Live Aid and Live 8. 'Put it in purely financial terms. Live Aid: $150 million. Live 8: $50 billion, per annum. But Live Aid had the "give me

---

* Carey was also the subject of an often-told apocryphal story concerning her ablutions. A roadie was seen leaving one of the Portaloos, and as he passed a group of PRs, said, in rather too loud a voice, 'I'd give that half an hour if I were you.' Two minutes later, Mariah Carey climbed into the same Portaloo, eliciting a huge round of applause when she exited a few minutes later.

your fuckin' money" moment. And Bowie introducing the famine film. Live 8 though . . . people never really got their head around the fact that all I needed was for you to be either there, or on the street, or watching it on TV. Just so I could say to the world's leaders, "There they are, they're watching you, answer to them." Now [Tony] Blair and [Gordon] Brown watched Live Aid, they say it influenced their whole political thing. Clinton says he saw it. Bush even says he saw a couple of hours . . . [pause] course he didn't. But these were Live Aid babies. And numbers are political. A million kids on the streets is political.'

It had been a great day, but it wasn't Live Aid. Nothing would be. Nothing could be. Live Aid was destined never to be repeated, as it was completely unrepeatable.

'It would cost a lot more to do Live Aid today,' said Harvey Goldsmith. 'It would be so much harder to do today, largely because of the politics between the groups. Everyone left it up to me to do the running order, principally because of the changeover times. But it would be much harder now. The media would be different, more intrusive. It was fine then because it was brand new and everyone kind of went, "You know what? It's kind of a cool idea, let's do it." Today it's all about money, everything today is about money. It has a whole different connotation to it. Not to say that people won't do it but it's certainly more difficult to do shows like this. The difficulty we have today ironically enough is that there isn't a big enough generation of new acts that have global consequence. Look at the big acts today and they're the same names from five years ago. There are no big new acts.

'Having said that, the music industry is still first in the queue when it comes to events such as this. Movie people get it, but not really, and the same with TV people, but people in the music industry are always there first. They still jump in immediately and offer their help and do it. And it's to their absolute credit that they can do that. Quite unusual. So Live Aid changed a lot of things. Most for the good. I always say it was the end of creativity because when the media took over, they started deciding which acts they would go for and which they wouldn't, which pushed a lot of people to the margins. The media started being responsible for making stars.'

Live Aid changed the way large-scale stadium events were staged, changed the way money was raised, changed the way TV treated music, changed the way the media treated rock stars, and in a way kick-started the era of celebrity culture, and brought the world a little closer together, with the wealthy helping the poor. Of course, the money may not have always got where it was meant to, but it opened up channels of communication, channels of aid, and would result in Western governments debating the nature of Third World debt.

Live Aid did wonders for the concert business.

'Live music itself received the most extraordinary boost from this event, because the area circuit and the stadium circuit were still relatively new,' said Mark Ellen. 'It hadn't quite found its speed and it was still a difficult experience; you've got to find a babysitter and you've got to find a car park, and it's Wembley Arena and it wasn't built for rock music and it's not physically very satisfying, etc. There were lots of reasons why you might not want to go. But Live Aid looked great on television, and I think that a lot of people who had thought that their relationship with rock music might be over changed their minds that day.'

'After Live Aid, everyone wanted to play stadiums, and it certainly gave the stadium business a lift,' said Harvey Goldsmith. 'We also proved that you could have a real global TV event. We got 160 countries to buy into the global jukebox idea, and 90 per cent of them showed the whole thing. None of them had ever done that before. We also changed the way people gave money. We changed the way event-type shows could work. We brought the world closer together by having three shows – not two, because everyone always forgets it started in Australia. And over quite a short period we actually changed the way the money was used and granted on an international level across the board.

'The one thing that I personally failed to do was create a database which all of the agencies would subscribe to and feed into, but that didn't work out. So it wasn't replicated. With all of the will in the world, I could not get the agencies to do it. They just refused to do it. I thought if ever there was a legacy that we could create, having a global database with that information would absolutely make life a lot easier for everybody. I couldn't get it through, because they are all businesses that compete with each other.'

The Band Aid trust still exists, with five of the original six trustees (CBS and PolyGram boss Maurice Oberstein died in 2001), and still spends around £1 million pounds a year, from what it receives in donations. The trust doesn't advertise, or lobby, and while most people think it's a dormant organisation, it still involves itself in African projects (schools, hospices, etc.). Civil war and weather patterns continue to be an issue in Sahel, and this is where Band Aid still focuses its efforts.

'We part fund, put pressure on governments, get competitive quotes, and funnel money,' said Harvey Goldsmith. 'Our modus operandi is that we insist that the local population operate actively and continue running whatever the activity is. That it isn't one of the NGOs who goes in there, puts it all in, shows them how to do it and then leaves them high and dry without help, unfortunately a lot of which happens. And that continues to this day. And we're quite rigid on how we invest and what we go into. We look for projects where they can then evolve, where villages can work with other villages to develop. We try very hard to get the best value and more importantly best practice. We know that Western values in relation to food, and to some extent medicine, which work here often don't work there. So we've learnt the structure of how. We work through all of the agencies that work in the area because we don't have any full-time employees. We never set ourselves up to be a competitive NGO. All we ever wanted to do was collect the money, give it out the best way possible and as fast as we could. That was it, goodbye. But then money kept coming in so we had to continue with it.'

As for Geldof – a man who, after Live Aid, was such an acceptable mainstream celebrity that he was asked to turn on the Oxford Street Christmas lights – when asked at the end of the decade whether he had any regrets, he said, 'The obvious thing is that I wish I'd never had to do Live Aid. I'm a bit frightened that people will only remember a pop concert, and not the fact that it was to do with millions upon millions of people who were potentially going to die, and because of a pop concert some of them were kept alive. And starvation is still rampant, for no good reason that I can see, so there's a deep regret about that.

'There are personal regrets. I wish that the break-up of the band had been friendlier. But I can't have many regrets, because I've been to almost everywhere in the world in this period, seen and done things that I guess most people will never get to see or do.

'But ultimately I will probably remember the Eighties for having my two daughters. That's what I'll remember and enjoy most.'

In 2012 Geldof said that he was convinced he could have enjoyed a solo career on the scale of Sting and Paul Weller if his commitment to fund-raising hadn't got in the way. He told the *Evening Standard* that it would have been 'criminally irresponsible' of him not to hold the events, but he does believe it totally damaged his music career. The activism just got in the way: 'It's completely damaged my ability to do the thing I love. If it hadn't happened I think I would have been able to make the transition from the Boomtown Rats to a solo thing.' As Kevin Jackson said in the summer of 1990, in an article I'd commissioned for *Arena* to mark the release of Geldof's second solo album, *The Vegetarians Of Love*, 'Just as T. E. Lawrence could never live down his Arabian myth, so Geldof of Africa can never again hope to be seen as just another muse, even though there are signs that he might enjoy that less complicated status.'

Such huge events as Live Aid have become almost commonplace these days. As a *Daily Telegraph* critic, who was twenty-four when he attended Wembley, wrote on the twenty-fifth anniversary of the show, 'Between charity shows and festivals, reunion tours and televised concerts, it almost feels like anyone can see every band that ever existed (and press the red button for alternative angles).'

The excitement and amazement that a generation felt on seeing so many great acts perform on the same stage couldn't be replicated nowadays, and, as the *Telegraph* critic noted, it's unlikely that a contemporary twenty-four-year-old fan would feel quite so impressed. Compassion had never been seen or articulated on such a scale, donors never mobilised in such a way. Live Aid is remembered with such warmth, as it was such a magical event. Nothing like it had been attempted before, and while there would be many copycat events over the years, each was subject to the law of diminishing returns. Whenever there was a natural disaster, a relevant anniversary, a blighted minority or a mass charity drive, you'd only have to blink and there would be a random collection of A+, B+ and C- pop stars, followed by an even more random selection of TV soap stars, and ageing sports stars, eager to flaunt their craft and sing their little hearts out.

'Live Aid affected the music industry in many ways,' said Goldsmith. 'I think overall it generated a real feel-good factor and everybody felt that they had done something special. They had helped to create something that was different, that was special. I think the entire industry realised that this was quite unique. There was a glow and then the stars realised, as I had been saying for a long time, that they could use their power as heroes, and do exactly what they do and help other people. If we were to try and put Live Aid on today it would not only cost a lot more, there would be a lot more politics. The politics of the media and TV are really different today too.'

The press also changed.

'Before the event there wasn't that much fuss in the press, because at the time there wasn't much music in national papers,' said Goldsmith. 'In the States you had *Rolling Stone*, *Billboard* and *Cashbox*, and in the UK you had the music weeklies, but not much else. Newspapers never believed that music would sell papers. But the coming together of Live Aid and its effect, its global effect, suddenly the papers started giving space to music, and to celebrity in general. As a result of Live Aid, the papers started to give space to pop because they realised that actually there was a massive amount of people who were interested in it, and that pop stars and celebrities could sell papers. That's why they made such a thing out of it.'

Boy George was the main pivot that made papers realise that they could use various characters from pop music to re-commercialise their paper, either through employing a regular pop-music critic or gossipy pieces of music news which might make headline, front-page news.

'One of the negatives of the Live Aid legacy was the fact that the press took over after that,' said Goldsmith. 'To some extent they destroyed music and took it in a different direction. And that's why you've got a pop culture and the whole forced celebrity that really dominates today. That's why you've got Beyoncé and Cheryl Cole all over the front pages of the papers. Because of Live Aid. As for those hundreds of alternative bands, right underneath the underbelly, well, they don't really get a look-in unless they're off the wall or they get very lucky.'

One morning at the end of November 2012, Bob Geldof and I sat in the bar of the Chelsea Arts Club in London, sipping soft drinks and reminiscing about the biggest day in his life. He gets asked about it a lot – too much, in fact – and I could tell that much of the stuff he was dredging up had been dredged up before. But the day is too defining for him to treat it with disrespect for too long, and after ten minutes or so he was off, breaking each question down into bullet points, and answering with enthusiastic precision. Verbally, he wandered here, there and everywhere, and just when his ramblings got to a point when I thought I needed to correct him, and steer him back on course, he'd hold his hand up to stop me interrupting, and then veer back in the most enlightening and surprising way. Geldof not only knows how important Live Aid was, he knows how important it is now.

'Honestly, I don't have one,' he said, when we were putting on our coats and hats, and I asked him if he had one abiding image of the day. 'That's the truth. I could say to you it's when the Rats were on stage and I suddenly stopped and looked around, but I don't really think about that as Live Aid. That was a rock 'n' roll personal moment. The thing that I really remember was the look on all these very famous faces backstage, as there was absolutely a sense of exhilaration. When you do a festival, in general you tend to fuck off straight away. You think to yourself, I'd really like to see so and so, but then you think: fuck me, they're on in three hours and I've got to hang around, and anyway I've got to get out of my dressing room because it's needed for someone else. So you leave. But at Live Aid nearly everyone hung around. That's why, at the end of Live Aid, everyone's on fucking stage. They could have fucked off, but they're all there. That's odd. Nobody, I think, thought about that. There's no question that they wanted to be there, as when they came off their peers were clapping, and just going, "Great." It was a bit like a football match, in that respect, but is that my abiding image? My other big memory is the cock-up of trying to rehearse "Do They Know It's Christmas?", which most of them had never fucking heard, never mind [knowing] the words. That was farce, but again it's not my abiding image.

'Anything else? Well, Bowie massaged my back because I was in bits. That's a great personal moment, because he's a great personal fucking hero of mine, and always has been. How many people can say that David Bowie massaged their back and told you to be still and all that? Not bad. Paul McCartney and Pete Townshend hugely embarrassingly lifting me up. I was fucking mortified, and in the picture you can see me trying to get down, but actually in retrospect, to have that happen to you by the people who were entirely [responsible for] why you got into this business in the first place is pretty cool, personally speaking.

'But an abiding image? Well, the thing I remember more than anything is the feeling of fear that came through me again. I was just afraid the whole time, that's the truth of it. I thought I had bitten off more than I could chew and was going to get killed for it. It was going to be so bad that the Rats would never recover from it. I was going to fuck it up. It was going to be a grotesque failure. I'd say even more stupid things than I normally say. It wouldn't work at all. No one would give any money.

'Those were the things going through my mind. So there were three failures in my mind, personal, national, but much more importantly, failure on behalf of those in whose name we were doing the whole fucking thing in the first place. You know, it just wouldn't work and no one would bother: "Fuck off, it's a lovely day, we're off, we're going to the pub," or whatever. That was essentially it, the fear that it would all fuck up from start to finish. As we know, it was the very opposite, but that was nothing to do with me. It just was meant to be.'

13 July 1985 was one of the most extraordinary days in history, a day that by rights should never really have happened. But happen it did, changing

and reshaping the nature of our culture in the process. The Eighties are still remembered as the decade of glitz, the decade when the government and the private sector pulled up the ladder of society behind them, ignoring everyone below. It is a defining image, and one that sticks. However, Live Aid is testament to the fact that the Eighties were also full of compassion, and were a decade in which philanthropy entered a new, personal era. An era when people were quickly getting used to taking control of their own lives, and enjoying the emancipation that came with it. And what better way to enjoy your emancipation than by helping other people.

The Eighties are often characterised as being the decade of greed, the decade of the yuppie and the supremacy of Wall Street. But even if you were an eighteen-year-old gorblimey broker, the kind who wanted a big car and a bigger suit, you were not oblivious to compassion. For many, the Eighties were a decade characterised by overwhelming kindness and generosity.

Live Aid was the day of days, a weird anomaly of a day that set in motion a sequence of events that had such a huge effect on our lives that sometimes those effects appear incidental, often imperceptible. It remains one of the most extraordinary days in post-war history, the first cultural event that attempted to involve the whole world, or at least those parts of the world which had the ability to help those parts that couldn't help themselves. There are many defining days of the Eighties, flash points that pop up in every major conflict, from the Brixton riots to the miners' or print union strikes, from the Falklands to the arms race, from the fall of the Berlin Wall to the 1986 Libyan crisis. The entertainment world witnessed the coronation of Michael Jackson, the ascendancy of Madonna, and the global reach of Bruce Springsteen. It also ingested a lot of dodgy synth groups who tried to take over the world via MTV.

But if there is one day that lingers, one day that occurs to us whenever we think of the Eighties, it is bound to be Live Aid. Honestly, how could it not be?

Live Aid influenced such wide-reaching changes, and while it may have been a generational shift that moved pop into mainstream culture, the constituent parts of the concert changed the way we interpreted everyone from the Sex Pistols to the Spice Girls. You only have to look at the opening and closing ceremonies of the 2012 London Olympics to see how much has changed in the thirty years since Live Aid. Who would have thought that the Olympics would have celebrated Madness, Blur, the Kinks, Arctic Monkeys, Queen, Pink Floyd, George Michael, Dizzee Rascal, Tinie Tempah and Mike Oldfield's *Tubular Bells*? By 2012, popular culture had become mainstream culture, whether anyone liked it or not, while pageantry and pomp had been banished to the museums. Who would have thought that a bunch of Camden Town skinheads would have been performing at the Queen's official Jubilee concert? Who would have thought that London would have willingly celebrated mods, punks and cocaine-snorting supermodels? What Live Aid did was tell the world how great Britain is at pop, something that by 2012 was taken for granted.

Honestly, what were the poor old Brazilians going to do in four years' time – roll out a series of Astrud Gilberto tribute acts?

Seriously, what on earth were they going to do?

WHERE ARE THEY NOW?

Who could have dreamed in 1965 that the alternative society would eventually multiply to such extraordinary proportions that it becomes our mainstream

BILL GRAHAM

The Band of the Coldstream Guards

Formed in 1785, they are one of the oldest and best-known bands in the British Army, and still provide the music for the Changing of the Guard, the Festival of Remembrance, the Trooping of the Colour and Beating the Retreat. They increasingly travel the world on commercial tours, flying the flag, and selling good old British pageantry. Their 2011 album *Pride Of The Nation* featured 'Land Of Hope And Glory', 'Jerusalem', 'The British Grenadiers', 'Abide With Me' and more.

Status Quo

Through the refracted light of a thirty-year distance, Status Quo seem an almost quaint proposition. Like many bands who don't have hits any more (most of them), they still tour, although the band bears almost no resemblance to the one formed in London in 1967. The only original members are Francis Rossi and Rick Parfitt, and on stage they work their way through their back catalogue like two denim-clad cab drivers, albeit denim-clad cab drivers who have an almost royal glow; Status Quo are such a national institution that they have become as synonymous with Britain as Marmite, Boris Johnson or J. K. Rowling. 'Quo is never going to be the biggest band in the world,' Parfitt conceded in 1999, perhaps a little unnecessarily, 'but the level of success we've had is enough to fulfil everything that I could have wanted. I don't think we were cut out to be a U2 or a Rolling Stones. We're Quo. We are what we are.'

The Style Council

Weller would disband the Style Council and launch his solo career at the start of the Nineties. Things started well enough, with three or four albums that reinforced his rock credentials, and when Britpop reared its untucked shirt, he was anointed the Modfather, the Sta-Prest guvnor – older than Oasis's Gallagher brothers, younger than Macca, and capable of being more opinionated than all of them put together. Soon he would turn average (mod the plod), overburdened by expectation and encumbered by belligerence, a grumpy old punk in danger of turning into a generic pub-rocker. It all came good in the end, though, and in the last ten years he has re-established himself as not just a great songwriter, but also someone for whom experimentation is still an acceptable form of expression. Any retrospective is prismatic, yet Weller's is incontrovertible: in the Jam he reinvented social realism for the punk mob; in the Style Council he used his fame to subvert Eighties idealism; with his solo career he would go on to become someone for whom adulation was institutionalised. He is still a maze of contradictions – on the one hand he can write songs that display such sensitivity that you're almost not sure it's Weller singing ('Devotion', a song he wrote for a film about Manchester United's famous 'Busby Babes' and the 1958 plane crash in Munich that claimed eight of their lives, is as good as any John Sebastian song, a song as good as Paul McCartney's 'Distractions'), yet he refused to accept that the reason David Cameron liked 'Eton Rifles' so much was simply because he responded to its youthful rebellion. Weller's grace notes are not easy to spot, especially if you're only exposed to the gruff persona he exaggerates for interviews. In person, as in song, he is always trying to disguise his sensitive side, always wary of a sweet melody or a kind word. It's one of the reasons we compare him to Van Morrison, the curmudgeon's curmudgeon. It's perhaps this adolescent nature of his that makes him so particular, although it doesn't make him any easier to appreciate. Paul Weller is as likely to re-form his second band as he is his first, and in commercial terms there would be little mileage in the idea anyway. While it's quite possible that a reconfigured Jam could fill any O2 you care to mention for a week or two, the thought of the Style Council doing the same is an unlikely one (there are probably as many people out there who would want to pay good money to pay Mick Talbot to perform as would do the same for Andrew Ridgeley). The Style Council's records are surprisingly robust, though; many of them still sound like summer. In 2007 Weller's former friend Paolo Hewitt wrote an aggressively unauthorised biography of him, calling the songwriter boorish, violent, selfish and bullying. 'He had a brooding presence which fills the room to such an uncomfortable level that people are forced into silence.'

Bob Geldof

Bob Geldof says he is enjoying his sixties, although he says his fifties were pretty good fun too. 'I wasn't going to do anything like most people, at that age, now was I? But I survived. I still have hair. Still thin-ish, got some wedge. Not bad. When I was sixty I decided to have a big party. Coming into my sixties was different because, without question, it's the beginning of age. It's the long slide down, or the short slide, whatever may happen. I decided I'd kick it off anyway, so I had a big one again, and it was great fun. But they are the best decades, simply because when you're twenty-one, you get to see the receptionist, when you're sixty-one you get to see the CEO.' If you're Bob Geldof. 'I think anyway. You've got a track and you're talking to your generation and you've got something to say, and an idea, you'll get a hearing. By that time anyway, you've been through the vital wars, and your children, in theory, should have grown up. You'll have done the best you can in that area and they're on their way; not much you can do. You've done the career, as much as is possible for you. Hopefully you've got a bit of wedge and you're not too scared of what's coming down the track. If you survive the emotional wars, then you're in for a smooth glide. It gets better, I think. For all of those reasons, it just turned out to be good. In my fifties I was still playing music. I thought I was playing better music than I ever had. The last two records both were done in my fifties: nominated, won lots of awards, best reviews I ever had. Playing them was a pleasure, the band that I play with – forgive me – are just superb. They got a great review recently. Toronto was: "The best organic band we have seen since The Band"; given that they're a Canadian band, that's good.' His songs are still playlisted by FM radio, and occasionally turn up on TV in things such as *House* or *The West Wing*. 'Yes, you're right, when you get to a certain level in society, then more doors open to you and you can engage in what would seem to be ridiculous business ideas, or political ideas. For all those reasons, it's more satisfying than previous decades. Mortality doesn't beckon any more than it did in the past. Now you're in the realm of people getting ill, your friends retiring, your generation moving out of power, age, like the loss of beauty in women, makes them invisible. All that. I'm not sure what my audience expects from me now. When a poster goes up and it says, "Tonight: Bob Geldof", I'm sure people think, "Doing what?" It's not surprising that I'll be doing something, but people aren't exactly sure what it is I'll be doing. The records are still played on the radio, and I've got a fairly decent crowd around the world who pitch up, which is amazing. I started this forty years ago, almost. Who'd have fucking thought? I never thought about being in a band, and forty years later I'm still in one. Having said that, it's the only thing that interests me. I know that sounds crap and pathetic, without any question music is the thing I get more pleasure out of. I can do other shit, but that's a function. It's a facility. I love it. There's the physical exhaustion. There's the emotional catharsis. There's the psychological depletion. You leave the stage emptied, and I sleep very well on those nights. The best of all is, we pile into a bus, and there's smoking or eating or we're watching a movie or having a chat and a drink and then pile into one of those coffin bunks, and I'm doing something when I'm sleeping. I'm going somewhere. That is so profoundly stilling, it stills me. It gets more like that. I remember playing up in northern Italy, getting in a bus, drunk, falling asleep, and it's a sunny afternoon in Italy, did the gig, night-time, pull the curtain back in the morning, we're in Saltzburg and the snow is falling. Another world had happened overnight, and I'd done something, I'd gone somewhere. That's it; it's this terrible feeling of time slipping away.'

The Boomtown Rats

Let sleeping Rats lie.

Adam Ant

What could have been his redemption turned out to be his undoing, as Live Aid pretty much put a nail in Adam Ant's musical career. Not that he appeared to care, as he swanned off to Hollywood and forged a living as a jobbing actor. I don't know anyone who has ever seen a film or TV show with Ant in it, but he certainly kept busy. These days he still tours (and occasionally gets good reviews), yet his career has been completely overshadowed by his mental-health issues. As Ant was about to join the Here & Now tour (full of Eighties heritage acts) in 2002, he was charged with throwing a car alternator through a pub window and then threatening customers with an imitation firearm. A year later he was arrested again after a contretemps with a neighbour, and was then promptly sectioned.

Ultravox

As Midge Ure had already flirted with a solo career, Live Aid gave him the courage to leave Ultravox completely, so after various personnel changes the band officially split up in 1988. They would re-form twenty years later, for a tour and later some new material, none of which was in any danger of overshadowing anything they released in their heyday. Ure has said he regrets leaving the band, and in hindsight should have stayed after Live Aid, although it would have been difficult to see where they would have gone artistically, as one of the few bands to make electronica work at the end of the Eighties was Depeche Mode. And even their moment ended.

Spandau Ballet

While they weren't invited to play the closing ceremony of the London Olympics in 2012, 'Gold' was the unofficial anthem of the Games, and was in such heavy rotation on the BBC that one felt it was being used either as punctuation or as a metronome. Spandau also occupy another small pocket of popular culture, by having 'True' sampled on P. M. Dawn's classic 'Set Adrift On Memory Bliss', which was a massive hit in 1991. Gary Kemp remains a mensch, as well as a keen cyclist.

Elvis Costello

Punk's scarecrow singer-songwriter was long gone by 1985, but he was no less angry. His first half a dozen records were almost concept albums, with Costello moving through genres as though they were time zones – including lacerating tales of romantic frustrations, political expediency and hapless social climbing – and, confident of his instincts and virtuosity, he continued in this vein for thirty-five years, happy to dip in and out of styles, and collaborate at will (notably with Burt Bacharach on 1998's *Painted From Memory* and Allen Toussaint on 2006's *The River In Reverse*). *Blood & Chocolate* from 1986 is one of my very favourite records, and the concerts that Costello did to promote it rank as some of the best I've ever seen – his performance of 'I Want You' being one of the most chilling things I've ever seen or heard.

Nik Kershaw

Kershaw stopped performing not long after Live Aid, and concentrated instead on writing songs with and for other people – some rum, some not – including (deep breath): Chesney Hawkes, Elton John, Cliff Richard, Bonnie Tyler, Lulu, Ronan Keating, Jason Donovan, Genesis's Tony Banks, the Hollies, Colin Blunstone, Gary Barlow and Let Loose. He still tours and releases records, none of which ever trouble the charts.

Sade

As there are so many talentless ambitious people in the entertainment industry, it's increasingly rare, and correspondingly heart-warming, to see the way in which talented unambitious people approach their work. Sade Adu has never courted the press, has never gone to parties, and would never consider herself a celebrity. She also has a tendency to ignore her public by only releasing records every ten years or so. The flurry of activity around the 2010 album *Soldier Of Love* (her and the band's best record to date, twenty-six years after their debut) was completely uncharacteristic, involving, as it did, a world tour. On stage, she didn't appear to have aged at all.

Sting

It's easy to lampoon Sting, yet as an activist he is beyond criticism. In June 1986, Sting reunited with the Police for the last three shows of Amnesty's A Conspiracy of Hope concerts in the US. The same year he contributed a version of Billie Holiday's 'Strange Fruit' to a fund-raising compilation album entitled *Conspiracy Of Hope: Honouring Amnesty International's 25th Anniversary*. In 1988 he joined Peter Gabriel and Bruce Springsteen for the Human Rights Now! world tour. He then founded the Rainforest Foundation Fund, and has since performed benefit concerts such as the Concert for Walden Woods, Music for Montserrat, America: A Tribute to Heroes, the Leeuwin Estate Concert Series, Live 8, Live Earth, and Hope for Haiti, to name only a few. In November 2012, he appeared on *Hurricane Sandy: Coming Together*, to help raise funds for the American Red Cross in support of those affected by the storm which hit the US East Coast. Respect, Mr Sting.

Phil Collins

We eventually decided we'd had enough of Phil Collins, although it certainly took some time. He had three US number one songs in 1985, while *No Jacket Required* went on to win several Grammy awards, including Album of the Year. He continued touring and having hits by himself and with Genesis, and was one of the most successful performers of the Eighties. 'Another Day In Paradise' was the last number one US pop hit of the decade. On the release of his *Dance Into The Light* album in 1996, *Entertainment Weekly* said, 'Even Phil Collins must know that we all grew weary of Phil Collins.'

He appeared to spend much of the last decade with a chip on his shoulder, concerned that he wasn't taken seriously enough. Collins officially retired in March 2011. There is a secret society that meets monthly to pray that he keeps his word.

Howard Jones

Jones was already thirty by the time of Live Aid, and stardom had come to him late. He was lucky to appear on the bill, as his career would soon evaporate, and although he would hang around for a while, still brandishing his effervescent brand of optimistic synth-pop, the charts would tire of him. He would go on to write hit songs for other artists, played keyboards with Ringo Starr, and – along with Rick Astley, Kim Wilde, Paul Young, Midge Ure, Altered Images, Boy George, Nik Kershaw, Bananarama, ABC, et al. – play the Here & Now revival tour.

Bryan Ferry

Famed for his glacial working practices, Ferry has nevertheless released more than a tote bag full of albums since Live Aid, including *Bête Noire* (October 1987, UK number nine, US number sixty-three), *Taxi* (13 April 1993, UK number two, US number seventy-nine), *Mamouna* (5 September 1994, UK number eleven, US number ninety-four), *As Time Goes By* (15 October 1999, UK number sixteen, US number 199), *Frantic* (18 May 2002, UK number six, US number 189), *Dylanesque* (5 March 2007, UK number five, US number 117), and *Olympia* (26 October 2010, UK number nineteen, US number seventy-one). *Boys And Girls* remains his most successful US album.

Paul Young

Having steered clear of the whole Eighties revival-tour phenomenon (he had problems with his voice), Young finally succumbed and started touring regularly with the likes of Rick Astley, Bananarama and ABC. Asked if he still got groupies at the age of fifty, he said, 'Well, I don't know if you could call them groupies as such. These days, once they get your autograph, they just go home.' He is also something of a foodie, and has appeared on TV shows such as *Celebrity MasterChef* and *Hell's Kitchen*.

Alison Moyet

The Adele of her decade, after the gargantuan hits with Yazoo, and her early solo work – wonderful singles such as 'Love Resurrection', 'All Cried Out', 'Invisible' and 'That Ole Devil Called Love' – success stalled, proving that Live Aid was yet another high-water mark for Eighties pop. Still blessed with an astonishing voice, her remit appears uncertain.

U2

In 1967, with almost extraordinary prescience, Ellen Willis – who would go on to become the music critic of the *New Yorker* – wrote these words in *Cheetah*, which was once a serious competitor to *Rolling Stone*: 'The tenacity of the modern publicity apparatus often makes artists' personalities more familiar than their work, while its pervasiveness obscures the work of those who can't or won't be personalities. If there is an audience for images, artists will inevitably use the image as a medium – and some images are more original, more compelling, more relevant than others.' In the decades since Willis wrote them, these words, these sentiments, have described everyone from Bob Dylan to Lady Gaga, everyone who has tried to build a personality rather than disclose one. But while U2's image couldn't be more indelible, and while Bono's personality has been broadly drawn and interpreted for him for over thirty years, I've always had the sense that they have fallen over themselves to communicate their version of authenticity, however embarrassing that sometimes has been. U2 have spent over three decades building an edifice, yet they've always been at pains to show us the wiring, to tell us how they got to where they think they are at any given point. U2 have spent their career telling us not just why they do what they do, but how, too. Live Aid turned U2 into global superstars, and they were soon to become the biggest band in the world, a mantle secured by their 1987 *Joshua Tree* tour. As soon as the decade ended, they would completely reinvent themselves, and spent the

Nineties exploring their contrary 'disco' underbelly, with huge success. Towards the end of the Noughties they embarked upon the grandest touring spectacle ever mounted, the phenomenally successful 360 tour, the likes of which might never be seen again. There are nowadays too few bands who could command such a large audience on a regular basis, and fewer still who have the ambition, the wit and the sense of community of U2. Bono has also reinvented political activism through his commitment to various humanitarian causes, not least AIDS awareness and the ending of poverty in Africa. Using lobbying, the creation of political organisations, grass-roots activism and the co-opting of any microphone that happens to be in his vicinity, he has been about as proactive in this area as it's possible to be and still hold down a day job (although at times he has tested the patience of his other band members). His political strategy has always been one of inclusion and non-partisanship, while he has sought to influence many of those who have opposed him, including the religious and political right in the US. If ever a man was destined to lead a coalition, it is Bono, and only those suffering from political myopia would deny that he has not only been seriously successful in drawing attention to many of the issues he has campaigned for, but also seriously successful in terms of fund-raising and diverting political opinion.

Dire Straits

Mark Knopfler would soon tire of the big league, and break up the band in order to go solo. The two-year, 247-shows-in-over-a-hundred-different-cities tour on the back of 1985's *Brothers In Arms* convinced him that he didn't want to work at that scale. His last hurrah with the band was the *On Every Street* album in 1991, which included the knockabout rockabilly hit 'Calling Elvis'. In one way they were the perfect Eighties rock band as they sounded like a relief teacher's wet dream, all white man's overbite and headbands. Palaeontologists listening to Dire Straits discovered a new species of dinosaur in 2001, calling it *Masiakasaurus Knopfleri* in Knopfler's honour. 'The fact that it's a dinosaur is certainly apt,' he said, 'but I'm happy to report that I'm not in the least bit vicious.' If Knopfler could ever be persuaded to re-form, he could probably buy Wiltshire with the proceeds.

Queen

Who says one has to go quietly? Since Freddie Mercury's untimely death, the remaining members of Queen have experimented with various different frontmen, including George Michael and most recently Paul Rodgers, ex of Free and Bad Company. While you wouldn't begrudge them a last hurrah, none of these attempts have been especially edifying. They certainly conquered theatreland though, as *We Will Rock You*, the stage play based on the Queen story (produced and written with the help of Robert De Niro and Ben Elton) celebrated its tenth anniversary on 14 May 2012, becoming the longest-running musical at London's Dominion Theatre. It is still playing on five different continents.

David Bowie

One wonders what Howard Hughes's life would have been like had he been around during the days of email. Indeed, had email been around at the same time as him. I would imagine he would have used it every day, teasing his way through his vast empire like the Wizard of Oz. His life, in fact, would probably have been a lot like David Bowie's, or at least a lot like David Bowie's life is right now. Like Bowie, Hughes would have played the role of the arch manipulator, moving his armies, his money, and his ideas around him as though they were characters on a board game – or, given the nature of the medium we're discussing, avatars in a virtual world. These days David Bowie does just that, sitting either at his desk in Lower Manhattan, or looking out over his land in upstate New York, communicating to his teams with the minimum of fuss and the maximum of control.

Until January 2013, Bowie has been absent from our lives for nearly a decade, secretly keeping in contact with his lieutenants on a daily basis, requesting information or figures, or sending small orders regarding yet another project he'd been invited to participate in. A request he would no doubt politely decline. There had been no new records for ten years, and he had shown scant interest in continuing to be the custodian of his back catalogue, and yet Davie Bowie loomed large in our lives. He probably always will. He is ever-present, as his influence can be seen and heard all around us, every day. No musical figure has been so important in the last forty years, nor so inspirational. No one has touched so many people in so many different ways as Bowie has in the last four decades, forty years in which he has been absent for the last ten. Since his heart attacks in 2004, he greets every day with a resigned smile. The first attack happened on 25 June, backstage at a concert at the Hurricane Festival in Scheessel in Germany. He had emergency angioplasty surgery for a blocked artery, and there were rumours that he had a second attack the following day. These days Bowie lives in New York, on the top floor of a former chocolate factory in Lafayette Street, in an apartment designed by Jonathan Reed. Here he tends to his daughter Lexi, his website, his wife and – sporadically – his back catalogue. If you wander around NoHo you'll probably see him, in his quilted black Belstaff, skinny jeans, workman's boots and peaked cap, looking like a cross between a gamekeeper and Lou Reed circa 1966. Blending in with almost everyone around him, he's invisible. Unless you're looking for him, of course. On any day when the air is crisp and there's a chill between the builings, you can see Manhattan's downtown quilted army out in force, drinking peppermint mochas, shopping for clothes, or simply convening with their smartphones. They all dress in black quilted jackets, pea coats or puffas, with their collars pulled up, scarves tied in fat knots and buttons tightly fastened. Oh, and as it's winter, they'll be wearing sunglasses too, just in case. You can't miss them: they'll be wearing the black caps, and matching jeans, maybe with a pair of designer biker boots (Diker-Boots?), or some hybrid trainers. Oh, and they'll be carrying a manbag of some description, and maybe walking a dog (a little black one, sporting its own quilted jacket). These men are anything between sixteen and sixty, and not only do they all look the same, they all look like David Bowie. Until January 2013 he hadn't released a new album since 2003's *Reality* and not played live since 2006, when he sang onstage with Alicia Keys in New York City. He had given no indication he is likely to tour again. He had been asked to participate in most global pop events – Live 8, the Princess Diana tribute, Glastonbury, on an annual basis – but always turned them down, inferring that he would rather spend his time analysing his future rather than exploiting the past. David Cameron had asked him to participate in various events, as had the Royal Family, but he just hasn't been interested. He was also rather dismissive of his fan base's obsession with his other-worldliness. One of the many theories for his disappearance was his unhappiness with the way he now looks; having been one of the world's most famous handsome men, he had perhaps experienced the same panic that Marianne Faithfull had when she realised she was no longer beautiful. Looking back over his career since then, he has been surprisingly adept at ploughing a furrow for the ageing chameleon, and while it's been easier for the likes of Bob Dylan and Neil Young to grow old gracefully, there was a constant pressure on Bowie to keep reinventing himself as he got older. Paul McCartney could become an institution, the Rolling Stones could carry on being the Rolling Stones, and Elton John could continue morphing into ever more extravagant versions of himself. But what on earth was Bowie going to do? In the end he did what he had always done, which is keep moving, making records and films that occasionally worked, occasionally collapsed, but which were always interesting. In the Eighties, Bowie's cultural divining rod deserted him, and while he would go on to achieve a level of fame and commercial success that had eluded him in the Seventies, he was by no means as relevant. This was a combination of three things: firstly, he wasn't as hip as he had once been; secondly, the generation he had inspired were now copying him, and often making better records; and thirdly, his song-writing skills had temporarily deserted him. It is often said that Bowie was all fabrication, but I think we know that now, and it is something that he readily admits to. But he has always been able to harness genuine emotion to any vehicle he might be using to propel himself, however insincere his motivations might have appeared to be. Surprising his fans, the world media and even his management (who had been told about it just days beforehand), on 8 January 2013 Bowie released his first single in ten years, 'Where Are We Now?', on iTunes.

It was a beautiful, elegiac record, proving that not only was he not dead, but also that he had lost none of his ability to make the sort of music that makes us look forward at the same time as looking backwards. The album that followed, *The Next Day*, was just as powerful (if a little too long), while the 'CD' cover was yet another self-referential skit. Bowie's iconic creations will forever remain in aspic, and while the images he created throughout the Seventies have now reached saturation point, they remain as strong as they did when he first created them. You can copy Ziggy Stardust, Aladdin Sane or the Thin White Duke all you like; you can water them down, add a slapdash digital sheen, or simply use them as a rock 'n' roll template. But you can never better them. In the same way that Elvis inspired a host of snarly imitators – complete with greased quaff and truck-driver sideburns – so Bowie has inspired every pop chameleon from Gary Numan and Boy George to Madonna and Lady Gaga.

The Who

Pete Townshend and Roger Daltrey still tour under The Who flag, John Entwistle having died of a heart attack in a Las Vegas hotel room in 2002 – accompanied only by a hooker and a parcel of cocaine in a rock 'n' roll exit that could have been scripted by Matt Groening. In 2012 Townshend finally published his memoirs, *Who I Am*, an autobiography that was easily the equal of Keith Richards' *Life*, and which explored in some detail the events that led to his arrest in 2003 on child pornography charges. The Who released a lacklustre album in 2000, *Endless Wire*, that nevertheless sold in respectable numbers and did nothing to diminish the band's monumental standing. Even though Live Aid wasn't one of The Who's best performances, the intention, the intent, was plain for all to see, as it always is when The Who play. 'I'm not ashamed of praying on stage,' Townshend said in 2012. 'In a sense, we discovered the rock anthem through that. At the end of *Tommy* there's a prayer to a higher power – "Listening to you, I get the music" and "See me, feel me, touch me, heal me." Rock audiences of the late Sixties would always stand up. They would suddenly feel, "Ah! I see, we're gathered here in order to lose ourselves in this plea for grace."

And that's what the rock anthem is. Bono might think he's rallying the troops or something, but he's aware of the power of congregation. And Bruce Springsteen started to anthemise much, much more basic things, like, "We're driving through the streets of New Jersey and we feel like fucking God!"'

Elton John

The early Seventies are always held up as the decade in which Elton made his best records, that collection of extraordinary albums recorded between 1970 and 1975 – *Elton John* (1970), *Tumbleweed Connection* (1970), *Madman Across The Water* (1971), *Honky Chateau* (1972), *Don't Shoot Me I'm Only The Piano Player* (1973), *Goodbye Yellow Brick Road* (1973), *Caribou* (1974), and *Captain Fantastic And The Brown Dirt Cowboy* (1975) – and taken as a whole it is an impressive body of work. But he has had a forty-year career since then, producing another body of work that any major (and we're talking *major*) recording artist would be more than proud of. The thing is, Elton is in it to win it. He thinks you either go for it, or you bow out. There is nothing half-hearted about his appetite for success, which is why he has applied himself to each sector of the entertainment industry with such force. Think of *The Lion King, Billy Elliot,* the Vegas residencies, the soundtracks, the duets, and all the awards – the Oscar, the Golden Globe, the Tony, the Grammys, and the rest. Elton has had more careers than his roadies have had hot dinners. And then there are the songs, the ones that came after the 'canon', all the greatest hits sequels: 'Sorry Seems To Be The Hardest Word' (*Blue Moves*, 1976), 'Song For Guy' (*A Single Man,* 1978), 'Little Jeannie' (*21 At 33*, 1980), 'Just Like Belgium' (*The Fox*, 1981), 'Blue Eyes' (*Jump Up!,* 1982), 'I Guess That's Why They Call It The Blues' (*Too Low For Zero*, 1983), 'Sad Songs (Say So Much)' (*Breaking Hearts*, 1984), 'Nikita' (*Ice On Fire*, 1985), 'Sacrifice' (*Sleeping With The Past*, 1989), 'The One' (*The One*, 1992), 'Believe' (*Made In England*, 1995), 'Something About The Way You Look Tonight' (*The Big Picture*, 1997), 'This Train Don't Stop There Anymore' (*Songs From The West Coast*, 2001), and 'Tinderbox' (*The Captain And The Kid*, 2006) . . . for instance. And that's forgetting the 2003 remix of 'Are You Ready For Love'. *Songs From The West Coast* is a particularly good record, a collection of stark, plaintive, piano-led tunes that harks back to classic Elton albums such as *Madman Across The Water* and *Tumbleweed Connection*. Many of these songs echo the mood and arrangements of hits such as 'Tiny Dancer', 'Someone Saved My Life Tonight', 'Levon' and 'Mona Lisas And Mad Hatters'; these include 'I Want Love', which sounds like the great lost John Lennon single, and 'This Train . . .', which is as good a song as Elton and Bernie Taupin have ever written. The sound on *Songs From The West Coast* is closer to Lennon's *Plastic Ono Band* than any previous Elton John album, and is as far from the Princess Di version of 'Candle In The Wind' as the chalk hills of the South Downs are from the Cheddar Gorge. The use of 'Tiny Dancer' (possibly Elton's very best song) in Cameron Crowe's *Almost Famous* also introduced Elton to a whole new audience, one perhaps ignorant of his massive troubadour status in the early Seventies. I've interviewed Elton many, many times, but when I looked back at all my old interviews with him, I was struck by how much I focused on the luxuriant trappings of fame – the clothes, the houses, the art gallery, the excess. It's easy to get sidetracked by the things surrounding Elton, and always important to remember that he is – first and foremost – a songwriter and piano player. You only have to see him perform once to understand this. The acclaim, and the attention, and the fawning he expects – as one of the most famous men in the world it would be surprising if he didn't – but the real thrill he gets on stage is not from recognition, it's from his own performance, and from watching his fingers run up and down the keyboard, making people smile and cry and dance in the process. Elton is never happier than when performing, losing himself in the moment. At the turn of the century, he began making more naturalistic records, albums that reflected his growing disaffection with the pop industry, records that echoed earlier records like *Tumbleweed Connection* and *Madman Across The Water*. And in 2010 he started working with Leon Russell on an album of original material produced by T-Bone Burnett and featuring songs by Elton and Leon, as well as Burnett and Bernie Taupin. Having been out of touch for the best part of four decades, Elton listened to Leon's music while on safari in Africa in 2009 (he heard a vintage Russell song on his partner David Furnish's iPod), and was inspired enough to try and reconnect with his idol. The result, *The Union*, was a wonderful piece of work, and a real surprise. The album built on the sound, spontaneity and artifice-free feel of Elton's previous three albums – *Songs From The West Coast*, *Peachtree Road*, and *The Captain And The Kid* – relying more on artistry and musicianship rather than radio-friendly pop hooks. And because the album was written, sung and performed with Leon Russell – a man for whom gumbo funk had been a calling card for four decades – the record was a genuine evocation of early Seventies West Coast rock, the sort that finds space for R&B, country rock and gospel funk. Still passionate about music the way few big stars are, and passionate in his espousal of everyone from Hot Chip, Röyksopp and Crowded House, to Arcade Fire, the Scissor Sisters and Laura Marling, Elton still gets a new batch of CDs from the record store every Monday, and he still plays them all. 'I know what makes a number one record,' he said. 'I have a film company, a record company, an AIDs foundation, a publishing company, a management company. So, I have to know what's going on. I'm probably more informed than most heads of any other companies in the entertainment business. I have to be.' Elton has rarely played gigs like Live Aid since. 'I think Glastonbury is one of the nicest British institutions, but I don't like playing festivals very much,' he said. 'I like to be in control of my own environment, and I'm not sure I'd be a success. Part of me is afraid, and instinct says "no". I was asked to play there, but I was working. [Also] I wouldn't do it myself as I'm sure I'd get the piss taken out of me. And why would I want to do that? I'd rather play the Troubadour.' In 1992 he set up the Elton John AIDS Foundation, which has so far raised over $200 million for people living with the disease in over fifty countries. He was knighted in 1998.

George Michael

At the closing ceremony of the London 2012 Olympics, Michael was accused of doing an 'Adam Ant' by promoting his new single. The decidedly tune-free 'White Light', which detailed his near-death battle the previous year with pneumonia. The Twittersphere was not amused.

Paul McCartney

Charles Shulz's *Peanuts* cartoon strip is something that tends not to resonate very much with me. I doubt if it resonates with many people. After all, its rather trite homilies are the sort of thing appreciated by a select bunch: largely by overly sentimental senior citizens, lovesick teenagers or prepubescent girls looking for scrapbook alternatives to their torn-out photographs of Zac Ephron, Robert Pattinson or One Direction. Come to think of it, maybe *Peanuts* isn't so popular with them either any more. However, there is one strip that has always stayed with me, even though I haven't seen it for over thirty years. This is the one where the much-beleaguered Linus says the following to his pal Charlie Brown: 'Charlie, you know that one day of your life will always be better than any other?' 'Sure,' says Charlie Brown, 'everybody knows that. Why do you ask?' 'Well,' says Linus, 'what if you've already had it?' If you were a cynical person, you might think that this is a question that Paul McCartney asks himself on a regular basis. Come on, seriously. What could possibly top having five records in the American top ten? What could top playing Shea Stadium to the loudest crowd in history? Or making *Sgt Pepper*? Or 'Hey Jude'? Or 'Let It Be'? What on earth could possibly top being revered by an entire generation? Or two. What could top being – along with David Bailey, the Rolling Stones and Michael Caine – pretty much responsible for the Sixties? What could top being a Beatle? Here is a man who gave his name to the Ramones (Paul Ramone being McCartney's old stage name), who effortlessly recorded duets with Michael Jackson, whose much-lauded song 'Yesterday' is the most popular of all time (3,000-plus mangled cover versions and counting), who conjured up the bass part for John Lennon's 'Come Together' in a jot, whose performance at Super Bowl XXXIX was watched by a live TV audience of 86 million, whose first concert in Moscow took on all the trappings of a state visit, including a more-than-warm welcome from Vladimir Putin. However, the thing about McCartney is that just when he thinks he's had the best day of his life – his 'Elvis' day – along comes another to put it in the shade. As if conquering the world with the Beatles wasn't enough, McCartney then conquered the world again with Wings, then again as a solo artist, every now and then setting new records, new standards for popular entertainers. He has had more number one hits than anyone else in the world (including Madonna), has made more money than any other entertainer (and that includes Madonna again), and – with or without John Lennon – is responsible for the most important catalogue of songs ever produced. After a fifty-year career in which his fame has only occasionally ever been overshadowed by presidents, despots and royalty, he is now justly acknowledged as the only copper-bottomed elder statesman of pop.

Bernard Watson

A true Live Aid enigma, this eighteen-year-old high school graduate from Miami Beach had no professional experience, yet had slept outside the JFK Stadium for nearly a week before the show, and somehow persuaded Bill Graham to give him a slot on the bill. He opened the US leg of Live Aid by performing Bob Dylan's 'All I Really Want To Do', although there is no video record of this, while some people say he actually performed a self-written song called 'Interview'. Watson disappeared immediately afterwards, becoming the forgotten precursor to the biggest mediated event of all time.

Joan Baez

As a figurehead of peaceful activism, Baez would tour on behalf of many other causes, including Amnesty International's 1986 A Conspiracy of Hope tour and their subsequent Human Rights Now! In 1989, after the Tiananmen Square massacre in Beijing she wrote and released the song 'China' to condemn the Chinese authorities, in 2009 she created a special version of 'We Shall Overcome' containing a few lines of Persian lyrics in support of peaceful Iranian protests, and has repeatedly campaigned – amongst many other things – against the death penalty. She continues to be driven by causes.

The Hooters

Who the fuck *were* the Hooters? Well, they hailed from Philadelphia, which was one of the main reasons they were at Live Aid. After that, they played at The Wall Concert in Berlin in 1990, before going on hiatus in 1995.

The Four Tops

Their best days were already well behind them by the time of Live Aid, although they were still an impressive stage act. Levi Stubbs, Abdul 'Duke' Fakir, Renaldo 'Obie' Benson and Lawrence Payton had been together since 1953 and the group lasted until 1997 without a single change in personnel. By rights they should have become the Three Tops when Payton died that year, the Two Tops in 2000 when Stubbs suffered a stroke, and the One Top in 2005 after Benson died of lung cancer. But they are still performing today as the Four Tops (often playing with the Temptations), although Fakir is now the only surviving founding member of the group.

Billy Ocean

West Ham supporter Ocean (born in the Caribbean he moved to Romford when he was eight) had had a run of hits by the time he performed at Live Aid, with 'Caribbean Queen' winning a Grammy for Best Male R&B Vocal Performance in 1985. In October 2007 he started touring again, and shocked himself by how successful he was.

Black Sabbath

Having invented heavy metal and survived the forty-odd years since, Ozzy Osbourne has been there, done it, done everyone else's, and all but done himself in. As the man says himself, he's been in so many 'fucking' rehabs he could write the Egon Ronay guidebook. Since Live Aid, Osbourne has become something of a national treasure – he is now a TV star, an agony uncle, and the punchline to a thousand different rock 'n' roll jokes. His self-deprecation is legendary: 'I always feel like I am on the dark side of the tracks,' he told *GQ*'s David Furnish in 2004. 'I feel I'm no good. I can't read. I can't concentrate and I can remember fuck all. I have no faith in my ability to judge things. Everything that I think is good is bad, and everything that I think is bad is good.'

Run-DMC

Founded in 1981, Run-DMC were the first hip-hop group to have a gold album (*Run-DMC*, 1984), a platinum record (*King Of Rock*, 1985) and a multi-platinum album (*Raising Hell*, 1986). They were also the first hip-hop band to be nominated for a Grammy, and to appear on *American Bandstand* and the cover of *Rolling Stone*. Their 1986 *Raising Hell* tour, which also featured the Beastie Boys and LL Cool J, is a thing of legend.

Rick Springfield

Because of 'Jessie's Girl' and due to his performance in the long-running TV series *General Hospital*, Springfield was a massive star in the States but almost unknown in the UK. This is still the case, even though he has appeared in several episodes of *Californication*.

REO Speedwagon

Named after a US light motor truck, this wholly American band had actually formed at the end of the Sixties, only becoming truly successful in the early Eighties. Live Aid was the high-water mark for them (even though they only played the show en route to another, in Milwaukee), and by the end of the decade their best days had long gone. They can still be seen pumping out their hits at fairs and carnivals, occasionally teaming up with other rock bands of their era (Styx, for instance) in order to try and leverage audiences. Their monster hit 'Keep On Loving You' can occasionally be heard in movie scenes, and in every karaoke bar from Bournemouth to Beijing.

Crosby, Stills & Nash

To many they are the American Beatles, a band so immersed in Sixties counter-culture that they embody all that was good about it. They have been fervently political, had tabloid-worthy drug problems, and the sort

423

of push-me-pull-you careers that would make most TV soap operas blush. They have also made some extraordinary records, although few of them were made after 1985. What they have had is a career of interpretation and reinterpretation, reconfiguring their wonderful songs for audiences old and new. One should never forget that they were responsible for an entire microclimate of California singer-songwriters.

Judas Priest

Birmingham's second most famous heavy metal band had already had a sixteen-year career by the time of Live Aid, and for the remainder of the Eighties would add synthesisers to their repertoire in order to try and acclimatise to the requirements of a genre bastardised by MTV. They adopted a more outlandish stage presence, which often featured singer Rob Halford riding on stage on a Harley-Davidson, dressed in motorcycle leathers and mirrored shades (Halford can be credited with introducing the S&M leather-and-studs look into heavy metal). Even though they have officially retired, they still occasionally perform, and in 2011 appeared in the finale of the tenth season of *American Idol*.

Bryan Adams

A cookie-cutter rock star he may have been, but he knew exactly who his audience were and why they liked him. A *GQ* journalist once spent a week with him writing a song, and when Adams was presented with some potential lyrics, he scored through all the words his fans wouldn't get. He still has a decent live business, gets heavy rotation on digital rock radio and has a successful parallel career as a photographer. It's this second passion that has earned him a reputation as the nicest man in the business. In the early Nineties, his six-minute-thirty-four-seconds ballad '(Everything I Do) I Do It For You', from the Kevin Costner film *Robin Hood: Prince Of Thieves*, spent seven weeks at number one in the US and an unprecedented sixteen weeks at number one in the UK. Somewhere that song is still playing.

The Beach Boys

Culturally bankrupt for well over a decade before Live Aid, the Beach Boys were one of those heritage acts who had become more reductive the more you saw of them. Brian Wilson, however, slowly moved from the margins to the centre of the culture, and when – under the tutelage of Darian Sahanaja of the Wondermints, among others – he started touring *Pet Sounds* and a revamped *Smile* as solo tours, the shows became almost religious experiences. The *Pet Sounds* gigs at the Royal Festival Hall in 2002 in particular – where rows and rows of men of a certain age were in floods of tears – have become almost legendary. Half a century after inventing the California Dream, Brian Wilson is finally living it. In his primary-coloured Hawaiian shirts and standard-issue Ray-Bans, he can be found cruising along Mulholland Drive, high up in the hills above his sprawling adobe-style Beverly Hills home, listening to oldies stations and wallowing in the security of the present and the serenity of the sunshine. Having survived half a lifetime of drug abuse, drug damage, psychoanalysis and stultifying medication, Wilson is now trying to enjoy all the things he espoused when he first started making music with the Beach Boys fifty years ago. He still suffers from a schizoaffective disorder, a mental condition that means he hears voices in his head and suffers terrible bouts of depression. So he lives day to day, trying to replace all his bad old memories with bankable new ones. He rarely listens to his old records, as he's unsure what sort of memories will cloud his mind. But when the good ones come, and when a record comes on the radio he likes, he embraces them: 'Each one brings back a different kind of memory. Sometimes sadness, but most of the time it brings back a good feeling – sunshine and ocean. The Beach Boys were all about sunshine and ocean.' Wilson is always living in the past. He is still working on ideas for yet another stage in his rehabilitation, this time a concept album called *Pleasure Island: A Rock Fantasy*. 'It's about some guys who took a hike, and they found a place called Pleasure Island,' said Wilson. 'And they met all kind of chicks, and they went on rides and – it's just a concept. I haven't developed it yet. I think people are going to love it – it could be the best thing I've ever done.'

George Thorogood and the Destroyers

The guitarist has been touring for thirty-five years, playing what he calls a fusion of roots rock, roots blues and endless boogie. In his world, longevity is the benchmark of success. 'Anything that makes money or anything that's good will stick around,' he said. 'Why is Budweiser beer still on top?' In 2012, Thorogood was named one of the Fifty Most Influential Delawareans of the Past Fifty Years. No, really.

Simple Minds

Singer Jim Kerr once said their music was built for stadiums, yet they didn't appear to have enough fans to fill them on a regular basis. Listening to 'Promised You A Miracle' thirty years after it was recorded, you wonder why they didn't carve out a bigger career for themselves, but in the end their material didn't have enough ambition, imagination or narrative depth. The tunes weren't so good either. They still tour, although all you have ever really needed to know about Simple Minds is the fact that 'Don't You Forget About Me', by some distance their biggest hit, was written by someone else. *Graffiti Soul* in 2009 gave the band their first UK top-ten placing for fourteen years. But as Jim Kerr said in 2012, 'It's really not such a bad life.'

The Pretenders

We have reached a stage in the development of pop when a group can sound almost exactly like they did when they were first starting out. This is not just the result of rapidly improving studio wizardry – proving to their fan base that they can still sound like they did the day they first rushed out of the traps – but also the desire to recapture that first flush of fame, when their records had the blessing of novelty as well as distinction. The Pretenders are one such example, and their 2010 record, *Break Up The Concrete*, doesn't sound so very different from their first, thirty years ago, or indeed from how they sounded at Live Aid. The album came with a 'doubled-up' best-of CD, containing everything from 'Back On The Chain Gang' and 'Kid', to 'Message Of Love' and 'I'll Stand By You'. It also contained a song that had previously passed me by, a small masterpiece (well, a masterpiece if you like the Pretenders) called 'Night In My Veins'. In 1994 Chrissie Hynde – who to all intents and purposes is the Pretenders – felt the band needed a hit, and so drafted in seasoned songwriters Billy Steinberg and Tom Kelly, who wrote songs to order (they were responsible for 'True Colors' for Cyndi Lauper, and 'Eternal Flame' for the Bangles). Their biggest success was the worldwide hit 'I'll Stand By You', although that always sounded a little too much like Bryan Adams for my liking; it's a revelation that they also co-wrote 'Night In My Veins'. With lines such as 'He's got his hands in my hair and his lips everywhere/He's got me up against the back of a pick-up truck/Either side of the neon glare/It's just the night under my skin . . . slippin' it in . . .' it sounded as though Hynde was lost in a maelstrom of lust, a rare and very welcome display of female sexuality. '"I'll Stand By You" felt a little generic,' said Steinberg, 'and I know that Chrissie felt that way, too, to some extent. But "Night In My Veins" really felt like a great Pretenders rocker.' Not just that, but one of the most vivid, as well as libidinous songs she has ever sung. It's as though she suddenly walked into one of those photographs by Gregory Crewdson, a seemingly ordinary suburban landscape masking nefarious goings-on. It whispered sex. And sounded just like any other song the Pretenders have recorded in the last thirty years.

Santana

By 1985 Carlos Santana's band were in a kind of hiatus, being neither the band who had stunned the world with their performance at Woodstock and then with hits like 'Samba Pa Ti', 'Oye Como Va' and 'Black Magic Woman', nor the comeback kings who made 'Smooth' in 1999. Bill Graham had to convince Bob Geldof to put them on the bill, although their performance was proof positive that they could still cut it live when it mattered.

Pat Metheny

No other fusion guitarist who has relied so heavily on the Roland GR-300 guitar synthesiser has won nineteen Grammy awards (ten of them consecutively, with the Pat Metheny Group). Still, he is best remembered for his soundtrack for *The Falcon and the Snowman,* in the year of Live Aid, which included the collaboration with David Bowie, 'This Is Not America'.

Ashford & Simpson

Having turned from songwriters into performers, the duo had their biggest hit in 1984, 'Solid (As A Rock)', the song they performed at Live Aid. Latterly they opened a restaurant, Sugar Bar in New York City, and worked as DJs on the New York radio station WRKS. Ashford died in 2011, of complications from throat cancer.

Teddy Pendergrass

The sole representative of the Philadelphia Sound (Pendergrass was the lead singer of Harold Melvin & the Blue Notes before successfully going solo), three years before Live Aid, at the age of thirty-two, he had been paralysed in a car accident when the brakes failed on his 1981 Rolls-Royce Silver Spirit. He kept recording after the crash, even though he was a quadraplegic, eventually retiring in 2006.

Madonna

In 1985 it looked as though Madonna was on her way to global domination, something she achieved, and maintained for longer than almost any other performer in pop. In fact, there's nothing 'almost' about it. Her relentless drive and ambition have not only made her the pre-eminent act of the last thirty years (mathematically, at least), but her obsession with reinvention, and latterly with the idea of perpetual youth (surely by now she must be an expert in cryogenics), has meant her career has become a masterclass, almost a blueprint for survival. She remains the quintessential brittle disco maven. I was a member of the *Observer* team that sent Martin Amis to New York in 1992 to interview her about her coffee-table porno book, *Sex,* although Amis ended up interviewing the book rather than her as he was deemed by her people to be too famous. 'In the old, benighted, pre-modern days,' said Amis, 'a new book was normally sent to the reviewer, encased in a jiffy-bag or, under exceptionally glamorous circumstances, a Federal Express wallet.

But Madonna is perhaps the most postmodern personage on the planet, so in this case the reviewer was sent to the book, by supersonic aeroplane.'

Tom Petty and the Heartbreakers

Like feathers on a freeway, Tom Petty's songs are meant to bounce around your car as you cruise down the highway on a journey to the past. They actively encourage nostalgia, songs you're meant to play as you're driving home from work. Or out into the desert. Or, like I said, back to the Sixties. Petty took a bit of the Byrds, some power chords (when they emerged in the mid-Seventies they were practically considered punks in their homeland), and built a sound based on the Big Jangle. It was corny as hell, but the tunes were good, even the Eighties ones produced by Jeff Lynne (the only man who can make a snare-drum smack last four beats, and not in a good way). It didn't hurt that Petty looked cute (a bit like Brian Jones crossed with a chipmunk). The first album is the best (*Tom Petty And The Heartbreakers*, 1976), but then none of the following should be ignored: *You're Gonna Get It!* (1978), *Damn The Torpedoes* (1979) and, for post-Live Aid work, *Full Moon Fever* (1989, a solo album), and *Into The Great Wide Open* (1991).

Kenny Loggins

What could be more 'Eighties' than the sight of Kevin Bacon expressively and defiantly 'rock dancing' to Loggins' appalling 'Footloose' in the 1984 film of the same name? As high concept as any Hollywood film from the early Eighties – local town bans dancing and rock music! – the film was a camp classic of its day, like *Top Gun* (which also included Loggins' 'Danger Zone') and *Over the Top* ('Meet Me Halfway'). Has since reunited with ex-partner Jim Messina. Altogether now, 'Loose, footloose, kick off your Sunday shoes . . .'

The Cars

Because of 'Drive', the band have become so closely associated with Live Aid that they needn't have performed in the first place. They would never again be so popular, and after a few more hits, disbanded to pursue those dreaded words, 'solo projects'. They would re-form in 2011 with some success, although like many groups from their era who have chosen to re-form, the zeitgeist remains impervious. Did they re-form in a forest, did the tree fall, did anyone notice, etc.

Neil Young

Like Bob Dylan, in the years since Live Aid, Young Neil has just got stronger and stronger, and the material he's released in the last thirty years is just as good as – and some of it better than – anything he did before. In 1985 he was actually at a low ebb, having only recently been sued by his record company, Geffen, for making music 'unrepresentative' of himself. Having spent most of the Eighties experimenting, the records started getting better, sounding older, and deeper. He's made so many great albums since 1985, although it would be difficult to top 1990's *Ragged Glory*, arguably the best Crazy Horse album ever made. Young has spent his life holding on to the memory palace that is the hippie dream, something that was evident from his rambling musings in his 2012 memoir *Waging Heavy Peace*. Bemoaning the fracturing of the coloured glass of Sixties idealism, and the squandering of old-school rock 'n' roll passion, on his recent album *Passionate Pill* he says that he had loved Picasso until 'a tech giant came along and turned him into wallpaper'. Wary of dementia, and having had some MRI scans showing some disturbing 'cloudy stuff', Young recently quit drinking and smoking weed.

Power Station

Live Aid was both their coming-out party and their swansong, as the band folded soon afterwards. Even though the band was started on a whim, they made some startling records, and Michael Des Barres was never a good enough replacement for Robert Palmer (who sang on them). They briefly reconvened a decade later, with a modicum of success.

Thompson Twins

'The three haircuts' were on top of their game at Live Aid, even being joined on stage by Madonna, yet singer Tom Bailey would have a nervous breakdown, and the hits soon dried up. The late Eighties weren't kind to the band, and they finally threw in the funny hat in 1993. Some say that – largely because of the way they looked – they became heroes to disaffected youth, although it wasn't made clear if those same disaffected youth had actually heard their records.

Eric Clapton

Whenever I find myself listening to Clapton, I always feel as though I ought to be in a car commercial. Not an ad for one of those little city runabouts, not a Skoda Fabia, not a Chevrolet Matiz or a Renault Laguna or one of those miniature Citroëns that look as though they were designed – like *Glamour* magazine – to fit into your handbag as well as your life. No, I mean the sort of ads for proper German behemoths, the gas-guzzling, road-hogging monsters like a Mercedes S Class, a serious BMW or any of the new Audis. A few years ago I went to see Clapton play the Hampton Court Palace Festival, principally because I'd never seen him perform a non-blues show before, and secondly because of the venue. At the time, stately-home rock was everywhere (everywhere they had stately homes, that is), with everyone from Bryan Ferry, Jools Holland and Van Morrison to Texas, Elton John and the Pretenders playing the sort of lovingly tended manicured lawns that were usually reserved solely for croquet. Catering for a demographic that no longer wanted to queue up outside overcrowded venues in inhospitable, dangerous parts of town, these concerts offered Arcadian surroundings, the type of service you'd find at the opera, and – most importantly – car parks the size of Wales. Also, this was the only gig I'd ever been to where they gave you a blanket to cover your knees in case it got cold. The money shot was a perfectly reconstructed 'Layla', which every person should see Clapton play at least once in their lives. And instead of disguising his most famous tune, like some artists might do – acknowledging its existence, but subverting it so as to appear modern and cool – he played it straight, and had everyone swaying.

Led Zeppelin

Since their extraordinary 2005 reunion at the O2 in London (a rock group as reimagined by David Lean), Jimmy Page has been urging Robert Plant to re-form the band properly, but as Plant still has a tractionable solo career (his 2007 *Raising Sand* album with Alison Krauss won plaudits from all corners), he has never taken the bait. A film of the O2 show was finally released in 2012, and shows the band picking up where they left off in 1982 when they officially split up, the standard-bearers for old white men playing the blues. They are still so embarrassed about their woeful Live Aid performance that they have refused to allow it to be released in any official form; however, anyone who is interested only has to click on to YouTube to see just how bad they were.

Duran Duran

They were never particularly fashionable – even when they were meant to be fashionable themselves, ironically – yet they made classic pop that defied (and annoyed) the critics. Even if you hated what they stood for – and many did, quite vociferously – it was difficult objectively to say that they didn't write extremely good songs: 'Is There Something I Should Know', 'Rio', 'Save A Prayer', 'Skin Trade', etc. They continued in this vein for some time after 1985, without any great success, but continued to write the occasional song worthy of their prime: 'Ordinary Day', 'Come Undone', 'What Happens Tomorrow' and 'Box Full 'O Honey'. Yes, admittedly Duran were responsible for *Thank You*, an album of cover versions that included a misguided attempt at Public Enemy's '911 Is A Joke', but their cover of Led Zeppelin's title track is actually a lot better than it ought to be, and Duran almost make it sound like an original. In 2010 Mark Ronson, the T-Bone Burnett of the digital age, produced *All You Need Is Now*, a Duran album which he envisaged as the follow-up to *Rio*, and which sounded like it too. It contained a song called 'Girl Panic' which was so good it appeared to suggest an ability to be transported immediately back to 1985.

Patti LaBelle

She was rather a random guest at Live Aid, being neither a proper star at the time, nor an A+ heritage act. She had recently been in vogue due to her inclusion on the *Beverly Hills Cop* soundtrack in 1984 (both 'New Attitude' and 'Stir It Up' were big hits). She went down well, though, and although she was criticised for singing too loudly during the 'We Are The World' finale, she managed to get a TV special out of it. The following year she had a massive hit with Michael McDonald, 'On Your Own'. She has since had a full career, on record, on stage and on television. She has also released a selection of cookbooks, and for a while even had her own wig collection, Especially Yours.

Hall & Oates

The music industry's most successful duo would never be bigger than they were in 1985, having just come off a tour supporting their 1984 album *Big Bam Boom* (featuring the original version of one of the decade's best 12" remixes, the truly epic 'Out Of Touch'). They made a soul album recorded live at the Apollo, there was a hiatus while Hall went solo, and then they staggered back with songs that, although almost the equal of everything before 1984, didn't go down so well with their fan base. They still tour and make albums, some of which are as good as anything they did before 1985, including their 2004 album of blue-eyed covers, *Our Kind Of Soul*.

David Ruffin and Eddie Kendricks

Having had their careers briefly resuscitated by Hall & Oates, the former Temptations singers would die within a year of each other, Ruffin in 1991 (aged fifty, from a cocaine overdose) and Kendricks a year later (aged fifty-two), from lung cancer.

Mick Jagger

Old giblet lips and his merry gang of mercenaries have been analysed by so many people over the years, although I've always liked what David Bailey said to me in 2010: 'The Stones have had a much longer career than anyone expected,' he said. 'They're like blues artists. Just before he died, Joe Strummer told me he was worried that he was too old to be doing what he was doing. I told him it was a racial thing, and that if he had been black and ninety years old then nobody would care. Which is what the Stones have done. But because Joe was white and middle class, he was hung up about the concept that old white people can't play rock 'n' roll. But if he had been a B. B. King, or a Willie Dixon, or a John Lee Hooker, nobody would think twice. That's what the Stones have carved out for themselves, and they can carry on until they die.' After fifty years as a Rolling Stone Jagger still hasn't lost his sense of humour though, and wanted to call their fiftieth anniversary tour in 2012 'Fuck Off.' However, 'No one went for that,' he said. As the *New York Times* said, since the late Eighties, when the band pulled themselves together to make *Steel Wheels* and return to the stadium circuit, arguably every tour and album has been largely a victory lap for what they accomplished in their first twenty years. 'It's the Rolling Stones on stage,' said Jagger. 'You know what it's like. They do "Honky Tonk Women". They do "Satisfaction". People coming to a fiftieth-anniversary show want some kind of predictability.' The Stones released yet another greatest-hits package in 2012, *GRRR!*, with a cartoon rubber-lipped gorilla on the cover. It contained two new songs, one of which, 'Doom And Gloom', the *NME* described as "Gimme Shelter" for the Wii generation.' Grandfathers will more than likely never look so cool.

Tina Turner

The diva was in full turnaround by the time of Live Aid, having rebuilt her career since divorcing Ike Turner. Since 1983 (when she released her version of 'Let's Stay Together') there had been a constant stream of hits as she quickly took on a hallowed status. The year of Live Aid was also her 'Elvis Year', as her 1984 album *Private Dancer* was still producing hits, and she starred in the Mel Gibson action movie *Mad Max Beyond Thunderdome*. After this her career was on cruise control, as she became celebrated, feted, and on occasions even worshipped. She has sold over 180 million records, and still occasionally pops out to sing. In 2008, Turner left semi-retirement to embark on her Tina!: Fiftieth Anniversary Tour, making a fortune in the process. As for her late ex-husband, one record executive, on observing the whale-shaped television and sofa with octopus tentacles in his living room, was moved to utter: 'Hey, so you can spend $70,000 at Woolworths.'

Bob Dylan

Since 1985 Dylan has continued to have an incalculable effect on the culture, moving between styles and genres and producing some truly extraordinary records, not least in the last fifteen years. He has received Grammys, Golden Globes, Academy Awards, been inducted into the Rock 'n' roll Hall of Fame, the Nashville Songwriters Hall of Fame, and the Songwriters Hall of Fame. In 2008 the Pulitzer Prize jury gave him a special citation for 'his profound impact on popular music and American culture, marked by lyrical compositions of extraordinary poetic power'. In May 2012, Dylan received the Presidential Medal of Freedom from President Barack Obama, and later that year released what many consider to be his best record since *Blood On The Tracks*: *Tempest*. The former *GQ* critic Alexis Petridis had this to say about the record: 'The music is the same stew of beautifully played blues, rockabilly, folk and country as every Dylan album for the last twelve years: styles you might call pre-rock or, perhaps more pertinently, pre-him. Dylan, it seems, is determined to see out his days playing pop music from the era before Bob Dylan changed pop music for good.' Now, while it would be a lie to say that I like everything he's recorded, I think even Bob Dylan's most fervent fans would have trouble doing the same. He has, let's face it, been resolutely erratic in his output. Which, incidentally, is why so many people like him. He is a genius, we like to say. Flawed, but genuinely gifted. Sort of like Picasso – if Picasso had worn black cowboy hats and opaque shades, and deliberately released such unrepresentative records that they would challenge the allegiance of even his most ardent supporters. Yes, we all like the surreal, alliterative lyrics and the 'thin, wild mercury sound' of *Blonde On Blonde*, 'kinetic rock 'n' roll as glimpsed through the smoky prism of French symbolist poetry and abstracted beat romanticism'. But is there anyone out there who likes *Self Portrait* or *Saved*? Then came the 2009 Christmas CD, a record that sounded as though it were recorded for a bet, or as a joke, or quite possibly both. I played it in the car when it came out, and my youngest daughter Georgia immediately said, 'Is he trying to sound as though he can't sing?' People have said worse, of course. A friend says that when the batteries used to run down on his Walkman, Bob Dylan still sounded the same. Another once said that if Dylan's voice was a fight, they'd stop it in the first round . . . Georgia's stinging rebuke was echoed a few minutes later by the car's CD player, which duly ejected the disc, sending it tumbling to the floor. 'See, even the car doesn't like it.' Her dislike of Dylan – 'The only thing I like about him is his name,' she'll say, before asking for some pocket money – has now become a family trope, and she brings his name up with increasing regularity. A few months after the rejection by our car, as we were walking by a neighbour's garden, my wife pointed out the CDs he'd used to scare the birds away from his peas. 'Should we get some of those?' I asked. 'Only if they're Bob Dylan's,' Georgia said.

Keith Richards

Who would have thought that Keith Richards would turn out to be one of the defining musical icons of the last twenty years? Who would have thought that, decades after first achieving success, he would spend the Nineties and Noughties being revered as not just an elder statesman of rock, but also something approaching a national folk hero? An ancient guitar hero with slurred speech, inconsistent playing, and arthritic joints. Seriously now, who would have thought it? Yet here he is, the most iconic musical entertainer of his generation, a man who looks like Leatherface in the original *Texas Chainsaw Massacre* – not just a guitarist, but a film star, playing Johnny Depp's father in *At World's End*, and a best-selling author: *Life* being one of the world's three greatest rock autobiographies (the others being Bob Dylan's *Chronicles Vol. 1* and Pete Townshend's *Who I Am*).

'I always thought that Keith was in a world of his own,' said David Bailey. 'Keith was always Keith. Keith has always been to me the personification of rock 'n' roll. He has never changed, he's never given a fuck, he's straight down the line. And he stuck to his guns more than the punks ever did. I loved it when they asked him to perform at the concert for Princess Diana and he said, "No, sorry, didn't know the chick."' Just before the Stones' 2012 tour he was reminded that Bob Dylan, Paul McCartney and The Who were also going out on the road. 'What can you say?' said Richards. 'It's a hell of a generation.' There was more. 'When you're supported by millions all over the world, you can either go nuts, or try to feed off the goodwill. I always felt that it was my job to give back to them as much as possible. I want to make better records, better shows. So it's about reciprocation – there are millions of fans, and if you get that feedback, especially from an early age, it's indescribable. It's the same with the Beatles, and John Lennon in particular. It's something you have to handle all the time. I've never taken it for granted. I just happened to be at the right place at the right time.'

Ronnie Wood

Continually playing the perpetual adolescent, the reformed Jack the Lad who many people think isn't even a proper Rolling Stone even though he's been with the band for forty years, Wood has carved himself out a niche as rock 'n' roll's favourite rogue. And while Keith Richards is still, in his own words, 'polytoxic', Wood has intermittently given up the booze, and taken up the brush, regularly exhibiting his paintings all over the world. He also wrote a book, although according to Keith, 'I think he tossed it off. Even Ronnie would admit that. Ronnie's got a much better story to tell than that book, that's all I can say.'

Lionel Richie

Now, while I think it's fair to call Little Richard the black Liberace, I always thought it was a bit rum that Richie was once called the black Barry Manilow, even if he did sport a Manilowesque proboscis. In 1985 Richie wrote and performed the theme song for the film *White Nights*, 'Say You,

Say Me', and the following year had hits with 'Dancing On The Ceiling', 'Ballerina Girl' and 'Se La'. The king of the closed question – 'Hello, is it me you're looking for?' 'Er, not as such' – Richie remains a slow-dance perennial. Recently he has become something of a sensation in the Arab States, and has performed in Dubai, Qatar, Libya and Morocco. ABC News said, 'Grown Iraqi men get misty-eyed by the mere mention of his name.'

Appendix

London, Wembley Stadium

Coldstream Guards: 'Royal Salute', 'God Save The Queen' (12:00 GMT).

Status Quo: 'Rockin' All Over The World', 'Caroline', 'Don't Waste My Time' (12:02).

The Style Council: 'You're The Best Thing', 'Big Boss Groove', 'Internationalists', 'Walls Come Tumbling Down' (12:19).

The Boomtown Rats: 'I Don't Like Mondays', 'Drag Me Down', 'Rat Trap' (12:44).

Adam Ant: 'Vive Le Rock' (13:00).

Ultravox: 'Reap The Wild Wind', 'Dancing With Tears In My Eyes', 'One Small Day', 'Vienna' (13:16).

Spandau Ballet: 'Only When You Leave', 'True', 'Virgin' (13:47).

Elvis Costello: 'All You Need Is Love' (14:07).

Nik Kershaw: 'Wide Boy', 'Don Quixote', 'The Riddle', 'Wouldn't It Be Good' (14:22).

Sade: 'Why Can't We Live Together', 'Your Love Is King', 'Is It A Crime' (14:55).

Sting and Phil Collins (with Branford Marsalis): 'Roxanne', 'Driven To Tears', 'Against All Odds (Take A Look At Me Now)', 'Message In A Bottle', 'In The Air Tonight', 'Long Long Way To Go', 'Every Breath You Take' (15:18).

Howard Jones: 'Hide And Seek' (15:50).

Bryan Ferry: 'Sensation', 'Boys And Girls', 'Slave To Love', 'Jealous Guy' (16:07).

Paul Young: 'Do They Know It's Christmas?'/'Come Back And Stay', 'That's The Way Love Is' (with Alison Moyet), 'Every Time You Go Away' (16:38).

U2: 'Sunday Bloody Sunday', 'Bad' (17:20).

Dire Straits: 'Money For Nothing' (with Sting), 'Sultans Of Swing' (18:00).

Queen: 'Bohemian Rhapsody'/'Radio Ga Ga', 'Hammer To Fall', 'Crazy Little Thing Called Love', 'We Will Rock You'/'We Are The Champions' (18:44).

David Bowie: 'TVC 15', 'Rebel Rebel', 'Modern Love', 'Heroes' (19:22).

The Who: 'My Generation'/'Pinball Wizard', 'Love, Reign O'er Me', 'Won't Get Fooled Again' (20:00).

Elton John: 'I'm Still Standing', 'Bennie And The Jets', 'Rocket Man', 'Don't Go Breaking My Heart' (with Kiki Dee), 'Don't Let The Sun Go Down On Me" (with George Michael and backing vocals by Andrew Ridgeley), 'Can I Get A Witness' (20:50).

Freddie Mercury and Brian May: 'Is This The World We Created?' (21:48).

Paul McCartney: 'Let It Be' (21:51).

Band Aid: 'Do They Know It's Christmas?' (21:54).

Philadelphia, JFK Stadium

Bernard Watson: 'All I Really Want To Do' (13:51 GMT).

Joan Baez: 'Amazing Grace'/'We Are The World' (14:02).

The Hooters: 'And We Danced', 'All You Zombies' (14:12).

Four Tops: 'Shake Me, Wake Me (When It's Over)', 'Bernadette', 'It's The Same Old Song', 'Reach Out I'll Be There', 'I Can't Help Myself (Sugar Pie, Honey Bunch)' (14:33).

Billy Ocean: 'Caribbean Queen', 'Loverboy' (14:45).

Black Sabbath: 'Children Of The Grave', 'Iron Man', 'Paranoid' (14:52).

Run-DMC: 'Jam Master Jay', 'King Of Rock' (15:12).

Rick Springfield: 'Love Somebody', 'State Of The Heart', 'Human Touch' (15:30).

REO Speedwagon: 'Can't Fight This Feeling', 'Roll With The Changes' (15:47).

Crosby, Stills And Nash: 'Southern Cross', 'Teach Your Children', 'Suite: Judy Blue Eyes' (16:15).

Judas Priest: 'Living After Midnight', 'The Green Manalishi (With The Two-Pronged Crown)', 'You've Got Another Thing Comin'' (16:26).

Bryan Adams: 'Kids Wanna Rock', 'Summer Of '69', 'Tears Are Not Enough', 'Cuts Like A Knife' (17:02).

The Beach Boys: 'California Girls', 'Help Me, Rhonda', 'Wouldn't It Be Nice', 'Good Vibrations', 'Surfin' USA' (17:40).

George Thorogood and the Destroyers: 'Who Do You Love' (with Bo Diddley), 'The Sky Is Crying', 'Madison Blues' (with Albert Collins) (18:26).

Simple Minds: 'Ghost Dancing', 'Don't You (Forget About Me)', 'Promised You A Miracle' (19:07).

The Pretenders: 'Time The Avenger', 'Message Of Love', 'Stop Your Sobbing', 'Back On The Chain Gang', 'Middle Of The Road' (19:41).

Santana and Pat Metheny: 'Brotherhood', 'Primera Invasion', 'Open Invitation', 'By The Pool'/'Right Now' (20:21).

Ashford & Simpson: 'Solid', 'Reach Out And Touch (Somebody's Hand)' (with Teddy Pendergrass) (20:57).

Madonna: 'Holiday', 'Into The Groove', 'Love Makes The World Go Round' (21:27).

Tom Petty and The Heartbreakers: 'American Girl', 'The Waiting', 'Rebels', 'Refugee' (22:14).

Kenny Loggins: 'Footloose' (22:30).

The Cars: 'You Might Think', 'Drive', 'Just What I Needed', 'Heartbeat City' (22:49).

Neil Young: 'Sugar Mountain', 'The Needle And The Damage Done', 'Helpless', 'Nothing Is Perfect (In God's Perfect Plan)', 'Powderfinger' (23:07).

Power Station: 'Murderess', 'Get It On' (23:43).

Thompson Twins: 'Hold Me Now', 'Revolution' (with Madonna, Steve Stevens and Nile Rodgers) (00:21).

Eric Clapton (with Phil Collins): 'White Room', 'She's Waiting', 'Layla' (00:39).

Phil Collins: 'Against All Odds (Take A Look At Me Now)', 'In The Air Tonight' (01:04).

Led Zeppelin: 'Rock And Roll', 'Whole Lotta Love', 'Stairway To Heaven' (01:10).

Crosby, Stills, Nash & Young: 'Only Love Can Break Your Heart', 'Daylight Again', 'Find The Cost Of Freedom' (01:40).

Duran Duran: 'A View To A Kill', 'Union Of The Snake', 'Save A Prayer', 'The Reflex' (01:45).

Patti LaBelle: 'New Attitude', 'Imagine', 'Forever Young', 'Stir It Up', 'Over The Rainbow', 'Why Can't I Get It Over' (02:20).

Hall & Oates: 'Out Of Touch', 'Maneater', 'Get Ready' (with Eddie Kendricks), 'Ain't Too Proud To Beg' (with David Ruffin), 'The Way You Do The Things You Do', 'My Girl' (with Eddie Kendricks and David Ruffin) (02:50).

Mick Jagger (with Hall & Oates/Eddie Kendricks/David Ruffin): 'Lonely At The Top', 'Just Another Night', 'Miss You', 'State Of Shock', 'It's Only Rock 'n' Roll (But I Like It)' (with Tina Turner) (03:15).

Bob Dylan (with Keith Richards and Ronnie Wood): 'Ballad Of Hollis Brown', 'When The Ship Comes In', 'Blowin' In The Wind' (03:39).

USA For Africa: 'We Are The World' (03:55).

Bibliography

The Greatest Show on Earth, Peter Hillmore, Sidgwick & Jackson, 1985

Is That It?, Bob Geldof, Sidgwick & Jackson, 1986

Tell Me Why, Tim Riley, Knopf, 1988

Unforgettable Fire: The Story of U2, Eamon Dunphy, Grand Central, 1988

From Matt Black to Memphis and Back Again, edited by Deyan Sudjic, Architecture Design & Technology Press, 1989

Beatlesongs, William J. Dowlding, Fireside, 1989

One of Us, Hugo Young, Macmillan, 1989/1991

Conversations With Tom Wolfe, edited by Dorothy Scura, University Press of Mississippi, 1990

Bare, George Michael and Tony Parsons, Penguin, 1990

Revolution In the Head: The Beatles' Records and the Sixties, Ian MacDonald, Fourth Estate, 1994

Summer of Love: The Making of Sgt Pepper, George Martin, Macmillan, 1994

Peter York's Eighties, Peter York, BBC, 1995

Tom Wolfe, William McKeen, Clemson University, 1995

Take It Like a Man, Boy George, Sidgwick & Jackson, 1995

England Is Mine, Michael Bracewell, HarperCollins, 1997

Many Years From Now, Paul McCartney and Barry Miles, Henry Holt & Co., 1997

The Last Party; Studio 54, Disco, and the Culture of the Night, Anthony Haden-Guest, William Morrow & Co., 1997

The Beatles Diary Volume 1: The Beatles Years, Omnibus Press, 1998

Queen: The Definitive Biography, Laura Jackson, Piatkus, 1999

Appetite for Destruction, Mick Wall, Orion, 2000

The Whispering Years, Bob Harris, BBC Worldwide, 2001

Shakey, Jimmy McDonough, Jonathan Cape, 2002

If I Was . . . , Midge Ure, Virgin, 2004

XS All Areas, Francis Rossi and Rick Parfitt, Sidgwick & Jackson, 2004

Bill Graham Presents, Bill Graham and Robert Greenfield, Da Capo Press, 2004

The Beatles Literary Anthology, edited by Mike Evans, Plexus, 2004

The Road Taken, Michael Buerk, Hutchinson, 2004

Who's Afraid of Tom Wolfe: How New Journalism Rewrote the World, Marc
     Weingarten, Aurum Press, 2005

The Beatles: The Biography, Bob Spitz, Little, Brown, 2005

Magical Mystery Tours: My Life with the Beatles, Tony Bramwell, Robson Books,
     2005

The Beatles: Film & TV Chronicle 1961–1970, Jorg Pieper and Volker Path,
     Premium Publishing, 2005

U2 by U2, HarperCollins, 2006

Stand & Deliver: The Autobiography, Adam Ant, Sidgwick & Jackson, 2006

The Ghost of '66, Martin Peters, Orion, 2006

*Re-make/Re-model: Art, Pop, Fashion and the Making of Roxy Music, 1953–
     1972*, Michael Bracewell, 2007

The Autobiography, Eric Clapton, Century, 2007

The Diana Chronicles, Tina Brown, Arrow, 2007

Under Their Thumb, Bill German, Aurum Press, 2009

I Am Ozzy, Ozzy Osbourne, Grand Central, 2009

Is This the Real Life? The Untold Story Of Queen, Mark Blake, Da Capo, 2010

Rejoice! Rejoice! Britain in the Eighties, Alwyn W. Turner, Aurum Press, 2010

My First New York, edited by David Haskell and Adam Moss, Ecco, 2010

Freddie Mercury, Laura Jackson, Piatkus, 2011

Queen: The Complete Works, Georg Purvis, Titan, 2011

Starman, Paul Trynka, Little, Brown, 2011

Le Freak, Nile Rodgers, Little, Brown, 2011

No Off Switch, Andy Kershaw, Serpent's Tail, 2011

Freddie Mercury: The Definitive Biography, Lesley-Ann Jones, Hodder &
     Stoughton, 2011

No Such Thing As Society, Andy McSmith, Constable, 2011

The Quotable Hitchens: From Alcohol to Zionism, edited by Windsor Mann, 2011

I Want My MTV: The Uncensored Story of the Music Video Revolution, Rob
     Tannenbaum and Craig Marks, Dutton, 2011

Hope and Glory, Stuart Maconie, Ebury Press, 2011

Live Aid, Pete Smith, Penn & Ink, 2012
From the Ground Up, Dylan Jones and Ralph Larmann, Random House, 2012
Love is the Cure, Elton John, Hodder & Stoughton, 2012
Who I Am, Pete Townshend, HarperCollins, 2012
In the Pleasure Groove: Love, Death and Duran Duran, John Taylor, Sphere, 2012
Desert Island Discs: Seventy Years of Castaways, Sean Magee, Bantam Press, 2012
Rod, The Autobiography, Rod Stewart, Century, 2012
Going to Sea in a Sieve, Danny Baker, Weidenfeld & Nicolson, 2012
London In the Sixties, Rainer Metzger, Thames & Hudson, 2012

Picture Credits

Integrated Images

Live Aid Stage: © Trinity Mirror/Mirrorpix / Alamy
The Jam: Chris Walter, Wire Image, Getty
Arthur Scargill: SSPL/Manchester Daily Express, Getty
Brenda Ann Spencer: © Bettmann/CORBIS
The Specials: © Philip Grey/Lebrecht Music & Arts/Corbis
Brixton riots: © Gérard Rancinan/Sygma/Corbis
Miami Vice: Tom Gates, Getty
Tom Wolfe: Ulf Anderson, Getty
Bono & crowd: Dave Hogan, Hulton/Getty
Richard Gere & Herb Ritts: Ron Gallela Ltd, Getty
Harvey Goldsmith: Mick Hutson, Redferns/Getty
Jack Nicholson & Bette Midler: Ron Gallela Ltd, Getty

Plate Section Images

Brixton Riots: Keystone, Hulton/Getty
Boomtown Rats: Finn Costello, Redferns/Getty
Band Aid single: © Jane Smith, Alamy
Live Aid ticket: Phil Dent, Redferns/Getty
Freddie Mercury: Georges DeKeerle, Getty
Bowie & Jagger: RB, Redferns/Getty
Ed Koch: © Owen Franken/CORBIS
Margaret Thatcher and Bob Geldof: SSPL/Manchester Daily Express, Getty
Bryan Ferry: Phil Dent, Redferns/Getty
Red Wedge: Keystone, Stinger/Getty
Steve Rubell, Michael Jackson, Steve Tyler & Cherie Curry: Bobby Bank, Wire Image/Getty
Madonna: Ron Gallela Ltd, Getty
Ray Petri: © Jamie Morgan
Ronnie Wood, Bob Dylan & Keith Richards: Ebet Roberts, Redferns/Getty
Geldof in Sport Aid plane: © Jacques Langevin/Sygma/Corbis
Michael Jackson: Dave Hogan, Getty
Diana's Funeral: Ken Goff, Time &Life Images, Getty
Tony Blair & Gordon Brown: Steve Eason, Hulton/Getty
Live 8: Pool, Getty
Other images courtesy of the author.

The publisher has made all reasonable effort to contact copyright holders for permission and apologises for any omission or error in the credits given. Corrections may be made to future reprints.

Acknowledgements

would like to thank Trevor Dolby, Harvey Goldsmith, Bob Geldof, Bono, Mark Ellen, Gary Kemp, David Bowie, Paul Weller, Keith Richards, Sir Bernard Ingham, Sir Elton John, David Cameron, Sir Paul McCartney, John Taylor, Andrew Hale, Paul McGuinness, Robin Derrick, Kathryn Flett, Robert Sandall, Bryan Ferry, Jane Carter, Sting, Ted Cummings, Alan Edwards, Luke Lloyd Davies, Spas Roussev, David Walliams, Gary Farrow, Susan Hunter, Bernard Doherty, Tabatha Leggett and Richard Campbell Breeden, all of whom were tremendously helpful in their own way. Thanks obviously to Sarah Walter, for her invaluable support, as ever, as well as to Edie and Georgia. I would also like to thank Ed Victor and his magnificent team at Ed Victor Ltd, namely Linda Van, Sophie Hicks, Edina Imrik, Maggie Phillips, Sarah Williams, Morag O'Brien, Rebecca Jones, Charlie Campbell, Hitesh Shah, Siobhan Kelly, Juliet Kavanagh, Sarah Williams and Mary Rees. Then there are huge thanks to Nicholas Coleridge and Jonathan Newhouse. And of course to Stephanie 'Frisky' Sleap. Many of the quotes here are the result of brand-new interviews with most of the principals, although I've also repurposed (OK, stolen) various quotes that originally appeared in many of the following magazines, documentaries and newspapers; others were simply good for background: *Against All Odds, Arena, Bio, Blitz, Campaign, Daily Mail, Daily Mirror, Daily Telegraph, Details, East Village Eye, The Economist, Egg, Esquire, Evening Standard, The Face, Financial Times, GQ, Guardian, i-D, Independent, Independent on Sunday, Interview, London Daily News, Los Angeles Times, Melody Maker, Mojo, NME, New York Times, News on Sunday, New Yorker, Number One, Observer, Paper, Playboy, Q, Quietus.com, Radio Times, Record Mirror, Ritz, Rockin' All Over the World, Rolling Stone, Smart, Smash Hits, Spin, Sun, Sunday Telegraph, Sunday Times, Time, Time Out, The Times, Uncut, Vanity Fair, Variety, Viz, Vogue, Vox, Wall Street Journal, Washington Post* and *The Word.* Unsurprisingly, Wikipedia has also been useful . . .

Index